Software Architecture

Oliver Vogel • Ingo Arnold • Arif Chughtai
Timo Kehrer

Software Architecture

A Comprehensive Framework and Guide
for Practitioners

 Springer

All Authors
authors@software-architecture-book.org

Oliver Vogel
oliver.vogel@software-architecture-book.
org

Ingo Arnold
ingo.arnold@software-architecture-book.
org

Arif Chughtai
arif.chughtai@software-architecture-
book.org

Timo Kehrer
timo.kehrer@software-architecture-book.
org

Translator
Tracey Duffy
TSD Translations
TraceyDuffy@tsdtranslations.org

Copyright © 2009 by Spektrum Akademischer Verlag, Heidelberg, Germany.
Title of the German original: Software-Architektur. Grundlagen - Konzepte - Praxis
ISBN: 978-3-8274-1933-0
All rights reserved.

ISBN 978-3-642-42788-6   ISBN 978-3-642-19736-9 (eBook)
DOI 10.1007/978-3-642-19736-9
Springer New York Dordrecht Heidelberg London

ACM Codes: D.2, K.6

© Springer-Verlag Berlin Heidelberg 2011
Softcover re-print of the Hardcover 1st edition 2011

Cover Design Editor: KünkelLopka GmbH

Printed on acid-free paper

Springer is part of Springer Science+Business Media (www.springer.com)

Foreword

"The architect should be equipped with knowledge of many branches of study and varied kinds of learning, for it is by his judgement that all work done by the other arts is put to test." Thus opens Chapter I in Marcus Vitruvius Pollio's seminal text, "*The Ten Books on Architecture*" [1]. Readers unfamiliar with Vitruvius' work may find it surprising to learn that it was published in the first century B.C., long before anyone even dreamt of such a thing as software. It is, in fact, the oldest known engineering text. Yet, this nugget of wisdom from a two thousand-year-old text resonates fully today, spanning the full continuum of technological evolution and the growth of engineering knowledge up to our modern world of software.

Vitruvius goes on: "This knowledge is the child of practice and theory" and, yet further, "[i]t follows, therefore, that architects who have aimed at acquiring manual skill without scholarship have never been able to reach a position of authority to correspond to their pains, while those who relied only upon theories and scholarship were obviously hunting the shadow, not the substance."

I cannot think of more apt set of quotations for introducing this book on software architecture. Architects, as Vitruvius tells us, must possess not only the requisite technical knowledge of their domain (i.e., the theory), but they must *understand* it, and, true understanding comes only with direct experience (i.e., practice). Moreover, architects must take a broad perspective that encompasses many varied facets of the systems they are designing: more than just the technical issues and solutions, but also the social, economic, and even psychological factors that are at play. It has been my experience in close to forty years of industrial software development that the primary difference between a competent software architect and a skilled software developer is that architects see beyond the technology. Architects perceive a software system not as a Java or C program or even as software, but as an integral part of a greater system that serves a particular business or technical purpose. Consequently, good software architects are individuals who care deeply about the system and recognize the value that it provides, which means that in the process of design they must learn to become domain experts, but ones distinguished by a deep understanding of computing technology and its capabilities.

The authors of this book are fully cognisant of what makes a true software architect—based on their long-term experience as practitioners. They teach us not only about the fundamental technical tricks of the trade (WITH WHAT) but also the equally important aspects (WHAT, WHERE, WHY, and WHO) and, last but not least, HOW all of these can be combined to produce a software design that hits the sweet spot. In this, the book distinguishes itself from numerous other books on software architecture—it covers the full spectrum of concerns facing an architect.

I think that we are fortunate to finally have such a comprehensive treatment of the topic at our disposal. For practicing architects, this book can serve as a handy reference—a convenient reminder and check list. For aspiring software architects, it will expose and demystify some of the less well-known but crucial aspects involved in the architectural practice and, perhaps, help identify the gaps they may need to fill to become *bona fide* heirs of Vitruvius' long-standing legacy of engineering excellence.

Bran Selic
Malina Software Corp., Ottawa, Canada

Reference

[1] Vitruvius, "The Ten Books on Architecture," (translated by Morris Hicky Morgan), Dover Publications, Inc., New York, 1960.

Foreword

For many years now I have been leading the *IT Architect Profession* program at IBM in Europe. It is my job to support the development of IT architects and to ensure that they keep their knowledge up-to-date. Increasing numbers of customers and competitors are interested in building up their own architecture skills. The Open Group, a technology-independent and provider-independent consortium, has been offering the *Open Group Information Technology Architect Certification Program* since 2006. Many of our customers and competitors already use it to evaluate the qualifications of their employees.

Architecture skills are becoming increasingly important

In this context I am excited about the new edition of this book. It describes and explains very clearly and in a well-structured way what architects of IT systems do and what IT or software architecture is all about. The book therefore offers a good basis for familiarizing yourself with the topic and improving your architecture skills. It fits perfectly with the current trend that I see both in The Open Group and with our customers and competitors. It reflects the way of thinking that we have been promoting and demanding for many years at IBM.

This book helps you to build up and expand these skills

It is a very good time for IT architects. The trends in IT and technology are developing ever further and ever faster. A software architecture as the basis for the development of IT systems has become increasingly important in dealing with these rapid changes. Not least the whole discussion around the topic of service-oriented architecture (SOA) has made that more than clear.

The time is ripe to get into this exciting topic...

I can therefore highly recommend this book for anyone who has recognized the necessity of dealing with the topic of software architecture. It provides a comprehensive starting point for conscious architectural thinking.

...and develop an architectural awareness

Karin Dürmeyer
IBM Distinguished Engineer
IBM IOT Northeast IT Architect Profession Leader

Preface

In everyday IT work, the term "software architecture," or "architecture" in general, has become ever-present, and due to its enormous relevance for project success, can no longer be ignored. Business cards show job titles such as Security Architect, Data Architect, System Architect, or even Enterprise Architect. We create documents with the title "Solution architecture" for customers, for example, or customers themselves request architecture from suppliers. Although the term "architecture" is used so frequently, on closer inspection, it is clear that architects, project leaders, developers, and other stakeholders do not share a common understanding of the term.

As a term, architecture is ever-present ...

For some of us, "architecture" is the selection and use of a technology; for others, "architecture" is a process; for many, "the architecture" is a folder with drawings containing geometrical figures connected to one another; for others again, "architecture" may be everything that "the architect" produces—whatever this may be. In its practical use, the term "architecture" covers quite a broad scope—that is, it is not defined or understood uniformly. This often makes it difficult for several people to work together and communicate efficiently in the architecture domain and in daily working life.

... and interpreted in lots of different ways ...

When we decided to write a book about software architecture some years ago, we started our project by initially taking stock. We quickly learned that even within a strictly limited group of experienced software architects, it was not as easy to clearly define software architecture itself as we had expected. We realized that, even though we all had years of experience in designing, describing, or verifying software architectures, we did not have a uniform, precise understanding of the architecture domain.

... initially even within the team of authors

We became more and more aware of how important it was to develop a common understanding and vocabulary. An architecture framework that establishes a common, uniform terminology would allow us to look at and explain the architecture topic discriminatingly. This type of holistic framework was something we had always been looking for in our professional careers.

Our desire for an architecture framework ...

We looked back to the time when we ourselves were primarily software developers and were confronted with the term "software architecture" for the first time. At this point in time, "software architecture" was a very abstract term for us, and it was difficult for us to really grasp what it meant. There was no intuitive architecture framework available that would have enabled us to understand this

... and orientation

important field of topics. Theory and practice concentrated primarily on individual aspects of architecture and did not allow a holistic understanding. We therefore tried to find order amongst the architecture chaos ourselves. For a long time, we had all been subconsciously or intuitively looking for a framework that covers the important dimensions of the architecture domain. At the beginning of our journey through the IT world, we needed a lot of technical and detailed knowledge. We therefore concentrated on acquiring knowledge about techniques and technologies, process models, methods, and organizations. In the course of our professional life and thus throughout our educational journey, each one of us, constantly and partly without being aware of it, derived *his* understanding of the architecture domain from this collection of isolated individual insights. With this book project, we had finally arrived at the point where we could reconcile our individual understandings, bring them together to formulate a common understanding, and make this the core of our book.

Our architectural thinking developed over time

We all knew that there is *no one* architecture examination that gives *the one* architecture certificate that you can pass or acquire in order to then be able to call yourself a certified architect. In the course of our lives as computer scientists, we had all already worked in lots of roles. As analysts, software developers, testers, project leaders, designers, or enterprise architects, we knew that architecture has many faces and that the architecture aspect is decisively important for many roles—not solely for the role of the architect. Our experience was also that, in addition to further technical education, we first had to gather sufficient practical experience before we could start to think "architecturally."

Our book vision

The primary goal of our book is to give readers orientation in the architecture domain. In our view, many books about architecture focus too heavily on the topic of technology. Other books concentrate on architecture documentation and nomenclatures and their related techniques. Some other books look at solution patterns for architecture problems. And finally, relevant computer magazines regularly cover reports on project experiences in which the architecture aspect of a solution presented is very often the factor that gives the article its substance. However, in our opinion at least, hardly any of these works attempt to give the reader a comprehensive orientation in the topic of architecture. Most of the books we know concentrate only on selected sub-areas of architecture. And the few books that cover architecture more broadly still lack more or less a thorough structure that provides orientation, or rather, a book architecture.

Our challenges

We thus faced two great challenges. The first challenge was to design a book structure that addressed the aspects of orientation, theory, and practice—for us, all of these aspects are equally important. Our second challenge was to develop and describe a software architecture model that then allowed us to work through the multi-dimensional nature of this topic appropriately and to use it as a stable core for our book. The result of this initial and fundamental work was the architecture of the book itself. We describe this in detail in Chap. 2 and it is structured as follows:

> Explanation of the architecture dimensions (e.g., requirements in the context of architecture) based on a holistic architecture framework.
> Presentation of the parts of the individual architecture dimensions relevant in practice.
> Practical application of the architecture contents covered in the book.

This book is thus the result of our desire for a work that structures the topics around architecture sensibly, is based on practice, and that conveys corresponding practical experience. In particular, the book is independent of any specific technology and is timeless. For us therefore, this book belongs to that group of fundamental works that provides you with a stable and future-proof reference system that goes beyond current technological trends. The task that we set ourselves with writing this book was not easy—it required all of the authors to look at the topic of architecture intensively and in great depth beyond the otherwise usual level of considering different aspects in isolation. In the time in which we produced this book, we learned a lot. We discussed and debated with one another. As a result of working together on this book, we gained a lot of new and valuable knowledge and a common understanding of architecture.

Our book

You now hold our understanding of architecture in your hands. We hope that our claim of arranging and explaining the topic of architecture for you, and anchoring it in practical examples, will help you in your dealings with this interesting and important area of your working life or your studies.

The first edition of this book appeared on the German-speaking market in autumn 2005. In our view, the great success that the first edition enjoyed was connected to the fact that at this time, conceptual, planning, educational, or organizational contributions in IT had gained importance to the extent that specialized technical knowledge was outsourced to countries with pay structures and an expert basis that further encouraged this trend. From then on, the role of the architect, with its holistic and integrative view of the IT challenges, formed the spearhead of a new generation of training profiles within computer science and neighboring domains. This had a corresponding positive effect on the sales of our fundamental work.

History of the book and the English version

The high demand for the first edition of our book meant that we were able to offer our German-speaking readers a revised and updated second edition of the book in 2008.

In the meantime, we received numerous requests from non-German-speaking colleagues to provide an English translation of our book. All of the authors work in an international, primarily English-speaking environment, and, thanks to presentations at IT conferences or university contacts, have regular exchanges with English-speaking colleagues. We therefore quickly agreed when we received a request from Springer for a further revised version of our book—this time in English. We used the opportunity of producing an English translation to improve the contents further based on reader feedback, our practical experience, and current IT developments, such as cloud computing.

Although the translation and the repeated revision of this third edition cost our translator and us as authors many hours of our free time, we are all happy that we took advantage of this opportunity. In particular, we are delighted to finally be able to offer our book to a global audience.

Our thanks

At this point we would like to thank everyone who gave us the freedom to work on this project and who supported us. This includes our partners and children, our friends and colleagues, our employers and superiors. We would like to thank all of those who gave up their time for us and constantly gave us new strength.

Our sincere thanks also go to our translator, Tracey Duffy. With her extremely professional and team-oriented approach and her great talent for technical translation, she provided us with continuous support in realizing this translation project. Her assistance enabled us to meet our high quality standards, and to do so highly efficiently and right on schedule.

Finally, we would like to thank Ralf Gerstner at Springer, who provided us with continuous and professional support in producing this third edition of our book, and who did so with great patience.

Contents

About the Authors

Oliver Vogel is a certified Enterprise and IT Architect with IBM Switzerland. He leads, coaches, and acts as consultant for international projects in architecture topics such as architectural design, implementation, evaluation, and governance. He is also the worldwide IBM Enterprise Architecture Education leader.

Ingo Arnold is a Global Enterprise Architect with Novartis, Switzerland. In addition to his role at Novartis, Ingo is an Associate Professor at the Universities of Basel, Switzerland, and Lörrach, Germany. He is also a well-known speaker at IT conferences, where he holds presentations on topics such as SOA, IT Security, and IT Governance for international audiences.

Arif Chughtai has been a successful freelance IT consultant and IT trainer for more than 10 years. His specialist fields include software architecture, service-oriented architectures, object-oriented software development, and model-driven software development. He regularly shares his expert knowledge in lectures, presentations, and technical articles.

Timo Kehrer is a scientific employee at the Software Engineering Group of the University of Siegen, Germany. He is currently researching model-based software development, model comparison, model version management, and model evolution.

1 | Introduction

This chapter positions the topic of software architecture and provides important basic information. Firstly we will explain the relevance of architecture for developing IT systems. This is fundamental information for the following chapters. We will then show what the concept "architecture" covers in IT. The chapter closes with an overview of the structure of the book, the intended target audience, and the contents of the book. After reading this chapter you will know what architecture means and comprises in IT. You will also know the main aims of our book and how to use it.

Overview

1.1 Starting Position and Aims of the Book

Software is complex and becoming even more so

The desire to implement increasingly complex requirements faster and more cost-effectively, whilst maintaining the same level of software quality, and the complexity of maintaining (global) widely ramified, interlinked IT systems, have put the topic of software architecture increasingly into the spotlight for some years now. This applies not only to commercial business software but also to all other IT domains, for example, embedded systems, mobile communication, or social networks. However, due to the unstructured way in which software is still frequently developed even today, it is difficult to deal with the complexity of software appropriately. You can only successfully overcome the challenge this complexity presents by applying a systematic process that provides structure. Architecture is a deciding factor in this process.

Software architecture has a key position

Architecture has taken up a key position in the successful development of software. The way software is developed is currently changing. In the past, the central element of a developer's role was manual programming. Now, the ability to deal with architectures and to create them is becoming an increasingly important aspect of a developer's job. This aspect is also evident from the different options that now exist for obtaining certification as an architect (see Chapter 7).

Evolution of software development

You can trace these changes in software development if you look at its evolution. During the course of this evolution, a developer first worked at the level of bits and bytes, for example. The developer's activity then shifted to increasingly abstract levels (assembler, procedural programming languages, object-oriented programming languages, etc.). These allowed the developer to perform increasingly complex tasks and implement increasingly complex requirements. As a consequence, the current evolution steps in software development contain model-based and highly architecture-centric concepts such as model-driven software development (MDSD) (see Section 6.2.6), service-oriented architectures (SOA) (see Section 6.4.11), business process modeling (BPM), and the very latest topic, cloud computing (see Section 6.4.13). The awareness for technical quality and the desire to measure it are also increasing. Modern software development tools increasingly take this desire into account and offer corresponding functionality. You can use metrics (e.g., number of dependencies between system building blocks) to check whether developers are considering architecturally significant aspects sufficiently.

Our motivation I: Give orientation for architecture

The motivation to write a book about software architecture arose from the challenges and problems in software development that we, the authors, have been encountering in our professional lives for some years. Two issues are particularly important: firstly, what exactly does architecture cover? We often see a lack of orientation when architecture is a topic on the agenda for projects. Everyone knows that architecture is a very important topic and should therefore be "done." However, people often do not know what it means exactly, or there is no clear consensus. When people involved in the project talk about architecture, it is often the case that each person understands something different. For some, architecture is the schematic diagrams (box and line diagrams) shown on presentation slides. For others, architecture means defining the signatures of methods and functions. The lack of orientation is often expressed in the following questions:

> How can you assess whether a supposed architecture presented to you is actually architecture?
> How can you determine the quality of an architecture?
> How do you create an architecture?
> How does the thing "architecture," that you have to deliver, manifest itself?
> What do you use to create an architecture?
> What is architecture?
> What is expected of you as an architect or developer when you are asked to create an architecture?
> When and where does architecture take place?
> Who is responsible for architecture?
> Why do you need to create an architecture?

With our book, we want to give people active in the IT field orientation in the topic of architecture. This is because we have observed that many developers and architects are preoccupied with the questions listed above. Also, we have not yet been able to find a book about architecture that offers a clearly structured, comprehensive, and focused introduction to the topic—at least, not in the way that we have often wished.

The second important issue is the poor technical quality of software, which is the result of not considering architecture (for example, when you have to rewrite a large part of the source code to take account of new customer requirements).

Our motivation II: Improve software quality

Every IT system has an architecture. But is this an architecture that has been deliberately planned, or has it arisen more or less unconsciously and randomly? The aim should be to achieve a workable architecture. However, a workable architecture does not just "happen"—it has to be developed deliberately [Bredemeyer 2002]. Due to the great importance of architecture for the software quality and the project success, it is very important to have architecture firmly fixed in thought and to thus develop an understanding for it. Helping you to establish architectural thinking and conveying the understanding required to do this are the central aims of our book.

Our book conveys understanding for architectural thinking

At the beginning there is a "wish list" …

How do architects, developers, and other people involved in projects frequently experience the process of a software development project? We are sure that the following scenario will not be completely new to you. A project generally begins with recording the customer's requirements as quickly as possible in the form of a "wish list". The aim is then to convert this wish list into source code equally fast. There is not a lot of time for questioning the wish list. The focus is on a user interface that satisfies the customer's requirements and is outwardly effective (but not necessarily user-friendly). This gives the customer something tangible quickly, and you can show the customer that you are in control of the situation.

… followed by a "concept" …

Before the points on the wish list can be distributed to the individual developers for processing, the "lead developer" creates a more or less technical and accepted "concept" for the software to be developed based on the wish list. The developers use this concept as instructions.

… changes are suddenly necessary …

During realization—at the latest when requirements change or new requirements suddenly arise—the first shortcomings of the concept appear.

… the project has to deviate from the concept …

In the source code, the developers now have to deviate from the concept and take matters into their own hands. What they do is not documented in the concept because there, of course, nothing is changed "officially". This is because you have already "sold" the concept to the customer in perfectly designed presentations with convincing diagrams. There is also no time to change the concept and the customer would not understand or accept this.

…. the inevitable result: a big ball of mud!

The original concept and the actual source code become increasingly different. The documentation of the concept soon becomes just a pretty cover. Systematic structures that the software once contained are now covered in patchwork. Over the course of time, the software mushrooms into an unfathomable creation along the lines of the big ball of mud pattern [Foote and Yoder 1999], also known as "kludge" [Bredemeyer 2002]:

Why did the software have to end as a big ball of mud?

At some point, you reach the situation where nobody knows exactly why and how the system works. You are just happy that it does work. Maintenance and implementation of new requirements become a bigger nightmare with every version of the software and cost a lot of time and nerves. How did things get so far? After all, you had a concept! Is the wish list to blame? Is there something wrong with the concept? How can you prevent a software becoming a big ball of mud? We asked ourselves these and many other questions and searched for answers. Many of the answers that we present in our book resulted from the fact that, often, insufficient attention is given to architecture when IT systems are created.

Figure 1.1-1: Software structures out of control (big ball of mud)

The project scenario above is not an exaggeration—it is a widespread reality. There are also other scenarios, and they all end in a big ball of mud. Most IT projects fail to some extent. Only around 30% of these projects can claim to conclude successfully [Standish 2009] despite increasingly progressive technologies (e.g., Java EE) and concepts (e.g., SOA). The failure of a project is evident from the project exceeding the time or budget limits, or the customer being unhappy with the product delivered. Projects may even be canceled [Yourdon 2004]. Since the 1960s, this situation has been known as the "software crisis" [Dijkstra 1972]. It first became evident through the immense progress of hardware infrastructure and the related, almost infinite possibilities that opened up for software development. There are many reasons for the software crisis. They include inadequate architectures.

Many IT projects fail

In building construction, it is a well-known fact that sooner or later, if you do not have a well-planned architecture, you will encounter problems. If you were to

A well-known fact in building construction

build a house without first defining the architecture, you would quickly encounter problems with statics, stability, integration in the communal infrastructure (e.g., electricity and water), etc. To stay with the building construction analogy: often, when you "construct" an IT system, you start by defining the approximate overall dimensions, and then, if at all, think quickly about the allocation of rooms and the number of floors. Everything else (e.g., statics and infrastructure for power and water) is supposed to somehow just happen "during construction". The "advance planning" is documented on a scrap of paper and then "off you go". You dig out the space for the foundations, make the molds for the concrete blocks, mix the concrete, and so on. Over time, fundamental errors gradually appear and you have difficulty correcting them or you cannot correct them at all. For example, you realize that the space for the foundations is the wrong size for the concrete blocks you have made. A counterproductive operational hectic follows, in which the situation usually just gets worse.

Symptoms of poor architectures

Unfortunately, the consequences of poor architecture in IT often only appear after a considerable delay. Serious problems may only arise when you go live with a system for the first time, or when it is already in use and you have to adapt it for new requirements. An architecture that arises without being planned—i.e., that simply develops over time—leads to considerable problems in the creation, delivery, and operation of a system. The following selection of symptoms can potentially indicate a poor architecture:

> Results of the analysis are not deliberately considered.
> Overview is missing.
> Complexity runs out of control.
> Planning becomes more difficult.
> Early recognition of risk factors is barely possible.
> Reuse of knowledge and system building blocks becomes more difficult.
> Flexibility is restricted.
> Maintainability becomes more difficult.
> Problems with integration.
> Performance is bad.
> Architecture documentation is insufficient.
> Learning curve for understanding the architecture is too high.
> Functionality is redundant.
> Development cycles (e.g., translation times) are too long.
> System building blocks (e.g., classes) have numerous, unnecessary dependencies to one another.
> System building blocks that cover many different responsibilities and are therefore difficult to maintain or reuse ("monster building blocks").
> System building blocks whose implementation details are known in the entire system.
> Numerous system building blocks have to be adapted when there is a change anywhere in the system (e.g., database or user interface).

Even if you have worked out an architecture thoroughly, this is no guarantee that none of the problems listed above will occur. On one hand, this is because poor architecture is only one of many factors for the software crisis (others are, for example, users' lack of awareness for quality or an unsatisfactory IT strategy in the enterprise). On the other hand, successfully creating architectures is no easy challenge due to the inherent complexity of IT systems; on the contrary, as well as having a broad technical knowledge and well-founded experience, those responsible have to take a whole series of other aspects into account (e.g., stakeholders and requirements).

Inherent complexity

To introduce and "sell" the main features of an architecture to a non-technical audience (e.g., managers and even lead architects) in an early stage of an IT project, it is often very helpful to work with so-called marchitectures (marketing architectures). These architectures usually take the form of presentation slides with a series of graphical diagrams and keywords. However, all of the other (technical) elements that make up a real architecture are missing. Marchitectures become a problem if you use them in place of a real architecture later on in the project, thus diverting the term "architecture" from its intended use. This is because the primary aim of a marchitecture is to sell something—it does not contain any definable technical "nutritional value" for software developers. You cannot use it as an adequate explanatory model for a system you are developing and the developers will therefore not accept it. In this case, during the software development, an architecture develops more or less unplanned and unconsciously depending on the abilities of the developers.

Marchitectures

1.2 What is Software Architecture?

In the context of software, architecture is a relatively new discipline. Conscious architectural thinking in software development has only been around for a few decades [Shaw and Garlan 1996]. This is why there are still contradictory opinions on what exactly architecture means. Furthermore, in contrast to physical objects such as buildings, rooms, or even hardware, where it is obvious that these need and contain an architecture, this is not immediately evident for software systems. The result is that in the context of software, architecture is difficult to comprehend. In spite of this, people involved in software development projects are confronted with architecture on a daily basis even though they do not notice it. Architecture is implicitly always an aspect of software and you cannot eliminate it or ignore it—doing so leads to the negative consequences described in the previous section.

Architecture is difficult to comprehend

Faced with this knowledge, the reasons why architecture has to be in a conflicting relationship with the business side become clearer. If there are numerous questions and uncertainties about architecture on the IT side, this situation is

Architecture and the business side

even more strongly defined on the business side. It is often difficult to convey to the business that there is such a thing as architecture for software. In addition, it is difficult for the business to imagine what direct (financial) benefits an architecture would provide, since investments in architecture only pay off or can only be written off in the medium to long-term. This implies that architecture generally does not bring any benefits until the medium or long-term (e.g., better maintainability), and is therefore only useful for projects with a corresponding long-term time horizon for the system life cycle, corresponding complex requirements, and corresponding high risks with regard to resources, project size, etc. (see Figure 1.2-1). The business is therefore often not prepared to bear the extra costs connected to architecture (often for political reasons, for example, the creation or maintenance of artificial costs in software development). Unfortunately there is no universal solution for overcoming this challenge. Essentially, the issue is making the return on investment (ROI) of architecture tangible for the business. One option is to point out the higher financial costs (for example, due to an increased maintenance effort) caused by neglecting architecture, and which can be avoided in the medium-term, to the business at an early stage. In addition to ROI, as a result of globalization, compliance is now also at the top of the agenda for the business. Here you have to show the connection between architecture and the fulfillment of requirements with reference to IT compliance (for example, the implementation of security aspects with regard to data protection laws).

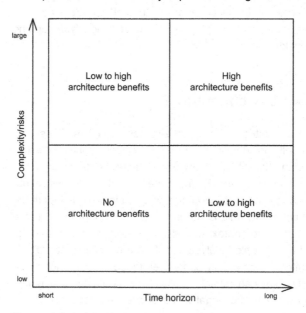

Figure 1.2-1: *Criteria for evaluating the benefits of architecture*

Focus on people

Architecture is not a purely technological issue. It also has numerous social and organizational aspects (see Chapter 7) that can influence the success of an architecture and thus an entire project considerably. Therefore, in our perception of architecture, which is the basis of this book, the focus is on the people involved, and in particular, the architect (see Chapter 2).

It is not easy to define architecture as strictly as facts from mathematics or economics, for example. Our definition of architecture, as we present it in Section 3.2, should be understood as an intuitive clarification of the term "architecture" based on our experiences and impressions of architecture in our daily project work. Your project reality may well produce a definition that is different to ours in parts. There are numerous definitions of the term "architecture" in IT [SEI 2010]. This shows that it is a challenge to find one definition that is recognized universally. If you bear in mind that architecture is an important topic in many computer science disciplines (e.g., software architecture, data architecture, security architecture, etc., see Chapter 3) and comes into play at different levels of abstraction (see Chapter 4), it becomes clear why it is difficult to find a universally valid definition that does not overflow. The following sections prepare the way for our definition of architecture.

Numerous definitions

Regardless of the type of IT system you are developing, in order to define the fundamental parts (and thus the supporting pillars), the architecture always considers the requirements the system must satisfy (see Chapter 5). The architecture does not define the details of the system to be developed [Buschmann et al. 1996]. With regard to a system, an architecture answers the following questions:
> Which requirements are the structuring and decisions based on?
> Which are the major logical and physical system building blocks?
> How are the system building blocks related to one another?
> What responsibilities do the system building blocks have?
> What interfaces do the system building blocks have?
> How are the system building blocks grouped or layered?
> What are the specifications and criteria used to divide the system into building blocks?

Architecture defines the supporting pillars and not the details

Architecture thus contains all fundamental specifications and agreements triggered by requirements.

Architecture stretches from the analysis of the problem domain of a system right up to the realization of the system (see Chapter 8). It is not present at the level of abstraction of fine-grained structures such as classes or algorithms; instead, it is present at the level of systems, that is, coarse-grained structures, such as components or subsystems (see Chapter 4). Nevertheless, there is not always a strict separation between the aspects of fine-grained and coarse-grained structures. This means that the border is sometimes blurred.

Where does architecture stop?

Architecture makes complexity easier to understand

An important characteristic of architecture is that it makes complexity easier to control. It does this by showing only the main aspects of a system and not going into detail. This enables you to get an overview of a system quickly.

Decisions with system-wide consequences

The definition of what makes up the fundamental parts of the system and what the details are is subjective or context-specific [Fowler 2005]. The fundamental parts are the things that you cannot subsequently change without great effort. These are structures and decisions that play a decisive role for the development of a system over time [Fowler 2005]. Examples are the specification of how system building blocks exchange data with one another or the selection of the technology platform (e.g., JEE or .NET). Architecturally significant specifications of this kind have an effect across the entire system starting from the respective architecture level (see Chapter 4). This is in contrast to architecturally insignificant specifications (for example, specific implementation of a function or method) that only have a local effect on a system [Bredemeyer and Malan 2010]. The architecturally significant structures and decisions, as well as the procedures needed to determine these specifications, are some of the main topics of this book.

Architecture in the context of IT

Our book covers architecture that stretches across the creation, delivery, and operation of software of every kind. This means that the architecture we discuss has points in common with other architecture disciplines, for example, data architecture. We do not cover these in detail in our book; we look at them only to the extent of the points they have in common with software architecture. When we refer to IT in the book, we are not restricting ourselves exclusively to software; we also mean implicitly the whole spectrum of IT, in which software is only one part, even though it is a very important part. Chapter 3 discusses the term "architecture" in more detail. It answers the questions raised above, and develops the definition or perception of architecture that we use in our book.

1.3 Reader Guide

1.3.1 Book Structure

Architecture is an extensive topic

Within information technology, architecture is not a clearly delineated or structured topic in the way that, for example, formal languages or data structures are. It is a topic that affects various domains of information technology. Architecture uses well-known information technology concepts (e.g., interfaces) and raises new, separate concepts (e.g., *architecture patterns*). These new concepts take up, use, and connect the already well-known information technology concepts.

Structuring the topic "architecture"

One of our first challenges in writing this book was to create the fundamental structure (i.e., the architecture) for the book. To do this, we had to structure the topic "architecture" such that you can use our book as an orientation aid that allows you to acquire the knowledge you require efficiently, without getting lost in this big topic.

The clear and thorough structuring of the topic "architecture" and the focus on this topic in its entire breadth, without slipping into areas that are not (immediately) connected to architecture, distinguishes our book from various other books on this topic. This clear direction is a priceless advantage for you in dealing with this extensive topic.

Unique properties of our book

In our book, we structure the topic of architecture using a so-called orientation framework. Based on simple questions (WHAT, WHERE, WHY, etc.), the framework classifies architecture knowledge into domains. In Chapter 2, we establish and describe the (architecture) orientation framework. The resulting book architecture (see Figure 1.3-1) leads to the following basic structuring of our book:

Book architecture

> *Part I—Architecture overview and orientation:* Gives a first overview of architecture and describes the framework that defines the architecture for the second part of the book.
> *Part II—Architecture knowledge:* Describes in detail what architecture contains and conveys theoretical knowledge of architecture.
> *Part III—Appendix:* Contains the glossary, list of abbreviations, bibliography, and the index.

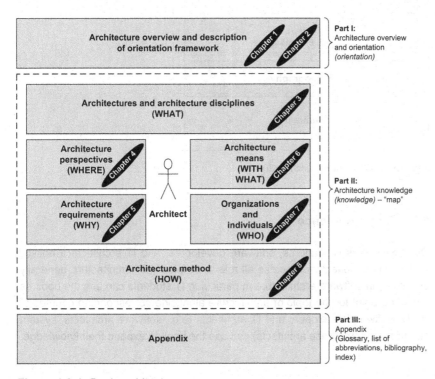

Figure 1.3-1: Book architecture

The part of the book architecture labeled "map" in Figure 1.3-1 (Part II) is the architecture orientation framework and your orientation aid for the second part of the book.

Chapter architecture

In our book each chapter follows the structure shown in Figure 1.3-2. Each chapter in the second part begins with this map. The area of the map covered in the respective chapter is highlighted in dark gray. The map is followed by a concept map (except Chapter 1), giving an overview of the main concepts that the chapter or section covers in detail in context. In Chapters 6 and 8, each individual section has its own concept map. Each chapter closes with a summary and a bibliography (in Chapters 6 and 8 at the end of the individual sections). In addition, Chapter 8 also contains checklists for the various activities of an architect at the end of each section and before the bibliography.

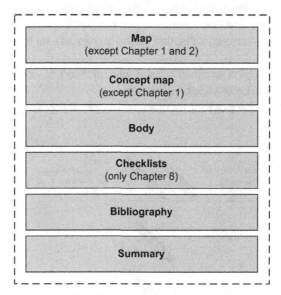

Figure 1.3-2: Chapter architecture

1.3.2 Target Audience

IT students, software developers, IT architects and IT manager

Our book offers IT students, software developers, and IT architects a holistic and consistent orientation across all relevant topics in IT architecture generally as well as in software architecture in particular. IT students can use the book as a starting point for the topic of architecture alongside corresponding courses of study. Software developers and IT architects (e.g., software architects, system architects, or enterprise architects) can use the book to expand their knowledge.

IT managers (e.g., IT project leads, CIOs, or CTOs) can use our book as a reference work for specific topics to acquire a basic understanding of architecture.

1.3.3 Chapter Overview

Table 1.3-1 gives an overview of the contents of the individual chapters. They are described in more detail in Section 1.3.4.

Table 1.3-1: Chapter overview

Part	Chapter	Contents
I Architecture overview and orientation	1 Introduction	Motivation and introduction
	2 Architecture Orientation Framework	Book architecture
II Architecture knowledge	3 Architectures and Architecture Disciplines (WHAT)	Architecture definition
	4 Architecture Perspectives (WHERE)	Architecture models
	5 Architecture Requirements (WHY)	Architecture and requirements
	6 Architecture Means (WITH WHAT)	Architecturally significant techniques and technologies
	7 Organizations and Individuals (WHO)	Social and organizational aspects of architecture and architect roles
	8 Architecture Method (HOW)	Architecture in the development process and architecture knowledge applied in a case study
III Appendix	–	Glossary, bibliography, list of abbreviations, and index

Chapter 2 is a must for all readers. It describes and defines the architecture of our book and is therefore the prerequisite for the basic understanding of our book.

Part I: Chapter 2 is a must

The chapters in the second part of the book do not strictly build on one another. You can read them in any order.

Part II: Read in any order

If architecture is more or less a new topic for you, we recommend that in addition to Chapters 1 and 2, you read the following chapters in this order: Chapters 3, 4, 5, and finally in no specific order, Chapters 6, 7, and 8 (see Figure 1.3-3).

IT students: Recommended chapters

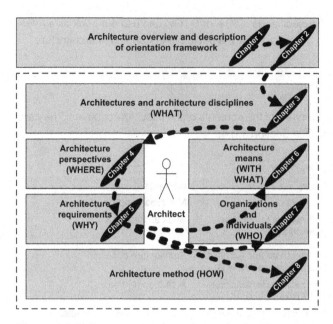

Figure 1.3-3: Recommended reading order for IT students

Software developers: Recommended chapters

As a software developer you should focus on the non-technology aspects of architecture. Therefore, we recommend that in addition to Chapters 1 and 2, you read the following chapters in this order: Chapters 3 and 8 and finally in no specific order, Chapters 4, 5, 6 and 7 (see Figure 1.3-4).

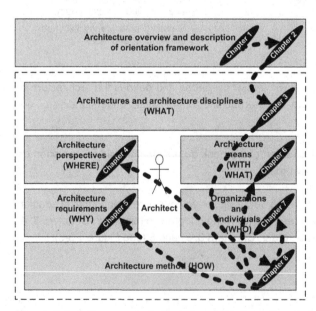

Figure 1.3-4: Recommended reading order for software developers

We have observed that IT architects often need to supplement their knowledge with information about social and organizational aspects. Therefore, we recommend that in addition to Chapters 1 and 2, you read Chapters 7 and 8 and optionally in no specific order, Chapters 3, 4, 5, and 6 (see Figure 1.3-5).

IT Architects: Recommended chapters

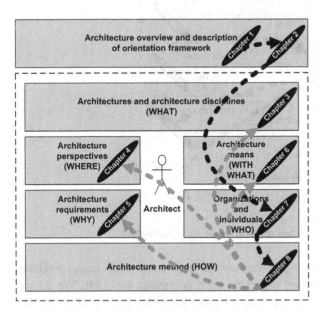

Figure 1.3-5: Recommended reading order for IT architects

As an IT manager, it is important that you know that architecture is important in the organizational context too and that you have an overview of the most important aspects of software architecture. Therefore, we recommend that in addition to Chapters 1 and 2, you read the following chapters in this order: Chapters 3 and 4 and in no specific order, Chapters 5, 7, 8, and optionally Chapter 6 (see Figure 1.3-6).

IT managers: Recommended chapters

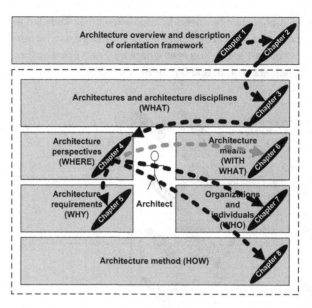

Figure 1.3-6: Recommended reading order for IT managers

Unified Modeling Language (UML) is used

In many of the diagrams in this book we use Unified Modeling Language (UML) version 2 (UML2). Readers should therefore be familiar with UML. We do not introduce UML in detail in this book. If you are interested and would like further information, see [Booch et al. 2005].

Basics of software development are not presented

We do not cover basic concepts of software development and technologies mentioned in connection with architecture in detail—we look only at their architectural aspects. The bibliography at the end of the individual chapters (in Chapters 6 and 8 at the end of the individual sections) and in the Appendix provide details of further sources of information.

Basic orientation for architecture

You will not find solutions or a collection of guides for technology-specific architecture problems, such as the separation of business logic and persistence logic in the context of Java EE in our book. A range of recommended works are already available for these topics. The primary aim of our book is to give you basic orientation in architecture. This orientation is the unconditional prerequisite for enabling you to solve (technology-) specific architecture problems.

Disclaimer

In our book, whenever the masculine gender is used, both men and women are included.

1.3.4 Chapters in Detail

The first part of the book provides a first overview of the topic "architecture" and establishes the architecture orientation framework that defines the architecture for the second part of the book.

Part I: Architecture overview and orientation

This chapter delivers the motivation and basics for the topic "software architecture". Firstly we explain the relevance of architecture for developing IT systems. This is fundamental information for the following chapters in the book. We then show what the concept "architecture" covers in the context of IT. The chapter closes with an overview of the structure of the book, the intended target audience, and the contents of the book. After reading this chapter you will know what architecture means and what it comprises in the context of IT. You will also know why we wrote this book and what the main aims of our book are. And of course, you will know how to use the book.

Chapter 1— Introduction

In Chapter 2 we present an architecture framework. It provides orientation by positioning the significant elements of architecture in an architecture orientation framework using simple question words. The focal point of the orientation framework is the role of the architect. We also use the framework to convey knowledge and experience throughout the rest of the book. It enables you to think about architecture in a structured way and provides you with orientation.

Chapter 2— Architecture orientation framework

The second part of the book covers essential architecture knowledge. We structure and convey this knowledge based on the architecture orientation framework previously introduced.

Part II: Architecture knowledge

The third chapter covers the *WHAT dimension* of the architecture orientation framework. It conveys a basic understanding of architecture. We also present the significant building blocks that make up a system and their relationships to one another. Since the nature of systems and systems thinking are essential for your work as an architect, we also position these concepts in the context of architecture. After reading this chapter, you will be able to explain the general nature of architecture, differentiate between individual architecture disciplines and the most important building blocks of systems, as well as describe their relationships with one another.

Chapter 3— Architectures and Architecture Disciplines (WHAT)

Chapter 4 looks at the *WHERE dimension* of the architecture orientation framework. It explains the levels of abstraction at which you are active as an architect and how architecture is demonstrated at these levels. We also present architecture views that you can use at these levels of abstraction to make it easier to manage the different aspects and the resulting complexity of an architecture. After reading this chapter, you will be able to differentiate between the relevant ar-

Chapter 4— Architecture Perspectives (WHERE)

chitectural levels of abstraction and use them. Using architecture views, you will also be able to consider and process specific different aspects of an architecture.

Chapter 5—Architecture Requirements (WHY)

Chapter 5 covers the *WHY dimension* of the architecture orientation framework. In the center of this dimension are requirements. They define the IT system to be created and restrict your creative scope as an architect. There are different types of requirements at different architecture levels. In order to be able to use your creative scope, you have to know the different types of requirements and their relationships to one another and the architecture levels—these topics are covered in this chapter. After reading this chapter, you will be able to name the most important types of requirements, understand their relationships, and place them in the context of architecture.

Chapter 6—Architecture Means (WITH WHAT)

Chapter 6 looks at the *WITH WHAT dimension* of the architecture orientation framework and presents basic concepts and technologies that belong to a software architect's toolbox. After reading this chapter, you will have an idea of the means you can use to assess, describe, create, and develop architectures.

Chapter 7—Organizations and Individuals (WHO)

Chapter 7 looks at the *WHO dimension* of the architecture orientation framework more closely. We show organizational and social influencing factors that affect the architecture of a system and that can influence the work of an architect. We also provide basic knowledge about groups and their dynamics. In addition, we define the role of the architect. Applying the knowledge contained within this dimension enables you to understand the relevance of the influencing factors mentioned, describe the role of an architect, consider the processes of group dynamics, and act accordingly.

Chapter 8—Architecture Method (HOW)

Chapter 8 concentrates on the *HOW dimension* of the architecture orientation framework. Firstly we present knowledge about development processes that is relevant for you as an architect, before describing your individual activities during the creation of a system at a general level. We then make this more concrete using a real world example. This approach connects the orientation framework to the contents of the previous chapters. It enables you to understand how to apply the information presented in the other chapters to a concrete problem.

Part III: Appendix

The Appendix contains supplementary information and aids for using the book in the form of a glossary, list of abbreviations, bibliography, and index.

More information at www.software-architecture-book.org

At **www.software-architecture-book.org**, you can find more information about the book and in the future, various additional contributions on the topic of software architecture. We welcome any contribution you would like to make. You can send us these contributions and your opinion (hints, criticisms, praise, etc.) of our book by sending an e-mail to **authors@software-architecture-book.org**. We look forward to hearing from you.

1.4 Summary

> Complexity (IT systems and requirements) is the main reason for software architecture becoming so important over the past years.
> The way software is developed is currently changing. The ability to deal with architectures and to create them is becoming an increasingly important aspect of a developer's job.
> The current evolution steps in software development contain model-based and highly architecture-centric concepts.
> We often see a lack of orientation when architecture is a topic on the agenda for projects.
> With our book, we want to give people active in the IT field orientation on the topic of architecture.
> Every IT system has an architecture.
> A workable architecture does not just "happen"—it has to be developed deliberately [Bredemeyer 2002].
> Most IT projects fail to some extent. Only around 30% of these projects can claim to conclude successfully [Standish 2009].
> Unfortunately, the consequences of poor architecture in IT often only appear after a considerable delay.
> In the context of software, architecture is a relatively new discipline.
> Architecture is only useful for projects with a long-term time horizon, complex requirements, and corresponding high risks.
> Architecture is not a purely technological issue. It also has numerous social and organizational aspects (see Chapter 7).
> An architecture always defines the fundamental parts and thus the supporting pillars but not the details of the system to be developed [Buschmann et al. 1996].
> In our book, we structure the topic of architecture using a so-called orientation framework.
> Our book offers IT students, software developers, IT architects, and IT managers a holistic and consistent orientation across all relevant topics in IT architecture generally as well as in software architecture in particular.
> Chapter 2 of our book is a must for all readers. It describes and defines the architecture of our book and is therefore the prerequisite for the basic understanding of our book.

**Summary:
Introduction**

Further Reading

Further reading: Software architecture

[Bredemeyer 2002]
Bredemeyer, Dana, *Introduction to Software Architecture*, http://www.bredemeyer.com/papers.htm, 2002

[Bredemeyer and Malan 2010]
Bredemeyer, Dana; Malan, Ruth, *Visual Architecting Action Guide Book*, http://www.ruthmalan.com/, 2010

[Shaw and Garlan 1996]
Shaw, Mary; Garlan, David, *Software Architecture - Perspectives on an Emerging Discipline*, Prentice Hall, Upper Saddle River, N. J., 1996

[SEI 2010]
Carnegie Mellon University Software Engineering Institute, *Community Software Architecture Definitions*
http://www.sei.cmu.edu/architecture/start/community.cfm, 2010

Further reading: Software architecture means

[Booch et al. 2005]
Booch, Grady; Rumbaugh James; Jacobson, *The Unified Modeling Language*, Addison-Wesley, Amsterdam, 2005

[Buschmann et al. 1996]
Buschmann, Frank; Meunier, Regine; Rohnert, Hans; Sommerlad, Peter; Stal, Michael, *Pattern-Oriented Software Architecture Vol. 1, A System of Patterns*, John Wiley & Sons, New York, 1996

Further reading: IT projects, development processes and methods

[Dijkstra 1972]
Dijkstra, Edsger W., *The Humble Programmer, Communications of the ACM*, 1972

[Fowler 2005]
Fowler, Martin, *The New Methodology*, http://www.martinfowler.com/articles/newMethodology.html, 2005

[Foote and Yoder 1999]
Foot, Brian; Yoder, Joseph, *Big Ball of Mud*, http://www.laputan.org/mud/mud.html, 1999

[Standish 2009]
The Standish Group International Inc., *The CHAOS Summary 2009*, http://www.
standishgroup.com/newsroom/chaos_2009.php, 2009

[Yourdon 2004]
Yourdon, Edward, *Death March*, Prentice Hall, New York, 2004d

2 | Architecture Orientation Framework

In this chapter we present an explanatory model for dealing with architecture. This model provides orientation by positioning the significant elements of architecture in an architecture orientation framework using simple question words. The focal point of this framework is the role of the architect. We also use the framework to convey knowledge and experience throughout the rest of the book. It enables you to think about architecture in a structured way and to orient yourself.

Overview

Basic concepts of the architecture orientation framework

Figure 2-1 shows the basic concepts covered in this chapter and visualizes how they relate to each other.

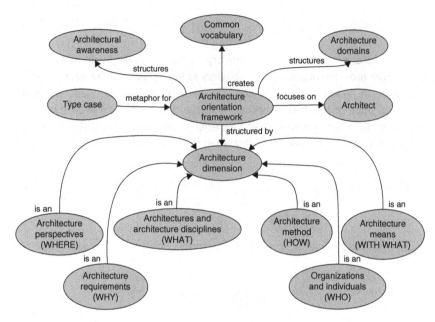

Figure 2-1: Basic concepts of the orientation framework

2.1 Motivation

Varied and dynamic environment

Architects work in a very varied and dynamic environment. New technologies are flooding onto the market, new tools promise increases in efficiency and productivity, lean methodologies promise risk-free project management, and new architecture concepts, such as service orientation and cloud computing, claim to reduce the inherent complexity of IT systems. As an architect, you must be able to understand, classify, and finally assess all of these developments and new features in order to select a suitable solution for your specific problem. You must therefore arrange and classify such new topics accordingly and compare them with your existing knowledge. In addition to mastering this flood of information, your tasks include making architectural decisions, defining guidelines, and managing your team professionally. You must also take on board customer requirements, analyze them, and design viable architectures. The selection of suitable products, and therefore the communication with suppliers, is also an important part of your role.

Develop architectural awareness

To be successful in this environment, you must be aware of these varied aspects—you must develop an *architectural awareness* that enables you to classify, evaluate, and put all aspects into an overarching and holistic architectural context. Every architect develops such a way of thinking about architecture over the course of his or her career. It reflects your understanding of architecture and enables you to structure your daily work. The quality of this awareness is relevant strategically and in the long term, since an architectural awareness is a basis for life-long learning and thus for being a successful architect. Concrete knowledge is of course important, but it can be learned and has a shorter life than an architectural awareness. Without this understanding, it is difficult to position, apply, and assess knowledge. During the course of your activities, you will also undergo experiences that you have to classify in the same way as your concrete knowledge. This will enable you to make better decisions in the future based on your wealth of experience, and to make these decisions more easily and more consciously.

Architectural awareness should be structured like a type case into which you can sort new experiences and new things learned, and retrieve them as and when they are required. "Learned" refers to the knowledge aspect of practicing as an architect. Architecture principles, styles, and patterns, but also specific platforms, such as JEE and .NET, fall into this category. "Experienced" covers specific experiences from the real world, for example, whether one of the afore-mentioned platforms works in practice, or how to deal with tensions within a project team. To stay with our metaphor, the type case supports the orderly arrangement of parts, where each section is a container for elements that share certain characteristics—thus a specific classification that they all have in common. This enables you to derive the general characteristics of new information learned and new experiences gained from the understanding of the characteristics of the section into which you have sorted them.

Structure architectural awareness

The structure of the architecture type case should take into account your varied fields of activities. It must therefore consider architecture in its entirety, and not, for example, restrict itself to primarily technical aspects. It is therefore important to place you the architect at the center of the consideration. The type case should also enable you to open further sections within a section, to guide your awareness to further structuring paths within a section, and to develop the type case further over time. In addition, despite having to be comprehensive and extensible, it must still be intuitive and understandable so that you can use it efficiently. You will only be able to act successfully in practice if you can explain the layout and structure of your architecture type case, and thus your holistic understanding of architecture, in simple words.

Define architectural structuring characteristics

The type case represents a basic model for explaining the architecture domain and spans the framework within which you operate as an architect. Based on the previously defined requirements for comprehensiveness, extensibility, simplic-

Derive the architecture orientation framework

ity, and understanding, the following sections present an architecture orientation framework that can be viewed as a type case.

2.2 Overview of the Framework

Basis of the architecture orientation framework

The framework presented below has arisen from visualizing the daily life of an architect and considering the requirements formulated in the previous section. A framework should be simple. It is therefore important to restrict yourself to the few most important dimensions, or rather main sections in the sense of the type case metaphor. However, at the same time, these dimensions should be extensive enough to be able to describe the varied nature of architecture. It should also be possible to subdivide the dimensions further in a useful way so that you can extend the framework. The framework must also be easy to understand and based on practice. So what distinguishes an architect in practice? In principle, you provide answers to questions and problems put to you by customers, team members, suppliers, or even questions you pose yourself. Therefore, an architecture orientation framework with a structure based on open question words is a sensible and practical approach.

Question words as main dimensions

The main dimensions of the framework are:

Table 2.2-1: *Dimensions of the architecture orientation framework*

Question word	Dimension	Explanation
WHAT	Architectures and architecture disciplines	The WHAT dimension contains basic principles and definitions of architecture. It therefore lays the basis for working as an architect. It also classifies architecture according to the various fields of activity in which architects work (e.g., software architecture, data architecture, or security architecture). Fundamental knowledge and experience belong to the WHAT dimension.
WHERE	Architecture perspectives	The WHERE dimension covers the different levels at which architecture takes place and the views with which architecture can be described. The use of different perspectives enables you to concentrate on one problem at a time. You use this dimension to include different ways of looking at things.
WHY	Architecture requirements	The WHY dimension is dedicated to the requirements IT systems must satisfy in general and architectures in particular. From the wealth of requirements you are confronted with, you must be able to identify those that are architecturally significant and design an architecture that meets these requirements. In the WHY dimension, you can arrange the requirements an architecture must satisfy.

Question word	Dimension	Explanation
WITH WHAT	Architecture means	The WITH WHAT dimension structures the different architecture means you can use whilst carrying out your trade. It thus enables you to classify different architecture means.
WHO	Organizations and individuals	The WHO dimension looks at the role of the architect and the influence of individuals and organizations on architecture. It examines the interaction between organizations, individuals, and architecture more closely. Considering this dimension allows you to act successfully. In the WHO dimension, you can include knowledge and experience from your social and organizational environment.
HOW	Architecture method	The HOW dimension structures the architecture method. It details the most important architectural activities that you perform during your work. Here you can store proven methods and access them again as and when necessary.

The framework can be visualized as shown in Figure 2.2-1. This image places you, the architect, at the center, and we use it repeatedly throughout the book to place the topic in question in the context of the framework, thus providing you with better orientation.

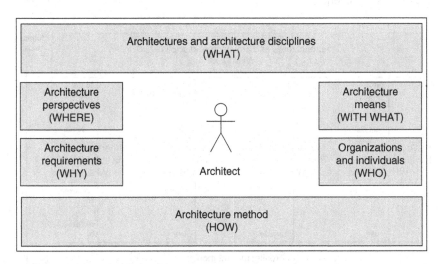

Figure 2.2-1: *Overview of the architecture orientation framework*

A framework structured according to the question words specified enables you to ask basic questions and thus in practice, enables simple and systematic orientation. Architectural activity can thus take place based on an explanatory model in

Framework in action

which you are aware of the different dimensions at any given time. In the course of a project, for example, during analysis, design, and implementation, you will continually ask yourself which means (WITH WHAT) to use in which way (HOW) to realize a specific requirement (WHY). For example, you document the desire for a distributed architecture during the analysis by holding a requirements analysis workshop (HOW), document it in a requirements document (WITH WHAT), and you guarantee it in the architecture design by using a corresponding architecture pattern (WITH WHAT). In addition, depending on the architecture discipline (WHAT), you will, for example, use different perspectives (WHERE) to consider relevant aspects of the IT system for the current activity. It is not possible to assign all aspects uniquely to one and only one dimension, since the aspects themselves are multi-dimensional. Methods such as the Unified Software Development Process (USDP) are a good example of this. They define, for example, a basic process on one hand, and on the other, document the means with which a system is realized and the perspectives from which it can be considered. In the sense of our architecture orientation framework, you should generally assign such methods to the HOW dimension and the other process-independent elements of the methods to the other dimensions. For orientation purposes, it is important that you establish criteria that enable you to make assignments to the dimensions. The basic question you have to answer is: *"What is the essence of the topic under consideration?"* Once you have answered the question, you can make an assignment.

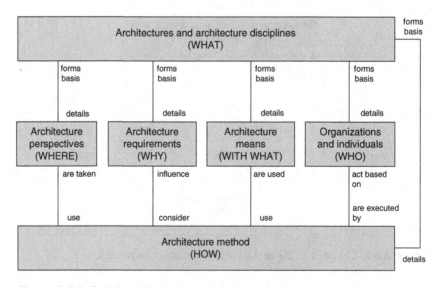

Figure 2.2-2: *Relationships between the dimensions*

The individual dimensions of the framework are related (see Figure 2.2-2). The WHAT dimension forms the basis for all other dimensions since it contains the basic architecture knowledge and important architecture definitions. All other dimensions detail the basic principles contained in the WHAT dimension. In an architecture method (HOW dimension), the elements of the other dimensions are also put into a methodological and time context. For example, an architecture method describes which architecture perspectives (WHERE dimension) have to be applied and which architecture means (WITH WHAT dimension) have to be selected to fulfill specific architecture requirements (WHY dimension). The architecture method also describes which activities are to be performed. Individuals (WHO dimension) base their actions on the method.

Relationships between the dimensions

Using this framework, you can establish a common vocabulary and understanding, which makes communication within the team easier. It therefore not only benefits individual architects in arranging their architectural thoughts, but also makes collaboration with others more efficient, since a common framework can reduce misunderstandings. The framework can therefore be a catalyst for successful collaboration within the team. Of course, the framework merely represents one possible model for thinking about architecture and arranging your thoughts. In our experience, however, the model is very practical and makes daily work easier. The following sections give an overview of the individual dimensions of the architecture orientation framework.

Common vocabulary and practical suitability

2.3 Architectures and Architecture Disciplines (WHAT)

The WHAT dimension is dedicated to basic architecture knowledge. The elements of this dimension enable you to explain the nature of architecture, define architecture, and relate architecture to other IT domains and non-IT domains, such as building architecture. With a good understanding of the basic terminology outlined here, you have the basis for understanding and working with the other dimensions.

WHAT dimension represents the foundation

Designing architectures successfully is a challenge given the inherent complexity of IT systems. Today, architectures must recognize the usual requirements such as reliability, availability, and scalability, and in addition, offer a basis for realizing functional requirements. You are thus faced with the challenge of considering various architectural influencing factors, such as functional and qualitative aspects, and balancing them out sufficiently for the specific problem at hand. In addition to a well-founded basic architectural knowledge, you also need deeper knowledge of specialist fields. For example, for the integration of IT systems, you must have a very good understanding of the integration platform to be implemented and possible integration approaches, such as message-based or

Varied aspects

process-based integration. This need for specialist knowledge has led to the establishment of various *architecture disciplines*. During the course of your career, you will generally decide to specialize in one of these disciplines. An architecture is thus often created as a team effort through the collaboration of architects from the individual disciplines.

Architecture disciplines

Therefore, in the WHAT dimension, in addition to looking at the basic principles of software architecture in detail, we briefly present further architecture disciplines. We do this in an overview in order to position the disciplines within the architecture orientation framework and to separate them from one another. We will look at the following disciplines:

> Software architecture
> Data architecture
> Integration architecture
> Network architecture
> Security architecture
> System management architecture
> Enterprise architecture

We will examine the contents of the WHAT dimension in more detail in Chapter 3.

2.4 Architecture Perspectives (WHERE)

Concentration on perspectives

Architectural thinking and practice are complex. Psychological studies indicate that people can only process 7 ± 2 units of information simultaneously [Miller 1956]. Added together, the quantity of information covered by all aspects of an architecture vastly exceeds this figure. It is therefore extremely difficult to grasp the building blocks of a system, how they are grouped, how they interact, how they are distributed, and their behavior at runtime all at once. To be successful despite the restrictions of human understanding, you have to reduce the complexity by examining only one manageable part of an architecture at any one time.

Architecture levels

Architecture can take place at different levels. It is therefore important to always be clear about the level you are dealing with. This is the only way of applying useful means and disciplines for the architecture level in question. The levels possible range from organizations to systems all the way down to individual building blocks.

Architecture views and models

At each level, you can take different *architecture views* of a system. In their entirety, the views give a complementary image of the architecture to be implemented. *Architecture view models* enable you to look at architectures systematically and in a way that reduces their complexity for this purpose. They group relevant views from which architectures are to be considered into one model, thus enabling them to be shown in their entirety. The *4 + 1 view* from Kruchten [Kruchten 2000] is an example of an architecture view model. Architecture frameworks, such as the *Zachman Framework* [Zachman 1987] and the *Reference Model for Open Distributed Processing (RM-ODP)* [ISO10746 1998], also contain architecture view models.

Chapter 4 discusses the individual architecture levels and views. It also takes a closer look at the different views of the architecture models mentioned.

2.5 Architecture Requirements (WHY)

For companies, information technology (IT) is a significant means for realizing their business strategies and supporting their operations. You therefore design IT systems and, as a consequence, architectures, not for their own purpose but with a specific business purpose in mind. The primary motivation for architecture is thus not technological elegance but the specific and long-term added value for the business. Of course, you can only achieve this added value if the IT system satisfies the functional requirements placed on it. However, an IT system that satisfies the functional requirements but does not appreciate the non-functional requirements will have no real benefit for the business. An e-commerce shop that satisfies all functional requirements but crashes with a high number of simultaneous users will not support the real business strategy and will probably not deliver any added value.

Architecture is not an end in itself

You must therefore ensure that the requirements placed on an IT system are supported by the underlying architecture of that system. It is essential that you know different types of requirements and their implications for architecture. In principle, there are functional and non-functional requirements. We can differentiate between the following types of requirements:
> Organizational requirements
> System requirements
> Building block requirements
> Development time requirements
> Runtime requirements
> Organizational constraints

Types of requirements

The WHY dimension identifies and explains the different types of requirements. You can only design IT systems "fit for purpose" when you are aware of the different *requirements* and take them into account when practicing as an architect. We will discuss these different types of requirements in detail in Chapter 5.

Relevance of architecture requirements

2.6 Architecture Means (WITH WHAT)

Elements of the WITH WHAT dimension

This dimension is dedicated to the means you use to design and implement your solutions. Using the type case metaphor, this section contains lots of smaller subsections in order to structure the large number of *architecture means* and make orientation easier. During the course of your career, you will continually add new means to these sections and remove obsolete ones. A means becomes obsolete when it is no longer relevant. The spectrum of possible architecture means ranges from fundamental principles to concrete technologies.

Principles

There are elementary means, which, when used and considered, are extremely relevant in establishing successful architectures. These belong to the category of *architecture principles*. One means in this category is the *separation of concerns principle*. Its aim is to clearly separate the responsibilities of building blocks. For example, a building block for visualizing data should not be responsible for saving it in a database. *Architecture principles* are important long term and should accompany every architectural activity. They embody fundamental architecture experiences.

Basic concepts

To ensure that architecture principles are also taken into account in an architecture, you can apply basic *concepts* that support these principles accordingly. You must therefore look at the different concepts and select the appropriate ones depending on the problem at hand. The architecture concepts include basic design and realization paradigms, such as object orientation and component orientation. Means that are based entirely on modeling and generation, such as model-driven software development or model-driven architecture [OMG 2010c], are also elements of this sub-dimension.

Tactics, styles, and patterns

In addition to considering elementary principles and concepts, we recommend having proven architecture solutions in your toolbox so that you can reuse them for similar problems. These solutions, which are based on *architecture principles*, belong to the family of *architecture tactics, styles,* and *patterns*. An *architecture tactic* helps you to get a first idea about a design problem. You can then develop this idea further. You can also use *styles* and *patterns*, for example, as further means. An *architecture style* documents a proven and successful way of structuring an architecture. Every style has specific characteristics and is a template for the design of the actual architecture. An *architecture style* is also an efficient documentation and communication tool, since the properties of the style used can be understood independently of the actual purpose of the system. There are various options for documenting *architecture styles*. One proven and recommended form is the documentation of the style as an *architecture pattern*. An *architecture pattern* describes *architecture styles* using a general structure. The authors of POSA1 and POSA2 have made a considerable contribution in this area [Buschmann et al. 1996; Schmidt et al. 2000]. For example, one *architecture style* described in pattern form is the *layers architecture pattern*. It documents the arrangement of system building blocks at different levels. This arrangement achieves a clear separation of responsibilities and avoids a monolithic architecture [Buschmann et al. 1996]. The classic arrangement of presentation logic, business logic, and persistence logic on different layers is a well-known application of this pattern. Architecture styles and patterns are similar means with a different form of description.

A further type of means is *basic architectures*. Basic architectures use the previously identified architecture means in a larger context. Examples of such basic architectures are:

> Cloud Computing Architectures
> Dataflow architecture
> Layered architecture
> Middleware architecture
> n-tier architecture
> Rich client architecture
> Service Oriented Architectures
> Thin client architecture

Basic architectures

Knowing these basic architectures enables you to expand your architecture knowledge and understanding—and thus arrive at an effective software architecture more quickly.

Architectures of complex systems have to solve several different architecture problems, or rather, balance them out appropriately. Therefore, several *architecture patterns* are used in combination. *Architecture patterns* are also architecture means that do not relate to any specific problem area. That is, they do not address, for example, specific characteristics of a call center architecture. Relying solely on *architecture patterns* to design a solution for such an architecture is therefore not sufficient. It is much more important to include complete architecture solutions in your toolbox as references. These *reference architectures* describe solutions that have been designed for a specific problem domain using different *architecture styles* or *architecture patterns*. They therefore reflect the highest degree of reusability of architectural knowledge and experience.

Reference architectures

One very important factor in the success and acceptance of an architecture is that everyone involved (customer, project lead, software developer, etc.) understands and supports it. It is therefore essential that you communicate your ideas and approaches and model the architecture according to these ideas and approaches. To achieve this, you have to use the correct means to express the architecture.

Modeling means

These means can vary depending on the target group. For example, for a bid presentation, it may be sufficient to visualize the significant building blocks of an architecture using graphical elements. However, you will need more expressive means for the architecture design in order to exclude misunderstandings and take account of all significant architecture aspects, such as the structure and dynamics of an architecture. The means used in this context are used to model the architecture and belong to the family of *architecture modeling means*. One example of a widespread, standardized modeling means is the Unified Modeling Language (UML) from the Object Management Group [OMG 2007a].

Technologies

In addition to the architecture structures themselves, the selection of technologies that carry and support the architecture design in the actual implementation is a further important influencing factor for a successful architecture. Therefore, one of the trays of your toolbox should be dedicated to these *basic technologies*. Add new technologies to your toolbox frequently and remove technologies that have become obsolete. Databases, transaction monitors, and middleware can be included in this sub-dimension, for example. Furthermore, to implement an architecture successfully, it is very important that you know possible target platforms and consider their strengths and weaknesses when actually realizing the architecture on a concrete platform. Target platforms, such as Sun's Java Enterprise Edition or Microsoft's .NET, belong to the category of *component platforms* and are important design means for implementing architecture requirements such as scalability, availability, and reliability by providing elementary basic functionality.

Chapter 6 covers these topics

The realization and conscious use of these means make architectural activity easier and contribute considerably to the success of an architecture. Chapter 6 looks more closely at the WITH WHAT dimension, examining the individual architecture means in more detail. In this book, we restrict ourselves primarily to IT-related means. It is, however, also possible to place other means in this dimension, such as presentation and discussion techniques. These are useful for you in your communication with stakeholders.

2.7 Organizations and Individuals (WHO)

Interaction and communication as an architecture activity

Architectures are created by people. As an architect, you interact and communicate with many different groups of people in order to design an architecture. For example, you work closely with the customer and end users of the system to be developed in order to extract the architecturally significant requirements from the requirements placed on the system. You are also the first contact person for project leads, supporting them in the creation of project plans and effort estimations. You also lead project teams from a technical point of view, and act as the communicator and motivator of the architecture to be implemented.

To manage these tasks successfully, you need more than well-founded skills in technical and methodological topics. You must also have good social skills. Even the most elegant technical architecture idea cannot be realized if you cannot convince your team and customer of the idea. Unfortunately, not enough importance is placed on social skills in the role of an architect today, even though as far back as 1968 Melvin Conway raised the theory that an architecture is defined to a considerable extent by organizational influences [Conway 1968]. It is very important to be aware of these organizational influences and the required social skills. This is one of the key differentiators that make a technical specialist an architect.

Relevance of social skills

The *WHO dimension* addresses these social skills and thus outlines the role of an architect in organizations and teams. On one hand it covers general topics such as group dynamics processes, factors for well functioning teams, and the interdependencies of organizations and teams. On the other hand, it presents topics that have arisen from concrete project experiences. These include, for example, *organizational patterns*. Organizational patterns describe successful options for cooperation between roles in projects [Coplien and Harrison 2004]. Chapter 7 looks at these topics in detail.

Elements of the WHO dimension

2.8 Architecture Method (HOW)

As an architect, your objective is to design an architecture that can be used as a foundation for realizing a system. To achieve this objective, you have access to various architecture means, can vary their level of abstraction, and can communicate with different partners such as project leads, developers, and analysts. However, considering these options does not guarantee that you will meet your objective. Even if you realize a system successfully once, it does not mean that you will experience the same success next time. You can only be successful in the long term if you are able to repeat your architectural activities systematically. Therefore, it is very important to be aware of proven methodological approaches and be able to apply them repeatedly. The *HOW dimension* is dedicated to these methodological approaches, or rather the question "what do I have to do to design and implement an architecture?" We will therefore present a general architecture method.

Systematic and repeatable activity

The architecture method contains the following activities that must be executed when you design an architecture:
> Creating the system vision
> Understanding the requirements
> Designing the architecture
> Implementing the architecture
> Communicating the architecture

Architecture activities

You can perform the activities several times within an iterative development process.

Activity-specific relevance of other dimensions

Depending on which activity you are currently performing, elements of the other *dimensions* have an effect on the architecture to different degrees. For example, you should use different means and perspectives depending on the activity at hand. In *understanding the requirements*, for example, it is particularly important to select the architecturally significant requirements from the requirements placed on the system.

We will look at this topic in more detail in Chapter 8.

2.9 Summary

Summary: Architecture orientation framework

> The architecture orientation framework structures architecture using the dimensions WHAT, WHERE, WHY, WITH WHAT, WHO, and HOW.
> The WHAT dimension (architectures and architecture disciplines) contains basic principles and definitions of architecture. It therefore lays the basis for working as an architect.
> The WHERE dimension (architecture perspectives) covers the different levels at which architecture takes place and the views that make architecture tangible.
> The WHY dimension (architecture requirements) is dedicated to the requirements placed on IT systems in general and architectures in particular.
> The WITH WHAT dimension (architecture means) structures the different architecture means you can use whilst practicing as an architect.
> The WHO dimension (organizations and individuals) looks at the role of the architect and the influence of individuals and organizations on architecture.
> The HOW dimension (architecture method) structures the architectural process. It details the most important architectural activities that you perform during your work.

Further Reading

Further reading: Architecture styles and patterns

[Buschmann et al. 1996]
Buschmann, Frank; Meunier, Regine; Rohnert, Hans; Sommerlad, Peter; Stal, Michael, *Pattern-Oriented Software Architecture Vol. 1, A System of Patterns*, John Wiley & Sons, New York, 1996

[Schmidt et al. 2000]
Schmidt, Douglas C.; Rohnert, Hans; Stal, Michael; Buschmann, Frank, *Pattern-Oriented Software Architecture Vol. 2, Patterns for Concurrent and Networked Objects*, John Wiley & Sons, New York, 2000

[Kruchten 2000]
Kruchten, Philippe, *The Rational Unified Process - An Introduction Second Edition*, Addison-Wesley, Boston, 2000

[ISO10746 1998]
International Organization for Standardization, *Information technology – Open Distributed Processing – Reference model: Overview*, http://www.iso.org/iso/en/CatalogueDetailPage.CatalogueDetail?CSNUMBER=20696&ICS1=35&ICS2=80&ICS3=, 1998

[Zachman 1987]
Zachman, John, A., *A Framework for Information Systems Architecture*, IBM Publication, 1987

[OMG 2007a]
Object Management Group, *UML 2.1.2 Superstructure Specification*, http://www.omg.org/spec/UML/2.1.2/Infrastructure/, 2007

[OMG 2010c]
Object Management Group, *Model Driven Architecture*, http://www.omg.org/mda/, 2010

[Miller 1956]
Miller, G., *The Magical Number Seven, Plus Or Minus Two: Some Limits on Our Capacity for Processing Information*, The Psychological Review, 63(2), 81-97, 1956

Further reading: Architecture views and framework

Further reading: UML

Further reading: Miscellaneous

3 | Architectures and Architecture Disciplines (WHAT)

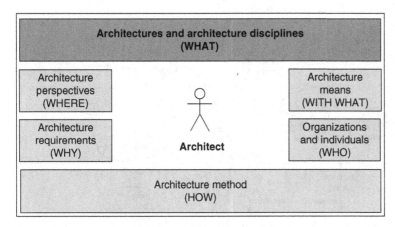

Figure 3-1: *Positioning of the chapter in the orientation framework*

In this chapter we look at the *WHAT dimension* of the architecture orientation framework. It conveys a basic understanding of architecture. We also present the significant building blocks that make up a system and their relationships to one another. Since the nature of systems and systems thinking are essential for your work as an architect, we also position these concepts in the context of architecture. After reading this chapter, you will be able to explain the general nature of architecture, differentiate between individual architecture disciplines and the most important building blocks of systems, and describe their relationships with one another.

Overview

Figure 3-2 shows the basic concepts that we will look at in this chapter and visualizes how they relate to each other.

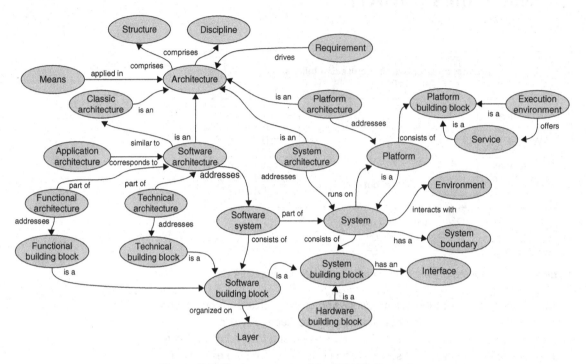

Figure 3-2: Basic concepts of the WHAT dimension

3.1 Classic Architecture as Starting Point

General meaning of architecture

This section explains what is generally understood under the term "architecture". Using this understanding as a base, later in this chapter we will discuss software architecture. The classic architecture of buildings and constructions is the starting point for this examination. The American Heritage Dictionary offers possible definitions of architecture in its classic meaning:

Classic architecture definition

> The art and science of designing and erecting buildings
> A style and method of design and construction
> Orderly arrangement of parts

According to this definition, architecture is both an art and a science, dealing with both designing and erecting buildings. It does not concentrate solely on planning the building. It extends right up to the realization of the building. Furthermore, a key result of the architecture activity is the arranging or orderly arrangement of parts of the building. Architecture thus makes important statements about the structure of the building. The definition states further that architecture styles and methods are elements of architecture. They represent architectural experience that you use in your work. Architecture is therefore not merely the structure of a building, but also the way of approaching something.

There is no unique definition of the term "architecture". For some, "architecture" is the structure of a building or an IT/software system; for others, the activities performed by people in designing the structure. To make the differentiation between the actual architectural process and the structural aspects of architecture clearer, in this book we will treat the activity as an architecture discipline.

Architecture comprises structure and activity

Architectures are generally created based on requirements (e.g., the desire for simple housing) and using available means (e.g., building materials and tools). Seen from an historical perspective, in classic architecture the actual design was based initially on the principle of *trial and error*, and was generally ad hoc. This meant that every building had its own individual structure. An orderly arrangement of parts as a result of planned architecture was generally not the case. Architecture styles were only developed once architecture experiences were passed on verbally or in writing. Architecture is therefore always based on heuristics, or rather, architecture means and procedures that have proven themselves in the past. Architecture styles are therefore means for documenting tried and proven solutions for architectural problems. Figure 3.1-1 illustrates the influence of requirements and means on architecture.

Development of architecture

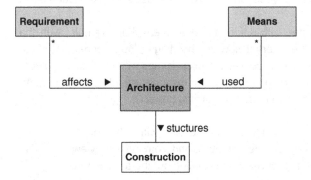

Figure 3.1-1: Requirements and means as influencing factors on architecture

An important thought leader in classic architecture was Marcus Vitruvius Pollio, a Roman architect from the first century BC. He wrote the work "*De architectura libri decem*," known today as "*The Ten Books on Architecture*" [Morgan 1960]. Vitruvius represented the theory that good architecture must satisfy the following requirements:

> Durability (*firmitas*)
> Usefulness (*utilitas*)
> Elegance (*venustas*)

Requirements placed on architecture

These requirements are still valid today. The *durability* of an architecture indicates whether it can satisfy future requirements and support further evolution. For example, a further floor can only be added to a house if such an extension was considered in the architectural design. The *usefulness* is a quality attribute regarding whether the architecture fulfills the specific requirements. For example, the architecture should plan the arrangement of doors in a house such that the rooms can be accessed. Finally, *elegance* expresses how the architecture is structured. The arrangement of the individual elements of the architecture is reflected in the *elegance*. Different architecture alternatives can implement the same requirements with a different degree of elegance.

Architecture as a compromise

An architecture is therefore created based on different requirements and is influenced by these requirements (see Figure 3.1-2).

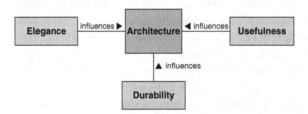

Figure 3.1-2: *Architecture influenced by classic requirements*

Architectures fulfill requirements to different degrees. They are therefore always a compromise and the result of your considerations and decisions (see Chapter 5).

Architect communicates with stakeholders

An architect communicates with different stakeholders. For example, with the customer he discusses the external view of a building or the arrangement of the rooms within the building. He discusses technical issues with other stakeholders involved in the construction of the building—for example, the electrical wiring. An architect therefore has a central role in a building project.

Architect uses different perspectives

An architect discusses one and the same building with different stakeholders (e.g., customer or foreman) at different levels and from different views. He also applies these different perspectives when working out the architecture.

Common features of classic architecture and software architecture

Classic architecture and software architecture have some features in common. We illustrate these below in a brief summary of the insights gained so far:
>   An architecture defines the arrangement of parts of a building or an IT system. In classic architecture, these are the fundamental parts [Perry and Wolf 1992]. The architecture therefore defines the fundamental parts, but not the details of the system to be developed [Buschmann et al. 1996].
>   An architect uses different views to present an architecture and his activities take place at different levels. The levels and views relevant for you as a software architect are presented in Chapter 4.

> Every architecture discipline must ensure balance between the architecture requirements. Therefore, just like a classic architect, a software architect must know the requirements that are relevant for the software architecture and take them into account in the architecture design. We will therefore discuss architecture requirements in more detail in Chapter 5.

> The manner of the arrangement is based on experience and embodies an architecture style. Architecture means are used during the design of the architecture. In software architecture, various means are used. We will present these in Chapter 6.

> An architect communicates and interacts with different stakeholders. He has a central role in the realization of a building project. This also applies for a software architect. Chapter 7 therefore looks at the social aspects of software architecture.

> The concrete action of arranging the parts is based on a method, and the architectural activity stretches from the design up to the implementation. The architectural process for designing a software architecture is covered in Chapter 8.

In the following section, we make the insights gained so far more concrete and apply them to software architecture.

3.2 From Classic Architecture to Software Architecture

As explained in the previous section, the general definition of architecture can also be applied to software architecture. Software architecture is concerned with the design and implementation of IT systems. From the viewpoint of architectural activity, software architecture covers the steps necessary to design and implement an architecture. With regard to the structural aspect of architecture, software architecture describes the structures of IT systems.

Software architecture and the classic architecture definition

> From this point on, the terms "IT system" and "system" are used synonymously provided no explicit differentiation is necessary.

IT system and system as synonym

Today, systems have many facets and you have to make decisions in architectural areas that exceed the pure software aspect. This means that, depending on the type of system, you may need to know the concrete hardware used very early in the software architecture design process. Consequently, a system as a whole consists of more than just software building blocks, and you have to have a sufficient understanding of the other building blocks. Therefore, here we will introduce a system definition that considers the holistic nature of systems:

Systems have many facets

Definition: System

> A system is a unit that consists of integrated software and hardware building blocks and exists for the purpose of fulfilling a functional objective. To achieve this objective, it communicates with its environment and must take account of the conditions defined by the environment.

Figure 3.2-1 shows the building blocks of a system.

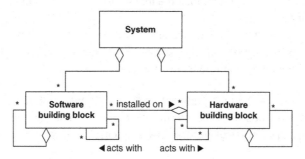

Figure 3.2-1: Building blocks of a system

The functional objective is described by the functional requirements placed on the system (see Chapter 5). The system definition intentionally stresses software *and* hardware building blocks to emphasize that a system is more than just software. A system's environment is the organization in which it is embedded. The system communicates with parts of the organization. These can be people as users of the system, or also other systems the system is connected to. Whether human users exist depends on the type of system. For example, a system for controlling an engine has no direct human user. However, it will definitely communicate with other systems in its environment. The organization sets the framework within which the system can act. For example, defined IT standards and development guidelines can be general conditions that the system has to consider in the broader sense. Of course, any existing standards and guidelines have to be considered during the design and implementation of the system.

Attempt at a definition of software architecture

In Chapter 1 we illustrated that there are a number of definitions for software architecture. This clearly shows how wide the field of interpretation and probably also confusion is in this area. As a result of this broad spectrum, in our opinion it is not possible to give one "correct" definition. For the purpose of this book, we have decided to find a definition that is based on our common understanding and that takes the afore-mentioned classic architecture definition into account. A corresponding definition must therefore cover both *the structure* and *the activity*.

Software architecture describes the software building blocks of a system. To be more precise, we can take a look at a definition that reflects the structural character of software architecture appropriately and that is widely used in literature and in practice. It is the definition of software architecture according to Bass et al. [Bass et al. 2003]:

"The software architecture of a program or computing system is the structure or structures of the system, which comprise software elements, the externally visible properties of those elements, and the relationships among them". (Note that Bass uses the term "element" for the parts of the architecture, whereas in this book we use the term "building block".)

Software architecture describes software building blocks

Definition: Software architecture of a system according to Bass et al.

This definition is very general. It does however contain the most important aspects of a software architecture:

> The software structure or structures of a system
> The software elements (or building blocks) of a system
> The properties of the software elements (or building blocks) of a system
> The relationships between the software elements (or building blocks) of a system

The definition states that a software architecture defines the software building blocks of a system. So which software building blocks does an architecture define? According to Perry and Wolf, these are the fundamental building blocks of a system [Perry and Wolf 1992]. In other words, the software building blocks that are of considerable importance for the system under construction. These can be key classes, interfaces, components, frameworks, subsystems, and modules (Chapter 6 looks at these terms in more detail). We intentionally do not specify them precisely here, since systems are very diverse and the specific designs of their software building blocks can therefore be very different. A clear differentiation between software architecture and design is very difficult. Drawing the correct boundary often depends on the corresponding experience of the architect and the viewpoint taken (see Chapter 4). The externally visible properties of software building blocks are the properties that can be perceived by other software building blocks. These include, for example, the functionality offered, the interfaces, and the performance of the software building blocks. The internal structure and characteristics of software building blocks are generally not taken into consideration in an architecture view, which is in principle a holistic view of a system (see Section 3.3).

Software building blocks of a system and their visible properties

In addition to naming the software building blocks, a software architecture also describes the structures between the software building blocks and the thus implied relationships. It is important to note that there is not "one" structure. De-

Software structure(s) of a system

pending on the perspective, different structures of a system are important and must be defined by an architecture. For example, a system always has a static and a dynamic structure. Therefore, when designing the architecture, you must consider different perspectives (see Chapter 4).

Definition: Architecture of software-intensive systems according to IEEE

A further important definition of architecture comes from the IEEE:

> Architecture is the fundamental organization of a system embodied in its components, their relationships to each other and to the environment and the principles guiding its design and evolution.

The IEEE introduced this definition in its standard 1471 [IEEE 2007], which covers the description of software-intensive systems. Software-intensive systems are systems whose character is defined to a large extent by software, but which do not consist solely of software.

Software architecture and the system environment

An important aspect of this definition is the explicit consideration of the environment of the system. This is a significant point that we will look at in more depth in Section 3.3 and Chapter 8.

Definition: Software architecture$_{structure}$

From the definition according to Bass and the definition according to the IEEE, we can derive the following definition of software architecture that acknowledges its structural character:

> The software architecture of a system is the structure or structures of the system, which comprise software building blocks, the externally visible properties of those building blocks, and the relationship among them and with their environment.

Software architecture as a discipline

With regard to the definition of classic architecture presented in Section 3.1, the previous definition of software architecture addresses only the *orderly arrangement of parts*. According to the classic definition however, architecture is much more than simply an architectural description of a system. It also comprises the actual architecture activity (in the classic architecture definition: *art and science*) that leads to the architecture of a system. Software architecture as a discipline is dedicated to this aspect:

Definition: Software architecture$_{discipline}$

> As a discipline, software architecture covers the architectural activities and the related decisions about the design and implementation of a software architecture.

In other words, as an architecture discipline, software architecture looks primarily at architectural activities as part of the analysis, design, and implementation of individual systems. Important activities are the identification and design of software building blocks, their interfaces, and their interactions. Usually, you break the system down recursively. You do this based on the requirements placed on the system and obtained during the analysis. The selection of principles on which the design and the evolution of a system are based is also an important aspect of this discipline. This is emphasized by the IEEE definition. In addition, your tasks as a software architect also include considering the underlying platform and selecting the distribution of the software building blocks. They also include selecting corresponding development methods and tools (see Chapter 8). In this context, Maier and Rechtin also use the term *architecting* to express the active aspect of architecture [Maier and Rechtin 2000].

For the purposes of this book, we have made a conscious decision to firstly separate the aspects structure and activity in definitions. Software architecture as a structure can be seen as the result of software architecture as a discipline. As a whole, software architecture comprises software architecture as a structure and software architecture as an activity or discipline:

Holistic view of software architecture

$$\text{Software architecture}_{total} = \text{Software architecture}_{structure} + \text{Software architecture}_{discipline}$$

When we subsequently talk about software architecture in the book, on one hand it means the result or software structure(s) of an IT system, and on the other, practicing as a software architect.

The overall architecture of a system takes into account both software building blocks and hardware building blocks. For completeness, we will therefore introduce a broader definition of system architecture:

Definition: System architecture

System architecture$_{structure}$: The system architecture of a system is the structure or structures of the system, which comprise building blocks (software and hardware building blocks), the externally visible properties of those building blocks, and the relationship among them and with their environment.

System architecture$_{discipline}$: As a discipline, system architecture covers the architectural activities and the related decisions about the design and implementation of a system architecture.

$$\text{Software architecture}_{total} = \text{Software architecture}_{structure} + \text{Software architecture}_{discipline}$$

There are many more architecture terms

In addition to the terms "software architecture" and "system architecture", many more architecture terms are used in practice and in literature. These include terms such as "technical architecture", "functional architecture", and "platform architecture". The terms are generally not clearly defined and are used indiscriminately. We will therefore look at these terms more closely below and try to find definitions that fit practice. Figure 3.2-2 illustrates the different architecture terms and places them in relation to the building blocks of a system.

The software architecture is part of a system architecture. It structures the software building blocks of a system. If we look more closely at the software architecture, we discover that it takes into account both functional and technical aspects. We therefore often talk about a functional and a technical architecture.

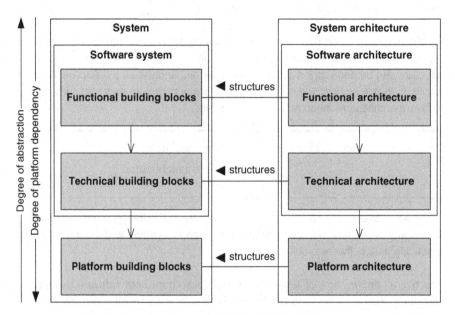

Figure 3.2-2: *Architecture terms and their relationships*

Functional architecture

Functional architecture arises from the domain or problem area for which the system is being developed. It divides the system into functional building blocks and is driven by the character of the domain and the functional requirements placed on the system. For example, in an order processing solution, we could identify the following functional building blocks: order entry, order management, and customer management. The degree of abstraction of functional architecture is high and its platform dependency is low. The functional architecture is based on the technical architecture.

Technical architecture

In its original sense, the technical architecture is domain-independent and is dedicated primarily to the realization of non-functional requirements or qualities. It defines technical building blocks for non-functional aspects, such as logging, auditing, security, reference data, persistence, and transaction management. The technical building blocks use services from the platform and encapsulate them such that they can be used in a platform-independent way by functional building blocks. The degree of abstraction of a technical architecture is lower than that of a functional architecture. Conversely, the platform dependency of a technical architecture is higher. Technical architectures can generally be used for software systems of various domains, as they are domain-independent. The technical architecture also defines how functional building blocks are mapped onto the technical architecture. A coarse-grained functional building block can be broken down into a set of fine-grained functional building blocks. The resulting functional building blocks have a lower level of abstraction. For example, the technical architecture can be based on the model view controller pattern [Buschmann et al. 1996]. This splits the functional building block "order management" into a model building block, a view building block, and a controller building block.

To understand the term "platform architecture", we must first explain the term "platform" in more detail. For a detailed discussion of this term, see Section 3.4. At this point, it is sufficient to state that a platform is itself a system that can consist of software building blocks, and, where applicable, hardware building blocks. It is used to execute software building blocks of a system and offers services to them. The platform architecture therefore defines the platform building blocks and their structure. The technical building blocks use the platform building blocks. For examples of pure software platforms, see Section 6.7.5. JEE is a component platform, for example, and in turn can exist on different operating system platforms and hardware platforms.

Platform architecture

The explanations above are sufficient for an initial understanding of the terms "functional architecture", "technical architecture", and "platform architecture". However, in practice, it is not always easy to assign an architecture to one specific category. Platforms are becoming more powerful and no longer provide only services of a pure infrastructure nature, such as transaction management or persistence. Platforms are now being created that offer functional basic functionality. For example, a portal platform will also offer personalization, syndication, or campaign management. The platform therefore already covers functional requirements. This means that it has both a functional and a technical character. It is also possible to imagine that a functional platform builds on a technical platform, and the actual software system in turn builds on the functional platform. The more useful the platform, that is, the more requirements that are already satisfied by the platform, the leaner the technical and functional architecture can be. Model-driven software development (see Section 6.2.6) and domain-specific modeling also contribute to this trend.

The crossover between functional, technical, and platform architecture is smooth

So, what was application architecture again?

Another term used in many ways in both practice and theory is "application architecture". For some people, the application architecture is the software architecture; for others, the functional architecture. In this book, we equate application architecture with software architecture.

Further architecture disciplines in IT

In addition to software architecture, IT contains further architecture disciplines. Amongst other things, this is because IT systems are becoming ever more complex, making specialization in one area essential. The examples given below are intended to make this clearer. The focus here is on an enterprise-related IT system. However, the problem is also transferable to other IT systems, such as embedded systems. The respective architecture discipline is given in parentheses.

> You can distribute different software building blocks of a system over different hardware and connect them via a network. Thus, in designing such an architecture, you must also consider network aspects (architecture discipline: *network architecture*).

> In addition, systems must communicate with one another to exchange data or to support cross-system business processes. This means that they must be integrated within the enterprise and across enterprise borders. The architecture of a system must therefore also acknowledge integrative aspects (architecture discipline: *integration architecture*).

> The quality of the data exchanged is very important for the success of an enterprise. Systems therefore often have the task of collecting existing data that is spread across an enterprise and making it available. When designing the architecture, you must also consider how this data is represented (architecture discipline: *data architecture*).

> The data a system exchanges and processes may contain highly sensitive information. You must therefore protect it against access by unauthorized third parties. A system must therefore guarantee this security, and you must provide for it in the system's architecture (architecture discipline: *security architecture*).

> It must also be possible to operate systems in a way sufficient to ensure the required availability and reliability. Therefore, you must also plan aspects relating to system operation in the architecture (architecture discipline: *system management architecture*).

> In addition, you must generally develop systems in accordance with predefined standards and guidelines defined within an enterprise (architecture discipline: *enterprise architecture*).

We will explain the architecture disciplines specified above briefly below for the purposes of differentiation.

Network architecture

Network architecture is concerned with the network infrastructure of systems. The main tasks of this discipline are the planning and design of the functions, services, building blocks, and protocols of a network.

Integration architecture is concerned with the planning and realization of integrative solutions. Its objective is connecting multiple applications or systems of one or more enterprises. Heterogeneous platforms, technologies, organizations, and data must be integrated.

Integration architecture

Data architecture encompasses the data-oriented aspects of a system. The design of logical and physical data models, the selection of persistence mechanisms (e.g., database or file system), the configuration of a database, and the design of a data warehouse are possible activities of this discipline.

Data architecture

A security architecture focuses on guaranteeing confidentiality, integrity, availability of systems or system landscapes, identity and authorization checks, and the verifiability and non-repudiation of security-relevant operations. Examples of tasks in this architecture discipline are the design and implementation of PKI infrastructures, the implementation of an enterprise-wide single sign-on solution, and the establishment of an identity management. The authentication and authorization of users within an application is another aspect of this discipline. The execution of tests to identify security vulnerabilities should also be assigned to this discipline.

Security architecture

System management architecture primarily contains the operational aspects of systems. Within this discipline, your tasks are designing operating strategies of centralized and decentralized system landscapes and defining service level agreements. A system management architecture also describes, for example, how a system is connected to a system management environment.

System management architecture

Enterprise architecture is a discipline that designs an enterprise-wide IT architecture taking into account business strategies, business processes, and business data. It comprises processes, application, data, and technologies for realizing the business strategy. Enterprise architecture also has the task of demonstrating and monitoring the transition process from the actual architecture to the planned target architecture. It therefore addresses the target architecture, the transition process, and the governance of this process. With regard to the example previously introduced, enterprise architecture defines the standards and guidelines around which you must orient yourself when designing systems. In classic architecture, the enterprise architecture would define the zoning plan.

Enterprise architecture

Enterprise architecture focuses not on the individual IT system but on the entirety of all IT systems of the enterprise or part of the enterprise under consideration (architecture of architectures). The questions that an enterprise architecture answers therefore relate to the system as a whole. There are also specific architecture models for enterprise architecture views. Examples are the Zachman Framework (see Section 4.2.1) and TOGAF(see Section 4.2.4).

Challenges of enterprise architecture

Some of the challenges an enterprise architecture faces are:
> Enterprise-wide motivation cannot be mapped directly onto the structural organization of the enterprise.
> The identification of standards and guidelines that are deemed to be relevant for enterprise architecture (organizational level).
> Implementation and operationalization of these standards and guidelines in the enterprise.
> Planning and management of the system portfolio of an enterprise.

No claim to completeness

The information here does not claim to be complete. However, the disciplines named in the *WHAT dimension* are considerably important in information technology—particularly in the area of enterprise-related IT systems.

Interaction of architecture disciplines

In their entirety, the architecture disciplines named can contribute to a system. With the increasing complexity and size of the system, sound knowledge in architecture disciplines other than software architecture is becoming ever more important. The tasks of the disciplines are often spread over many shoulders, making the architecture of a system a team effort. The main responsibility generally lies with you, the software architect. For consultation purposes and to discuss questions, you involve architects from other disciplines. The interaction of the architecture disciplines is shown in Figure 3.2-3.

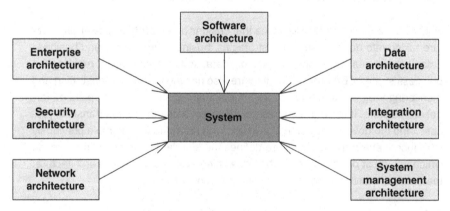

Figure 3.2-3: Interaction of architecture disciplines

It is not always easy to differentiate between the architecture disciplines. As a software architect, you will have to deal with all topics since any system to be realized can have aspects from the different disciplines.

3.3 Architecture and the System Concept

We have used the term "system" several times in the previous chapters, since architecture is generally concerned with systems, be they buildings, cities, landscapes, or IT systems. It is therefore important to understand the general properties of systems. A basic understanding of systems and thinking in systems is thus a prerequisite for acting successfully as a software architect. We will look at significant aspects of the system theory briefly in this section.

Architecture and systems

As a starting point for the explanations, we will use the following system definition derived from [Wikipedia 2011]:

Definition: System

> A system is a set of elements that are related to each other and interact in such a way that they can be seen as one unit that separates itself in this regard from the surrounding environment for a specific task, sense, or purpose.

According to this general definition, a system is a unit that consists of mutually interacting parts or system building blocks. A system can consist of subsystems or finely grained system building blocks and be structured hierarchically. In other words, a system can be seen as a system building block of other systems.

Systems consist of parts

A system has a system boundary that separates it from its environment (see Figure 3.3-1).

Systems have a system boundary

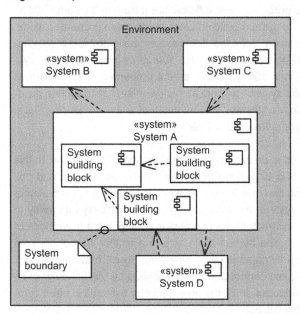

Figure 3.3-1: System in the context of its environment

Systems have objectives	A system always exists to achieve an objective. For example, a football team, as an organizational system, exists with the objective of winning the championship. In the same way, a project team forms with the objective of completing a project successfully and thus achieving the related objective. In turn, an IT system exists to achieve functional objectives (see Section 3.2).
Types of systems	Systems can interact with their environment and exchange information in order to achieve their objective. The example from Figure 3.3-1 shows that system A is dependent on information from system B, and provides system C with information. There is also bidirectional communication between system D and system A. Depending on whether a system interacts with its environment, the system theory differentiates between the following types of system:

> *Open systems* are in touch with and exchange information with their environment. The systems have to interact with their environment to be able to exist.

> *Closed systems* do not exchange information with their environment. They do, however, have an energetic relationship with their environment.

Do closed systems exist?	Closed systems are very rare in practice since systems always interact with their environment. As an example of a system in classic architecture, a house is generally connected to the power and water supply provided by its environment. Furthermore, the building of a road in development planning is always embedded in the overall road planning of its environment or road network.
Emergence of systems	One important finding of system theory is the emergence of systems. Emergence states that a system has properties that differentiate it from its system building blocks. Accordingly, no one system building block holds these properties alone. They arise from the interaction of the individual system building blocks. In other words, as a whole, the system is more than the sum of its individual parts (system building blocks) [Rechtin 1991]. The emergent properties of systems thus exist only at the level of the system, and not at the lower level of its system building blocks. With regard to architecture, this means that every *architecture level* has different emergent properties (see Chapter 4).
Examples of emergent systems	The formation of tornadoes is an example for the emergence of systems. In this context, the system building blocks are both moist, warm air masses and dry, cold air masses. A tornado can only be formed when these building blocks meet and interact. The whole system, the tornado, behaves completely differently to its building blocks. It has characteristics that clearly distinguish it from those of its system building blocks. The human brain acts in a similar way. It consists of many neurons, and is only capable of thinking when these neurons interact. Thus the behavior of systems cannot solely be explained by the behavior of its individual system building blocks. In IT, the emergence of systems is often demonstrated in large, complex projects.

The holistic view of systems looks at a system in its entirety. It concentrates on the emergent system properties that arise through the interaction of the system building blocks. This is the view that determines whether an architecture can be deemed stable, since statements about the overall behavior can only be made through an overall view. Figure 3.3-2 makes this approach, known as holism, clearer. The subsystems are seen as a black box.

Holism

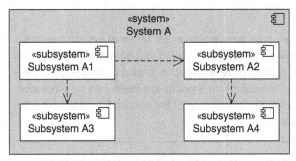

Figure 3.3-2: Holistic system view

In contrast to holism, in reductionism, the individual system building blocks are analyzed separately. With reference to Figure 3.3-2, this means, for example, that only subsystem A1, including its system building blocks, is explained in more detail (see Figure 3.3-3). This view enables a concrete analysis of the behavior and function of individual system building blocks. A subsystem is thus perceived as a white box. However, due to the inherent emergence of systems, it is not possible to determine the behavior of the whole system in this way.

Reductionism

Holism and reductionism should therefore be understood as complementary approaches. We can only make statements about the holistic behavior of the system (*holism*) when we know which system building blocks a system consists of (*reductionism*).

Holism and reductionism are complementary

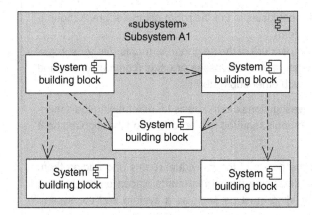

Figure 3.3-3: Reductionistic system view

Thinking in systems

Thinking in systems can be understood as *architectural thinking*. It looks at the significant building blocks of an architecture and their interaction, and makes statements about how the architecture can support requirements the system must satisfy. Furthermore, this approach reflects the use of architecture experience in the form of architecture styles. Architectural thinking is a method of looking at architecture based on specific objectives, with the focus on the holistic view.

Selecting the system boundary

In order to examine a system or its architecture in the sense of system theory, it is important to select the relevant system boundary. If you do not draw the system boundary appropriately, this may have a negative influence on the analysis—either too many or too few aspects of the system are taken into consideration. The following example illustrates the selection of the system boundary using the planning of a heating system.

Example for selecting the system boundary

A heating plant is a system with the objective of achieving comfort within a building, for example, a house. The building to be heated represents the system boundary. A heating plant consists of the system building blocks *energy supply*, *heat generator*, *heat distribution*, *heating areas*, and *regulation*. An individual room within the building can be seen as a subsystem that contains system building blocks of the whole system.

During the analysis, design, and implementation of a heating system, the first step involves reductionism. Each individual room is viewed as a system in order to subsequently create the whole system based on the individual rooms. The system boundary is therefore drawn tightly at the beginning deliberately in order to obtain a heating system that satisfies the heating requirements of each individual room. In the consideration of the rooms, the following aspects must be clarified, for example:

> Room use to determine the required internal temperature (requirement)

> Construction with heat insulation of the room perimeter areas (boundaries of the subsystem)

> Assumed room temperature of the neighboring rooms (further subsystems) in order to determine heat losses or gains (communication and energy exchange with other subsystems)

The results of these investigations are the basis for determining the dimensions of the heating elements required for the rooms and the required heat performance.

However, examining the needs of the individual rooms and adding them up is not sufficient to determine the requirements placed on the heating system. The whole building must be seen as a system and the system boundary shifted accordingly. It is therefore considered holistically. At the architecture level *building* it is important to know the location of the building and the related climate conditions, such as lowest external temperature and wind strength.

From the findings obtained through changing the system boundary, a heating system that satisfies the requirements of the entire building can be designed. If the system boundary is not changed, you get a heating system that cannot provide the building with enough heat, for example, or a system that is oversized and therefore uneconomical with regard to energy consumption.

3.4 Architecture and the Building Blocks of a System

In general, architecture is concerned with the structuring of system building blocks of a system. Software architecture focuses on the software building blocks of a system. Irrespective of the concrete architecture discipline that you focus on in information technology, it is important to know the basic types of system building blocks. This supports architectural thinking since, at a higher level of abstraction, it illustrates the building blocks that make up a system, how these building blocks are related, and the importance of the individual building blocks. This makes systems tangible and makes it possible to make decisions specific to individual building blocks.

Basic understanding of system building blocks

In addition, a common vocabulary is created, or rather, a common ontology that can be applied in all architecture disciplines of information technology. This improves the collaboration of architects from the individual disciplines since they have a common understanding of systems.

Common vocabulary

The architecture disciplines are concerned with different aspects of a system. Therefore, architects from the individual disciplines focus on different building blocks or aspects of building blocks in their activities—they look at building blocks from different perspectives. For example, a software architect looks at a software building block primarily with regard to its functionality, responsibility, and interfaces. In contrast, a security architect analyzes whether a software building block satisfies the security demands and, for example, does not use passwords stored in plain text.

Different views depending on the architecture discipline

In the model shown in Figure 3.4-1, we present the most important system building blocks and their relationships to one another. The focus is on simple illustration of the system building blocks relevant for architecture.

System building blocks and their relationships

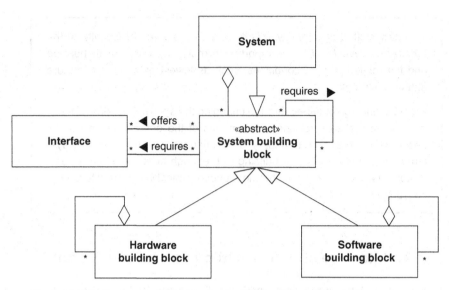

Figure 3.4-1: *System building blocks and their relationships*

System building block

The central concept in Figure 3.4-1 is the *system building block*. It represents the abstract type of all concrete building blocks of a system. It can require other system building blocks and can have one or more interfaces or require one or more interfaces of other system building blocks.

System

A *system* consists of system building blocks and is itself a building block. This means that a system can also contain subsystems.

Subsystem

Subsystems encapsulate coherent functionality and are self-contained. A subsystem therefore provides related functionality that satisfies some of the requirements placed on the system.

Software and hardware building blocks

Software and *hardware building blocks* are specializations of system building blocks. A hardware building block can require another hardware building block and can consist of hardware building blocks. For example, as a hardware building block, a personal computer consists of a motherboard, a graphic card, a network card, and many other hardware building blocks. Hardware building blocks also have interfaces.

MIS example

We will look at the relationships between the different system building blocks more closely in an example below. The main focus is on the software aspects of systems. One example is a Management Information System (MIS) for collecting and evaluating performance indicators. We will look at this example again in more detail in Chapter 8.

3 | Architectures and Architecture Disciplines (WHAT)

In the MIS, data that forms the basis for the calculation of the indicators has to be imported, for example, from other systems. The functionality required to do this can be encapsulated in an *import subsystem* and be used by other subsystems of the MIS. This example already shows that subsystems communicate with one another in order to fulfill the requirements of the system. In the case of the *import subsystem*, a *user interfaces subsystem*, which receives the user's request to perform an import, could communicate with the *import subsystem* and initiate an import (see Figure 3.4-2).

System building blocks require system building blocks

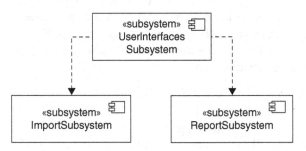

Figure 3.4-2: Subsystems require other subsystems

In addition, system building blocks can be further structures by means of composition, i.e., system building blocks can consist of other system building blocks. We will illustrate this using the subsystems of the MIS example again. One important functionality of the MIS is the generation of performance indicator reports. A *report subsystem* could be dedicated to this task. It may be appropriate to distribute reports using different publication channels, such as e-mail, HTML, or Adobe Portable Document Format (PDF). The logic for generating channel-specific reports can be provided by dedicated subsystems of the report subsystem (see Figure 3.4-3).

System building blocks consist of system building blocks

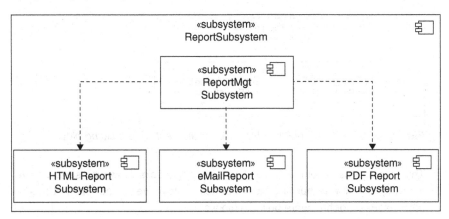

Figure 3.4-3: System building blocks consist of system building blocks

Access to system building blocks via interfaces

Systems consist of hardware and software building blocks. These building blocks have *implicit* or *explicit interfaces*. An interface defines a contract between the system building block that offers some functionality and the system building blocks that use it. It also defines the operations offered by the system building block. An *explicit* interface is detached from the actual system building block. The concept of the explicit interface is implemented, for example, by technologies such as Enterprise JavaBeans or web services. In contrast, *implicit* interfaces are direct parts of the system building block. A module written in the programming language C is an example of a system building block with an implicit interface. The *report subsystem* in our example system contains a software building block *ReportMgr,* which provides an interface for generating e-mail, HTML, or PDF reports for performance indicators. The user interfaces subsystem can use this interface to trigger the creation of reports.

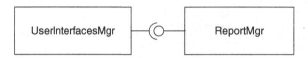

Figure 3.4-4: *System building blocks use system building blocks via interfaces*

The relationship shown in Figure 3.4-4 clearly shows that the software building block *UserInterfacesMgr* initiates the creation of reports via the interface of the *ReportMgr* building block.

Software building blocks consist of software building blocks

In the MIS, a *PDFReportMgr* is used to create PDF reports. It consists of further software building blocks, such as a *PDFReportCreatorROI* for generating a paragraph within a report that contains information on return on investment (see Figure 3.4-5).

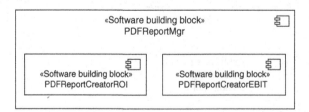

Figure 3.4-5: *Software building blocks consist of software building blocks*

This also applies of course for hardware building blocks. However, since we are focusing on software building blocks in this context, we will not present a concrete example for hardware building blocks.

A further important concept not contained in the model presented in Figure 3.4-1 is the arrangement of a system in *layers*. A system can be organized in layers that contain subsystems. A *layer* structures a system logically in hierarchy levels. Subsystems of a layer have common characteristics and responsibilities. They can only access subsystems of lower level layers. Depending on how strictly this convention is configured, it may even be the case that access only to the next lowest level is permitted. For a precise description of this principle, we refer to the layers architecture pattern [Buschmann et al. 1996].

Layers

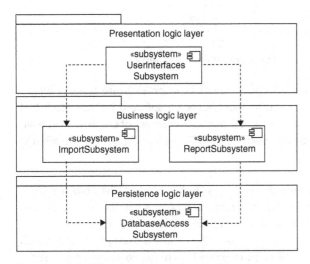

Figure 3.4-6: A system is organized in layers

Figure 3.4-6 illustrates the *layers* of the MIS example and the positioning of the *subsystems* depending on the task area. It is clear that the MIS is subdivided into a presentation logic layer, a business logic layer, and a persistence logic layer. The *import subsystem* and the *report subsystem* are located in the business logic layer. Both can be used by the *user interfaces subsystem* of the presentation logic layer.

So far we have presented the basic building blocks of a system. We will now extend the model introduced to include the platform aspect. This is presented in Figure 3.4-7.

A *platform* is a system that can consist of software and, if applicable, hardware building blocks. It is used to execute software building blocks of a system and is part of the holistic view of software architecture.

Platform

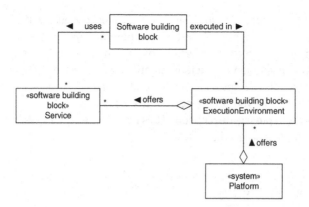

Figure 3.4-7: *Platform, execution environment, and service*

<table>
<tr><td>**Execution environment**</td><td>A platform provides *execution environments* in which software building blocks are executed. An execution environment is itself a software building block that provides services. For example, a JEE application server offers execution environments for JEE components such as Java Servlets or Enterprise JavaBeans (see Section 6.7.5).</td></tr>
<tr><td>**Services**</td><td>*Services* are also software building blocks. In this context, they provide basic functionality that is usually independent of any business functionality realized by the system. In other words, a service provides functionality for satisfying non-functional requirements. The building blocks of the MIS example require a JEE platform, for example. This offers services such as resource management, security, transaction control, or persistence.</td></tr>
</table>

Summary: Architectures and architecture disciplines

3.5 Summary

> Requirements and architecture means determine the structure of an architecture.
> A good architecture must be elegant, durable, and useful.
> A system is a unit that consists of integrated software and hardware building blocks for the purpose of fulfilling a functional objective. To achieve this objective, it communicates with its environment and must take account of the conditions defined by the environment.
> The software architecture of a program or computing system is the structure or structures of the system, which comprise software elements, the externally visible properties of those elements, and the relationships among them.

> As a discipline, software architecture covers the architectural activities and the related decisions about the design and implementation of a software architecture.
> Software architecture$_{total}$ = Software architecture$_{structure}$ + Software architecture$_{discipline}$
> Software architecture comprises the functional and technical architecture.
> The functional architecture arises from the functional domain or problem area for which the system is being developed. It divides the system into functional building blocks responsible for the realization of functionality.
> The technical architecture is domain-independent and is dedicated primarily to the realization of non-functional requirements or qualities. It defines technical building blocks for non-functional aspects, such as logging, auditing, security, reference data, persistence, and transaction management. The technical architecture also defines how functional building blocks are mapped onto the technical architecture.
> A platform is a system that can consist of software and, if applicable, hardware building blocks. It is used to execute software building blocks of a system and is part of the holistic view of software architecture.

Further Reading

[Morgan 1960]
Vitruvius, Morgan Morris (Übersetzer), *Ten Books on Architecture*, Dover Publications, 1960

[Bass et al. 2003]
Bass, Len; Clements, Paul; Kazman, Rick, *Software Architecture in Practice*, Second Edition, Addison-Wesley, New York, 2003

[Buschmann et al. 1996]
Buschmann, Frank; Meunier, Regine; Rohnert, Hans; Sommerlad, Peter; Stal, Michael, *Pattern-Oriented Software Architecture Vol. 1, A System of Patterns*, John Wiley & Sons, New York, 1996

[IEEE 2007]
IEEE, *Recommended Practice for Architectural Description of Software-intensive Systems,* http://www.iso-architecture.org/ieee-1471/, 2007

[Maier and Rechtin 2000]
Maier M.; Rechtin E., *The Art of Systems Architecting*, Second Edition, CRC Press, 2000

Further reading: Classic architecture

Further reading: Software architecture

[Perry and Wolf 1992]
Perry, Dewayne E.; Wolf, Alexander L., *Foundations for the Study of Software Architecture*, ACM SIGSOFT Software Engineering Notes, 17(4), October, 1992

[Rechtin 1991]
Rechtin, Eberhard, *Systems Architecting – Creating and building complex systems*, CRC Press, 1991

Further reading: Enterprise architecture

[Opengroup 2008a]
Opengroup, *The Open Group Architecture Framework*,
http://www.opengroup.org/togaf/, 2008

Further reading: System concept

[Wikipedia 2011]
Systemdefinition, http://en.wikipedia.org/wiki/System/, 2011

4 | Architecture Perspectives (WHERE)

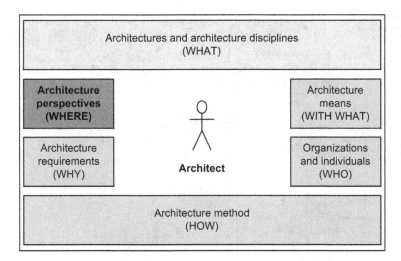

Figure 4-1: Positioning of the chapter in the architecture orientation framework

This chapter looks at the *WHERE dimension* of the architecture orientation framework. It explains the levels of abstraction at which you are active as an architect and how architecture is demonstrated at these levels. We also present architecture views that you can use at these levels of abstraction to make it easier to manage the different aspects and the resulting complexity of an architecture. After reading this chapter, you will be able to differentiate between the relevant architectural levels of abstraction and use them. Using architecture views, you will also be able to consider and process specific different aspects of an architecture.

Overview

Basic concepts of the WHERE dimension

Figure 4-2 shows the basic concepts covered in this chapter and visualizes how they connect.

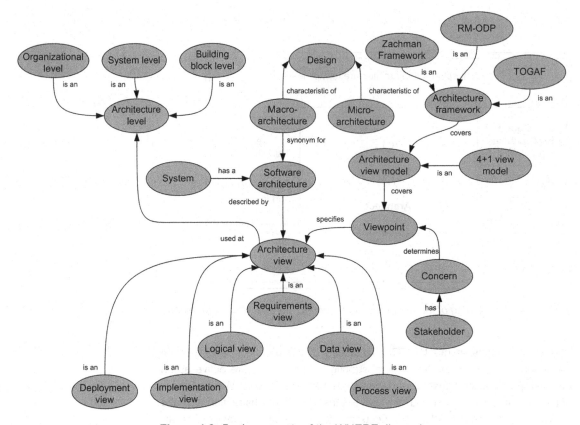

Figure 4-2: Basic concepts of the WHERE dimension

4.1 Architecture Levels

Looking at systems through a telescope

Imagine you are looking at a system through a telescope. You can change the level of detail at which you look at it using the zoom factor. Certain details of the system then become visible or hidden. We will use the example of city and building construction, as well as the transport infrastructure to make this clearer. If you could look at the earth from the ISS space station with a telescope and slowly zoom in, you could look at different architecture levels of city and building construction. You would move from the level of continents, through the level of countries, to the level of cities and districts, right down to the level of individual buildings and their floors. We can transpose this level scheme onto software architecture. Which architecture levels can we generally identify? We can answer this question by visualizing which external and internal contexts are generally present for an IT system and which degree of abstraction these contexts have respectively.

We will use the telescope metaphor again to develop the architecture levels. Imagine you want to look at an IT system through a telescope. However, before you can focus on a specific IT system, the telescope first shows you the external contexts of the IT system. First you see different organizations and how they collaborate in their different roles (clients, suppliers, partners, etc.). With the next telescope setting, you look at a specific organization more closely. You see the systems (employees, departments, IT systems, etc.) within the organization and how they are used and interact in the business processes of the organization. You increase the zoom factor of the telescope again and now you can look at a specific IT system of the organization in more detail. You see its interfaces, its functionality, and its users. Then you zoom inside the system. The telescope shows you the internal contexts of the system. You recognize the building blocks that make up the system (see Sections 3.3 and 3.4). You see their interfaces, responsibilities, and interactions. You then increase the zoom factor again and now you can see the internal workings of the system building blocks in detail. And you discover that the system building blocks are also made up of system building blocks. Later in this section we will explain more important facts about the internal workings of system building blocks when we discuss micro-architecture. Up to this point, you have been able to look at the following three basic architecture levels with the telescope:

Organizations, systems, and system building blocks

> **Organizational level:**
>   Here you can look at the organizations (e.g., departments and IT standards).

> **System level:**
>   Here you can look at the systems of the organizations (e.g., IT systems and their requirements).

> **Building block level:**
>   Here you can look at the building blocks of the systems (e.g., interfaces and data access objects).

Figure 4.1-1 shows the related architecture levels model that illustrates the relationships between the above-mentioned architecture levels and their context.

Architecture requirements (see Chapter 5) and decisions (see Section 3.2) at a specific level of abstraction from the point of view of an IT system are assigned to each architecture level. Along this level of abstraction, the architecture levels are arranged in a hierarchical order. Starting from the building block level, the

The architecture levels model in brief

level of abstraction increases. For example, the decision at the organizational level to integrate systems in the IT landscape of an organization using a standard middleware in future is located at a higher level of abstraction than the decision at system level as to how (e.g., using XML) to connect a concrete system to a specific middleware product (e.g., IBM WebSphere MQ). The architecture requirements and decisions at a lower, less abstract architecture level consider and detail the architectural specifications (requirements and decisions) at the next higher architecture level respectively. Requirements and decisions that apply across an organization are located at the organizational level. At system level, the specifications of the organizational level are taken into account in the requirements and decisions regarding the IT systems of an organization. Finally, at the lowest architecture level, the building block level, the specifications of the system level are the basis for requirements and decisions that affect the building blocks (see Section 3.4) of a system.

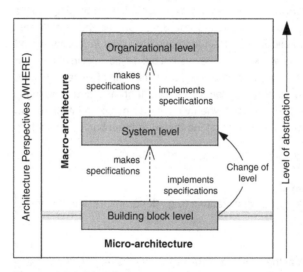

Figure 4.1-1: *Model of the basic architecture levels*

Consideration of architecture levels has a positive influence on the architecture quality

Using architecture levels, as an architect you are more aware of the forces that generally always influence architecture and the origins of these forces. At building block level, forces from the system level affect architecture, and at system level, forces from the organizational level. Being aware of this enables you to manage any problems and questions that arise when you are creating an architecture uniformly and to avoid mixing different aspects. For example, the question of how systems should exchange their data should not be answered at the building block level in the design of a functional building block such as "Customer". Instead, it should be answered at the organizational level or system level uniformly for all functional building blocks. Considering architecture levels therefore leads to an architecture that is more uniform and consistent. To summarize, the consideration of architecture levels leads to architectures of a much higher quality for the following reasons:

> Architecture problems and aspects are assigned to suitable levels and are therefore easier to handle and can be treated uniformly [Brown et al. 1998].
> Different architecture problems and aspects are not mixed but handled separately with the respective appropriate means.
> Influences on architecture exist explicitly and are therefore easier to understand and consider.

As an architect you have to deal with and solve specific problems at each architecture level. For example: at the organizational level, business processes; at the system level, system use cases; and at building block level, the creation of system building blocks that implement the building block use cases. At all of the architecture levels specified, you must take the architecture principles discussed in Chapter 6 into account—the principle of high cohesion (see Section 6.1), for example. At the organizational level, the steps within business processes should always be highly coherent with one another. For example, a business process "Enter order" should not contain any steps from the business process "Issue invoice." At system level, this applies for the steps within the system use cases. At building block level, high cohesion is applied, for example, to system building blocks such as components or classes that realize the system use cases by providing coherent functionality. Disregarding these principles generally leads to numerous unnecessary dependencies, incorrect assignments of responsibilities, and redundancies in the artefacts (e.g., class diagrams or source code) assigned to the architecture levels. Above all, this has a negative effect on the implementation of non-functional requirements (see Chapter 5) and thus the software quality.

Architecture principles must be followed at all architecture levels

The levels presented thus far are the basic architecture levels. For the purposes of this book, this level of detail is sufficient. However, if required, each of the architecture levels named can be divided into further architecture levels. The Software Design Level Model (SDLM) [Brown et al. 1998] has a similar structure, but splits the system level, for example, into the following three architecture levels: systems, applications, and frameworks.

Architecture levels can be subdivided further

Before we can explain the architecture levels in detail, we must first discuss the meaning of the terms "macro-architecture" and "micro-architecture" from Figure 4.1-1. Both terms are connected to the term "design". This term is a central term, because you perform your various activities (see Chapter 8) in the context of the different architecture levels with the aim of working out a design for the architec-

What is (software) "design" exactly?

ture of a system. But what does "design" mean exactly? [IEEE 2010] defines the term "(software) design" as follows:

Definition: Software design

> Design is defined in [IEEE1990] as both "the process of defining the architecture, components, interfaces, and other characteristics of a system or component" and "the result of [that] process."

According to this explanation, design generally covers the following:
> The process (see Section 8.1) of defining the architecture, building blocks, interfaces, and other features of a system or a system building block.
> The result of this process.

A system or a system building block has numerous features and they are located at different levels of abstraction (levels of detail). Design should therefore take place at these different levels. It is not sufficient to talk about "design" only in general terms when designing a system; rather, you should consider the respective levels of abstraction. The following two further definitions from [IEEE 2010] provide a differentiated view of design:

Definition: Software architectural design

> Software architectural design (sometimes called top-level design): describing software's top-level structure and organization and identifying the various components.

Definition: Software detailed design

> Software detailed design: describing each component sufficiently to allow for its construction.

These explanations clearly show that design takes place at two different fundamental levels of abstraction. Based on [Brown et al. 1998], the architecture levels model therefore differentiates between:
> Macro-architecture
>   (software architecture, architectural design, top-level/high-level design)
> Micro-architecture
>   (detailed design)

To avoid ambiguities, you should therefore always differentiate between "design" in the general sense (as a generic term) and "design" in relation to levels of abstraction (macro-architecture or micro-architecture). Macro-architecture corresponds to software architecture (see Section 3.2) and therefore affects the architecture levels previously discussed (organizational level, system level, and building block level). In contrast, micro-architecture only affects part of the building block level.

What happens if the level of abstraction continues to decrease and the details increase? When does architecture cease and detailed design begin? The border between macro-architecture and micro-architecture is not always clear. It is also dependent on the view of the respective stakeholder and therefore cannot be defined uniquely.

Where is the border between macro-architecture and micro-architecture?

Macro-architecture covers the spectrum of the architecture levels to which architecturally relevant elements are assigned (organizational level and system level, as well as the part of the building block level on which fundamental system building blocks (see Section 3.3) are located): thus "large-scale" architecture. It covers aspects such as requirements, decisions, and structures at a high level of abstraction: for example, decisions with regard to important system interfaces. A concrete example is a system building block that acts as a facade for a group of associated system building blocks in accordance with the facade design pattern [Gamma et al. 1995].

Macro-architecture

In contrast, micro-architecture covers aspects with a lower level of abstraction. This is then the detailed design ("small-scale" architecture) closely associated with the source code with no fundamental influence on an architecture. That part of the building block level on which the non-fundamental system building blocks are located belongs to the field of micro-architecture. In Figure 4.1-1, this aspect is made clear by the fact that the building block level is on the border between macro-architecture and micro-architecture. Why are non-fundamental system building blocks assigned to the building block level at all? Fundamental system building blocks can themselves consist of fundamental system building blocks (see Section 3.3). A recursive decomposition of the system building blocks along this building block hierarchy leads to system building blocks whose level of abstraction is decreasing. At some point you reach non-fundamental system building blocks with a low level of abstraction. This is when the changeover from macro-architecture to micro-architecture takes place. The example of this in Figure 4.1-2 shows how the fundamental system building block B is firstly broken down into system building blocks B1, B2, etc. at the building block level (macro-architecture). Since these building blocks are also fundamental, we remain in the area of macro-architecture. The subsequent decomposition of system building block B2 leads to the system building blocks B2', B2'', etc. These building blocks are non-fundamental and to consider them, we move into the area of micro-architecture. A helper class for character string operations is a concrete example of a non-fundamental system building block. Decisions (e.g., on signatures, validity ranges for variables, design patterns, etc.) with regard to non-fundamental system building blocks are another concrete example for elements that are not architecturally relevant and therefore, like non-fundamental system building blocks, belong to the area of micro-architecture.

Micro-architecture

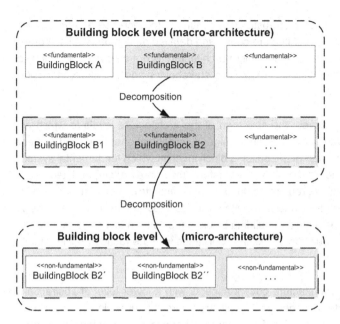

Figure 4.1-2: Macro-architecture and micro-architecture in context

4.1.1 Organizational Level

Zoning plans, business processes, and IT landscapes

At this architecture level we look at organizations (e.g., enterprises or institutions), their zoning plans, business processes, and IT landscapes as well as their interactions with other organizations (organization context). Here IT systems belong to the actors (departments, employees, systems, etc.) involved in the business process of an organization. The internal structure of the IT systems is of no interest. Treat individual IT systems as black boxes. For example, you could assign the description of a business process for order processing in an organization, with all of its systems (e.g., customer department, accounting, materials or goods management), to the organizational level.

IT standards and guidelines

Furthermore, in the context of the organizational level, there are requirements an organization must satisfy as well as IT standards and guidelines to be used and complied with across the organization (see Chapter 5). One example would be the IT guideline to use XML for the data exchange between different systems, without any specification of concrete XML technologies, such as XML parsers etc. These specifications enable systems from different organizations or different systems within an organization to work together to provide integrated services.

You will have to deal with the following problems in particular at the organizational level:

> IT-supported implementation of cross-organizational processes (e.g., Supply Chain Management)
> Enterprise architecture (see Section 3.2)
> Enterprise Application Integration (EAI)
> Service-oriented architectures (see Section 6.4)

Problems across an organization

As far as these problems are concerned, architectural decisions must go beyond the view of an individual system and are therefore oriented across an organization. These decisions cover, for example, the specification of IT standards to be used. For example, technologies such as JEE or architecture patterns such as Model-View-Controller (MVC) can be specified for architectures of systems across an organization [Fowler 2003]. Examples are: clinics with patient data management, health insurance billing, and medical information system, or the Internet with all of its IT standards and guidelines.

4.1.2 System Level

At system level we look at (zoom in on) the IT systems of organizations. The internal structure of the systems is only important in as far as their subsystems are concerned. Treat the individual systems or their subsystems as black boxes. The focus is on the responsibilities, interfaces, and interactions of the systems with their context. The main elements at system level are:

IT systems of organizations

> Requirements the systems must satisfy (see Section 5.3)
> System contexts of the systems (see Section 8.3)
> Subsystems of the systems (see Section 3.4)

One of the artefacts you create and assign to the system level is the architecture vision or architecture overview (see Section 8.3). In the example from Figure 4.1-3, we first look at the system under construction, system A, in the context of its peripheral systems U1, U2, and U3. We then perform a first decomposition for system A. This results in a series of subsystems (A1', A2', A1", etc.). However, because these subsystems are also systems (see Section 3.3), we are still moving at system level and now assign the subsystems to the logical layers X and Y (see Section 6.3).

System context and subsystems

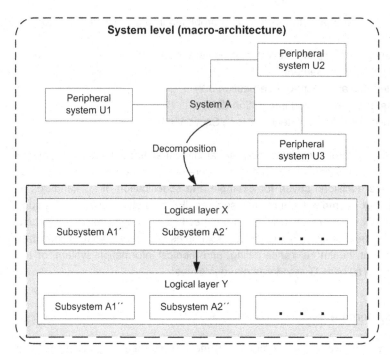

Figure 4.1-3: Relationship between system level, system context, and subsystems

4.1.3 Building Block Level

Building blocks of the subsystems

At the building block level in macro-architecture we look at the internal structure of the individual subsystems. We zoom into the subsystems (white box) by breaking them down into software building blocks (see Section 3.4). We move from the system level to the building block level. Significant aspects you must consider at the building block level are the responsibilities of the system building blocks, their interfaces, and their interactions with one another. The example from Figure 4.1-4 shows the decomposition for subsystem B into the fundamental building blocks B1, B2, etc. Since we are now looking at software building blocks, we move from the system level down to the building block level.

Change of level between building block level and system level

In very large systems, the system building blocks that result from the decomposition of a subsystem may also be subsystems instead of software building blocks. In this case, we change level: from the building block level back to the system level. There we treat the system building blocks as systems, starting with the system context etc. (as described above). Therefore, at this point, the architecture levels model is recursive. This aspect is shown in Figure 4.1-1 by the change of level arrow from the building block level back to the system level. The example

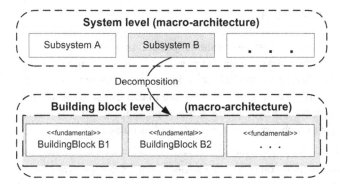

Figure 4.1-4: Relationship between system level and building block level

from Figure 4.1-5 looks at subsystem B. The decomposition of this subsystem initially leads to the building block level, as is usual for subsystems (see also Figure 4.1-4). There we look at the assumed software building blocks B1, B2, etc. and discover that these are actually subsystems. Therefore, to look at system building block B2 further, we switch back to the system level.

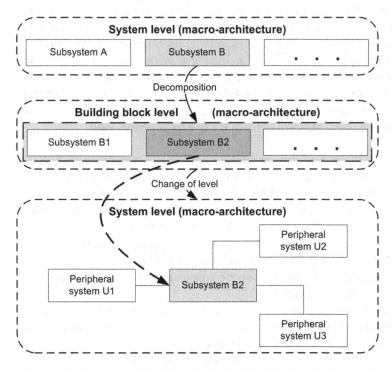

Figure 4.1-5: Change of level from building block level to system level

4.2 Architecture Views

Architecture views make complex systems understandable

Understanding all aspects of complex systems (people, building constructions, IT systems etc.) completely at all times is not possible at least for human perception. It would also be impractical to attempt to do this, because not all aspects of a system are relevant all of the time. It therefore makes sense to be able to look at only those aspects of a system that are of interest at a given time. For IT systems, the concept of architecture views exists for this purpose:

Definition: Architecture view

> > A view is a representation of a whole system from the perspective of a set of concerns [IEEE 2007].
> > A view is a representation of a coherent set of architectural elements, as written by and read by system stakeholders [Bass et al. 2003].

Architecture views are motivated by stakeholders

Both definitions clearly show the most important property of architecture views: they are motivated by stakeholders of a system ("...a set of concerns... " and "... read by system stakeholders"). In this context, a set of concerns means different questions about a specific aspect. One aspect might be, for example, the structures of a system. Different concerns can be connected to this aspect; for example, which building blocks are present, or what the interfaces look like. An architecture view is therefore used by specific stakeholders (see Section 8.7). It thus sensibly shows only those aspects of a system that are important for those specific stakeholders. One aspect might be, for example, requirements. An architecture view that covers this aspect would cover all artefacts referring to requirements. Section 8.4 contains examples of this. Clients or domain experts are examples of stakeholders who would use a requirements view.

Architecture views according to IEEE

In addition to the above-mentioned definition, with its 1471 standard [IEEE 2007] IEEE has laid down further fundamental principles regarding architecture views. This standard is concerned with the description of software-intensive systems and initially, was a standard only for architecture documentation (see Section 8.7). The overview (following [IEEE 2007]) for the context of architecture views in Figure 4.2-1 shows important concepts related to architecture views:

> Stakeholders have different concerns with regard to a system, or rather, its architecture. Based on their specific concerns, different stakeholders each adopt a specific viewpoint.
> A specific architecture view (e.g., data view) is available to stakeholders from each respective viewpoint (different angles). It is defined by the viewpoint and refers to a set of specific concerns.
> Each architecture view has a reference to exactly one viewpoint.
> Architecture views essentially determine the content and structure of architecture documentation (see Section 8.7).

A concern is generally defined as follows [Oxford English Dictionary 2007]:

Definition: Concern

/noun: 6, A matter that affects or touches one; a subject that excites one's interest, attention or care.

Concerns generally

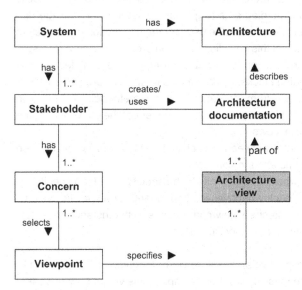

Figure 4.2-1: *Architecture views in context [IEEE 2007]*

According to this definition, a concern is something that affects you and that you have to pay attention to. Applied to an IT system, this can be any of the following:
> Requirements
  (e.g., the system must save data automatically at specific intervals)
> Worries
  (e.g., the worry that the decision to use a specific technology platform for a system can lead to a dead end in an important future market)
> Goals
  (e.g., the system should increase productivity by 15%)

In the broadest sense, therefore, concerns are also requirements. However, concerns often do not fulfill the criteria that requirements (see Chapter 5) must satisfy.

Architecture views consider those concerns that correspond to the general generic questions about a system, or rather, its architecture. Examples are:
> What are the requirements for the system?
> Which logical building blocks does the system consist of?

**Concerns and
architecture views**

> What interfaces do the system building blocks have?
> How do the system building blocks interact?

Viewpoint

With regard to architecture views, there must be a differentiation between their specification and their concrete use as an instance of their specification. For example, the specification for an architecture view of logical system building blocks can specify that specific UML diagrams (e.g., class diagram and package diagram) and specific standard texts are to be used for the description of the system building blocks. An instance of this specification as an architecture view on a specific system would then show a series of UML diagrams and textual descriptions of the logical system building blocks. Specifications of architecture views can be more or less comprehensive (from the name up to the methodological creation of a view). [IEEE 2007] introduced the important concept of the viewpoint for the specification of architecture views:

> [IEEE 2007] differentiates between an architecture view and its specification with regard to the terms and the concepts.
> In [IEEE 2007], a viewpoint corresponds to the specification for a specific architecture view (e.g., deployment view) independently of a specific system.
> In [IEEE 2007], an architecture view corresponds to the instance of its corresponding specification for a specific system.

Viewpoints specify the respective architecture views for given concerns, or rather, how you should create these views. For example, a viewpoint may represent the question "which of the system's structures are the logical structures?" For the corresponding architecture views, this viewpoint can define the architecture modeling means (see Section 6.6) to be used and the rules to be applied.

For architecture views, viewpoints specify:
> Name
> Stakeholders and their concerns
> What is to be documented (documentation subjects)

For the creation of architecture views, viewpoints specify:
> Architecture modeling means to be used
> Templates/patterns
> Best practices
> Methods
> Guidelines

Viewpoints make handling views easier

The use of viewpoints makes it easier to handle architecture views: generic aspects in the creation of architecture views are easier to reuse and you do not have to redefine them redundantly for every system. Viewpoints provide you with a framework or template for creating architecture views. However, creating viewpoints is not a trivial matter. For more information on viewpoints, see [Rozanski and Woods 2005].

Why are architecture views so important and how do you work with them? You need architecture views because different groups of stakeholders are involved with an architecture—but only with the parts (views) of an architecture that are interesting for them. If these views are not available, then the different stakeholders do not understand the architecture or do not understand it correctly. Therefore, a specific architecture view should deliver a specific abstraction of the architecture of a system that the stakeholders affected can understand. For example, the use cases are interesting for business analysts, but not the technical details of the building blocks of the system. They will therefore work with the corresponding architecture view that covers the use cases. However, this only works if you have explicitly considered architecture views from the very beginning when you created or documented (see Section 8.7) an architecture. If this is not the case, the business analysts would have to search for the use cases in the documentation "jungle".

Relevance of architecture views

Architecture covers different aspects of a system, such as interfaces of system building blocks or the interactions of system building blocks. However, in the architectural activities (see Section 8.2), at any given time only some of these aspects are relevant—it would be unmanageable to always have to consider all of these aspects simultaneously. This is another reason why architecture views are necessary. They are a means that enable you to focus on a specific problem at an appropriate time or to separate different aspects of the architecture of a system from one another. This aspect also shows how architecture views help you to handle the complexity in the context of architecture. For example, in the architectural activity "understanding the requirements" (see Section 8.4), you can focus on the architecturally significant use cases without having to also consider how specific system building blocks realize the use cases technically. The situation described is similar to the architecture of buildings. There, architecture views are also required in the form of plans for the arrangement of rooms, electrical cabling, water cables, etc. in order to obtain a clear and usable architecture. Depending on the activity, only the specific plans required for the specialists responsible in each case are used.

Architecture views and the development process

In order for you to work practically with architecture views, they should be separate. The dependencies between them determine the order in which you develop them. Ideally, you do this iteratively, i.e., they can evolve: you do not have to completely develop one architecture view before you can develop other dependent architecture views. Sometimes you can also (if the dependencies permit this) dedicate yourself to one architecture view while other architecture views are already being developed further. Thus you can sometimes create architecture views in parallel.

Develop architecture views in a specific order

Architecture view models

An architecture view model represents the grouping of different viewpoints. In practice various architecture view models already exist (e.g., the architecture view model from the 4+1 view model). These are partially domain-specific and each specifies different architecture views usefully aligned with one another for practical use. Architecture frameworks also exist (e.g., Reference Model for Open Distributed Processing (RM-ODP), the Zachman Framework, or The Open Group Architecture Framework (TOGAF)). These comprise architecture view models and also standards, best practices, tool support, or even methods for architects. Architecture frameworks are frequently designed for enterprise architecture. However, this section focuses on architecture view models and does not discuss other elements of architecture frameworks.

Reuse of proven viewpoints

A considerable advantage in the use of existing, standardized architecture view models is on one hand that you reuse viewpoints that have proven their usefulness time and again in practice. On the other hand, as an architect you are freed from the effort of having to develop your own architecture view model as well as specifying the architecture views, documentation, guidelines, rules, tools, etc.

Architecture view models make architecture tangible

Architecture view models cover all relevant architecture views and thus enable you to make the architecture tangible and visible. An architecture must cover very different aspects of a system: for example, on one hand the logical building blocks of the system, and on the other hand, the physical deployment of these building blocks. These aspects are examples of views of an architecture. Architecture view models enable you to manage the complexity of the architecture of a system. You create and document an architecture based on the architecture views of an architecture view model using the architecture modeling means presented in Section 6.6. To provide for different views for an architecture in the design, you have to base an architecture on an architecture view model from the very beginning.

The quality of the specifications of architecture views is important

For architecture view models, the quality of the specifications for each architecture view is very important. These specifications should therefore cover the following points [Kruchten 2000]:

> Context of the architecture view
> System building blocks that the architecture view focuses on and their relationships
> Principles for structuring an architecture view
> Relationships of an architecture view to other architecture views
> Procedure for creating an architecture view

A good architecture distinguishes itself amongst other things by the fact that no architecturally relevant aspects are missing and the complexity has nonetheless been reduced. Using an architecture view model, you can check whether an architecture covers all relevant aspects of a system as required. A complete architecture contains all relevant architecture views and is therefore multi-dimensional. If you create an architecture based on an architecture view model from the very beginning, then you are less likely to forget important architecturally relevant points and therefore not take them into account in the architecture.

Architecture view models improve the quality of the architecture

Which relevant architecture views should an architecture view model specify? Following [Rozanski and Woods 2005], [Bredemeyer and Malan 2010], and [Larman 2002], we recommend that you always plan at least the following basic architecture views:

Basic architecture views

> *Conceptual view:* This architecture view describes the system building blocks and their relationships to one another without going into detail about, for example, interfaces. It is therefore suitable for conveying an architecture to non-technical stakeholders.
> *Logical view:* This architecture view describes the system building blocks and their relationships to one another in detail. The system building blocks and their relationships, or communication mechanisms, are specified precisely. This is necessary for the technical realization. This architecture view is therefore directed towards technical stakeholders. The conceptual view may be part of the logical view and therefore not represented explicitly. In this case the logical view partially addresses non-technical stakeholders.
> *Execution view:* This architecture view describes the physical deployment of the system building blocks at runtime in detail. It is also directed towards technical stakeholders.

The architecture views presented show static and dynamic structures of a system. However, the basic architecture views are not sufficient for a "real" architecture view model as further aspects, such as requirements, data, or the development environment, are not specifically considered. To take these further aspects into account specifically, you would have to assign them to one of the three basic architecture views. This would have a negative effect on the coherence of the views (e.g., you would have to assign the aspect "development environment" to the logical view or execution view). Therefore, the architecture view models presented below add to and refine the basic views.

Basic architecture views are not sufficient

Before we look more closely at the three most important representatives of architecture view models used in practice, we will present a common architecture view model to simplify the handling of view models. This architecture view model abstracts from the views of the architecture view models subsequently handled and covers viewpoints that specify the name, the stakeholders and their con-

Common architecture view model

cerns, and the important artefacts for the architecture views used. In the concrete architecture view models the architecture views may have different names or be split or grouped again. However, for your activities as an architect, it is vitally important that you use architecture views or an architecture view model. Which architecture view model you use is not so important. Figure 4.2-2 shows the common architecture view model that has arisen following the architecture views from [IEEE 2007], [Rozanski and Woods 2005], and [Kruchten 2000].

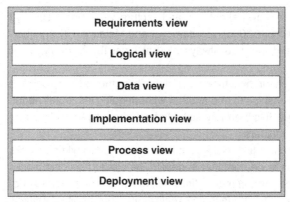

Figure 4.2-2: *Common architecture view model*

Requirements view

Table 4.2-1 shows the viewpoint of the requirements view by way of example.

Table 4.2-1: *Viewpoint of the requirements view*

Requirements view	
Purpose	Documentation of the architecture requirements
Stakeholders	Architects, developers, customers, management, domain experts, testers, project lead
Concern(s)	What does the business context of the system look like?
	What are the essential requirements the system must satisfy?
Artefacts	Business opportunities and problem description
	Stakeholders
	Business processes
	Requirements
	Guidelines

Examples of artefacts for the requirements view are Tables 8.3-1, 8.3-2, 8.4-2, and 8.4-3.

Table 4.2-2 shows the viewpoint of the logical view by way of example.

Logical view

Table 4.2-2: Viewpoint of the logical view

Logical view	
Purpose	Documentation of the architecture design
Stakeholders	Architects, developers, domain experts
Concern(s)	Which are the logical structures of the system?
Artefacts	Architecture overview/vision
	System context
	Key abstractions (with behavior)
	Functional system building blocks
	Technical system building blocks
	Guidelines

Examples of artefacts for the logical view are Figures 8.3-4, 8.5-4, 8.5-5, and 8.5-11 as well as Table 8.5-2.

Table 4.2-3 shows the viewpoint of the data view by way of example.

Data view

Table 4.2-3: Viewpoint of the data view

Data view	
Purpose	Documentation of aspects with regard to saving, manipulating, managing, and distributing data
Stakeholders	(Data) architects, developers
Concern(s)	Which are the data structures and data flows of the system?
Artefacts	Key abstractions (without behavior)
	Data models
	Data flows
	Guidelines

An example of an artefact of the data view is Table 8.5-6.

Implementation view　　Table 4.2-4 shows the viewpoint of the implementation view by way of example.

Table 4.2-4: Viewpoint of the implementation view

Implementation view	
Purpose	Documentation of the implementation structure and the implementation infrastructure
Stakeholders	Architects, developers, configuration managers, test managers, testers
Concern(s)	What do the implementation structure and the implementation infrastructure look like?
Artefacts	Implementation structure
	Guidelines

Process view　　Table 4.2-5 shows the viewpoint of the process view by way of example.

Table 4.2-5: Viewpoint of the process view

Process view	
Purpose	Documentation of the control and coordination of concurrent building blocks
Stakeholders	Architects, developers
Concern(s)	Which are the concurrent building blocks of a system?
Artefacts	Processes and threads
	Interprocess communication
	State model
	Guidelines

Deployment view　　Table 4.2-6 shows the viewpoint of the deployment view by way of example.

Table 4.2-6: Viewpoint of the deployment view

Deployment view	
Purpose	Documentation of the physical deployment of software building blocks
Stakeholders	Architects, developers, operation
Concern(s)	How are the software building blocks of a system deployed to hardware building blocks and how are they operated?
Artefacts	Installation and configuration
	Network topology
	Network protocols
	Operating environment
	Guidelines

Figure 8.5-13 shows an example of an artefact of the deployment view.

Architecture views do not build on each other sequentially in a specific order. Rather, the dependencies between the architecture views have many layers. Information from one architecture view is used in other architecture views. The requirements view is the central point because requirements are the starting point for all activities. Therefore, all architecture views are unidirectionally dependent on the requirements view. There are further, transparent, unidirectional dependencies between the realization view and the logical or data view, as well as between the deployment view and the implementation view.

Dependencies between architecture views are not trivial

In a concrete case, additional architecture views can be necessary and/or certain architecture views specified by an architecture view model are not relevant. You can and should therefore adapt the common architecture view model and the concrete architecture view models presented afterwards as required. For example, add a security or test view.

Architecture view models can be adjusted

The following architecture frameworks represent three important architecture view models frequently used in practice:
> Zachman Framework
> Reference Model for Open Distributed Processing (RM-ODP)
> 4+1 view model
> The Open Group Architecture Framework (TOGAF)

Overview of important architecture view models

Table 4.2-7 maps the architecture views of the common view model onto the architecture views of these architecture models. Analog architecture views are partially differentiated between the architecture view models with regard to their contents.

Table 4.2-7: Architecture views of the most important architecture view models

View model / Architecture view (common)	Zachman Framework	RM-ODP	4+1 view model	TOGAF
Requirements view	Business and context view	Enterprise view	Use case view	Business Architecture View
Logical view	System view	System view	Logical view	Software Engineering View
Data view	System view	Information view	Data view	Data Flow View

View model Architecture view (common)	Zachman Framework	RM-ODP	4+1 view model	TOGAF
Implementation view	Technology view	Technology view	Implementation view	Not available
Process view	Integration and runtime view	Construction view	Process view	Not available
Deployment view	Integration and runtime view	Construction view	Deployment view	System Engineering View

4.2.1 Zachman Framework

Father of the architecture view models

The Zachman Framework [Zachman 1987] is an architecture framework whose architecture view model can be seen as the father of the common architecture view models today. It was developed in 1987 by John Zachman at IBM, and was intended to describe the architecture of organizations (e.g., enterprises) without necessarily discussing IT. The Zachman Framework first describes an organization abstractly to then show the "implementation" of the organization step-by-step. As a result of its generic structure, the Zachman Framework has also proven itself to be suitable for describing IT architectures across organizations.

Matrix of architecture views and view aspects

In its current structural level, the Zachman Framework recognizes six general architecture views and six view aspects orthogonal to the architecture views. In the form of a matrix, architecture views and view aspects are the core of the architecture view model. With this matrix up to 36 specific architecture views are possible. For a concrete architecture, you should first configure the Zachman Framework, since it is a reference model, by making a selection according to relevance from the possible architecture views.

Suitable for enterprise architectures

The Zachman Framework, as a domain-independent and technology-independent architecture framework, can be used as the basis for an architecture for any type of system. Due to its orientation on aspects that apply across an entire organization, this framework is ideal for enterprise architectures (see Section 3.2). For more simple architectures, you would have to put in additional effort to reduce the complexity of its architecture view model.

Basic principles

The architecture view model of the Zachman Framework builds on the following basic principles:

> Systems can be modeled completely by describing the answers to the following questions: why? who? what? how? where? when? (view aspects).
> Six architecture views cover all essential models for the development of a system.
> Higher level architecture views adopt the restrictions of their lower level architecture views.
> Columns in the matrix represent different abstractions to reduce the complexity of a model.
> Columns have no order.
> Lines, columns, and cells are unique.
> Different instances of a framework can use themselves recursively.

Figure 4.2-3 shows the six architecture views and the related six view aspects of the Zachman Framework.

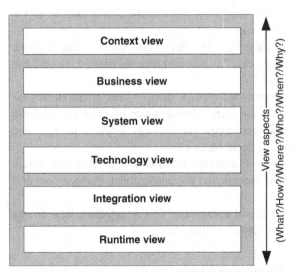

Figure 4.2-3: Architecture views in the Zachman Framework

Before we look more closely at the individual architecture views of the Zachman Framework, we should first explain the view aspects orthogonal to the architecture views:

> *What (data):* Describes the data. Examples are business objects, database tables, or field definitions.
> *How (functions):* Describes the functionality. Examples are business processes, application functionality, or computer functionality.
> *Where (network):* Shows nodes and their relationships in an organizational network. Examples are distributed objects, memory addresses, or message exchange.

View aspects

> *Who (persons):* Describes the persons with reference to an organization. Examples are stakeholders for functional requirements, roles and responsibilities in business processes, or access rights to system functionalities.
> *When (time):* Describes performance-relevant time or event dependencies between the resources of an organization. An example is the distribution of time windows for business processes.
> *Why (motivation):* Describes the organizational objectives and their subjects. Examples are business plans, standards for business processes, or technology standards for business rules.

Architecture views

We will now explain the individual architecture views in the Zachman Framework. The context and system views have a business focus, the other architecture views have a technical focus:

> *Context view (planning, scope):* This architecture view is concerned with the basic requirements and is the basis for estimations with regard to the cost, scope, and functionality of a system.
> *Business view (business model):* This architecture view shows all of the business entities and processes.
> *System view (system model):* This view determines the data and functions that realize the business model. The requirements are defined in detail and logical models are created.
> *Technology view (realization, technology model):* This architecture view is concerned with the technological implementation of a system. It covers technology selection and technology management, physical models, and the realization with concrete technologies.
> *Integration view (deployment, detailed representations):* This architecture view looks at deployment aspects and the configuration management of a system.
> *Runtime view (use, functioning enterprise):* This architecture view covers the operation of a system within an organization.

4.2.2 Reference Model for Open Distributed Processing

Generic reference model

The Reference Model for Open Distributed Processing (RM-ODP) is an architecture framework developed by ISO (International Organization for Standardization) and ITU (International Telecommunication Union). RM-ODP provides an architecture view model that has been an international standard for architecture view models in the form of a generic reference model [ISO10746 1998] since 1996. RM-ODP is tailored to distributed object-based systems. However, it also delivers a general architecture view model that can be used for other types of systems. This model was created in a standardization procedure that lasted many years.

Due to its generic view model, specific architecture view models can be instantiated from RM-ODP. It is used as a metameta-architecture view model. For example, it is applied in the 4+1 view model of the Unified Software Development Process (USDP) or the Object Management Architecture (OMA) from OMG [Malveau and Mowbray 2001]. Figure 4.2-4 shows the architecture views defined in RM-ODP.

Template for specific architecture view models

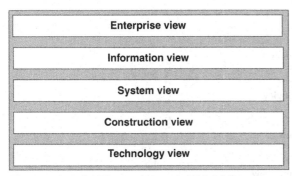

Figure 4.2-4: Architecture views in RM-ODP

The architecture views of RM-ODP each provide the complete object-oriented model of a system for their context. The main aim of RM-ODP is architectures that are independent of deployment and implementation aspects as far as possible in order to achieve systems that implement the non-functional requirements (see Chapter 5) optimally. The architecture views of RM-ODP are described below:

Architecture views

> *Enterprise view:* This architecture view looks at architecture from the viewpoint of the problem domain. The core factor is the business model from the management and end user view. This architecture view ensures that an architecture considers the requirements.

> *Information view:* This architecture view describes the structure and meaning of the information to be processed as well as its processing.

> *System view (computational viewpoint):* In this architecture view the focus is on the definition of the interfaces of deployable system building blocks (components and subsystems) of a system.

> *Construction view (engineering viewpoint):* This architecture view looks at the distributed interactions between system building blocks for the purpose of processing information and providing functionality.

> *Technology view:* The focus in this architecture view is on the technological implementation of the architecture described by the other architecture views.

4.2.3 4+1 View Model

The 4+1 view model [Kruchten 2000] was created at the end of the 1990s in the USDP (Unified Software Development Process) environment. Figure 4.2-5 illustrates the architecture views defined in this architecture view model.

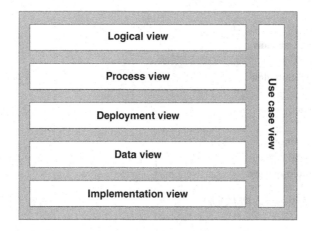

Figure 4.2-5: *Architecture views in the 4+1 view model*

Architecture views

In the beginning, this architecture view model planned a total of 5 architecture views. The data view came later [Larman 2002]. However, the name "4+1 view model" was retained. The individual views of the 4+1 view model are described below:

> *Use case view:* This architecture view is central in the 4+1 view model. The 4+1 view model states that all architectural decisions must be based on the use cases of the system concerned. This architecture view covers the most important use cases and is used as the basis for the other architecture views and for validating them.
> *Logical view:* This architecture view looks at the implementation of the functional requirements. It covers the most important system building blocks (subsystems, components, classes, etc.) and their interactions.
> *Implementation view:* This architecture view is concerned with the organization and management of the static artefacts (source code, graphics, etc.) in packages, layers, etc.
> *Data view:* This architecture view describes data models and looks at the mapping between system building blocks and persistent data.
> *Process view:* The behavior and deployment of the system at runtime are the topics in this architecture view. The focus is on parallel processing and competing accesses.

> *Deployment view:* This architecture view describes how the static artefacts from the implementation view are deployed physically.

4.2.4 The Open Group Architecture Framework

The Open Group Architecture Framework (TOGAF) was developed by The Open Group [Opengroup 2010] based on the Technical Architecture Framework for Information Management (TAFIM) of the United States Department of Defense. It has been available on the market since 1995. Since then, TOGAF has been subject to continuous further development and is now available in version 9. It is a comprehensive and widely used architecture framework for developing enterprise architectures. TOGAF comprises a method (Architecture Development Method (ADM)), a framework for defining the structural content of architecture (Architecture Content Framework (ACF)), as well as tools, reference models, and taxonomies. Numerous best practices, principles, guidelines, and technologies also play a part.

Focus on enterprise architecture

Through the ACF, TOGAF provides numerous recommendations, guidelines, procedures, and classifications for creating and using viewpoints and architecture views. It adapts the ISO/IEC 42010:2007 standard [IEEE 2007] and also recommends this standard for creating viewpoints and architecture views. In the ACF, TOGAF defines different viewpoints for developing architecture views for enterprise architecture. It also defines architecture views for IT systems. These architecture views are illustrated in Figure 4.2-6 and described in an overview below.

Viewpoints and architecture views based on ISO/IEC 42010:2007

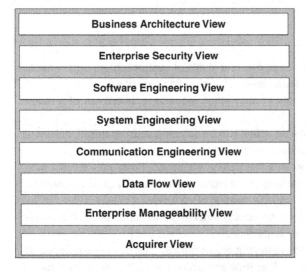

Figure 4.2-6: Architecture views in TOGAF

Architecture views are recommendations

Since TOGAF can also be combined with other architecture view models (e.g., architecture view model of the Zachman Framework), the following architecture views for IT systems defined in TOGAF represent recommendations:

> *Business Architecture View:* This architecture view is concerned with aspects of the system user. It focuses on human actors, processes, functionality, business information, usability, and performance. The aim is to achieve a comprehensive understanding of the functional requirements.
> *Enterprise Security View:* This architecture view covers typical questions regarding security (access protection, handling of threats, etc.).
> *Software Engineering View:* This architecture view provides guidelines for developing software systems. Here, reference is made in particular to the following: development processes, modularity, reuse, portability, migration, interoperability, and distribution.
> *System Engineering View:* In this architecture view the focus is on the distribution of the software building blocks to the hardware building blocks and on models for their interaction (e.g., client/server).
> *Communication Engineering View:* This architecture view supports the planning and design of networks with regard to infrastructure (e.g., LAN) and communication (e.g., OSI).
> *Data Flow View:* This architecture view covers aspects around modeling and the processing of persistent data.
> *Enterprise Manageability View:* This architecture view is concerned with the aspects operation, administration, and management of IT systems.
> *Acquirer View:* This architecture view provides requirements, guidelines, and procedures for acquiring commercial off-the-shelf (COTS) building blocks.

4.3 Summary

Summary: Architecture levels

> Architecture takes place at different levels of abstraction. As an arc-hitect you should consider these levels of abstraction explicitly.
> Taking account of levels of abstraction leads to architectures of a much higher quality.
> Three basic levels of abstraction can be differentiated: organizational level, system level, and building block level.
> Architecture levels are in a hierarchical sequence. From the view of a system, the organizational level is the highest level of abstraction, followed by the system level and then the building block level.
> At lower architecture levels requirements and decisions from higher architecture levels must be concsidered
> At organizational level we look at organizations, their business processes, and IT landscapes as well as their interactions with other organizations.

> At system level we look at the IT systems of organizations. The individual systems and their subsystems are treated as black boxes. The focus is on the interfaces and interactions of the systems with their context.
> At building block level we look at the building blocks of the individual subsystems, their responsibilities, their interfaces, as well as their interactions.
> Macro-architecture (software architecture) covers the spectrum of the architecture levels to which architecturally relevant ele-ments are assigned.
> Micro-architecture ("small-scale" architecture) covers aspects with a lower level of abstraction. This is then the detailed de-sign no fundamental influence on an architecture.
> If a system building block is a non-fundamental building block, at building block level we switch from macro-architecture to micro-architecture.

> Architecture views can be used to look at specific aspects of an IT system. They make it easier to manage the complexity of all aspects of an IT system.
> The aspects considered in architecture views depend on the respective stakeholder and his or her current activity in the creation of an IT system.
> Architecture views are specified using viewpoints.
> An architecture viewpoint is the specifica-tion of an architecture view and covers stakeholders and their concerns, as well as artefacts. The creation of an architecture view can also be specified.
> Following basic architecture views exist: re-quirements view, logical view, data view, implementation view, process view, and deployment view.
> To ensure the quality of the architecture, it is important to create or describe an archi-tecture on the basis of architecture views from the very beginning.
> It is not necessary to define architecture viewpoints from scratch; you can use exist-ing architecture view models. These al-ready cover all viewpoints relevant for prac-tice.
> The architecture view models relevant in practice include the 4+1 view model and the architecture view models of the architecture frameworks Zachman Framework, Reference Model for Open Distributed Processing (RM-ODP) and The Open Group Architecture Framework (TOGAF).

Summary:
Architecture views

Further Reading

[Brown et al. 1998]
Brown, William, J.; Malveau, Raphael, C.; McCormick III, Hays, W., "Skip"; Mowbray, Thomas, J., *Anti Patterns – Refactoring Software Architectures, and Projects in Crisis*, John Wiley & Sons, New York, 1998

Further reading:
Architecture levels

[Fowler 2005b]
Fowler, Martin, *The New Methodology*, http://www.martinfowler.com/articles/newMethodology.html, 2005

[IEEE 2010]
IEEE, *Guide to the Software Engineering Body of Knowledge*, http://www.swebok.org/, 2010

**Further reading:
Architecture views**

[Bass et al. 2003]
Bass, Len; Clements, Paul; Kazman, Rick, *Software Architecture in Practice*, Second Edition, Addison-Wesley, New York, 2003

[Bredemeyer und Malan 2010]
Bredemeyer, Dana; Malan, Ruth, *Visual Architecting Action Guide Book*, http://www.ruthmalan.com/, 2010

[Rozanski and Woods 2005]
Rozanski, Nick und Woods, Eoin, *Software Systems Architecture*, Addison-Wesley, 2005

[IEEE 2007]
IEEE, *Recommended Practice for Architectural Description of Software-intensive Systems*, http://www.iso-architecture.org/ieee-1471/, 2007

[ISO10746 1998]
International Organization for Standardization, Information technology, *Open Distributed Processing – Reference model: Overview*, http://www.iso.org/iso/en/CatalogueDetailPage.CatalogueDetail?CSNUMBER=20696&ICS1=35&ICS2=80&ICS3=, 1998

[Kruchten 2000]
Kruchten, Philippe, *The Rational Unified Process - An Introduction* Second Edition, Addison-Wesley, Boston, 2000

[Larman 2002]
Larman, Craig, *Applying UML and Patterns – An Introduction to Object-Oriented Analysis and Design and the Unified Process*, Second Edition, Prentice Hall PTR, Upper Saddle River, NJ, 2002

[Opengroup 2010]
Opengroup, *The Open Group Architecture Framework*, http://www.opengroup.org/togaf/, 2010

[Rozanski and Woods 2005]
Rozanski, Nick und Woods, Eoin, *Software Systems Architecture*, Addison-Wesley, 2005

[Zachman 1987]
Zachman, John, A., *A Framework for Information Systems Architecture*, IBM Publication, 1987

5 | Architecture Requirements (WHY)

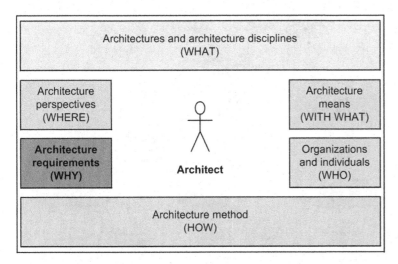

Figure 5-1: Positioning of the chapter in the architecture orientation framework

This chapter looks at the *WHY dimension* of the architecture orientation framework. In the center of this dimension are requirements. They define the IT system to be created and restrict your creative scope as an architect. There are different types of requirements at different architecture levels. In order to be able to use your creative scope, you have to know the different types of requirements and their relationships to one another and the architecture levels—these topics are covered in this chapter. After reading this chapter, you will be able to name the most important types of requirements, understand their relationships, and place them in the context of architecture. In Section 6.3.1, we will discuss requirement patterns as a methodological tool that enables you to systematically develop "good" requirements.

Overview

Basic concepts of the WHY dimension

Figure 5-2 shows the basic concepts covered in this chapter and visualizes how they relate to one another.

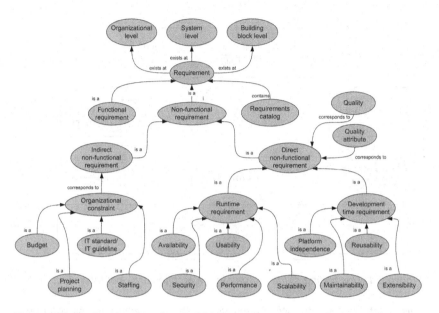

Figure 5-2: Basic concepts of the WHY dimension

5.1 Requirements Characteristics and Types

Requirements as motivators

If you ask an architect why he chose a particular architectural solution, in most cases he will reply: "The requirement was to ...." That is, the architecture is the result of requirements that were known at the beginning of a project or that arose over time (see Section 3.1). The architecture does not arise randomly. Rather, the different requirements represent the conditions or influences under which the system and the related architecture are created (see Figure 5.1-1).

Requirements are forces

Metaphorically speaking, requirements are forces that have an effect on and form the system. These forces have an effect in different directions, at different times, and to different degrees. The system must be created such that it can fulfill the given requirements. It is similar to a bone. In a bone, the fine bone structures form along the lines of influence of the external forces and balance these out. In the same way, the architecture defines the basic structure of the system to balance out the forces of the requirements affecting the system. For more information about forces in the context of architecture patterns, see Section 6.3.

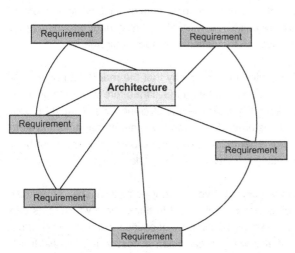

Figure 5.1-1: *Architecture influenced by requirements*

One definition of requirements comes from the IEEE [IEEE 1990]:

**Definition:
Requirement**

> A requirement is:
>
> (1) A condition or capability needed by a user to solve a problem or achieve an objective.
> (2) A condition or capability that must be met or possessed by a system or system component to satisfy a contract, standard, specification, or other formally imposed document.
> (3) A documented representation of a condition or capability as in (1) or (2).

This is a very broad definition of a requirement. The requirement "the system must be fast," whilst corresponding to the definition, is not precise enough to enable you to derive an architecture from it. Therefore, requirements must also have the properties outlined below [Wiegers 2003]. They give requirements the necessary precision and you can use them as a basis for an architecture.

Every requirement must be correct. However, only a stakeholder can assess whether this is the case. A stakeholder can be a user, sponsor, or client, for example. Therefore, you must include the various stakeholders in the identification of the requirements from the very beginning.

Correct

Feasible

It must be possible to realize the requirement under the given conditions and with the means available. To ensure this, someone with technical understanding (e.g., the architect) should be involved in the definition of the requirements.

Unambiguous

A requirement must be formulated in such a way that the reader can only draw one conclusion from it. Simple and clear language is therefore very helpful in the formulation of the requirements. For example, the statement that it must be possible to manage all relevant customer data in the customer management system is not an unambiguous requirement. To make it more precise, there must be a clear definition of what constitutes "relevant customer data."

Verifiable

Even the best requirement is useless if you cannot verify it reliably. Therefore, it is important when formulating the requirement to think about which tests can be used to verify it. The requirement that in 90% of cases the initial screen must appear within 5 seconds after a website has been accessed is a verifiable requirement. You can verify it with an appropriate test tool (e.g., Apache JMeter) that accesses the website and causes a corresponding load on the system, for example.

Requirements catalog

However, a system is defined not by a single requirement but by an entire catalog of requirements. A requirements catalog as a whole must also have the following properties:

Complete

The requirements catalog should be as complete as possible in order to provide a well-rounded picture of the overall system. But what are the criteria for completeness? One good option is to have a third party check that the requirements are complete. Often, the requirement definition only covers the standard processes. However, the requirements must also cover error situations. What happens for example, if information is delivered incorrectly or an order has been released by mistake? The requirements should also cover these possible scenarios [Cockburn 2000].

Consistent

The set of requirements must agree within itself and individual requirements must not contradict each other. If contradictions arise, only the stakeholders can help to remove them. However, it is your task as the architect to critically question the requirements placed on the architecture and to point out any inconsistencies. For example, the desire for high performance from a client/server system (see Section 6.4.4) coupled with the wish for low network bandwidth between the client and the server can be contradictory. This is always the case if physical properties of the network prevent the achievement of the required performance.

Overview of requirements

In order to consider requirements based on specific objectives when practicing as an architect, you must be able to differentiate between different types of requirements.

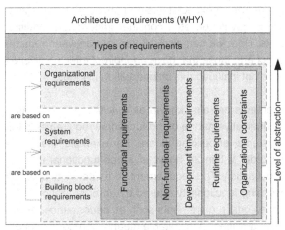

Figure 5.1-2: Requirements types

Figure 5.1-2 shows that requirements can generally be categorized into functional and non-functional requirements. These can be directed towards organizations (*organizational requirements*), systems (*system requirements*), and building blocks (*building block requirements*).

Functional requirements define required functionalities. Organizations, systems, and building blocks can fulfill functional requirements. Table 5.1-1 gives an overview of the different types of functional requirements.

Functional requirements

Table 5.1-1: Overview of types of functional requirements

Type of requirement	Description
Functional organizational requirements	Functional organizational requirements represent the functional requirements placed on organizations by, for example, their customers, employees, business partners, or by authorities. The desire of customers to place orders with the organization is an example of this type of requirement. A further example is the desire of employees to receive their wages from the organization. Organizations can also subject themselves to requirements. For example, an organization can require that an IT system for entering orders must exist in order to support order entry using IT.
Functional system requirements	Functional system requirements express the concrete functional needs of stakeholders or systems that interact with the system concerned. The desire of the user of a system to be able to enter an order in the system is an example of this type of requirement.
Functional building block requirements	Functional building block requirements represent functional properties that a system building block must possess for the system to be able to fulfill its requirements. The desire of a building block to be able to create PDF documents by calling up a service from another building block is an example of this type of requirement (see Section 3.4).

Non-functional requirements

Non-functional requirements represent expectations and necessities that stakeholders (client, user, architect, developer, etc.) consider important in addition to the functional requirements. Here we can also differentiate between requirements that have a direct effect and those that have an indirect effect. However, for reasons of clarity, we have not included this differentiation in Figure 5.1-2.

Direct non-functional requirements (qualities)

Direct non-functional requirements are also known as *qualities* or *quality attributes*, since they reflect the qualitative nature of the functional requirements fulfilled by organizations, IT systems, or building blocks. For example, the desire of customers to receive an order within 24 hours is a non-functional requirement that an organization must satisfy. This requirement corresponds to a quality desired from an *order processing* functionality offered by an organization. With regard to IT systems, non-functional requirements such as performance, extensibility, and reusability express qualities. One suitable means for recording qualities in a systematic manner are quality attribute scenarios, which we will briefly discuss in Section 6.3.1.

Indirect non-functional requirements (constraints)

Indirect non-functional requirements have an effect on the way you realize the required functionalities and qualities. They represent specifications or facts that you must adhere to or take into account. In this context therefore, we often speak of constraints. The budget available for the implementation of an IT system and legal regulations are examples of constraints. The budget specifies the financial scope within which you can implement the IT system, and you must comply with legal regulations.

Relevance of non-functional requirements

Non-functional requirements must be satisfied in order for the functionalities of an organization, system, or building block to be accepted. Despite this, insufficient attention is often paid to non-functional requirements since the focus is clearly placed on the functional requirements. It is your task as the architect to make stakeholders aware of this, since the architecture itself is significantly important in satisfying the non-functional requirements. By making the stakeholders aware of this issue, you can ensure that time is planned in the early stages of a project for considering non-functional requirements.

In addition to differentiating between qualities and constraints, we can break down the class of non-functional requirements even further. Table 5.1-2 gives an overview of the different types of non-functional requirements.

Table 5.1-2: Overview of the types of non-functional requirements

Type of requirement	Description
Development time requirements	Development time requirements express qualities and constraints that have to be considered mainly during the development of a system. These include classic quality attributes such as extensibility, reusability, or platform independence. Specifications about technologies to be used are a further example of this type of requirement.
Runtime requirements	Runtime requirements contain expectations with regard to the behavior of a system at runtime. These include requirements such as availability, stability, and performance. They are primarily visible at runtime. Runtime requirements are usually direct and relate to specific quality attributes.
Organizational constraints	Organizational constraints include specifications such as budget and time-to-market. Another example is the restrictions that the knowledge and experience within the development/project team place on the design of the architecture. Organizational constraints are usually indirect non-functional requirements.

Building block requirements, system requirements, and organizational requirements build on one another (see Figure 5.1-2). You can derive system requirements from organizational requirements, and in turn, building block requirements from system requirements. Generally, organizational requirements that are to be supported by IT should be completely covered by system requirements. System requirements should equally be covered by building block requirements. By linking the requirements, you can verify both the transparency and the completeness of the requirements.

Relationships between types of requirements

You cannot always assign non-functional requirements to development time or runtime uniquely. It is important to point out when the non-functional requirement mainly takes effect and when it must therefore be considered. If, for example, you consider the non-functional requirement for extensibility at development time in the design of an architecture, you can add new functionality at runtime. This means that extensibility is visible at both development time and runtime. However, you must consider it primarily at development time.

Differentiation between development time requirements and runtime requirements

Requirements can be described in different levels of detail. For example, the somewhat unspecific desire for a system for entering orders can be expressed by the organizational requirement "We must have a system in which employees can enter orders." Using this as a basis, you can describe a system requirement in the form of a system use case. The use case documents in detail how users

Level of detail of requirements

want to enter orders in an order entry system. The level of detail of a system to be realized therefore increases from the organizational requirements down to the building block requirements.

Requirements and their mutual influences

Requirements do not affect only the architecture—they also affect each other. The task of the architecture is to balance out these mutual influences and effects as well as possible (see Section 8.5). The knowledge that exists within a project team and the performance (see Section 5.5) required from the system can thus influence each other. High performance suggests a concurrent architecture, for example, but it may be the case that the people involved in the development project have no experience in concurrent programming. You have various options for dealing with the conflict between these two requirements. One option would be to integrate additional project team members with the required profile. A second alternative is to use architecture means such as application servers that simplify the use of a concurrent architecture. You have to decide which of the alternatives available best balances out the mutual influences between the individual requirements.

5.2 Organizational Requirements

The classification scheme presented in Section 5.1 enables you to classify individual requirements and place them in relationship to one another. It enables you to get an overview at the start of your work. In this section, we will explain organizational requirements, system requirements, and building block requirements in more detail. We will then look more closely at the non-functional types of requirements. In particular, we will focus on systems. We will therefore discuss some requirements often met in practice in more detail. However, the information should not be considered exhaustive.

Requirements placed on the organization

Organizational requirements represent requirements placed on organizations. They can be traced back to the environment of the organization (see Section 7.2), which specifies functional and non-functional requirements that the organization must satisfy.

Functional organizational requirements

Functional organizational requirements refer to services that the organization offers. The desire of customers to be able to place orders with the organization is an example of a functional organizational requirement.

Non-functional organizational requirements

Non-functional organizational requirements express the standard of quality that the environment demands in the fulfillment of the functional organizational requirements. Delivery within 24 hours or a two year guarantee time are examples of non-functional organizational requirements.

An organization can decide to use IT systems to fulfill the requirements placed on it. It can therefore express its own organizational requirements that reflect the demand on IT systems to be developed. For example, a company manufactures computers. The individual computers are always tailored precisely to the wishes of the individual customer. The employees in the order entry department are constantly overwhelmed by a flood of new orders. This volume can only be handled by an extremely high work input. The high work input and the related stress for the employees has been identified as a problem. During the problem analysis, it becomes clear that the high work input is the result of a number of constantly recurring manual steps. To support the employees in the order entry department in fulfilling their tasks, the organization decides to implement an IT system to solve the problem. The system should ease the burden on the employees by automating as many of the manual steps as possible. The organization therefore formulates an organizational requirement for an IT system for order entry.

Organization defines organizational requirements

IT standards and guidelines are specifications across an organization that IT systems being developed within the organization must satisfy. These specifications can be functional or non-functional. The mandatory use of JEE as a component platform is an example of a non-functional organizational requirement that can be defined as an IT standard or guideline. The principles of proper accounting state, for example, that it must be possible to create statements of accounts. The ability to create statements of accounts is an example of a functional organizational requirement that can also be seen as a guideline valid for the entire organization. Therefore, appropriate functionality must be planned in IT systems.

IT standards and guidelines

5.3 System Requirements

System requirements describe requirements placed on systems. The internal structure of the new system is out of scope for the consideration of the system requirements.

Functional system requirements are based on functional organizational requirements. The focus is on functionalities that a user or another system expects from the system. Applied to the example of the new system for entering orders, a functional system requirement documented in a system use case could be, for example, "Create a new order." This system requirement describes the individual activities the user performs with the system under construction. Functional system requirements are expressed in concrete building blocks of a system. For the

Functional system requirements

order entry example, this means that the order entry system contains building blocks such as the user dialog control, order processing, and persistence. These enable users to enter an order. A functional requirement is therefore always reflected in concrete functional behavior of the system.

Non-functional system requirements

Typical non-functional system requirements are performance, availability, extensibility, and platform independence. The fulfillment of non-functional requirements is a further important criterion for the acceptance of a system being developed. It is very difficult and sometimes impossible to localize non-functional requirements in one system. For example, there is no system building block that is responsible for extensibility. Extensibility results from a series of principles, such as encapsulation, that are widely distributed over different parts of the system (see Section 6.1). To account for the requirement for extensibility, the system can contain dedicated extension points that you must plan in the architecture. In our order entry scenario, one requirement that the order entry system must satisfy could be that in a next release, customers can call up the status of their order via the Internet. This potential extension must already be accounted for in the software architecture of the system. It is the non-functional system requirements that are often forgotten or neglected, since the client and the user focus on the functional system requirements. The client is therefore often unwilling to bear higher costs for the necessary architecture design. This is where you, the architect, are needed. You have to recognize which non-functional requirements have to be explicitly considered. The architecture must implement the non-functional requirements. This does not happen by accident—you have to take it into account in the architecture design from the very beginning.

5.4 Building Block Requirements

Building block requirements define the functional and non-functional requirements that the building blocks of a system must satisfy.

Functional building block requirements

Functional building block requirements define the functionalities expected of a building block. For example, one possible functional building block requirement that a data access building block of the order entry system must satisfy could be as follows: the data access building block allows searches for customer objects using the customer number and customer name.

Non-functional building block requirements

You can also formulate general non-functional requirements for building blocks. For example, the data access building block may have to satisfy the following development time requirement: building blocks from the business logic layer must be offered an interface in accordance with the Data Access Object pattern [Alur et al. 2003]. Therefore, the data access building block must implement the Data Access Object pattern. This building block requirement can be traced back to a system requirement for independence from the database management system used.

5.5 Qualities and Constraints

Qualities and constraints complement the requirement levels organization, system, and building block. We differentiate between qualities that have an effect at runtime and those that affect primarily development time. In addition, constraints have mostly an indirect influence on the architecture. Note that quality attributes often cannot be clearly assigned to just one of the categories runtime, development time, or constraints.

Runtime requirements are non-functional requirements that the system must satisfy at runtime. They therefore have a special meaning for the system and describe qualities that influence the client or user's acceptance of the system. Typical runtime requirements are availability, performance, usability, and security.

Qualities at runtime

Availability is expressed in the relationship of the downtimes to the uptimes. The fewer the downtimes compared to the uptimes, the higher the availability of the system. The architecture has two options for achieving the best possible availability. Firstly it can try to minimize the frequency of downtimes so that they occur as infrequently as possible. The second option relates to the length of the downtimes. If a system is not available due to an error, the architecture should enable the cause of the error to be located and removed as quickly as possible. Thus the architecture contributes to reducing the length of the downtime.

Availability

Systems must be able to cope with increasing loads. In other words, they must react appropriately to an increasing load in order to be able to offer their services to a defined level of quality. For example, a message service must not crash if the number of requests increases heavily due to an important new feature. There is a general differentiation between *vertical* and *horizontal* scalability. In the case of the former, for example, a server is replaced with a more powerful server. In the case of horizontal scalability, the load is distributed across several servers.

Scalability

A system always reacts to external events. Performance describes the capability of a system to do so within a certain time frame. There are two ways of expressing the performance of a system. It can be measured using the number of events a system can process within a specific period. The second option is to measure the average time the system needs to process an event. The performance of a

Performance

system is generally determined by the communication at its internal and external interfaces. The architecture thus makes a considerable contribution to system performance through the definition of the interfaces between the individual functional building blocks.

Usability

The usability of a system is a measure of the extent to which the user experiences the operation of the system as efficient, ergonomic, and satisfactory. You must select a suitable architecture in order to achieve sufficient system usability (see Section 6.4). A significant architecture decision here is the choice between a rich client architecture and a thin client architecture (see Section 6.4.6). To enable users with disabilities to also use the system, the architecture may be required to support different user interfaces (e.g., a voice-controlled user interface). There may also be a requirement for users to be able to work with the system in an offline mode. This is often the case for field employees so that they can enter orders on their laptop and synchronize with an order entry server at a later point in time. You must define this usability requirement explicitly in the architecture. A good architecture for the presentation logic of a system can also make it easier to develop a user interface with regard to extensibility, reusability, and consistency. The architecture can also include the basic mechanisms for error handling in a system. This also benefits the visual part of the error handling processes.

Security

Security is a non-functional requirement with a pervasive nature. It expects, for example, a system to refuse unauthorized access but grant authenticated users access to system resources for which they have the relevant authorization. Aspects we can identify in this context are: confidentiality, authentication, integrity, privacy, non-repudiation, and intrusion protection. Security is a very important topic. Security architecture is a separate architecture discipline (see Section 3.2) for which there are various basic architectures (see Section 6.4.12).

Requirements relevant at development time

Development time requirements refer to the architecture means that are to be used. On one hand, these include the means to be used in the IT system. However, they also include the means used in the creation of the IT system. These requirements therefore have an effect above all during the development of the system. Examples of development time requirements are platform independence, reusability, scalability, and maintainability. The specification of specific technologies (e.g., JEE or .NET) is also an example of this type of requirement.

Platform independence

A common requirement is the ability to operate a system on different platforms (see Section 3.4). For example, it can be possible to install a system on different JEE component platforms (e.g., IBM WebSphere Application Server and JBoss Application Server). The task of the architecture is to enable these different combinations by using appropriate architecture means (see Chapter 6). For example, you can separate the platform-specific system building blocks from the platform-independent building blocks using the principle of modularization. Platform independence is also often referred to as portability.

The use of appropriate architecture means can be leveraged to achieve platform independence. Furthermore, architecture means can contribute to reusing existing building blocks in subsequent developments or other systems in order to reduce the development effort. The non-functional requirement of reusability considers this topic. It can define that you should design building blocks so that they can be reused and that you should reuse existing building blocks. The topic of software reuse is covered extensively in [Chughtai and Vogel 2001].

Reusability

The lifecycle of a system extends beyond the initial development. Once you have put a system into operation, errors are identified that need to be corrected, and new requirements arise that the current status of the system cannot cover. Hence, you must correct system errors and implement new requirements. The non-functional requirement of *maintainability* is concerned primarily with correcting errors, whilst *extensibility* is concerned mainly with the implementation of new requirements and the replacement of system building blocks. The easier it is to correct an error, the easier it is to maintain the system. An easily maintainable system consists of system building blocks with high cohesion. The lower the coupling between system building blocks, the better the extensibility of the system. To achieve good maintainability and good extensibility therefore, apply the principles of high cohesion (see Section 6.1.2) and loose coupling (see Section 6.1.1).

Maintainability and extensibility

At first glance, organizational constraints are the responsibility of the project lead, since they cover topics such as budget, deadlines, and organizational structures. However, they also influence architecture. If the architecture does not consider the influences of the organizational requirements, then an architecture may not be implemented at all (see Chapter 7).

Organizational constraints influence the architecture

The abilities and knowledge of the members of the project team always influence the architecture. They have experience with and knowledge of specific technologies and procedures. If an architecture does not take account of this wealth of experience, this can only be balanced out by additional effort. The additional effort arises either because new developers are brought into the project team, or the existing developers have to be trained in the new technologies. It is therefore important that you know which technologies have been used previously in a project team and what the development process looks like. With this knowledge, the architecture can take account of these organizational constraints.

Staffing

Project planning

Development projects often have tight deadlines that you can only maintain by using existing third party products. In this case, the architecture must integrate these products in the overall system. The functionalities and interfaces of these prefabricated building blocks thus influence the division of the overall system into individual building blocks.

Budget

Every development project has a budget that also influences the architecture. Each technology is subject to different costs. These may be procurement costs or expenses for training in a new technology. The architecture must take account of the budget available by orienting the technology selection and the implementation of the requirements around this budget.

5.6 Requirements in the Context of Architecture

Requirements and architecture dimensions

In this section, we will look at the types of requirements previously introduced in the context of architecture. We will place them in context to the other dimensions of the architecture orientation framework. Figure 5.6-1 visualizes this architecture context. The different architecture levels from Chapter 4 are the central structuring schema. The important elements of the architecture dimensions are positioned at the different architecture levels. This enables us to consider the elements at a uniform level of abstraction. The level of abstraction decreases from the organizational level down to the building block level. In other words, the level of detail of a system to be realized, or its architecture, increases from the top to the bottom. Elements at the organizational level are valid across the organization as a whole. In contrast, elements at the system level refer directly to a system and elements at the building block level correspondingly to building blocks of a system (see Chapter 4). Figure 5.6-1 illustrates the types of requirements in the context of architecture.

Architecturally significant requirements

Architecturally significant requirements are generally all requirements that have a considerable influence on the design of the architecture. Unfortunately, it is not possible to define these universally for all projects. They are different in each individual case. The benefit, risk, and effect of a requirement can be identification characteristics for architecturally significant requirements. For more information on this topic, see Section 8.4.

Requirements and architecture perspectives

Requirements can be situated at different architecture levels. Requirements at one architecture level are based on requirements at the architecture level above it.

Organizational requirements at the organizational level express requirements placed on the organization by customers, business partners, employees, or authorities. These requirements can make it necessary for systems to support or fulfill the requirements at the organizational level. Furthermore, IT standards and guidelines valid across the whole organization are also situated at this level.

Requirements at the organizational level

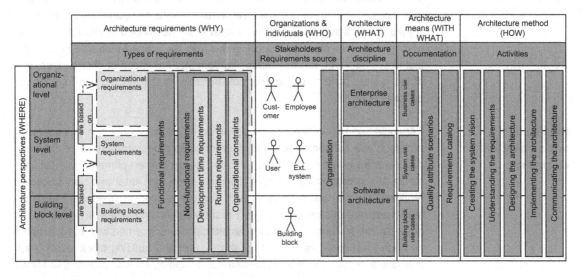

Figure 5.6-1: Requirements in the context of architecture

At system level, the focus is on systems and the functions and qualities they provide. The system requirements are based on organizational requirements. Using our example of the system for entering orders, at system level, the concrete functional requirements placed on the system can be derived from the functional organizational requirement that such a system should exist. Furthermore, the development time requirement that systems within the organization must be realized based on JEE can be expressed, for example, at the organizational level. This means that the system has to consider JSP, Java Servlets, and EJB APIs, for example.

Requirements at system level

At the last level, the building block level, the building block requirements address the internal structure of the system by describing the requirements according to specific building blocks, their functionalities, and their non-functional properties. For the order processing example, this means that at building block level, a building block requirement describes the requirements placed on a building block to write and read orders in a database (*functional requirements*) that must be realized using JDBC (*non-functional requirement*). Based on the JEE example introduced, the non-functional building block requirements would specify that building

Requirements at building block level

blocks must be realized using JEE building blocks (e.g., JSPs, JSFs, Servlets, EJBs).

Requirements and organizations/ individuals

Various stakeholders formulate requirements. For example, organizational requirements result from the wishes of customers, employees, business partners, or authorities. In addition, the organization itself formulates IT standards and guidelines at the organizational level. In turn, system requirements can be assigned to the actual users of the system to be developed or the systems with which the system interacts. Specifications from the organization also have an effect at system level. Building block requirements are based on the requirements of the system building blocks that collaborate with the system building block in question.

Requirements and architecture disciplines

Depending on the architecture discipline (see Chapter 3) in which you act as an architect, you are confronted with different types of requirements. For example, if you are an enterprise architect, you will be concerned primarily with requirements at the organizational level. These include functional and non-functional requirements that are defined as part of an enterprise architecture. These requirements are expressed through IT standards and guidelines laid down by the organization. In contrast, software architecture is concerned with the functional and non-functional requirements of the system and building block levels. As a software architect, you are responsible for designing an architecture that allows the building of a system that satisfies the requirements placed on it. This also includes taking into account the IT standards and guidelines specified. Your activity focuses on the system to be designed.

Requirements and architecture means

You can use various means to document requirements (see Section 6.6). Use cases are a good means of describing functional requirements at all architecture levels. You can formulate organizational requirements as *business use cases,* system requirements as *system use cases*, and building block requirements as *component use cases*. This classification of use cases originates from Alistair Cockburn [Cockburn 2000]. In this context a "component" is a system building block. At system and building block level, we often find quality attribute scenarios for describing non-functional requirements (see Section 6.3.1). In principle, you can of course also use quality attribute scenarios at organizational level to document non-functional requirements placed on organizations. Requirements catalogs are used at all levels.

Requirements and architecture method

Requirements play an important role in an architecture method. Thus you are involved in formulating the system vision and the requirements it contains (activity: *creating the system vision*). You must also understand the architecturally significant requirements placed on the system (activity: *understanding the require-*

ments) in order to design a suitable architecture (activity: *designing the architecture*). The software architecture will allow, for example, for dedicated subsystems or software building blocks that are responsible for fulfilling the functional requirements defined. The use of suitable architecture means in a software architecture also ensures that non-functional requirements such as extensibility and platform independence are guaranteed. You must also ensure the requirements are realized (activity: *implementing the architecture*). You will also demonstrate to the stakeholders how the architecture satisfies the architecturally significant requirements (activity: *communicating the architecture*). The architectural activities are covered in more detail in Chapter 8.

5.7 Summary

> Requirements are forces that define the IT system to be created and restrict the creative freedom of the architect.
> A requirement is a system capability that the user needs to solve a problem or achieve an objective. Alternatively, a requirement is a capability that the system must possess in order to fulfill a contract, standard, specification, or other formal document.
> Various stakeholders formulate requirements.
> Requirements must be correct, feasible, unambiguous, and verifiable.
> Requirements can be categorized into functional and non-functional requirements.
> Functional requirements define required functionalities.
> Functional organizational requirements represent the functional requirements placed on organizations by, for example, their customers, employees, business partners, or by authorities.
> Functional system requirements express the concrete functional needs of stakeholders or systems that interact with the system concerned.
> Functional building block requirements represent functional properties that a system building block must offer for the system to be able to fulfill its requirements.
> Non-functional requirements represent expectations and necessities that stakeholders consider important in addition to the functional requirements.
> Direct non-functional requirements are also known as qualities or quality attributes.
> Indirect non-functional requirements represent specifications or given facts that you must adhere to or consider. Here we often speak of constraints.
> Development time requirements express qualities and constraints that have to be considered mainly during the development of a system.

Summary: Architecture requirements

> Runtime requirements contain expectations with regard to the behavior of a system at runtime.
> Organizational constraints include specifications such as budget and time-to-market.
> Architecturally significant requirements are requirements that have a considerable influence on the design of the architecture.
> Requirements can appear on different architecture levels (organizational level, system level, building block level). Requirements at one architecture level are based on requirements at the architecture level above it.
> Depending on the architecture discipline in which you act as an architect, you are confronted with different types of requirements.
> Requirements can be documented with different means. Use cases are a good means of describing functional requirements at all architecture levels.
> As part of an architecture method, requirements play an important role in all activities of an architect.

Further Reading

**Further reading:
Architecture
requirements**

[Chughtai and Vogel 2001]
Chughtai, Arif; Vogel, Oliver, *Software-Wiederverwendung*, Theoretische Grundlagen, Vorteile und realistische Beurteilung, http://www.ovogel.de, 2001 (available in German language only)

[Cockburn 2000]
Cockburn, Alistair, *Writing Effective Use Cases*, Addison-Wesley, New York, 2000

[Wiegers 2003]
Wiegers, Karl E., *Software Requirements*, Second Edition, Microsoft Press, 2003

6 | Architecture Means (WITH WHAT)

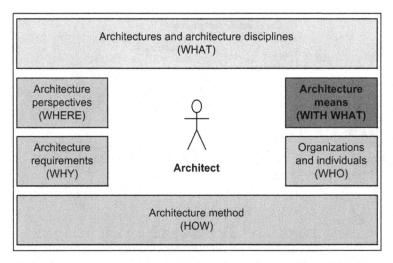

Figure 6-1: Positioning of the chapter in the architecture orientation framework

This chapter looks at the *WITH WHAT dimension* of the architecture orientation framework and presents basic concepts and techniques that belong to a software architect's toolbox. After reading this chapter, you will have an idea of the means you can use to assess, describe, create, and develop architectures (Figure 6-1).

Overview

Sections 6.1, 6.2.1–6.2.5, 6.2.7, 6.3.2–6.3.5, 6.4.1–6.4.10, 6.6.3, 6.7.1–6.7.4 and 6.7.6 are based on the work by Prof. Dr. Uwe Zdun for the German Edition of this book.

Basic concepts of the WITH WHAT dimension

Figure 6-2 gives an overview of how the topics presented in this chapter are related. As you can see, we will look at basic architecture means first: principles, concepts, patterns, styles, and tactics. We will then discuss further means that you can use to implement the basic means.

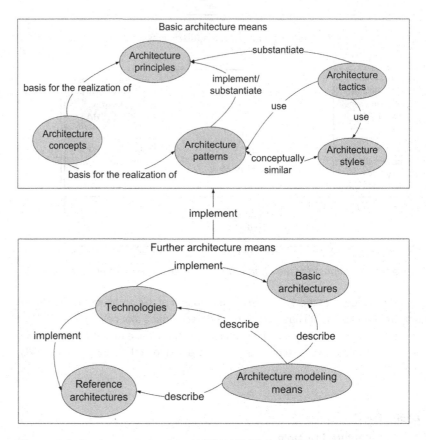

Figure 6-2: *Basic concepts of the WITH WHAT dimension*

Principles such as loose coupling or high cohesion are very general guidelines. Basic concepts such as object orientation or aspect orientation make these principles more concrete and provide a basis for realizing the principles. Tactics make general principles more concrete by offering guidelines based on quality attributes. Patterns and styles, which are very similar concepts, have even more concrete and detailed guidelines. Architecture patterns and architecture styles offer detailed approaches to support concrete design decisions.

The architecture means named so far abstract from concrete domains, technologies, and technology approaches. The further architecture means represent more concrete specifications in these areas. Basic architectures, such as layered architectures, n-tier architectures, or architectures based on component containers are concrete guidelines that enable you to structure entire systems. Reference architectures describe general architectural approaches for concrete domains, often combined with specific technology approaches. Architecture modeling means such as UML, domain-specific languages, or architecture description languages are tools for modeling and documenting architectures. And finally, we will discuss the current most important architecture technologies—that is, technologies such as platforms and infrastructures that are fundamentally important for a system's architecture.

Different types of architecture means influence the architecture under construction in different ways. Figure 6-3 makes this clear. The influence increases from the architecture principles (see Section 6.1) right up to the reference architectures (see Section 6.5).

The influence of architecture means should be considered

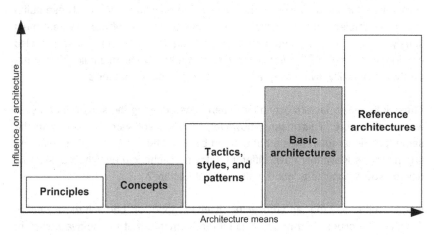

Figure 6-3: Influence of architecture means

Architecture principles are proven guidelines that you should apply when developing or modifying an architecture. However, they say nothing about how you should apply these principles in concrete cases. In contrast, reference architectures clearly indicate what a concrete architecture should look like. The degree of structuring thus increases. The degree of reuse also increases since you can use proven, concrete architecture knowledge. This is an advantage as it means you do not have to "reinvent the wheel." However, reference architectures also anticipate many decisions and this reduces your freedom as an architect. As long

How do means influence the architecture?

as you can apply the reference architecture directly to the concrete problem, this is not an issue. For example, depending on the scope, a reference architecture can cover both the functional architecture and the technical architecture. However, the use of the technical aspects of a reference architecture requires that all constraints formulated also permit the use of the technologies defined by the reference architecture. If this is not the case, there is a part of the reference architecture that you cannot use. You must therefore find a balance between the specifications resulting from architecture means and the concrete problem. When identifying the architecture means, we recommend that you look at those with a high degree of reusability first. You should only use more basic means (architecture principles) if there are no higher value means (e.g., basic and reference architectures) available.

6.1 Architecture Principles

Factors that influence an architecture

As explained in the previous chapters, software architecture is primarily concerned with the building blocks of a system and how they interact. These building blocks implement the functional requirements that a software system must satisfy. There are also many non-functional requirements, and these are also important: for example, performance, time to market, costs, maintainability, reusability, modifiability, availability, and simplicity (see also Chapter 3).

These influencing factors play a large part in determining the structure of a software architecture. This means, however, that two software systems with the same technical requirements but created by two different architects in different organizations inevitably have different software architectures. The question is, how do you recognize a "good" software architecture?

Good and bad architectures

It is difficult to say that an architecture itself is "good" or "bad"—it merely fulfills the given functional and non-functional requirements that the software system must satisfy more or less well. In other words: the architectures represent different variants of their systems' quality attributes. For example, a highly flexible and configurable server architecture may be very suitable for an application server. However, in some circumstances the same architecture—compared to a more inflexible architecture—can be highly problematic for a server in the field of embedded systems. On one hand the high flexibility is not really necessary in embedded systems, and on the other hand, the more flexible architecture is also clearly more complex and requires more memory, computing power, and other resources.

Architecture principles

There are, however, general principles that you should consider when designing a software architecture. In this section we will explain some central architecture principles in more detail. These principles look at different architectural questions and problems. There are two main problems that are important for almost all of the principles covered below: reducing the complexity of an architecture and increasing the flexibility (or modifiability) of an architecture.

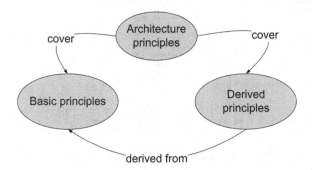

Figure 6.1-1: *Overview of the architecture principles*

Figure 6.1-1 provides a first overview of the architecture principles. It covers basic principles and principles derived from these basic principles. Figure 6.1-2 shows the basic principles and their relationship to one another in detail. Figure 6.1-3 gives an overview of the derived principles. The individual principles and their relationships are explained below.

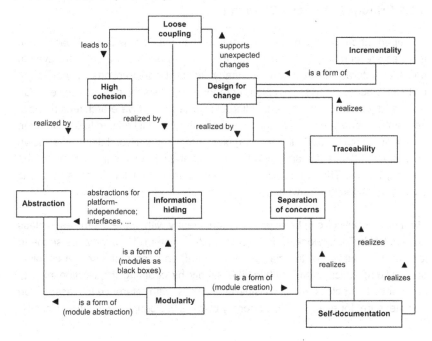

Figure 6.1-2: *Overview of the architecture principles*

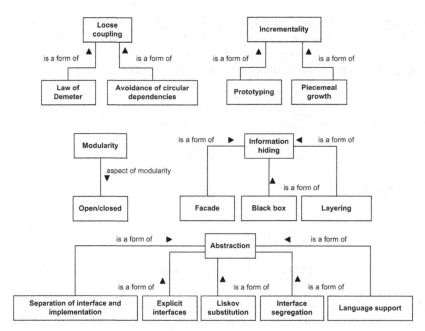

Figure 6.1-3: Overview of special variants of some architecture principles

6.1.1 Principle of Loose Coupling

Coupling

An important core of the definition of software architecture is that software architectures are primarily concerned with the building blocks of a software system and their interaction. You can use many different constructions to realize the building blocks, such as modules, components, classes, procedures, etc. On one hand you can look at the building blocks of the software architecture independently of one another—on the other hand they are still related to one another. The relationship between the building blocks of a software architecture is known as *coupling*. It is particularly important as it characterizes the interactions of the building blocks. These interactions are vitally important for all considerations from the architectural viewpoint.

The term "coupling" can be explained more clearly with some examples. A class is a central building block of an object-oriented system. Thus it makes sense to look at the coupling of the classes. In general, you can measure the coupling of a building block of the architecture simply by counting the relationships to another building block under consideration. Thus, with reference to classes, you can measure, for example, how strongly classes are coupled with other classes.

You do this by determining the number of other classes in a relationship with a given class.

This simple coupling metric gives you a first impression about the coupling in an architecture. However, it is also important to consider how the building blocks of an architecture are coupled. Please note that even though coupling is most often understood as two building blocks "calling", "including", or "knowing" each other, there are many other ways of how building blocks may have established strong mutual inter-dependencies. Different realizations of a relationship between the building blocks often mean dependencies of different strengths. A common type system, for example, may bind two building blocks together without having this ever interact, directly. Let us assume that two classes require common data. Three examples of types of coupling (there are many more types) are:

> The classes can mutually access each other's (private) data. This is a very strong form of coupling since you can no longer change one of the classes without considering the other.

> A weaker coupling is present if the classes communicate via a global data structure. The direct dependencies between the classes are released and outsourced to the global data structure. Despite this, the coupling is still very strong: all changes that affect the global data also affect all classes that work with the data.

> If the classes only communicate via method parameters, the coupling is considerably lower: the methods involved contain only essential data. Changes to this data coupling therefore only cause local changes to the relevant methods of the classes involved.

Two building blocks that work on the same level of abstraction without ever explicitly using each other, is another example. There are many more examples of comparably "invisible" coupling-relationships that may exist between building blocks due to some sort of shared assumptions or views of their worlds. Therefore call-measures may give you first indications of how loosely coupled two building blocks are—but this may by far not be sufficient for a final coupling-conclusion.

Coupling metrics can also be considered for other architecture views and types of building blocks. Another useful view is the consideration of the object and call structures at runtime. Here we can say that object x has a high coupling to object y if it frequently calls y.

The principle of loose coupling states that the coupling between system building blocks should be kept as low as possible (see Figure 6.1-4). This principle is concerned with the problem that, to understand and change a building block, it

Principle of loose coupling

is often necessary to understand or change other building blocks [Yourdon and Constantine 1978]. The assumption is that these quality attributes are positively influenced by loose coupling.

One aim of loose coupling is therefore to keep the complexity of structures low: the less strongly a building block is coupled with other building blocks, the easier it is to understand the building block without having to understand lots of other building blocks at the same time. A second aim is to increase the modifiability of the architecture: the less building blocks are affected by a change in another building block due to strong coupling, and the looser the existing relationships, the easier it is to change individual building blocks locally—without considering their environment.

Relationship to other principles

As you can see, loose coupling enables design for change, a further important principle of software architecture. Loose coupling also leads to the principle of high cohesion. If you keep the external relationships "loose," a direct consequence is frequently that the building blocks are designed with stronger internal connections.

You can achieve loose coupling particularly by implementing the following principles: abstraction, separation of concerns, and information hiding. The introduction of interface abstractions is an important aspect here. You separate the concerns "interface" and "implementation" and hide implementation information behind the interfaces. To achieve loose coupling, you should then try to keep the number of interface elements as low as possible and also restrict the frequency of the exchange of information via interfaces. Generally, building blocks of an architecture should only communicate via well-defined interfaces. This enables abstraction and also enables you to control the coupling of system building blocks.

Law of Demeter

A principle related to loose coupling is the Law of Demeter [Lieberherr and Holland 1989]. It states: A system building block should only use closely related building blocks ("don't talk to strangers"). This is particularly important since people can only retain a limited amount of information in their short-term memory. Thus it makes sense not to overload system building blocks with too much external information in order to increase their ability to be understood.

Avoid circular dependencies

An important sub-principle of loose coupling is the avoidance of circular dependencies between the building blocks of a system. This is because circular dependencies involve a particularly high coupling of the building blocks. Circular dependencies are the cause of many problems in software development, for example, deadlocks and complicated modifiability. An important architectural problem here is that none of the circularly dependent building blocks can be understood or tested without understanding or testing the entire cycle. This means that it is difficult to divide up the development of such building blocks.

Instead of circular dependencies, the relationships of the building blocks should follow the so-called Hollywood Principle: "don't call us, we'll call you"—that is, they should be loosely coupled. This is also known as Inversion of Control.

Inversion of Control (Hollywood Principle)

Dependency Inversion is an application of Inversion of Control or loose coupling: one building block defines an interface with which it works and other building blocks realize the interface.

Dependency Inversion

Dependency Injection is a further application of the Inversion of Control. It transfers the responsibility for the creation and linking of building blocks to an externally configurable framework in order to reduce the coupling to the environment of the building block. This makes it easier to manage dependencies.

Dependency Injection

6.1.2 Principle of High Cohesion

Coupling is concerned with the dependencies between different building blocks of an architecture. However, a building block itself often consists of several parts. For example, a class consists of variables and methods. The dependencies within a system building block are called *cohesion*. Ultimately, cohesion is a measure of how much a given building block is self-contained, semantically.

Cohesion

Cohesion can also be explained more clearly with examples. With reference to the methods of a class, you can measure the cohesion by the call relationships of the methods of this class among each other. In the runtime view, object x has a high cohesion if it frequently calls itself.

The cohesion within a system building block should be as high as possible (see Figure 6.1-4). As with loose coupling, the issue here is the local modifiability of system building blocks and their ability to be understood [Yourdon and Constantine 1978]. If a system building block unites all features relevant for understanding and changing it in its description, you can change it without having to understand or change other system building blocks. But only in case of semantically correct dependencies within a system building block high cohesion is given. For example even though the number of call relationships between methods of a given class may indicate high cohesion, this is by far not a proof of semantically correct relationships. There are often "invisible" semantic relationships that tie building blocks (eg., methods, classes, or modules) together even though no explicit call relationship exists. An example of high cohesion are two methods

Principle of high cohesion

that both operate on the same understanding of what a "customer", or "product" is—but never call each other, explicitly.

Relationship to loose coupling

Coupling and cohesion are normally interdependent. The following generally applies: the higher the cohesion of individual building blocks in an architecture, the lower the coupling between the building blocks. This relationship is illustrated in Figure 6.1-4.

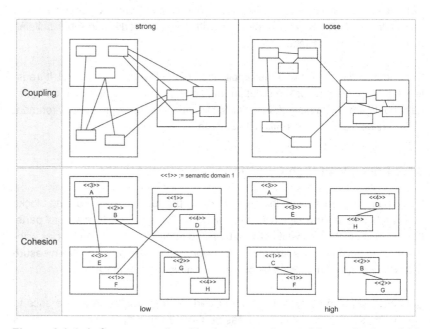

Figure 6.1-4: *Left, an example with strong coupling and low cohesion; right, loose coupling and high cohesion are implemented*

An architecture with loose coupling and high cohesion is suitable if you want to understand the entire structure of the software system quickly.

Relationship to other principles

High cohesion often leads to loose coupling and vice versa—thus in many cases these two principles are interdependent. You can achieve high cohesion particularly by implementing the following principles: abstraction, separation of concerns, and information hiding. You can also achieve it by encapsulating related requirements in one system building block. Specifically, this means that you apply separation of concerns and information hiding in the design. Related requirements tend towards a high need for communication. They should therefore be part of the same system building block in order to increase the cohesion of that building block. The building block should hide all internal details from the outside world in order to keep the coupling loose. Architectures with high cohesion enable you to consider the individual system building blocks as black boxes that you can modify and exchange independently of one another.

6.1.3 Principle of Design for Change

The principle of design for change [Parnas 1994] is a very general principle. It is concerned with the problem that software is constantly changing and changes are often difficult to foresee. However, some software architectures tend to cope better with changes than others. The idea behind design for change is that you plan foreseeable changes in advance within the architecture.

The idea of design for change

To fulfill this principle, you should first try to design the architecture such that it is easy to manage probable changes to a software system. For example, you can collect and consider more extensive requirements in advance. Ambiguities in requirement specifications can indicate more extensive functionality requirements to come, for example. These are often simply further developments that can be expected. For example, if a functionality has not been implemented for cost reasons, under certain circumstances you can expect that this functionality could be implemented in one of the next versions of the system.

Expected changes

Alternatively, when you are designing a new architecture, you can take account of experiences from the design of similar architectures. You can thus plan changes that are often required for one system type in the development of a new, similar architecture. You should therefore design an architecture such that it can easily manage expected changes.

The changes discussed thus far can be expected—at least if the architect has the corresponding experience. However, there are also changes that cannot be expected. It is usually difficult to plan changes generally if they cannot be foreseen, since the design for change also entails disadvantages. A more extensive design takes time and leads to a higher implementation effort, for example. Highly flexible architectures often have disadvantages compared to more simple architectures. For example, resource consumption (e.g., performance and memory) can be higher than with more inflexible architectures. You should therefore be careful when using a design for change in places where you are not sure that this change will really be required at some point.

Unexpected changes

In general you can achieve a design for change by consequently applying the principle of loose coupling in an architecture. Examples of known architecture approaches in this area are service-oriented architectures (see Section 6.4.11) or aspect orientation (AOP) [Kiczales et al. 1997] (see Section 6.2). In general,

Relationship to loose coupling

use loosely coupled structures for quick modifiability at specific points of an architecture without having to replicate the change at a number of other points.

Loosely coupled architectures can have disadvantages such as higher complexity or increased resource consumption if they are used incorrectly. You should therefore use them specifically where you suspect there may be frequent changes. In particular, these are places where changes often occur or where many different aspects of an architecture come together (so-called "hot spots" of an architecture [Pree 1995]).

Examples for the use of loose coupling for managing unexpected changes

For example, in distributed object middleware systems, such as CORBA or web service implementations, the evaluation of the distributed call is one such hot spot. Most middleware systems have a so-called broker architecture [Buschmann et al. 1996], as shown in Figure 6.1-5 (following [Völter et al. 2004]). Here you can see several call interfaces where new change requirements such as security concerns, logging, transactions, and many more often have to be implemented. These points are therefore the hot spots of the broker architecture.

If the middleware provides an abstraction that enables you to change the hot spots easily, you can probably also implement domain-specific changes that are difficult to foresee there.

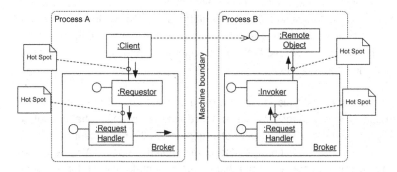

Figure 6.1-5: Hot spots of a broker architecture

As a second example for managing unexpected changes, you should consider a component architecture. Regardless of the actual functionality, here you can assume that the configuration of the components will change often. Therefore it is a good idea not to "hard code" the aspect "configuration of components." Instead, use an easily modifiable abstraction for configuration options, for example, a scripting language or XML configuration options.

In both examples loose coupling was used to increase the modifiability of the architecture. You can also implement the design for change through other principles, such as abstraction, modularity, separation of concerns, and information hiding. These principles are also important in the implementation of loose coupling.

Relationship to other principles

You can also use many other principles for design for change. For example, you can separate the aspect "documentation of the architecture" from the system and automate it. This means you can "force" the developers to describe the architectural structures in the code. This leads to the implementation of the principle of self-documentation. It also increases the modifiability of the system since the architectural role of an architecture building block to be changed is clear for the developer during the change [Parnas 1994].

6.1.4 Separation of Concerns Principle

The separation of concerns principle generally states that you should separate different aspects of a problem and deal with each of these sub-problems individually. Separation of concerns is a general software engineering principle used not only in software architecture but in many other areas of software engineering. It can be traced back to the Roman principle of "divide and conquer"—a general principle used in many situations of daily life to resolve difficulties. In general, separation of concerns reduces the complexity of a problem and enables you to divide up the processing.

The idea of separation of concerns

In software architecture, you use separation of concerns to break down a software system into a structure of system building blocks. It can also be applied in a number of other software architecture areas. These include:
> Breaking down the requirements placed on a software architecture.
> Breaking down a complex architecture description into views of the architecture.
> Breaking down the organizational responsibilities for the software architecture.
> Breaking down the processes for the creation of a software architecture into sub-processes.

We will now look at perhaps the most important use of separation of concerns in software architecture as an example: supporting modularization. This primarily means identifying parts of a software system responsible for specific concerns, aspects, or tasks and encapsulating them as separate system building blocks. The purpose of this is to break down the complex entire system into understandable and manageable individual parts. Breaking down the entire system into rela-

Use of separation of concerns for modularization

tively independent individual parts also enables you to distribute responsibilities for different system parts and thus several developers can work on the software system in parallel. The central idea behind this is to achieve as loose a coupling of the building blocks of an architecture as possible by modularizing them.

Decomposition criteria

The functionality requirements are often considered as criteria for the decomposition of a software system. That is, every building block identified fulfills a specific functionality. However, there are other decomposition criteria. For example, you can identify building blocks that are reusable as far as possible and thus apply reuse as a central decomposition criterion.

Example of a decomposition

A simple example could be a software system that processes orders in an enterprise. This system must accept the order from the processor via a user interface and query the database of available articles. It must then check the entries made by the processor and after a successful check, forward the entries to the supplier. During these steps it has to access the supplier database and the order must be archived in the order database. If we assume this system has been implemented with a monolithic architecture, this would throw up a whole series of problems such as the following:

> The system would be very complex and difficult to understand.
> It would not be easy to divide up different parts of the system for work purposes since changes at one point would not be independent of changes at other points.
> It would be difficult to make changes to the system. For example, to implement a further user interface the complete system would have to be searched for user interface code.
> Individual parts of the systems could not be reused.

These problems would not occur if you designed the system according to the separation of concerns principle. For example, you could divide the system up into the following building blocks: user interface, order processing, general database access, database access for the articles database, database access for the supplier database, and database access for the order database.

Separation of functional and technical parts

In software architecture, it is difficult to consider separation of concerns one-dimensionally. For example, in the example above, the decomposition was based on the functionality, i.e., the functional parts. Other important aspects, such as performance, usability, resource consumption, additional services such as logging and transactions etc. were not explicitly considered.

You should generally try to achieve a *separation of functional and technical parts*. This enables you to separate functional abstractions from their concrete technical implementation. In other words, it promotes the further development of different building blocks on an evolutionary basis.

However, you can go one step further and look at dimensions other than just the functional and technical aspects. For example, in modularizing the architecture, you can separate the main functionality of *aspects* such as transaction management, security, logging, etc. You can also separate different quality attributes such as performance, usability, resource consumption, or flexibility from the functional concerns of the system.

Multi-dimensional separation of concerns and AOP

The explicit consideration of all of these dimensions is known as multi-dimensional separation of concerns [Tarr 2004]. Multi-dimensional separation of concerns is supported by various approaches. The most well-known one at the present time is aspect orientation [Kiczales et al. 1997]. It can compose the different aspects, split into separate building blocks and automated, into a ready-to-run system (see also Section 6.2).

6.1.5 Information Hiding Principle

Information hiding is a fundamental principle for structuring and understanding complex systems. The principle generally states that you only show a client that part of the total information that is really necessary for the client's task and you hide all remaining information. Since software architectures are inherently complex, this principle is enormously important in architectures being understandable.

The idea of information hiding

In a software architecture, information hiding is applied in the modularization of a system, for example. Design decisions are encapsulated in a system building block and made known externally through well-defined interfaces. However, the using system building block does not know how the system building block is realized. For example, object and component concepts have the concept of visibility of information, which is intended to support information hiding. Here there is a differentiation between public and private variables and operations: clients can only access public elements; private elements are hidden for clients.

Information hiding and modularization

A sub-aspect of information hiding is data hiding. This aspect is frequently implemented via object orientation, for example. Objects hide data with their methods (that is, all data is private and, where necessary, there are public methods for access). You can also realize data hiding using database interfaces or query languages.

Data hiding

Information hiding using a facade

Information hiding is not restricted to individual building blocks of a software architecture. It is also an important structuring principle for larger structures of the architecture. For example, the facade design pattern [Gamma et al. 1995] is used in many architectures. A facade is an object that protects an entire subsystem against direct access. It provides a common interface for the building blocks of a subsystem and this hides the subsystem that lies behind the building blocks. Figure 6.1-6 shows an example of a facade.

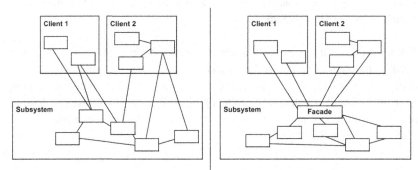

Figure 6.1-6: Left, a subsystem with direct relationships; right, the same subsystem with a facade

A typical example of a facade object is an interpreter. This usually consists of a number of building blocks that the clients do not see, such as parsers, implementation of language elements, byte code compilers, etc.

From this example we can see that information hiding is also used to implement loose coupling. In the previous example, the introduction of the facade design pattern made it possible to decouple the clients from the internal building blocks of the subsystem. This was achieved by hiding internal details of these building blocks.

Information hiding through the creation of layers

A layered architecture is usually structured such that each layer only sees the layer directly below it. This means that from the view of layer X, layer X-1 hides all of the layers below it. A layer should only be accessed via clear interfaces as far as this is possible. The using layer should not see any layer-specific objects or other implementation details of the lower layer being used. This then leads to data being exchanged between different layers via "neutral" data transfer objects, for example.

Example: Creation of layers in CORBA

A typical example is a distributed object system such as CORBA. A CORBA implementation hides the underlying protocol layers, the operating system APIs, the network, etc. as far as possible. It is itself divided into layers, such as the application layer, call layer, and the request handling layer. Figure 6.1-7 shows an example of a layer creation for a CORBA middleware.

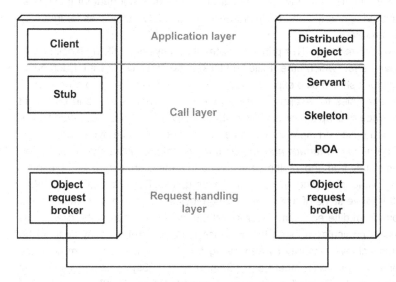

Figure 6.1-7: *Example of layer creation: CORBA middleware*

A further form of information hiding is the black box principle. It states that the internal details of a system building block should not be visible for the clients. Only the interface of the building block should be visible. This means that the internal details can be changed without clients being affected by the changes. The black box principle is frequently implemented via the interface abstraction principles. We will discuss these in the next section.

Black box principle

6.1.6 Abstraction Principles

Abstraction means focusing on aspects of a concept that are relevant for a specific purpose and neglecting unimportant details for this particular purpose. It thus follows that abstraction is a special case of separation of concerns: you separate the important details from the less important ones. Abstraction is a powerful concept that is applied in all possible engineering disciplines in order to understand and manage complex problems. It is also used in the creation of software: abstractions are used in programming languages, software processes, design methods, architecture description languages, etc.

The concept of abstraction

The field of software architecture contains some special sub-principles of abstraction that refer to interface abstractions. The result of the application of these

Sub-principles with a focus on interfaces

abstraction principles should be a *focus on the interfaces*: an architecture only really takes effect through the relationships of the building blocks of a system to one another. The interfaces of the building block are important for these relationships being created and for their quality. In detail, the principles for interface abstractions are:

> *Explicit interfaces:* This principle states that a system building block should clearly show which other building blocks it communicates with. Each building block should also explicitly say which interfaces it issues to clients. Typical examples for explicit interfaces are header files (e.g., as in C++) and interface description languages (IDL). A software architecture should be designed based on these interfaces and they should not be bypassed.

> *Separation of interface and implementation:* Interfaces should be described separately from the implementations so that the client can rely on the interface without knowing the implementation details. For example, you can use different versions of a system building block in parallel, or use implementations from different manufacturers without having to change the client. This makes particular sense if the interface is standardized. Many design patterns achieve flexibility by separating an abstract interface from concrete implementations (compare e.g., [Gamma et al. 1995]). This principle is also known as the Dependency Inversion principle [Martin 2000].

> *Liskov substitution principle* [Liskov 1988]: In inheritance abstractions, clients should be able to call up inheriting classes via the interface of the inheriting class' superclass. In particular, this principle ensures that a client can depend on all objects of a type (that is, also inherited) supporting the same interface. With this principle, it is important to note that many programming languages (including object-oriented languages) allow the principle to be violated through inheriting classes overwriting interfaces of inheriting classes' superclass. This becomes a problem when inheriting classes "hide" parts of the interface (make public parts private) and thus change the signature of an interface; for example, a method suddenly does not throw up any exceptions any more.

> *Interface Segregation Principle* [Martin 2000]: A client should never be based on an interface that it does not use. In particular, this also means that you should segregate complex interfaces that multiple client types are based on into multiple individual interfaces.

> *Language support for abstractions* [Meyer 1997]: Architectural abstractions, such as components or interfaces, should have language support in both the design language and the programming language. If this is not the case, it may be possible to extend the language with appropriate abstractions. The purpose of this is that the architect or developer should not have to map the abstractions time and again by hand. A further advantage is that you recognize system building blocks and interfaces syntactically in the program source code immediately.

> *Design by Contract* [Meyer 1997]: An important aspect of interface abstractions is that common interface abstractions only standardize the syntax but say nothing about the meaning of the relationship. The protocol used or the semantics of the operations and data remain open, for example. It is therefore your responsibility as the architect to document the meaning of a relationship. Self-documentation is a way of approaching this problem. Another possibility is *Design by Contract*. Here you specify suitable preconditions and post-conditions for the relationships as well as invariants that characterize the relationship more closely.

As explained above, interface abstractions are often used to realize loose coupling. You can also use other abstractions, such as aspects, components, classes, etc. for this goal—either directly or indirectly.

Relationship to other principles

The modularity principle is also closely related to abstractions since a useful modularization usually requires an implicit or an explicit module abstraction.

One aspect where abstraction is closely connected to information hiding is portability. It should be possible to use an architecture or its system building blocks in environments other than that in which they were created. One important aspect here is platform independence. Typically, abstractions that provide information hiding for platform details are used here. Examples are virtual machines that can run a byte code of a programming language on multiple operating systems, and database access layers that support database operations on different database products with a uniform interface.

6.1.7 Modularity Principle

The architecture should consist of well-defined system building blocks with clearly distinguishable functional responsibilities. This means that it should be easy to exchange the system building blocks and they should be self-contained. In particular, you use modularity to make the building blocks of an architecture modifiable, extensible, and reusable.

Originally, the modularity principle related primarily to composing individual operations. However, this is not sufficient to enable modifiable, extensible, and reusable structures in software architectures since individual operations are not autonomous, self-contained system building blocks. Individual operations usually have complex dependencies to other operations and to data. In contrast, the modularity principle states that you should strive for self-contained system building blocks with simple and stable architectural relationships.

The idea of modularity

You may have noticed that we have already mentioned modularity in the descriptions of some of the other principles. The modularity principle, as considered here in the context of software architecture, is indeed a particularly important combination of the principles of abstraction, separation of concerns, and information hiding, which we have already discussed. The modularity principle takes effect when these three principles are combined to implement the principles of loose coupling and high cohesion.

Modularity approaches

There are a number of approaches that support the modularity of a software architecture—for example, object orientation, component approaches, layered architectures, n-tier architectures, and many more. We will explain these in more detail later in this book.

Generally speaking, each architectural modularity approach should fulfill a number of criteria that characterize modularity. Seen from this angle, modularity is not only dependent on a special approach—rather, primarily on the design by the architect. For example, a procedural C system can have a highly modular architecture if the developers work in a disciplined way. In contrast, a system developed with a component approach such as EJB may be completely non-modular if the developers violate important principles of modularity.

Example of modularization

As an example for the modularization of a system we will use a heating control system. It is regulated by a central furnace control and must control a temperature sensor, a target temperature, the current room occupancy, and the heating times for every heated room. There is also an external temperature sensor for the entire building.

A completely non-modular design would group all of these elements in one algorithm that operates on a data structure. However, this would be difficult to understand, and changes to individual building blocks would entail considering the entire algorithm and the entire data structure.

A better design would be to split the system up into individual modular system building blocks, as in Figure 6.1-8, since each individual building block can now be considered independently of the others. Here, classes are used as modular system building blocks. However, this design has a big problem with regard to modularity: the class "heating control" is a so-called "God class"—a class in which all responsibilities of the system (or subsystem) are united. Even if the concerns are split up into modular system building blocks, their responsibilities are still united in the heating control. Practically every change to the system involves changing the God class and thus affects several responsibilities. It is also difficult to understand the different abstractions that are mixed in a God class.

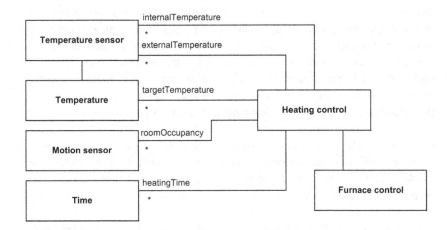

Figure 6.1-8: Example design with modular system building blocks, but still with a God class

God classes should be broken down using appropriate decomposition. As Figure 6.1-9 shows, this can be achieved in the example by introducing a "room" class. The heating control can now delegate the decision as to whether heating should be activated to the individual rooms. In turn, the rooms use their sub-building blocks to receive the corresponding information.

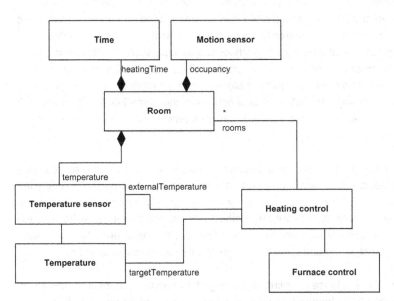

Figure 6.1-9: Example design with modular system building blocks, without a God class

Relationship to other principles	As already explained above, modularity is closely related to a series of other architecture principles. You can apply the two principles of separation of concerns and information hiding to implement the principle of modularity. Modularity is also closely connected to abstraction. You can support the modularity of a system using suitable module and interface abstractions, such as object models or component modules. However, it is still your task to find the correct decomposition—the approaches only help with the implementation of a design.
	Modularity aids loose coupling and high cohesion because it enables you to encapsulate related concerns in one modular system building block. You reduce the coupling between the system building blocks by using explicit interfaces between the building blocks.
Open/closed principle	One important aspect of modularity is the open/closed principle [Meyer 1997]. This principle states that system building blocks should be open for changes but closed for the use of their internal details by other system building blocks. You can generally achieve openness by applying the "Design for change" principle; you can achieve closed building blocks by using abstractions for stable interfaces and applying the information hiding principle.

6.1.8 Principle of Traceability

The idea of traceability	Guaranteeing the traceability of architectural structures and decisions is important to ensure that an architecture can be understood. It should therefore be possible to find the actual architectural structures, as they are implemented in the code, in other descriptions of an architecture as well, such as a design model or the requirement specification. Conversely, it should also be possible to assign a requirement to the system building blocks that implement it. Traceability should also exist amongst the different descriptions at the same level. For example, it should be possible to map different design views of the architecture on top of one another.
Approaches for traceability	Simple rules, such as noting architectural structures as such in the source code and in design documents (e.g., using comments) and consistently using the same names for the same building blocks can greatly improve the traceability. There are several approaches that offer further support for traceability. For example, you can embed metadata that references the requirements to a system building block in the code and thus make the requirements easy to find.
Relationship to other principles	Traceability aids loose coupling and design for change because it makes structures easier to understand and therefore more independent and modifiable.

6.1.9 Self-Documentation Principle

Self-documentation means that the architect or developer of a system building block should try to make every item of information about the system building block part of the system building block itself [Meyer 1997]. This supports design for change with regard to changing documentation and other additional information.

In daily business, documentation is often forgotten when small changes are made to the software. Thus the code, documentation, architecture descriptions, designs, and other descriptions of the software system quickly become inconsistent.

However, the self-documentation principle is also related to traceability: information that exists directly in the system building block can also be easily traced.

An important practical aspect of self-documentation is that such information can also be used to generate related documents that have to be created based on the code and other information. For example, the HTML description of an API can be generated automatically through a series of tools, such as JavaDoc.

The idea of self-documentation

6.1.10 Incrementality Principle

You should implement a first architecture design, as well as changes to an existing architecture, incrementally as far as possible. This is because software architectures are often highly complex. Thus, an attempt to design an entire system straight away often fails—for example, because you place too much value on incidental aspects or because important aspects are overlooked.

Such situations arise, for example, because architects and developers who are trained in technical software aspects often do not speak the same language as domain experts and because both sides often take some things for granted that are not immediately clear to a non-expert in the respective field.

To avoid this kind of misunderstanding, you should proceed incrementally and get frequent feedback. Resulting rules for the procedure are, for example:
> Delivering first versions of a system early
> Getting the opinion of real users of the system early
> Introducing new functionality step-by-step

The idea of incrementality

Incrementality therefore means applying the separation of concerns principle to the development steps in the development of the system.

Piecemeal growth

Piecemeal growth is a more extensive variant of incrementality. It is described by the architect Christopher Alexander [Alexander 1977] and can also be applied to software architectures. The idea is to let an architecture grow step-by-step. After every step there is an assessment that entails a decision about what to do next. This means that there is little or no planning in advance. Piecemeal growth is used in a software architecture context in the concepts refactoring and Extreme Programming, for example.

Prototyping

A further variant of incrementality is so-called prototyping. It often makes sense to develop simple prototypes first before developing a product in order to get to know the problem better. Sometimes you can convert these prototypes into products; sometimes it makes more sense to throw the prototype away and start again from the beginning. A prototype can still be very valuable since it gives the architect and the developer an understanding for the real problems of the domain. A possible middle way is an evolutionary prototype—that is, a prototype that you can develop into a product incrementally.

6.1.11 Further Architecture Principles

There are other general architecture principles that we will summarize briefly here:

> *Reference to use cases:* An architecture should not be created randomly; rather, its design should be based on the relevant use cases. This ensures that an architecture does not exceed the aim of the desired system.
> *Avoidance of superfluous complexity:* "Less is more" also applies to architecture. Unnecessarily complex architectures are prone to error and are not sufficiently understood.
> *Consistency:* An architecture should follow a standard set of rules from beginning to end: naming convention, communication of the system building blocks, structure of the interfaces, structure of the documentation, etc. This principle makes the development, understanding, and the implementation of an architecture easier.
> *Convention over Configuration:* Useful standard assumptions are made and only necessary adjustments have to be configured. This generally enables a developer to achieve a first result quickly and this result can be adjusted to the separate requirements step-by-step.

Summary

> There are two main problems that are important for almost all of the architecture principles: the reduction of the complexity of an architecture and the increase in the flexibility (or modifiability) of an architecture.
> The principles can be related to one another in a system.
> The principle of loose coupling is a central principle and states that the coupling between system building blocks should be kept as low as possible.
> Cohesion is a measurement of the dependencies within a system building block. The principle of high cohesion states that this cohesion should be as high as possible within a system building block.
> The principle of design for change states that you should try to design the architecture such that it is easy to manage the probable changes to a software system.
> The separation of concerns principle states that you must separate different aspects of a problem and deal with each individual problem part separately.
> The information hiding principle states that you only show a client that part of the total information that is really necessary for the client's task and hide all remaining information.
> Abstraction principles apply abstractions. Abstraction means focusing on aspects of a concept that are relevant for a specific purpose and neglecting unimportant details for this particular purpose.
> The modularity principle states that the architecture should consist of well-defined system building blocks with clearly distinguishable functional responsibilities.
> Guaranteeing the traceability of architectural structures and decisions is important to ensure that an architecture can be understood. It should therefore be possible to find the actual architectural structures, as they are implemented in the code or other artifacts.
> The self-documentation principle states that the architect or developer of a system building block should try to make every item of information about the system building block part of the system building block itself.
> The incrementality principle states that a first architecture design, as well as changes to an existing architecture, should be implemented incrementally as far as possible.
> There are further principles (e.g., Inversion of Control) which focus on special aspects of the principles mentioned above.

Summary:
Architecture
principles

6.2 Basic Architecture Concepts

In this section we will discuss important concepts that architects use today to implement architectures. Figure 6.2-1 gives an overview. The section starts with simple procedural approaches and then continues step-by-step to broader approaches such as aspect orientation, component orientation, and model-driven development. If you are already familiar with some of these areas, you can skip these parts. Here we will give a brief overview of the topics from the view of architecture to explain the terms used. For a complete introduction to the areas, see the further literature listed at the end of the section.

Firstly, for simplification, we will present the architecture means shown in Figure 6.2-1 from the perspective in which a new system is being created.

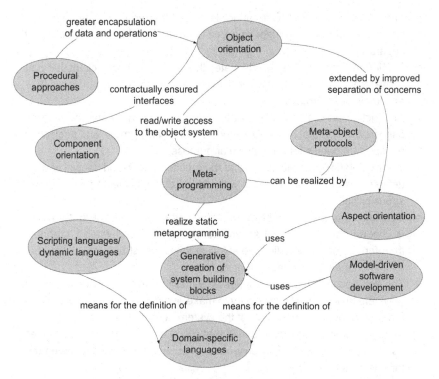

Figure 6.2-1: *Overview of the basic architecture concepts*

6.2.1 Procedural Approaches

Procedures are a traditional and widespread means of structuring architectures. They allow you to break down a complex algorithm into reusable individual algorithms. Procedures implement the separation of concerns principle because they allow you to break down a complex algorithmical problem into simpler sub-problems.

Overview of procedures

Today, procedures are still used in systems that are based on procedural programming languages such as C and COBOL, as well as in procedural distributed systems. Many object-oriented systems also allow procedural abstractions (such as static methods in Java) because sometimes, these are more suitable for structuring a system than objects and classes.

Note that there are many synonyms for "procedure," such as sub-program, function, routine, or operation.

The definition of a procedure consists of several parts:
> The *procedure name* is a designation that can be used to call the procedure externally.
> The *procedure parameters* are a number of values or references that can be transferred to the procedure. The procedure definition consists of formal parameters that each have a type and a name. When the procedure is called, current values are transferred for these parameters. These values must correspond to the types of the parameter definition. We can differentiate between call-by-reference parameters and call-by-value parameters. Call-by-reference parameters receive a reference to the data transferred. This means that a change to the data in the procedure implicitly causes a change in the calling validity range. In contrast, call-by-value parameters work with a copy of the data. This means that changes in the procedure have no influence on the data in the calling validity range.
> The *procedure return type* is used to return results data from the procedure to its clients.
> The *procedure body* specifies the algorithm to be executed when the procedure is called. When this happens, the current parameters specified are used (that is, the formal parameters are replaced by the current values). The result of the procedure must correspond to the return type.

Structure of a procedure

Figure 6.2-2 illustrates these terms using the example of a procedure definition and Figure 6.2-3 shows this procedure being called.

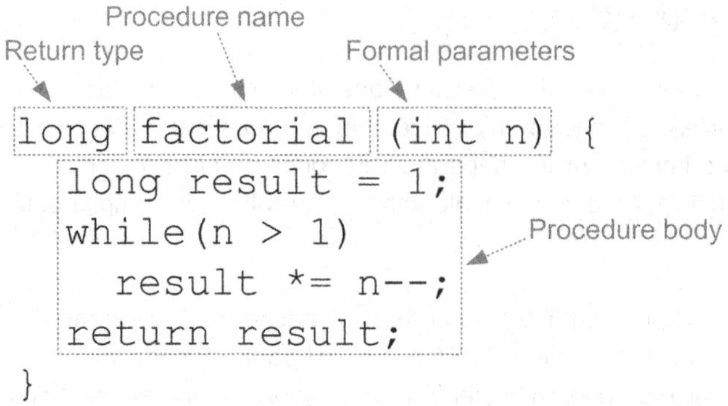

```
       Procedure name
Return type          Formal parameters

long  factorial  (int n)  {
    long result = 1;
    while (n > 1)                    Procedure body
        result *= n--;
    return result;
}
```

Figure 6.2-2: Example of a procedure definition

The first three elements of the procedure definition, that is, name, return type, and parameter, form the *interface* of the procedure, also known as the *procedure signature*. Using the interface as a basis, you can reuse procedures with other data or in another context.

Procedures mostly share a common (often global) data area with other proce-

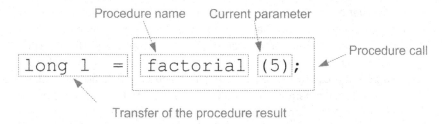

```
          Procedure name   Current parameter

long l  =   factorial  (5);          Procedure call

          Transfer of the procedure result
```

Figure 6.2-3: Example of a procedure call

Procedures and architecture principles

dures. These data areas are often used as a buffer and for communication with other procedures. If these data areas are addressed as global structures, procedures quickly become dependent on one another and it becomes difficult to re-use them in other contexts. Thus the principles of modularization and information hiding are quickly violated. This means that if you want to change one procedure, you have to change other procedures as well.

Procedural abstractions tend to produce architectures with large collections of procedures and related data structures in libraries. The interfaces are given by the signatures of the procedures contained in the library. Many procedural programming languages allow you to specify procedural interfaces through so-called header files at source code level, and to program against these interface definitions. You can use this means to implement the interface abstraction principles from Section 6.1, but this type of structuring of an architecture and its interfaces often makes it more difficult to create modifiable, extensible, and reusable structures. This is because individual procedures, linked to form a complex system, frequently have complex dependencies to other procedures and the data.

However, you can implement the architecture principles from Section 6.1 well in a procedural language. There are a number of successful systems with very good procedural architectures. However, there are also many examples of the opposite. Conclusion: it takes effort and a systematic design to implement all architecture principles well in a procedural programming language.

We can observe that the measures required to do this are recurring—this is described in the Object System Layer architecture pattern [Goedicke et al. 2000], which shows how you can replicate an object system within a procedural architecture.

Object-oriented designs in a procedural architecture

The observation that recurring abstractions lead to good procedural systems has led to object orientation, which makes it easier to implement the principles with corresponding language-supported abstractions (here, "language-supported" means both design languages and programming languages).

6.2.2 Object Orientation

Object orientation is based on the idea of bundling data processed by a series of related procedures together with these procedures. The procedures—called operations or methods in object orientation—can process their data exclusively. Thus, object orientation tries to implement the information hiding principle and the modularity principle directly.

The idea of object orientation

The idea is that objects should primarily map real world concepts. For example, an object can represent an author and store the author's data, such as name, address, etc. It then also provides the operations for changing and querying this data.

One important aspect of object orientation is classification. As a simple example let us take an author who publishes books in a publishing company. Publishing companies (and some books) have not just one author but several. Therefore, classification makes sense: the *class* "Author" can thus be seen as an abstraction for the recurring concern "Author." In object orientation, a class is defined

Classification and identity

once and can then be instantiated multiple times. Each object has its own data, i.e., the values of the attributes (also known as properties) specified by the class for itself exclusively in a separate dataspace and namespace. The object can access the operations defined by its class.

A further important concept in this context is object identity. As a set of objects from a class can be instantiated, it must be possible to differentiate between the elements of this set, i.e., the objects, at runtime. Therefore, every object has a unique object ID that identifies it. The object ID can be used to send object messages, that is, call operations of the object.

Figure 6.2-4 shows a UML class diagram with a class "Author" and two objects instantiated from this class in an object diagram. You can see that each of the derived objects has its own identity and its own values of the attributes defined by the class.

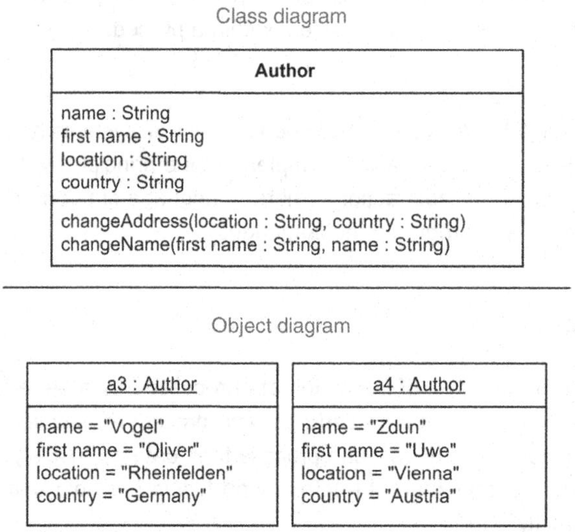

Class diagram

Author
name : String first name : String location : String country : String
changeAddress(location : String, country : String) changeName(first name : String, name : String)

Object diagram

a3 : Author	a4 : Author
name = "Vogel" first name = "Oliver" location = "Rheinfelden" country = "Germany"	name = "Zdun" first name = "Uwe" location = "Vienna" country = "Austria"

Figure 6.2-4: Example of a class diagram (top) and a related object diagram (bottom)

Relationships

Object-oriented concepts generally also offer a series of relationship abstractions that you can use to specify the possible interactions between objects more closely:

> *Association:* An object "knows" or "uses" another object that may be an instance of the same or any other class. That is, it saves the object ID of another object in its data and can thus call this object. For example, an author object can associate one or more books that the author has worked on.

> *Aggregation:* An object is part of another object. There are many types of "is part of" relationships. Object orientation differentiates between two types

of aggregation relationships: those that include the lifetime responsibility of the aggregating object for the aggregated objects (composition), and those that do not do this (aggregation). An example of an aggregation relationship is a "publishing company" class that aggregates the published books and authors. An example of a composition relationship is a "book" class that aggregates chapters.

> *Inheritance:* A class *X* is a specialization of another class *Y*. This means that all instances of *X* can also use the properties of *Y*. In this example, a further class "Editor" could be required. Like "Author," it would also have to manage a name and an address. The common properties and operations of "Editor" and "Author" can then be outsourced to a superclass "Person," which both classes inherit from.

> *Interfaces and abstract classes:* A class can implement an interface or inherit from an abstract class. In object orientation, you use a relationship like this to make interfaces explicit and to support the abstraction principles introduced in Section 6.1. This is because client classes can rely on the interface, but the implementation can change.

The additions to the example are shown in Figure 6.2-5 as a UML class diagram.

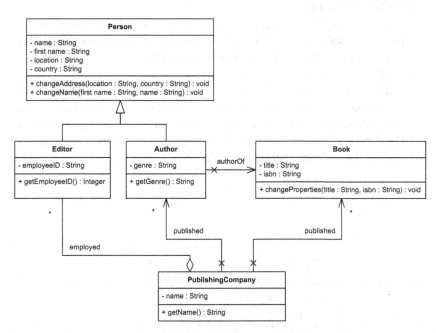

Figure 6.2-5: *Example of a class diagram with some relationships*

The concept of polymorphism in object orientation enables you to use objects and operations flexibly despite the fact that they are categorized into types through classes.

Polymorphism

Operations are always assigned to a specific type or class. Polymorphism ensures that the relevant operation is executed dependent on the class of a specific object. This is illustrated in Figure 6.2-6. Polymorphism enables you to achieve "connector compatibility" based on interfaces. How the connector is realized is irrelevant for the building blocks.

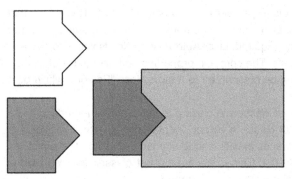

Figure 6.2-6: "Connector compatibility" through polymorphism

We can differentiate between:

> *Compile time polymorphism ("static" binding):* In compile time polymorphism, the static type of the object determines the operation called. This only works with object concepts that have static typing.

> *Runtime polymorphism ("dynamic" or "late" binding):* In contrast, runtime polymorphism determines the class of the object at runtime and then calls the operation on this class. The class found does not have to be identical to the static type. This means that the operation executed depends on the object connected. It is determined dynamically based on the object type at runtime. This is illustrated in Figure 6.2-7.

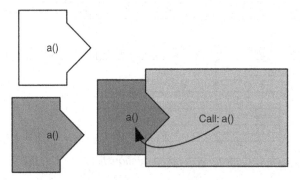

Figure 6.2-7: Runtime polymorphism

Runtime polymorphism is one of the most important parts of object orientation. This is easily explained with the example above. Let us assume that you want to access all persons employed at the publishing company. Without polymorphism, you would not be able to define this in a general form. Instead, you would have to first access the authors, then the editors, etc. Reusability would not be possible with such a solution and you would not be able to use the code for further extensions, such as adding other person types, without changing it.

It would therefore be difficult to implement the principles of loose coupling and design for change with object-oriented class concepts. Runtime polymorphism solves this problem. You can design the architecture based on superclasses and interfaces and the runtime system binds the concrete object types dynamically.

Object orientation and architecture principles

From an architecture point of view, object-oriented architectures are not dissimilar to procedural architectures. However, as a result of the additional abstractions, object orientation offers better support for modularization. Important abstraction principles have language support (in both programming and design languages). Better information hiding is achieved through the encapsulation of data and related operations.

All of this makes it easier to implement the principles from Section 6.1. However, as the architect, your challenge with object orientation is to design a suitable object-oriented model: it is not as easy as proposing a simple equation such as "object-oriented architecture = good architecture." For example, in object-oriented approaches, the important goal of reusability requires much more than classes and objects. In fact, object orientation only partly supports reusability. It is therefore important to understand object orientation correctly and to apply its technologies correctly.

Framework

Approaches for overcoming more complex object-oriented architectures are particularly important. One central approach in this context is the use of object-oriented *frameworks* [Johnson and Foote 1988].

A framework is a partially complete software system (or subsystem) that you instantiate. It thus defines an architecture for a family of (sub)systems and provides the fundamental building blocks of this architecture. The framework also defines the points where the framework can be adapted (so-called "hot spots" [Pree 1995]). Frameworks rely heavily on Inversion of Control (or the Hollywood Principle described in Section 6.1): instead of allowing the application to control the control flow, the control of parts of the system is left to the framework and only configurable parts are adapted using hot spots.

In object-oriented systems the framework consists of classes that you instantiate and abstract classes/interfaces that you make more concrete. You can map more specialized classes using inheritance from the classes specified. Late binding is particularly important for frameworks. It enables you to define the framework based on general types and still, for example, use derived classes through inheritance.

A further note: frameworks are not always object-oriented and many object-oriented frameworks also have non-object-oriented parts. However, it is still correct to mention frameworks here in the context of object orientation since the term "framework" was shaped primarily in this area.

Minimally-invasive frameworks

One disadvantage of the many specifications that frameworks make is that they restrict the architect's or developer's (architectural) freedom. Recently, some frameworks, such as Spring, have been trying to offer minimally-invasive solutions, such as Dependency Injection (see also Section 6.1) to partly alleviate this disadvantage.

Further approaches

In addition to frameworks, there is a series of other approaches intended to enable you to manage more complex object-oriented architectures. We will discuss some of them in this book—for example, object-oriented design patterns in Section 6.3. Design patterns are important in the development of frameworks and some patterns are frequently used in frameworks, for example, the "Template Method" design pattern [Gamma et al. 1995].

There are a number of object-oriented abstractions or abstractions that have arisen from object orientation. Later on we will discuss components, meta-objects, and aspects as examples for principles beyond the pure principles of object orientation.

6.2.3 Component Orientation

The "component" concept

Components are supposed to be reusable, self-contained building blocks of an architecture. Component orientation arose from the problem that objects implement the modularity principle, but are often too small to be used as reusable units.

Furthermore, we often want more extensive features from a reusable system building block: for example, additional non-functional requirements, such as different strategies for the recognition of assets or liabilities, or the concurrent provision of multiple identical component instances to increase scalability. However, such non-functional requirements are not part of the object-oriented approach.

Last but not least, in practice we often find units of reuse that do not correspond to the ideas of object orientation, for example, as a result of the existence of legacy systems. Here we find, for example, large procedural libraries that are seen as reusable units and thus have to be embedded in practical architectures in the design.

The concept of components is a very general concept that tries to solve this and similar problems. There are many definitions of components. Here we will use the definition of Clemens Szyperski [Szyperski 1998]:

> A software component is a unit of composition with contractually specified interfaces and explicit context dependencies only. A software component can be deployed independently and is subject to composition by third parties.

If we look at this definition more closely, we can see that it is very broad and means many things. The term "unit of composition" already states that the main purpose of a component is to collaborate and interact with other components. In order to do this, a component has one or more interfaces that act as a contract between the component and its environment. The interfaces of the component clearly define the services that the component provides. The component has no implicit dependencies: every element of the architecture that the component needs is also specified by the component—in particular, these are the other components that a component needs.

A component is self-contained and you can therefore use it independently of a special environment. In particular, this means that you do not have to change the component to use it, and using it does not entail changes to any other components.

An important point that these features of components enable is that a component is not only used by the persons that created it but also by third parties.

The definition intentionally covers many different concepts such as subsystems, DLLs, JavaBeans, ActiveX controls, JEE components, .NET components, CORBA components (CCM), component approaches of scripting languages (e.g., Tcl, Python, Perl), and many more. Of course, these approaches each implement the component concept to a different extent. In Section 6.4.10 we will take a closer look at component platforms as they are implemented by EJB, .NET, and CCM—since this basic architecture is very important in practice.

Example of component modeling

Figure 6.2-8 shows an example of component modeling with UML. A component "course" offers an interface for a component "student" and an interface for a component "manager." Both of the components need the respective interface. This is represented by the so-called *ball and socket* notation. "Manager" also has a relationship to the component "office" with the stereotype "uses." This means that the office component is necessary for the manager component to be implemented completely.

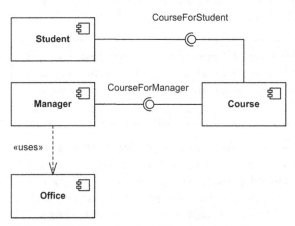

Figure 6.2-8: Example of a UML component diagram

Implementation of architecture principles

Component architectures primarily implement the principle of modularization. Components are often more loosely grained and/or more independent from their environment (that is, more loosely coupled) than objects. Another principle that many component architectures implement more strongly than objects is separation of concerns. The runtime environment separates technical and functional concerns and encapsulates them in different building blocks. The separation of these concerns enables you to develop them further independently of one another and you can reuse the technical concerns in different systems.

6.2.4 Metaprogramming

Basic concept

Many programming languages differentiate between the program as a set of executable instructions and the data with which the program operates. Actually, the programs themselves are also data. However, the program knows its data, but does not know itself. Metaprogramming changes this paradigm and allows the program access to itself.

In metaprogramming, programs are thus treated as data. Programs that use other programs (or themselves) as data are generally called metaprograms. Familiar examples of metaprograms are compilers, virtual machines, or interpreters that consider the program to be compiled or executed as data.

To enable a program to access itself, some programming languages provide a comfortable programming interface, also called meta-object protocol (MOP) [Kiczales et al. 1991]. There is a distinction between read and write access of a program to itself.

Meta-object protocol

With read access, also called introspection or reflection, the program can query type information, information about classes (attributes and operations), and inheritance hierarchies, for example. Often, you can also call dynamic methods and instantiate classes. Java reflection is a well-known example of read metaprogramming.

If a program has write access to itself, it can change class definitions, add and remove classes, or change class hierarchies, for example. CLOS, Smalltalk, Groovy and Tcl are examples of languages that permit write access at runtime. This access is also sometimes known as dynamic metaprogramming.

Some languages, such as Lisp or C++, have macro or template mechanisms that enable changes to the program using the preprocessor or the compiler. Mechanisms of this kind for changing a program at compile time are also partially grouped under the term "static metaprogramming." Note that some of these languages also allow you to modify the definition of language elements.

Static metaprograming

The idea of metaprogramming is to achieve a higher level of flexibility and control in software systems by means of an additional abstraction layer. The language instruments available for this are generally very powerful. However, some developers see them as difficult to understand or complex, in particular because the changes as a result of the metaprogramming must have been understood well in order to understand the actual program. In other words, metaprogramming can bring a lot of benefits but requires a lot of discipline from the developer.

Objectives and challenges

"Self-constructed" meta-architectures are also quite common—meta-architectures that are not supported by a language or runtime environment. For example, many analysis patterns use this (see, e.g., [Fowler 1996]), in particular to simulate dynamic typing. The reflection pattern [Buschmann et al. 1996] generally

The reflection pattern

shows how you can create a meta-architecture yourself. Figure 6.2-9 shows an example of such an architecture.

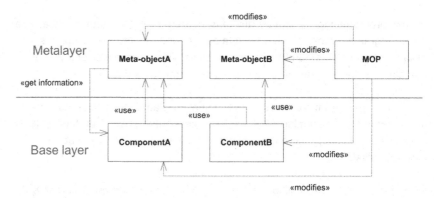

Figure 6.2-9: *Example of a "self-constructed" meta-architecture following the reflection pattern*

6.2.5 Generative Creation of System Building Blocks

Looking beyond software development, we can recognize that in other engineering disciplines, processes are always automated when certain recurring tasks have to be done in a similar way. The use of generative technologies in software development aims to adjust the degree of automation in the creation of software to that of other engineering disciplines. Below we will explain the use of generative technologies using an example, before continuing to discuss in simple terms how a generator works. We will also outline different generation technologies before briefly looking at the practical uses of generators.

Motivation

In software development, you often have to implement variants of a software system that are different in only a few details. The specific details of the individual variants can be functionally and technically motivated. One example of a functionally motivated variant creation is special customer requirements for a product that is being created for several customers simultaneously. A typical example of a technically motivated variant creation is the realization of an architecture on different component platforms (see Section 6.7.5). One main aim of software development is to achieve the highest possible proportion of reusable system building blocks. The variant creation briefly outlined here therefore always focuses on the adjustment of dedicated parts of a software to special requirements or specific functional or technical constraints. This adjustment can take place dynamically at runtime or statically at compile time. Possibilities for a dynamic adjustment are, for example, the descriptive adjustment of the system via configuration files or the concept of (dynamic) metaprogramming presented in Section 6.2.4. The concept of generative creation of system building blocks briefly outlined below represents a static solution option.

The aim of the generative creation of system building blocks and generative programming [Czarnecki and Eisenecker 2000] is to achieve a degree of automation comparable to that in other engineering disciplines in software development. Two important steps form the core of the generative approach. Firstly, the focus must be shifted from the design of an individual system to the design of a whole family of systems, or rather, from the design of an individual application building block to a set of similarly structured building blocks. The decisive criterion is the factoring out of the common, schematic parts of the applications of such a system family or the similarly structured system building blocks. In a second step, suitable technologies must be used to create these schematic parts automatically. This includes selecting means for precise, machine-readable specification of the system parts to be generated at the highest level of abstraction possible (such as the use of models, see Section 6.6). It also includes using generators that read the abstract specifications (*input*) and create the system building blocks to be generated (*output*) automatically (see Figure 6.2-10).

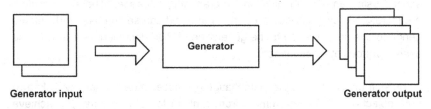

Generator input   Generator output

Figure 6.2-10: How a generator works: Generator input, generator, and generator output

There are various generation technologies for realizing the generation of system building blocks from abstract specifications as described above that we will not discuss in detail here. If you are interested and would like further information, see [Czarnecki and Eisenecker 2000]. We will briefly explain the most important generation technologies below.

The most widespread generation technology is implemented in *template-based generators*. In this context, a template (mostly text-based) consists primarily of two parts: one part enables you to access the (also mostly text-based) generator input. You can use patterns to define when the template is to be applied. The second part consists of a series of rules that control the generator output, that is, the manipulation of the template dependent on the generator input. Prominent examples are the Java Emitter Templates (JET) [Popma 2004a, b], the Velocity Project [Apache 2010b], or the transformation language XSLT (XSL Transformations) [W3C 2006].

XSLT is part of the Extensible Stylesheet Language (XSL) and is used to transform XML documents. The resulting document generally corresponds to XML syntax. However, you can create other text files and even binary files. An XSLT template has a pattern based on XPath (XML Path Language) [W3C 1999]. This pattern describes the nodes of the syntax tree of the XML source document it applies to. The template also has content that determines how the template is to create its part of the syntax tree of the XML target document. One application of the template-based generation described above is in the creation of PDF documents using XSL Formatting Objects (XSL-FO) [W3C 2006] and a suitable convertor, for example, the Apache Formatting Objects Processor (FOP) [Apache 2010a].

API-based generators

The iText project [iText 2010] is an alternative to the generation of PDF documents described above. It provides a Java class library for creating PDF documents. The entire structure of the document to be generated can thus be described using an API (Application Programming Interface). These generators are therefore known as *API-based generators*. Of course, the use of API-based generators is not restricted to the generation of PDF documents—they are also used in various other scenarios.

Frame technology and frame processors

If you shift the concept of the instantiation of classes (see Section 6.2.2) known from object-oriented programming from runtime to compile time, you achieve so-called *frame technology*. Frames are the counterpart of the object-oriented concept of the class and act as templates for source code fragments to be generated. They can be instantiated (any number of times) by the *frame processor*. Variable parts of the frames (slots) are bound to concrete values during instantiation. In a further step, through the use of corresponding instructions to the frame processor, you can generate more concrete source code from the frame instances. In contrast to the simple template-based generation technology, the values that the slots can accept on instantiation are not just character strings but can also represent frame instances, which enables the creation of entire hierarchies of frame instances. One representative of this generation technology is the ANGIE frame processor [DSTG 2010].

Inline generation

If the regular source code contains constructions that create further source code, intermediate code, or machine code during compilation, this is known as *inline generation*. One example of this generation technology is instructions to the preprocessor of a language. Examples of programming languages with a preprocessor are C or C++.

If the source code contains specifications and information (attributes) that a generator can evaluate and that go beyond the pure language elements of the programming language, this is known as a *generation approach based on code attributes*. A prominent example is the automatic creation of HTML documents using Javadoc annotations. Here, you use code attributes exclusively to generate additional artefacts such as documentation, deployment descriptors, database interfaces, etc. In contrast to inline generation, the source code itself is not changed.

Code attributes

The merging of self-contained, complete, independent source code fragments is known as code weaving. To do this you have to define how these different parts can be merged. One example of this generation technology is aspect-oriented programming (see Section 6.2.7).

Code weaving

The specification of abstract models as inputs for generators that use them to create less abstract building blocks of a system, as mentioned above, is a well-known concept in information technology. After all, a compiler can also be seen as a generator. Any differentiation between the two terms is very subtle and often not consistent in literature. In this book, a compiler is a special instance of a generator. It compiles programs formulated in a high-level language into less abstract executable code for a specific runtime environment. In contrast, the output of a generator does not restrict its output to executable code targeted at a defined runtime environment. A generator mostly creates system building blocks. A compiler takes these building blocks and compiles them into executable code. A generator can also create artefacts without the intention of executability, for example, configuration files or parts of documentation.

Compilers as special generators

The aim of using generative technologies is to create optimized outputs for a use case or problem. There are of course other ways of creating problem-specific or use case-specific outputs. The use of generative technologies should be preferred if, for various reasons, (for example, performance reasons or the more difficult maintainability of large configuration files) it is more difficult to use other means, such as metaprogramming or descriptive adjustment via configuration files. One area where generators are frequently used is in model-driven software development, described in Section 6.2.6.

Areas where generative technologies are used

When using code generation, it is important to estimate the effort required to create a generator. Additional abstractions such as templates, aspects, metadata, etc. potentially increase the complexity of the architecture of a system: the architecture can only be understood if these abstractions are understood as well. You should also consider this in weighing up the benefits of a generative approach. It usually makes sense to use a generator if you can use it in different places.

Practical considerations

6.2.6 Model-Driven Software Development

The basic idea of model-driven software development

Models are used in various ways in software development. Section 6.6.1 gives an overview of the possible usage scenarios and an introduction to the basic concepts of modeling. Model-driven software development (MDSD) occurs when models are used not only for documentation purposes but are also central artefacts of a ready-to-run system. In contrast to traditional development, where application logic is formulated in a 3GL programming language (such as Java, C#, or C++), here application logic is specified in models. These models must describe the functionality to be provided by the software as precisely and as expressively as possible. This is only possible if the elements of the model are defined with semantics that define a specific behavior at runtime or a specific software structure uniquely. At the beginning of this section we will give an overview of the core concepts and basic terms of the MDSD approach. We will then restrict the concepts presented to the *Model-Driven Architecture* (MDA) of OMG and explain the terms *function-centric MDSD* and *architecture-centric MDSD*. Finally, we will briefly discuss opportunities, goals, and challenges of the MDSD approach at the end of the section.

Domains and domain-specific languages

The starting point for a method according to MDSD is always a restricted area of knowledge or interest, usually known as a *domain* or *application domain*. The elements of a modeling language that can be used in any context (domain)—a "general purpose" modeling language—would be so abstract and problem-specific that they would be comparable to a conventional 3GL language. Defining a modeling language is only beneficial if model elements can represent the problem more concisely than 3GL programming languages. This is possible if the language is developed for a special domain. Modeling languages like this are known as domain-specific languages or DSLs (see Section 6.6.3).

Models at the level of abstraction of the application domains

The model of the system to be developed is at the center of the MDSD approach. It is at the application domain level of abstraction and is typically formulated using a domain-specific language (DSL) (see Section 6.6.3). The language defines the meaning of the model. The DSL, or more specifically its concrete syntax, can be either textual or graphical. You can also use tabular or other notations. Domain-specific languages and basic concepts and modeling terms are covered in detail in Section 6.6.1. Established DSLs such as Matlab/simulink [Mathworks 2010] or ASCET [Ascet 2005] can be found, for example, in automotive software engineering.

From the model to a ready-to-run application

There are basically two different options for achieving an executable application based on the model of the system: the direct interpretation of the models or their transformation into less abstract, executable target languages. Both options are briefly explained and discussed below.

In the case of interpretation, executable models are interpreted directly by a virtual machine without the compile interim step. The most prominent of these approaches is the OMG-driven initiative of an executable UML [Raistrick et al. 2004]. There are also numerous interesting research approaches, for example, the *Active Charts* project [ActiveCharts 2007]. Here, the behavior of active classes is modeled (and thus the program flow controlled) through activity diagrams interpreted at runtime.

Interpretive approach

In the case of the usual *generative approach* in practice, the compilation of the model into an executable application is usually achieved using one or more transformations. The code generation, i.e., the direct compilation of the model into an executable programming language is a special case in this context. From a technical point of view, in this case mostly generation templates are used, whereas in the case of a multi-level transformation process, mostly specialized model transformation technologies are used. For an overview of different approaches for transforming models, see [Czarnecki and Helsen 2006].

Generative approach

The interpretation of executable models is often criticized with the argument that the power of expression of such a modeling language must correspond to that of a generic General Purpose Language—it therefore does not focus on a specific application domain and thus brings no real added value compared to existing 3GL languages. If an application were to be specified completely using a model interpreted at runtime, this argument would have to be endorsed. However, you can use the interpretation of models to great benefit, particularly as a supplement to handwritten and generated source code parts and system building blocks. To a certain extent, we can compare a discussion of the advantages and disadvantages of both approaches with that of a comparison between static, compiled programming languages and dynamic, interpreted scripting languages (see Section 6.2.8). One example is the higher flexibility but worse runtime performance of interpreted languages.

Comparison between the interpretive and generative approache

So far, we have considered the generative approach presented above from the view of a procedure "from abstract to concrete" (*forward engineering*). You use transformation rules to compile the models into less abstract, mostly executable target languages. However, in practice, a complete generation of a ready-to-run application based on a domain-specific model is currently still restricted to a few application domains. Therefore, in an MDSD project, you should define suitable strategies for handling generated and non-generated system parts from the very beginning. One possible strategy is the strict separation of generated and non-generated system parts. A further solution strategy is the (automated) reduction of changes at a low level of abstraction (for example, the source code) to the models of the higher levels of abstraction. *Round-trip engineering* gener-

Round-trip engineering

ally means being able to make changes to two artefacts at different levels of abstraction, whereby the changes are propagated in both directions. The artefacts concerned are always synchronized and kept consistent. The extent to which round-trip engineering can be practiced usefully in the context of MDSD is in part heavily disputed amongst developers. It is not possible to make a general statement here. In the case of template-based generation approaches, you cannot automatically reduce the generated source code to the model on the basis of the domain semantics no longer visible in the source code (unless you are working with source code annotations). However, a synchronization of models at different levels of abstraction (for example, PIM and PSM) is definitely desirable. Whether you can implement this technically depends on the property of the bidirectionality of the transformation rules that transform the models into one another [Czarnecki and Helsen 2006].

The platform

In addition to the models and model transformations, model-driven development has a further central part: the platform. An MDSD platform consists of reusable, domain-specific building blocks and frameworks. In the field of enterprise systems, a good platform for MDSD consists of technical middleware such as COR-BA [OMG 2008a], Java EE [Oracle 2011c], or .NET [Microsoft 2009]. Building on this, the platform also contains a series of specific frameworks that provide the functional basic services as part of a specific domain. DSL and platform represent two sides of the same coin: the platform provides services; the DSL enables the simple, efficient, and correct use of these services. The rules for transforming the models into less abstract models or executable target languages contain the knowledge about the use of the platform. Figure 6.2-11 shows the typical structure of a platform as it is often used in connection with MDSD [Stahl and Völter 2006]. The contents of the individual layers vary from domain to domain, although the layering is identical everywhere from a practical point of view.

Function-centric vs. architecture-centric MDSD

The application domain and the correlated domain-specific language have a key position in MDSD. A domain can be functionally or technically motivated. In the case of functionally motivated domains, we therefore refer to function-centric MDSD. In the context of model-driven software development, the deciding aspect of a technically motivated domain is mostly the architecture of the application to be created. In the case of architecturally motivated domains, we therefore also refer to architecture-centric MDSD, which we will pay special attention to in this section.

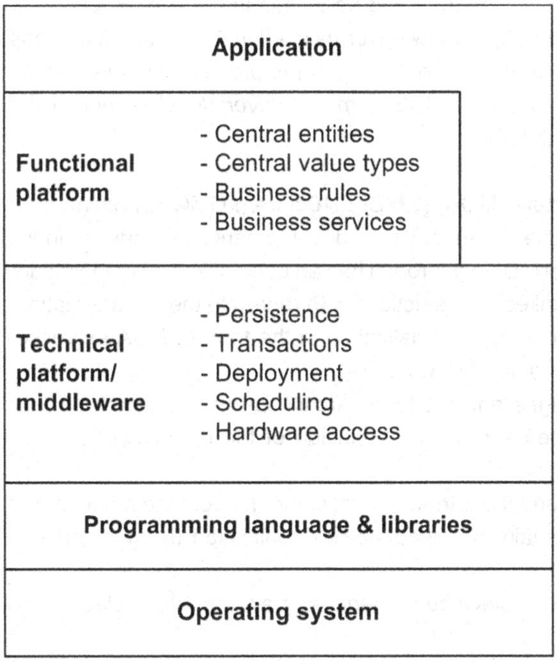

Application
Functional platform	- Central entities - Central value types - Business rules - Business services
Technical platform/ middleware	- Persistence - Transactions - Deployment - Scheduling - Hardware access
Programming language & libraries
Operating system

Figure 6.2-11: Typical MDSD platform in the field of enterprise systems. [Stahl and Völter 2006]

Following the explanations above, architecture-centric MDSD is therefore a specialization of MDSD with the following cornerstones:

> The domain is architecturally motivated: for example, "architecture for business software" or "component infrastructures for embedded systems."
> The metamodel of the DSL therefore contains the architecture abstractions.
> There is no demand to create the entire application automatically, only an implementation framework that contains the architectural infrastructure code (skeleton). The non-generated functional implementation code is implemented manually in the target language.

Cornerstones of architecture-centric MDSD

Note that is also useful to create an architecture metamodel without MDSD because it forces you to think about the software architecture systematically, which makes discovering inconsistencies in particular easier. We will discuss this aspect as part of architecture description languages (ADL) in Section 6.6.4.

Architecture metamodeling

Software developers use various terms and acronyms in the context of model-driven software development. The following terms used in this book are the most frequently used terms, but refer to all of the concepts presented in this section: *model-driven software development* (MDSD); *model-driven development* (MDD); *model-driven engineering* (MDE).

MDA standard as specialization of MDSD

The model-driven architecture (MDA) [OMG 2010c] from OMG is nothing more than a specialization of model-driven software development as introduced in this section. Whereas a general MDSD approach has an open selection of the modeling languages used and makes no restrictions with regard to the transformations into ready-to-run applications, the specialization in the form of MDA expresses itself in the standardization of the following:

> The modeling languages and modeling architecture to be used, i.e., the modeling means to be used for the definition of the domain-specific languages

> A multi-level process and the artefacts involved to get from the model based on the application domain to a ready-to-run application using a series of transformations

> The means to be used to describe the required transformation rules

The primary aims are interoperability between the tools used, and from a long-term perspective, the standardization of modeling languages for popular application domains. The following list gives an overview of those concepts introduced in this section for which MDA has more concrete views than the general MDSD approach [Stahl and Völter 2006].

UML and profiles

> *DSL:* MDA-conform DSLs are languages defined using MOF (meta-object facility, see Section 6.6). In practice, mostly UML profiles are used, i.e., adaptations of UML using stereotypes, tagged values, and constraints. Section 6.6.2 explains the extension possibilities of UML in more detail.

MOF

> *Modeling architecture:* Domain-specific languages in the form of UML profiles are embedded in the four-layer modeling architecture of OMG. The meta-object facility forms the metametamodel, that is, the uppermost instance of this modeling architecture. Section 6.6 covers modeling architectures in detail.

OCL

> *Specification of models:* You can use OCL (*Object Constraint Language*) and, since UML 2.0, *Action Semantics* to make models more precise and enrich them semantically or to make their behavior more specialized. Section 6.6.1 considers the aspect of static semantics from a theoretical viewpoint.

QVT

> *Transformations:* MDA-conform transformations should build on model transformation languages standardized in the *Query/Views/Transformation*

(QVT) [OMG 2008b] specification. There is no complete implementation of this specification available at this time.

> *PIM and PSM:* A core part of MDA is the concept of vertical separation of concerns (see also Section 6.2.7). That is, the specification of aspects of different levels of abstraction through different models. Platform-independent aspects are specified as part of PIM (*platform independent model*). PIM is mapped on one or more platform-specific models (PSM). PSM therefore represents the reference to a concrete platform.

PIM and PSM

The reasons for using model-driven software development can be varied. We will explain some of them below. The aim of MDA is above all to execute the same application logic on different platforms using different transformations. However, there are many other reasons for MDSD. For example, in the JEE environment, the development of software contains many, often recurring and error-prone steps. These can be automated very well using MDSD.

Opportunities and aims of model-driven software development

Model-driven software development requires the creation of an infrastructure consisting of DSL, modeling tools, generators, platforms, etc. You must also put considerable effort into the domain analysis in order to achieve a useful infrastructure. This effort is generally not worthwhile for a "one-time application"—it is only worthwhile if you use the infrastructure multiple times. This leads to the design of *software product lines* [Pohl et al. 2005] and *software factories* [Greenfield and Short 2004] through the identification of *program families* [Parnas 1976]. The family members of such a system family are distinguished by the fact that they have a number of functional or technical characteristics in common. They often use the same technical infrastructure. This means you can reuse them, and not just for building blocks and frameworks but also for metamodels, generators, transformations, etc. It is precisely these reuse possibilities that make MDSD worthwhile despite the additional effort for the creation of an MDSD infrastructure.

Software production lines, software factories, and program families

The closeness of the DSL to the domain makes it much easier to integrate specialists in the development. The prerequisite for this is that the DSL represents the domain well. You cannot achieve a DSL like this overnight—you need well-founded domain knowledge and experience in the definition of DSLs. An iterative approach is appropriate here (see Section 8.1).

Integration of domain experts

With regard to software architecture, MDSD has some useful „side-effects." Model transformations map constructions of the source metamodel on elements of the target metamodel [Czarnecki and Helsen 2006]. In order to formulate this mapping concisely, these two metamodels must contain a limited number of defined concepts. It must be possible to use rules to clearly state what has

Defined target architecture

to be mapped where. In the case of the transformation to the target platform, this means that the platform (or its architecture) must contain a limited number of defined concepts. This is one of the most important characteristics of good architecture. MDSD thus "forces" a well-defined architecture and supports the developers in developing conform to this architecture. Rules for dealing with the architecture are coded in the transformations.

We can summarize the major advantages of an MDSD-based process concisely using the following key points:
> Greater development efficiency
> Better integration of specialists
> Easier modifiability of software
> Improved (implementation of) software architecture
> Possibility for relatively simple porting of the business logic to other platforms

Problems in the context of MDSD

Supporters of model-driven software development often present its paradigm in a highly idealized way. Therefore, to complete this section, we will briefly look at existing problems in the context of model-driven software development.

Problems with existing SCM tools

Software configuration management (SCM) is an indispensable part of high quality software development. This also applies in the context of MDSD. Here you replace the source code of an application that is the focus of traditional procedures with models to a large extent. You can reproduce source code generated from the models at any time and it is less important in the context of SCM. In contrast, version control over the different models is essential. You can only use existing tools such as *CVS* or Subversion for versioning, parallel processing of models, for using typical repository functions (for example, difference analysis and the merging of concurrent versions) to a limited extent. Existing version management systems generally operate on the textual representation of the artefacts managed and you can thus use them generically. From a structural point of view, a text document is a sequence of text lines. The break between this simple structure and the actual structure of the artefacts managed (for example, the abstract syntax tree in the case of source code documents of a programming language) is generally reasonable and can usually be balanced out by the mental performance of the user. This does not generally apply to models. The break between the external presentation of a model in the form of graph-based diagrams and the physical representation (for example, in XMI format) is often enormous. Therefore, you cannot use existing SCM tools to manage models in a professional MDSD environment without further effort.

Different model types are also considerably different with regard to their structure, their semantics, and/or their notation. Whereas you can use text-based version management systems generically to manage artefacts of different programming languages, where management of models is concerned, in principle you require dedicated tools for each model type, possibly even for every diagram type. You have to adjust the display forms, the difference calculation [Kelter et al. 2005], and the conflict management during merging [Schmidt et al. 2009] to the model type or diagram type. A further problem that often exists in connection with languages that are not widespread is tooling (see Section 6.2.8).

Diversity of modeling languages

Going beyond the typical services of a configuration management system, you need suitable tools and methods to manage and control the evolution of different models. Of particular note here is the evolution of domain-specific languages. As already discussed, you do not create DSLs overnight—they are mostly the result of a high-quality iterative process. The evolution of the DSL is driven by the step-by-step refinement of the formal domain knowledge or by external requirements of an instable and constantly changing environment. This evolution results in considerable consequences, such as the adjustment (co-evolution) of the generators and transformation rules, but in particular the models already created. Suitable solutions are still being researched [Van Deursen et al. 2007].

Model evolution

6.2.7 Aspect Orientation

Aspect orientation [Kiczales et al. 1997] avoids so-called crosscutting concerns being spread across the code or the design. These are concerns that are general or go across the application logic. Instead, solutions are encapsulated in an aspect and thus separated from the system affected by the aspect. An aspect represents a concern that can be viewed separate to the actual application logic. In the discussion of component orientation, we have already mentioned some of these concerns as technical concerns, such as logging, security, activation, or lifetime management of components. Separating such aspects distributed over the code in naive implementations is the main task of aspect orientation. This means that aspect orientation realizes the principle of separation of concerns for these crosscutting concerns.

The idea of aspect orientation

As an example, Figure 6.2-12 shows three components in which the aspects persistence, logging, and synchronization are hard-coded. As shown by the dotted lines, these are the crosscutting concerns of the three components.

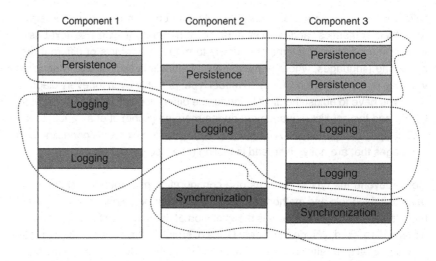

Figure 6.2-12: *Example of crosscutting concerns*

Aspect orientation avoids the problem of implementing crosscutting concerns spread across the code by encapsulating the concern as an aspect. The aspect is automatically woven into the system so that dir

ect intervention in the actual programs is not necessary—the developers of the system building blocks do not have to consider the aspect at all. This means that aspects are "non-invasive" [Filman and Friedman 2000] from the view of the program that the aspect is being added to.

Aspect orientation and metaprogramming

Being „non-invasive" is an important feature of aspect-oriented programming. Aspect orientation stems from metaprogramming. Note that some metaprogramming constructions can be extremely complex, since they make it difficult to understand the system without understanding the metacontext it is currently situated in. One example is Lisp macros. You can only understand a given Lisp system if you have previously considered the macros for this system. This is because the macros can change the meaning of the language elements. Aspect orientation avoids such constructions because you can consider the aspects and the system relatively independently of one another.

Aspect systems and their basic concepts

Aspect orientation is realized through systems for aspect-oriented programming (AOP). Popular AOP implementations, such as AspectJ [Kiczales et al. 2001], Hyper/J [Tarr 2004], JBoss AOP [Burke 2004], or AspectWerkz [Bonér and Vasseur 2004] realize this concept in very different ways and there are many AOP concepts still being developed. Internally, AOP concepts can be realized by metaprogramming, byte code manipulation, or generative programming. These realization technologies are explained in more detail in [Zdun 2004].

A well-known and now widespread example of a tool is AspectJ. AspectJ handles aspects at the language level of Java. To do this, it defines a series of language extensions that implement the above-mentioned concepts. From a purely technical point of view, the implementation works using source code or byte code manipulation. This means that the aspect code is statically "woven" with the core program (with a so-called "Aspect Weaver"—in other approaches, an "Aspect Composition Framework" is used to compose the aspects). AspectJ thus allows you to create Java byte code that contains the aspects, but the aspects and the core program are still separated in the source code. Figure 6.2-13 shows this process.

AspectJ

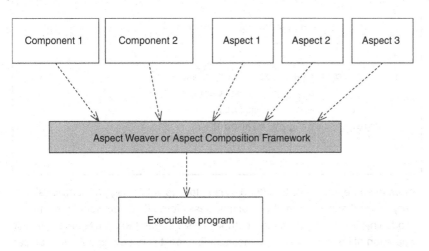

Figure 6.2-13: How an Aspect Weaver or Aspect Composition Framework works

All of the above-mentioned approaches have some common concepts that are however realized in different ways. Some cases also use different terminology. Here we will use the AspectJ terminology:

Concepts of aspect orientation

> *Join points* define the points in the program where the aspect can intervene at runtime.
> *Advices* define a behavior that the aspect can add to a program before, after, or instead of the execution of a join point.

> *Pointcuts* represent a number of join points at which a specific advice actually intervenes. In other words, the pointcut allows the developer to specify the connection between join points and advices for a specific application.
> *Introductions* represent structure changes to a program. For example, you can add a new interface or a new method to a class. In AspectJ, introductions are also denoted as intertype declarations.

Example with AspectJ

The following account class represents a simple example:

```
public class Account {
  String accountNumber;
  double credit;
  public void withdraw(double amount) {
    credit = credit - amount;
  }
  public void payIn(double amount) {
    credit = credit + amount;
  }
  public void transfer (double amount,
              account targetAccount) {
    credit = credit - amount;
    targetAccount.payIn(amount);
  }
}
```

Let us assume you want to extend these classes with a logging functionality at every method access in methods of this class. To do this, you would have to add a code line for logging to every method. This violates the architecture principle separation of concerns because the logging aspect is not encapsulated. You can use an aspect to remove this problem.

The example aspect below consists of an advice that starts with `before`, which means that the advice is executed before the join point. The pointcut `execution(* Account.*(..))` determines all join points considered: this means all method executions on an account with any arguments. Whenever such a join point is reached at runtime, the advice (the subsequent block in braces) is executed. The result is therefore that the method access of an Account is automatically logged as well.

```
public aspect AccountLogger {
  before(): execution(* Account.*(..)) {
    Logger.log(thisJoinPoint,
      thisJoinPoint.getArgs());
  }
}
```

6.2.8 Scripting Languages and Dynamic Languages

Scripting languages are originally programming languages for controlling software systems. They typically use a two-language approach. The core system is implemented in a programming language other than the scripting language, and the scripting language only takes over the composition of the system building blocks in a ready-to-run system. This has the advantage that the system user can compose the system building blocks flexibly and thus adapt the system to his or her needs without having to access the core system code.

Scripting languages are therefore often languages at a higher level of abstraction that are interpreted or compiled at runtime. In contrast, the languages composed by the scripting languages are typically compiled to native machine code. Typical examples are modern scripting languages, such as Perl, Python, Ruby, or Tcl, which are themselves implemented in C and typically compose C or C++ building blocks. As we can see from this example, scripting languages are usually embedded in the language that they compose. Apart from languages such as C or C++, many scripting languages today are also realized on the basis of languages that are executed with virtual machines, such as C# or Java.

The name scripting language comes from the fact that scripts were originally used in the area of batch jobs or shell scripts of the operating system. However, modern scripting languages are complete programming languages and entire systems are frequently implemented exclusively in these languages. In many cases, scripting languages are also used to initially create a quick prototype and then the prototype is migrated step-by-step in the language in which the scripting language is embedded.

As a result of their history, in some developer communities, scripting languages are seen as "hacker languages" and therefore have a bad image. The frequent use of such languages as independent programming languages also makes the term "scripting language" appear obsolete. For this reason, many of these languages position themselves today as *dynamic languages*. The languages are also partly positioned as *agile languages* to underline their frequent use in the context of agile development processes.

Dynamic languages are languages at a high level of abstraction that execute many tasks during runtime that other languages execute at compile time. Examples of these tasks are the parsing of the language, the addition of new code

Scripting languages

Dynamic languages

to the language, the extension of existing class definitions, procedure definitions, or data definitions, changing the type system, etc. Many dynamic languages are typed dynamically, but this is not a prerequisite for dynamic languages. In addition to the languages named from the scripting language environment, the dynamic languages also include in particular languages such as Lisp or Smalltalk (and their derivatives).

An important example of a dynamic language means is that variable types do not have to be declared—instead, they are determined automatically. For example, in the following Tcl code, the variable a initially receives an integer value and is bound to this data type internally (i.e., in the interpreter). With the subsequent new instruction, a receives a string value and is therefore automatically bound to this data type.

```
set a 1          ;# a is bound to the integer
set a "a b c"    ;# a is bound to the string
```

A further typical example for a dynamic language means is the possibility of using data specified in the language as code. We can explain this language means with the following Lisp example. In the example, a program fragment is transferred to variable a. This program fragment assigns the value 1 to variable b. Later, this program fragment is evaluated with the command eval. The consequence is that the code in variable a is executed dynamically and b receives the value 1.

```
setf a '(setf b 1))
; ...
; some time later
; ...
(eval a)
```

Closures are a further dynamic language means that originates from the area of functional programming languages. They are functions that when called, preserve the context in which they were defined. One example of this language means are Ruby blocks that preserve the context of their definition. In the following example, ntimes is transferred to b with the parameter 20. The dynamically transferred value for m is preserved in the block contained in ntimes. In contrast, the variable n changes from call to call.

```
def ntimes(m)
return proc{ |n| m * n }
end
```

```
b=ntimes(20)
b.call(1)   # returns 20
b.call(3)   # returns 60
```

Through their powerful means for language extension, dynamic languages and scripting languages are particularly well suited for implementing domain-specific languages. We have already discussed DSLs in Section 6.2.6 in the context of model-driven development. Section 6.6.3 discusses DSLs from the view of modeling. In dynamic languages, DSLs are not created *externally* but as *internal* language extensions of the existing language.

DSLs in dynamic languages

For example, no new parser is implemented for the DSL—the existing parser of the dynamic language is (extended and) used. DSLs are thus easy to realize with dynamic languages and you can use abstractions of the dynamic language in them. For example, it often makes sense to offer loops of the dynamic language in the DSL to cover cases where a code fragment is to be executed repeatedly. If you implement a new language (as is often the case in model-driven development), this reuse is not possible. However, the internal DSL has the disadvantage that language constructions that you do not want to provide to the domain experts are available. Preventing this completely requires a lot of effort in many dynamic languages.

Of course, you can combine both approaches. This means that you can use a DSL based on a dynamic language as a DSL for model-driven development. When executed, this type of DSL fills the model for the generator.

The article [Fowler 2005a] gives a more extensive overview of these topics.

Some of the dynamic languages, such as Ruby, Groovy, and Smalltalk are very popular in connection with so-called agile frameworks for web applications. Examples are Ruby on Rails, Grails, and Seaside. These frameworks use the dynamic language means amongst other things to accelerate the development of web applications and support rapid prototyping. For example, Ruby on Rails is primarily a series of DSLs for web applications. It is based on a framework that follows the model-view-controller pattern. Just like many other applications of dynamic languages, Ruby on Rails also follows the "Convention over Configuration Principle" (see Section 6.1). This means that useful standard assumptions are made and only necessary adjustments have to be configured. This generally enables a developer to achieve a first result quickly and this result can be adjusted to the separate requirements step-by-step.

Dynamic languages for web applications

Advantages of dynamic languages and scripting languages

The possibility of developing at a high level of abstraction in the scripting language, DSL, or dynamic language is the central advantage of these approaches. One sub-aspect of this advantage is that you can adjust the language to the problem at hand and thus use the most suitable language for the problem. If a two-language approach is used, you can use the scripting language or dynamic language for rapid prototyping.

Disadvantages of dynamic languages and scripting languages

However, there are also some disadvantages. Firstly, many scripting languages or dynamic languages have worse performance than languages such as C, C++, C#, or Java. A multi-language approach can have a negative effect, since you have to maintain all of the languages you use and in the long term, you need experts for all of them. A general problem with languages that are not widespread is tooling. For example, for many enterprises it does not make sense to use a language that has better performance in theory if there is insufficient support through IDEs. In the case of DSLs, you have to calculate in the development costs for a suitable tooling.

6.2.8 Summary

Summary: Basic architecture concepts

> Procedural approaches are a classic approach for structuring architectures and you use them in particular to break down a complex algorithm into reusable individual algorithms.
> Object orientation is based on the idea of bundling data that a series of related methods process together with these methods. Today, object orientation is a prevalent architecture concept.
> Component orientation offers components as reusable, self-contained building blocks of an architecture.
> Metaprogramming allows a program access to itself. Thus, the idea of metaprogramming is to achieve a higher level of flexibility and control in software systems by means of an additional abstraction layer.
> The objective of the generative creation of system building blocks is to increase the level of automation in the creation of software.
> Model-driven software development occurs when models are used not only for documentation purposes but are also central artefacts of a ready-to-run system.
> Aspect orientation avoids so-called crosscutting concerns being spread across the code or the design.
> Scripting languages and dynamic languages are languages at a high level of abstraction that execute many tasks during runtime that other languages execute at compile time.

6.3 Architecture Tactics, Styles, and Patterns

The principles discussed in Section 6.1 explain very generally how to design and (further) develop a "good" software architecture. Section 6.2 covers concepts that provide more concrete guidelines. However, just like the principles, they refer not to specific problems you face in designing an architecture but to the general problem of software design. This section looks at architecture tactics, styles, and patterns. What these three means have in common is that they describe principle solutions for specific recurring problems in architecture design. They do this in a way that can be applied to a number of cases. Tactics, styles, and patterns abstract from design decisions that have already been taken and that in similar contexts in the past, have led to successful software architectures. They therefore enable you to reuse design decisions.

Architecture tactics, styles, and patterns

Figure 6.3-1 illustrates the relationships of architecture tactics, architecture styles, and architecture patterns to principles and basic concepts. All three means help you to make principles more concrete and implement them, using the basic concepts in implementation. Patterns are the most general of the three means, as they are used not only in architecture but also in many other domains. They also offer the concept of the pattern language, which combines a number of related patterns. From a conceptual point of view, patterns and styles are very similar means. To implement architecture tactics, you often use styles and patterns.

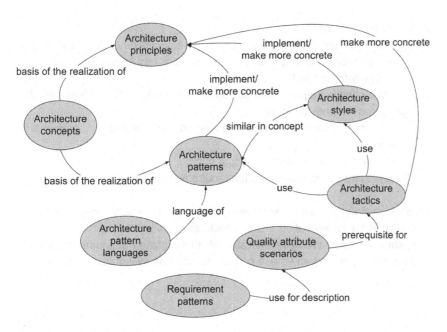

Figure 6.3-1: Overview of architecture tactics, styles, and patterns

6.3.1 Requirement Patterns

Requirement patterns cover frequently recurring requirements

A requirement pattern is a methodological tool that enables you to systematically develop "good" requirements (see Section 5.1). Like architecture patterns, requirement patterns refer to visibly recurring questions for which generally applicable solution proposals can be formulated. A requirement pattern can thus take the form of a template for concrete requirements of a specific requirements category.

Examples of requirement patterns

A project team will use a performance requirement pattern to define concrete requirements with regard to the performance required from a system. If there are also requirements for the system documentation, the team will formulate these very efficiently based on the corresponding documentation requirement pattern. Requirement patterns therefore help you to avoid having to redesign and reformulate frequently recurring requirements from scratch time and again. Let us assume that you are given the task of recording requirements that should precisely specify the security and privilege situation for a system. You will firstly look for requirement patterns in the security area. Examples are "user registration," "authentication," or "authorization." Each of these requirement patterns gives you a range of basic considerations, help, verification questions, etc. that you can use as a basis for devising your concrete system requirements. This process also enables architects with little experience to achieve complete and consistent specification aims when developing and verifying requirements.

Requirement patterns—characteristics and motivation

Requirement patterns...
> ...make the process of developing requirements very efficient and less prone to error since they offer you, for example, requirements that are 80% completely formulated
> ...often contain help on ideal solutions and strategies for dealing with the given requirement category
> ...indicate relationships to other requirement patterns and form pattern languages
> ...increase the consistency across a number of requirements since consistency is already an attribute at the requirement pattern level

Architecturally significant requirements and requirement patterns

From an architecture view, requirement patterns are a very effective means, in particular for incorporating the architecturally significant requirements in the problem analysis phase systematically. When integrating requirement patterns into the corresponding enterprise processes, you can systematically record the frequently underestimated non-functional requirements—the requirements that drive the architecture—and implement them in specifications.

With regard to the form for documenting requirement patterns, Withall [Withall 2007] suggests using the following structure:

> Basic details: Pattern abstract, domain, related patterns, pattern classifications, and pattern author.
> Applicability: Contexts within which the requirement pattern can be applied as well those contexts in which it cannot.
> Discussion: Description of all aspects to consider when writing a requirement of this type.
> Content: Main substance of the pattern—the 80%-ready requirement description.
> Template(s): A pre-defined starting point for writing a requirement of this type.
> Example(s): One or more representative requirements using this pattern.
> Extra requirements: List of additional requirements that often follow on from a requirement of this type.
> Considerations for development: References for architects on what usual responses to requirements of this type look like.
> Considerations for testing: Additional hints for testing this type of requirement.

Anatomy of requirement pattern descriptions according to Withall

In addition to Withall's suggested anatomy of requirement pattern descriptions, use case descriptions are also a suitable form of documentation, in particular for functional requirements.

Use cases document functional requirement patterns

Although the documentation of functional requirements, for example, in the form of use cases, is widespread in practice, quality attributes are rarely recorded systematically. One suitable means for recording them is quality attribute scenarios [Bass et al. 2003], which we will now briefly explain.

Quality attribute scenarios make the documentation of non-functional requirements systematic

Quality attribute scenarios are one possibility for analyzing the requirements as the basis for tactics (see Section 6.3.2). There are of course other means that you can use as the basis as well. A quality attribute scenario is an operational requirement with respect to a quality attribute. Table 6.3-1 introduces and explains the documentation schema for quality attribute scenarios.

Table 6.3-1: Documentation schema for quality attribute scenarios

Criterion	Meaning
Source	System or user that generates an event or stimulus.
Stimulus	Event to which the system must react.
Artefact	That part of the system affected by the event.
Context	Describes the context in which the event occurs. E.g.: "System is in normal state."
Reaction	Describes the activity that the stimulus triggers in the system. One possible reaction would be the rejection of the incident type and the writing of an entry to the operating log.
Reaction measurement	Describes the measurement as well as how the success or failure of the reaction is to be measured.

Quality attribute scenarios can be divided into scenario types according to quality attributes. For example, we can identify the following general scenario types [Bass et al. 2003]:

> Availability scenarios
> Modifiability scenarios
> Performance scenarios
> Security scenarios
> Testability scenarios
> Usability scenarios

6.3.2 Architecture Tactics

Informal introduction to architecture tactics

Architecture tactics provide guidelines for implementing the most varied quality attributes of the system under construction and its architecture. In principle therefore, an architecture tactic helps you to get a first idea about a design problem. You can then develop this idea further and can also use styles and patterns, for example, as further means.

Starting point: Analysis of quality attributes

The prerequisite for using architecture tactics is the analysis of quality attributes (see Section 6.3.1).

Now that we have presented the quality attribute scenarios (see Section 6.3.1) as one option for formulating an operational requirement with respect to a quality attribute, we can define the term "tactic" more precisely:

Definition: Architecture tactic according to Bass et al.

An architecture tactic is a design decision that influences the realization of the reaction of a quality attribute scenario.

Quality attribute scenarios increase the degree of formalization of requirements descriptions. In addition, by measuring their reactions, you can verify the quality of the realization of the tactic immediately.

As a supplement to the quality attribute scenario types, Bass et al. [Bass et al. 2003] offer a collection of general tactics for handling recurring problems for each scenario type. Therefore, for each scenario type, you can derive a general tactic that is refined by other, more concrete tactics that are alternatives to each other. As an example, Figure 6.3-2 gives an overview of modifiability tactics that are derived from the modifiability scenarios.

General and concrete architecture tactics according to Bass et al.

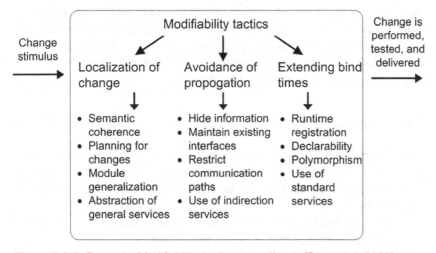

Figure 6.3-2: Example: Modifiability tactics according to [Bass et al. 2003]

As an architect, you use quality attribute scenarios and corresponding tactics to ensure that the non-functional requirements determined are complete. Furthermore, it seems obvious to connect architecturally significant use cases with architecturally significant qualities. To do this you should look at every architecturally significant use case with regard to the level of quality to which it has been realized. The greater the number of different quality features a use case has, the greater its architectural character. You can create quality attribute scenarios for each combination.

You should then investigate how to realize the quality attribute scenarios within the defined constraints. It sometimes becomes clear that this is not possible. In this case, you must point out these contradictions and show stakeholders alternatives.

Considering quality features within the given constraints

With reference to tactics, a quality attribute scenario is similar to the problem description and the context of a pattern. However, unlike the quality attribute scenarios, patterns have no analysis technology for analyzing concrete systems. Tactics are similar to the solution of a pattern but are generally described in much

Architecture tactics vs. architecture patterns and architecture styles

less detail. Like styles, however, tactics also cover only a very special application area and are therefore a more specialized architecture means than patterns. Tactics refer especially to quality attributes. Patterns also refer to quality attributes of the architecture but also have many other types of forces. For example, a pattern description can also contain forces that have no direct reference to architecture, such as the implementation of a design decision in the design process or strategic management considerations that can influence a design decision.

Therefore, it makes sense to use tactics to gain clarity about a general method and thus analyze quality attributes in general. Patterns and styles then offer concrete guidelines that enable you to define the design decision in detail. The specific forces that occur, for example, in a pattern and also encompass quality attributes help you in the design decision. For example, the decision for the change tactic "localization of the change" after further analysis of the requirements could lead to you introducing a layered architecture as described by the layers pattern or the layers style (see Section 6.4.1 for details).

6.3.3 Architecture Styles

Architecture styles

In this section we will discuss architecture styles. Shaw and Garlan [Shaw and Garlan 1996] define an architecture style as a pattern of the structural organization of a family of systems. For them, an architecture style consists of the following elements:
> A set of *building blocks* that fulfill specific functions at runtime
> A *topological arrangement* of these building blocks
> A set of *connectors* that regulate the communication and coordination between the building blocks
> A set of *semantic restrictions* that determine how building blocks and connectors can be connected to one another

Note that both the building blocks and the connectors of a style are mostly realized as independent building blocks of an architecture or a system.

An architecture style primarily reflects the fundamental structure of a software system and its properties. You can therefore use a style to categorize architectures. Furthermore, you can use styles to understand the consequences of a fundamental architecture and its variants.

Architecture styles vs. architecture patterns

It is very difficult to differentiate between architecture styles and architecture patterns—with the exception that they have different forms of description. The form of description for patterns covers many aspects that do not appear in the form of description for styles, such as the reasons for a design decision. Patterns are used not only in architecture but also in other areas, whereas styles are used only in this area. Many of the architecture styles documented by Shaw and Garlan have also been documented in the form of architecture patterns. For this reason, and because the concept of architecture styles is very similar to the concept of patterns, in the field of architecture you can use the terms "styles" and "patterns" synonymously.

Shaw and Garlan have cataloged some frequently used architecture styles. These are summarized and divided into categories in Figure 6.3-3.

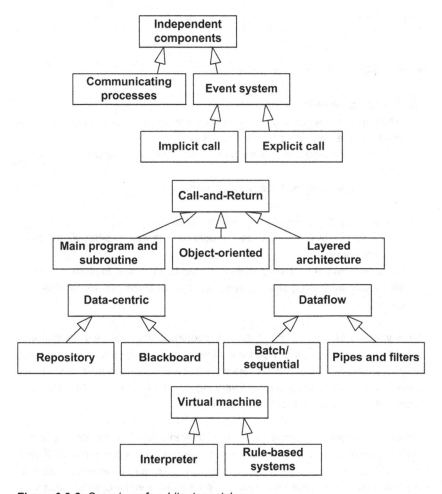

Figure 6.3-3: *Overview of architecture styles*

We will now look at the architecture style *Pipes and filters* as an example. The aim of this style is to describe a flexible architecture for the sequential processing of dataflows. Pipes and filters has one component type:

> *Filters* transform flows of input data into flows of output data incrementally.

Example of an architecture style: Pipes and filters

The style also has a connector type:
> *Pipes* move data from a filter output to a filter input.

The topological arrangement of these components and connectors is illustrated in Figure 6.3-4 with an example. One filter can provide several other filters with input data via several pipes. Processing continues (non-deterministically) until there is no further pipe connected to the last filter and thus the processing ends.

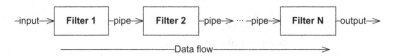

Figure 6.3-4: Pipes and filters architecture

The style has a series of invariants:
> Filters are independent processing components. External data is only entered into the system via inputs and outputs.
> One filter in a pipes and filters architecture does not know the identity of other filters.
> Filters can be combined in any order using pipes.

Typical examples of pipes and filters architectures are:
> UNIX Pipes, which connect UNIX programs with one another via interprocess communication.
> Compilers, which perform processing step-by-step and forward the result after each processing step respectively. Typical steps are lexical analysis, parsing, etc.

The advantage of a pipes and filters architecture is that it is very flexible with regard to the combination of pipes and filters. You can reuse filter components easily. It is easy to let pipes and filters work in parallel, for example, in separate processes or threads, since they are very independent of one another. This can increase the efficiency of the entire system.

However, there are also some possible disadvantages. The forwarding of the status between filters can involve a high effort and resource consumption. If data has to be transformed to be placed in the pipe, then unnecessary bidirectional transformations may occur. Debugging or the behavior in the case of errors can be more difficult than with other architectures because errors or debugging information has to be sent through the pipes.

In the POSA book [Buschmann et al. 1996], the pipes and filters style is also documented as an architecture pattern.

6.3.4 Architecture Patterns

Over the last years, patterns have become an important instrument for software developers and architects, particularly in the area of object orientation. In particular, the Gang of Four book (GoF) [Gamma et al. 1995], which is concerned with design patterns, and the POSA books [Buschmann et al. 1996; Schmidt et al. 2000], which deal with software architecture patterns, have made important contributions here. However, patterns also occur in many other areas of software development: for example, patterns for the analysis of domains [Fowler 1996], patterns for domain-driven design [Evans 2004], patterns for software organization [Coplien and Harrison 2004], or pedagogical patterns [Fricke and Völter 2000].

Architecture patterns in software engineering

The original pattern definition by Christopher Alexander—who originally introduced the pattern concept in classic architecture—states [Alexander 1977]:

Definition: Pattern according to Alexander

> A pattern is a three-part rule which expresses the relationship between a certain context, a problem, and a solution.

However, Alexander goes beyond this simple definition in many points. We will address these points in the next paragraphs. The somewhat longer definition by Coplien [Coplien 2004] offers a plausible summary of these points related to a software system:

Definition: Pattern according to Coplien

> Each pattern is a three-part rule that expresses the relationship between a certain context, a certain system of forces which occurs repeatedly in that context, and a certain software configuration which allows these forces to resolve themselves.

One very important point is that patterns are, in principle, solutions for recurring problems. This means that they have to be formulated so generally that a pattern can be applied not only for a specific problem but for a series of concrete problems. On the other hand, patterns are also a practical approach. This means that after reading the pattern, the reader should have a clear solution guideline for solving a concrete problem that fits the problem in the pattern description. However, the general solution described in the pattern must be adjusted to the concrete design situation.

Recurring problems and solutions

As the architect you should know the central design and architecture patterns as these represent the typically recurring solutions to the recurring problems in software architecture in general. You should also have a good knowledge of the design patterns and architecture patterns of the concrete technical and non-technical domains in which you are active. This is important as it enables you to solve problems of the same kind without having to "reinvent the wheel." Patterns are therefore a means of passing on established knowledge.

Patterns thus give architects and developers a common vocabulary to enable them to name recurring architecture structures. Once you have a deep knowledge of the central patterns in a domain, you will quickly see that these patterns frequently recur in given architectures. Therefore, patterns are also an important instrument for documenting and discussing software architectures. They enable you to recognize and name the common features in recurring architectural structures.

Known uses

It is important to note that patterns do not describe new ideas but represent proven solutions. This results in the general requirement that a software pattern must always have at least three *known uses* in real practical systems. Such known uses are often portrayed as part of the pattern to illustrate the practical benefit of the pattern to the reader.

Forces

An important part of every pattern is a system of forces. These forces are part of the problem solved by the pattern. They primarily build up pressure that is relieved by the solution. The solution must therefore establish a balance between the forces. This is illustrated in Figure 6.3-5. Of course, the pattern can only describe this balance in general terms. As the architect it is your task to work out the balance of the forces for a concrete solution in a design situation following the pattern. In the field of software architecture, the quality attributes (see Chapter 5) are often important forces for a solution. Figure 6.3-5 shows how the different forces, which are all typical quality attributes, influence a solution.

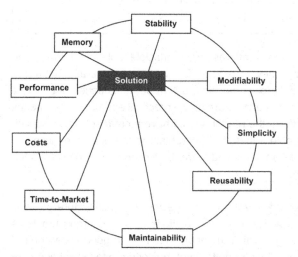

Figure 6.3-5: Quality attributes as forces that influence a solution

Not every solution offers a good balance between all the given forces in a problem situation. For example, a very efficient solution can drive the costs up or have a negative effect on resource consumption (as a result of the long development times for this special solution). In such cases, there may also be several patterns that solve a particular problem in different ways. For example, the Layers pattern [Buschmann et al. 1996] (see Section 6.4.1) and the Pipes and filters pattern [Buschmann et al. 1996] (see Section 6.4.2) can be alternatives for a design that divides responsibilities. Pipes and filters is a pattern with a positive effect on flexibility if you have to map relatively linear call sequences. Layers are more suitable, for example, when you have to compose complex structures of building blocks in an architecture in a way that they can be understood.

Consequences

In a pattern, the *consequences* of using the pattern are specified explicitly so that the reader can weigh up whether using it is viable and which positive and negative effects to expect.

A pattern should explicitly describe how the solution breaks down the forces and why the solution breaks down the forces in this specific way. Different pattern descriptions do this in different ways. In particular, however, the following are frequently specified: a detailed solution with examples, descriptions of the participants of the pattern, descriptions of the interaction of the parts of the pattern, variants of the pattern, and the relationship of the pattern to other patterns. You often find parts of the detailed solution that are very concrete, for example, in the form of UML diagrams or source code fragments. These illustrate the pattern. They should never be confused with the *pattern itself*, which is more general than all of these solution variants.

Detailed solution

In the context of software architecture, both design patterns and architecture patterns are very important. What they have in common is that they both generally present structural, technical solutions. You can therefore distinguish them from patterns that cover functional aspects (see, for example, [Fowler 1996] and [Evans 2004]). Patterns for functional aspects are often the basis for the domain-driven design of an analysis model. Design patterns and architecture patterns are thus frequently used in the implementation of the analysis model. In general, design patterns describe more specific design solutions that have a local effect, whereas architecture patterns tend to describe system structures that have an effect across the entire system. However, it is difficult to differentiate between these two categories of patterns.

Design and architecture patterns

For example, the pattern interpreter [Gamma et al. 1995] was originally presented as a design pattern and you can implement it using just a few classes. However, you can also use the same pattern as the basis for more complex architectures, for example, by using the interpreter as the architecture of an inter-preted programming language (see also: interpreter architecture style in [Shaw and Garlan 1996]).

Typical design patterns, like the patterns described in [Gamma et al. 1995], are often used as part of the solution of an architecture pattern. However, this is also not a general rule and depends on the concrete architecture and how the pattern is viewed.

Differentiation depends on the angle of consideration

You can see that the differentiation between design pattern and architecture pat-tern depends on the view of the person considering it and the purpose for which it is being considered.

Example: Proxy design pattern

Now we will consider two patterns as examples: the proxy design pattern and the broker architecture pattern. We will first outline the proxy pattern [Gamma et al. 1995, Buschmann et al. 1996].

Name:	Proxy
Context:	A client must access the operations of an instance of a specific class.
Problem:	Direct access to the operations of the class is not pos-sible, difficult, or inappropriate. For example, direct access may not be secure or efficient, or you are in a distributed environment. Here it may not be desirable for the physi-cal network address for the direct access to a distributed object to be hard-coded in the client. However, without this address, direct access via the network is not possible.
Forces:	Access to an instance of a specific class should be runtime-efficient and secure. This cannot be achieved with a direct call.
	Access to an instance of a specific class should be transparent from the view of the client. In particular, it should not be necessary to change the usual call be-havior or usual call syntax of the client.
	Client developers should know and assess possible ef-fects of a call. Complete transparency of the call be-havior from the view of the client can make this difficult.
Solution:	The client communicates with a placeholder, the proxy, instead of with an instance of the actual class. The proxy offers the same interface as the instances of the class that are to be called. Internally, the proxy forwards the call to an instance of this class. However, it can also implement additional functionalities, such as authenti-cation or the triggering of a distributed call.

Consequences:	A proxy offers the advantage that it decouples clients from the implementing instance. In a distributed environment, for example, this means that the client must not have the server network address hard-coded. The proxy thus increases the flexibility of the application because it enables a client to also influence the behavior of the "service" called by changing the proxy object. A proxy can increase the runtime efficiency, for example, by portraying the results in a cache and then delivering these instead of a renewed calculation.
	However, a proxy is also an additional indirection, i.e., at least one additional call. This means that the proxy slightly reduces the runtime efficiency. You should be cautious about using complex proxy variants because a complex logic in a proxy can produce a considerable effort, for example, with reference to resource consumption.

The basic structure of a proxy is usually implemented with just a few classes, as shown in Figure 6.3-6. The figure shows an example of a solution scheme—part of the pattern description—and not an example for the application of a proxy pattern for a concrete problem.

Proxy example

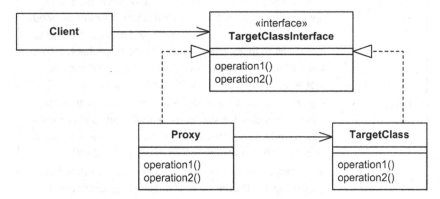

Figure 6.3-6: *An example of a solution scheme for a proxy*

Here you can see a proxy and a target class. Both implement the same interface. The proxy delegates calls to the target class using an association relationship. It can thus act as a placeholder for instances of the target class. The client therefore only has a reference to the interface as it should not know whether it is dealing with the proxy as a placeholder or with an instance of the target class.

A proxy is a typical design pattern. However, proxies can also be an important part of more complex architectures. For example, proxies are often part of the broker pattern [Buschmann et al. 1996; Völter et al. 2004]. We will describe this pattern as an example of an architecture pattern.

Example diagrams in patterns

An important note on the examples in pattern descriptions: the class diagrams (and other examples) in the pattern description are pure concept diagrams with concept classes that you do not have to or cannot implement one-to-one in "real" building blocks (e.g., classes) in the solution of a concrete problem. The examples therefore show the solution in principle, but a concrete implementation of the proxy pattern can have more than just a few classes or can even have fewer classes than described in the pattern.

Example: Broker architecture pattern

Name:	Broker
Context:	You want to design a distributed object system. This means that objects are to be made available in a server process and they are to be accessed by distributed clients via the network.
Problem:	A distributed system presents many challenges that do not occur in a local system that runs in a single process. An important challenge in this area is the communication via non-permitted networks—in contrast to local calls, a network can fail without the client or server failing. Furthermore, heterogeneous components must be brought into a coherent architecture and the distributed resources must be used efficiently. If developers from distributed applications had to master all of these challenges, they would probably forget the actual task in hand: developing a distributed application that solves the problems of the domain well.
Forces:	Communication via a network is more complex than local calls: connections have to be established, call parameters have to be sent via the network, and network-specific errors, such as network failure, must be dealt with.
	You want to avoid spreading aspects of distributed programming across the code of a distributed application.
	The network address and other parameters of the server should not be hard-coded in the client application. This is important to allow a distributed service to be realized by other servers without having to change the client.

Solution:	The outsourcing of all communication tasks to a broker separates the communication tasks of a distributed system from its application logic. The broker hides and controls the communication between the objects or components of the distributed system. On the client side, the broker establishes the distributed calls and then forwards them to the server. On the server side, it receives the request and establishes a call from it, which it then executes on a server object. In the same way the broker returns the response to the client. The broker takes over all details of the distributed communication, such as establishing the connection, marshaling the message (converting the data sent into the message format), etc., and hides these details from the client and the distributed object as far as possible.
Consequences:	A broker has the advantage that it abstracts from and simplifies distributed communication. The broker infrastructure can be reused by different distributed applications. Since the broker is responsible for finding the server or the distributed object via a symbolic name or an ID, it allows transparency of the location at which the distributed object is really situated in the network.
	A broker architecture typically has slightly worse performance and consumes more resources than a well-designed, distributed architecture in which static, distributed objects are connected directly to the network. A broker has a certain complexity that must be understood. For very simple applications, for example, in the area of embedded systems, more simple architectures may bring the same benefits as a broker architecture but are easier to maintain and to understand. For most other distributed systems, such as in the enterprise domain, the use of a broker is recommended.

Figure 6.3-7 gives an overview of the broker architecture (for more details, see [Buschmann et al. 1996; Völter et al. 2004]). You can see how a client communicates with a distributed object "virtually," but instead of addressing the object directly, directs the request to the broker.

Broker: Example architecture

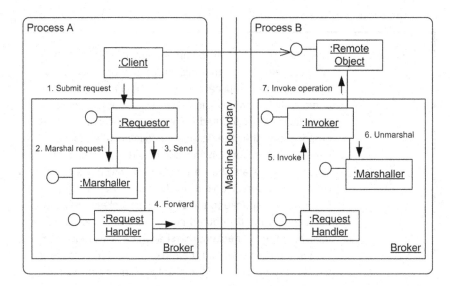

Figure 6.3-7: Example architecture of a broker for distributed objects

The broker contains a requestor, which, using a marshaller, converts the request into a form that can be transferred by the network. On the server side, again using a marshaller, the message is converted into a call and used by an invoker to call the distributed object. What you can clearly see here is that the broker pattern is made up of many other patterns that resolve the different individual tasks of the broker.

Proxy use in a broker

The proxy pattern described above is also often used in a broker. In order for the client to be able to access the interface of the distributed object, it requires a local placeholder that implements the same interface and forwards the call to the requestor. The client proxy [Völter et al. 2004], a variant of the proxy pattern for distributed object systems, takes over this task.

6.3.5 Pattern Languages

Complex pattern relationships

An individual pattern describes a solution to an individually recurring problem. However, in most use cases, the situation is more complex. This applies in classic architecture as well as in software architecture and other fields of application of patterns. Designing a software architecture typically involves several design problems that frequently occur together and are strongly related. For example, a pattern can be part of the solution of another pattern, or the context of a pattern is a situation in which another pattern was applied. Therefore, patterns are often described together, rather than isolated from one another. We can differentiate between the following ways of describing related patterns:

> *Related patterns:* In the simplest form, these relationships occur in individual patterns if these patterns are related to one or more other patterns. For ex-

ample, a pattern can describe which other patterns are alternatives or which other patterns are often applied in the same context.

> *Composite patterns:* A stronger type of pattern relationship is represented by composite patterns. These consist of one or more other patterns and add an increment to these individual solutions. An example of a composite pattern is the broker pattern described above. It is composed of a number of individual patterns in the area of design of distributed object systems.

> *Pattern systems:* Some authors describe pattern systems that, for example, are applied in the same domain or fulfill another classification criterion. One example is the POSA book [Buschmann et al. 1996], which describes a system of patterns in the field of software architecture.

> *Pattern languages:* In his original pattern definition, Alexander [Alexander 1977] strives for deeper relationships between the patterns than simple pattern systems. These deeper pattern relationships are described in pattern languages. We will look at these in more detail in the rest of this section.

A pattern language is a collection of semantically related patterns that offer solution principles for problems in a specific context. In particular, pattern languages focus on the relationships of the patterns in the language. In concrete terms, this means that the pattern descriptions are highly integrated—for example, by the fact that the context of one pattern takes up another pattern and that special value is placed on the description of the pattern interactions.

Pattern languages

Furthermore, Alexander [Alexander 1977] promotes a "generative" nature of a pattern language. The idea is that when you apply a pattern, a new context, in which other patterns of the pattern language can be applied, arises "automatically." Thus a better architecture arises step-by-step. Every incremental step in the further development leads to an improvement in the quality of the entire architecture. An example for the "generative" nature of a pattern language is given later in this section.

The domain-specific nature of a pattern language is very important for its application. In collections of individual patterns, it is often very difficult to determine when to use which pattern. A pattern language makes this consideration easier, since it presents the patterns in a coherent form. After every pattern application, the pattern description immediately shows which other patterns can be applied next, which patterns are alternatives to the given pattern, etc. These relationships are known as *pattern sequences*. The main idea behind this form of description is that the number of possible combinations of patterns in a pattern language is enormous, but the number of combinations that work is low.

Pattern sequences

Figure 6.3-8 shows an example of an extract from a pattern language that operates in the domain "development of distributed object systems" [Völter et al. 2004]. This means that this pattern language primarily describes the structure of OO-RPC middleware, such as CORBA, web service frameworks, .NET remoting,

Example of a pattern language

Java RMI, and many others. The illustration shows a section of this pattern language that is concerned with the basic patterns for realizing a broker architecture.

Using this example we can also explain the "generative" nature of the pattern language in more detail. If, for example, you begin an architecture design with the provision of a remote object, then you create a context in which you need an invoker to call remote objects. The invoker must be addressed from the client and must receive messages that both communication partners understand. This is the context in which you can apply the marshaller and requestor. On the other hand, both the client and the server must be connected to the network and operating system resources must be used efficiently, which leads to the use of client and server request handlers. In many cases the client should be able to refer to the interface of the remote object. This is described by the interface description and supported on the client side with a client proxy. Finally, the distributed errors must be handled and forwarded between the client and server, which leads to the use of the remoting error pattern.

From this example you can see that the patterns in this pattern language are closely related and their step-by-step integration leads to the realization of a complex broker architecture.

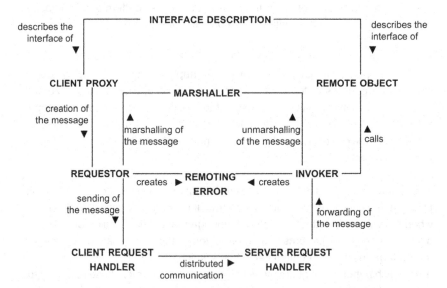

Figure 6.3-8: Overview of an extract of a pattern language for distributed object systems

Description of the pattern language example

The basic architecture of a typical broker therefore comprises a series of patterns. Firstly, the client proxy provides the interface of the remote object, as mentioned in the example above. The server developers can deliver this client proxy to the clients.

As an alternative that is often realized in the area of distributed systems, the client proxy can also be created on the client side. In order to realize this alternative, the client must know what the interface of the remote object is like—otherwise it is not possible to create the correct type of client proxy. The pattern interface description provides this information by describing the public interface of a remote object.

The requestor is responsible for creating the message and triggering the sending of the message. It must also wait for the result for the client. The client can also use the requestor directly, but in doing so it loses the call transparency that the client proxy pattern offers. Therefore, if you require call transparency, you should use a client proxy. The client proxy then uses the requestor internally. The client request handler is responsible for transferring the message via the network efficiently.

On the server side, the server request handler receives the message. It "listens" at the network port and waits for incoming messages. When messages come in, the server request handler forwards them to an invoker. The invoker transforms the message into a call again and thus calls the remote object.

The requestor and invoker use a marshaller for marshalling and unmarshalling the message automatically.

Errors that cannot occur in local calls can occur in the network and during the distributed call, for example, network failure. These special errors are forwarded by remoting errors that can be created anywhere in the call chain.

This brief outline should be sufficient to represent an extract from the architecture pattern language for distributed object systems. Actually, the pattern language describes a number of other patterns that occur in every broker architecture.

The role of the pattern in pattern languages

As the brief example clearly shows, the patterns in a pattern language normally describe *roles* rather than building blocks of a system. In some of the patterns mentioned above, some systems will contain exactly one building block that implements this pattern. However, the patterns are often distributed across several classes or an implementing class implements several patterns.

Despite this it is still easy to find the above-mentioned patterns in almost every OO-RPC middleware such as CORBA, web service frameworks, .NET remoting, Java RMI, etc. It is also easy to recognize the sequences and alternatives, i.e., how the patterns are related.

These are all decisive advantages in the application of pattern languages compared to the use of individual, isolated patterns. Pattern languages are thus becoming increasingly dominant in architecture pattern literature.

6.3.6 Summary

**Summary:
Architecture tactics, styles, and patterns**

> Requirement patterns describe when to use the pattern and how to write requirements based on it.
> A tactic is a design decision that influences the realization of the reaction of a quality attribute scenario.
> The prerequisite for using tactics is the analysis of the quality attributes. A suitable means for this is quality attribute scenarios.
> Quality attribute scenarios can be divided into scenario types according to quality attributes. Examples are: availability scenarios, changeability scenarios, performance scenarios, etc.
> An architecture style is a pattern of a structural organization of a family of systems.
> Architecture styles and architecture patterns are very similar concepts.
> A pattern is a three-part rule that expresses the relationship between a certain context, a certain system of forces which occurs repeatedly in that context, and a certain software configuration which allows these forces to resolve themselves.
> Patterns express the considerations behind a design decision and the consequences of such a decision.
> In the context of software architecture, both design patterns and architecture patterns are very important.
> A pattern language is a collection of patterns that solves the problems in a specific domain and/or in a specific context.
> In particular, pattern languages focus on the relationships of the patterns in the language.

6.4 Basic Architectures

Overview

This section covers some fundamental basic architectures that are used in many systems. To structure architecture, these basic architectures use the various architecture means discussed in the previous sections. They therefore represent more concrete architecture means that you can use to structure entire systems. We will first discuss simple basic architectures based on individual patterns and styles, such as layered architecture. For more details about the basic patterns and styles covered in this section, see [Avgeriou and Zdun 2005]. We will then discuss "larger" basic architectures, such as service-oriented architectures or security architectures.

Monolith

The "worst" form of architecture structure is often a *monolith*. In a monolith, the complete architecture specified during the design process is summarized in one single system building block. This type of architecture can only rarely implement the architecture principles from Section 6.1 well. For example, since you cannot consider different building blocks separately in a monolithic architecture structure, you cannot achieve separation of concerns. The same applies to loose coupling: in a monolith no building blocks are coupled, and therefore you cannot suitably implement loose coupling. Below we will explain some prototypical solutions that use a different architecture structure to the monolith. For suitable use cases, the basic architectures covered below implement the architecture principles better than a monolith.

Legacy systems that have often grown over decades are a typical example of monoliths. Here the business logic is often hard-coded and difficult to find because it is spread over the code and not documented. Typical symptoms of legacy systems as monoliths are:

> It is difficult to adjust the business logic to new requirements.
> Tests for new releases require a lot of effort and are long and drawn out.
> Small changes involve a large effort and endanger the stability of the entire system.
> Employees adapt their work processes to the behavior of the software and not vice versa.
> Only a few long-standing employees really know the software because the documentation is insufficient.

Example: Legacy systems as monoliths

One fundamental question you have to consider in deciding against a monolithic architecture is centralization versus decentralization. At many levels of the architecture design you have to ask yourself: Is it better to bundle a concern in one system building block (centralization) or to spread it over multiple system building blocks (decentralization)? The monolith represents an extreme form of centralization: everything is bundled in one single system building block. However, you generally have to weigh up centralization and decentralization and come to a compromise.

Compromise: Centralization versus decentralization

One clear advantage of decentralization is the often lower hardware costs. If you decentralize across several computers, then you can usually access more cost-effective hardware than if you bundle the software building blocks on a computer with great performance but which is therefore very expensive (the opposite can also be true). Decentralized architectures are also more flexible with regard to change and can cope better when individual building blocks fail, since usually the same building blocks are present redundantly. It is sometimes also simpler to structure the architecture based on tasks, since you can model the system landscape structurally following the responsibilities within the enterprise (or system environment).

Advantages of decentralization

In contrast, the advantages of centralization lie where the focus is on central tasks. For example, it is considerably easier to ensure the following in one central system: high data and IT security, logging, checks, monitoring, simple delivery of new software building blocks, etc. As a result, there are advantages with regard

Advantages of centralization

to the costs for personal supervision. Therefore, typical central tasks are: management of larger databases, network control, control of transaction processing, continual checking of hardware and software in the entire network, and delivery and provision of software building blocks. Further advantages of centralization are in some cases lower hardware costs (for example, when applications can be pooled on hardware) and lower costs for hardware energy consumption.

One important influencing factor in weighing up between centralization and decentralization is the use case in question. For example, if you are thinking of centralizing an enterprise-wide application system, then you will have to involve more sub-areas, systems, and stakeholders in the decision than if the centralization or decentralization relates only to one project or one department. However, as part of a consideration of an entire system at a physical and logical level, centralization and decentralization do not exclude each other—you can often use them in combination to take advantage of synergy effects. For example, you can implement an LDAP service on a distributed basis from a physical point of view, but logically a central directory service is provided.

Overview of basic architectures

The brief discussion of basic architectures below can only give an overview of important examples in current practice—the information should not be considered exhaustive. There are many other suitable basic architectures. Figure 6.4-1 gives an overview of the basic architectures covered.

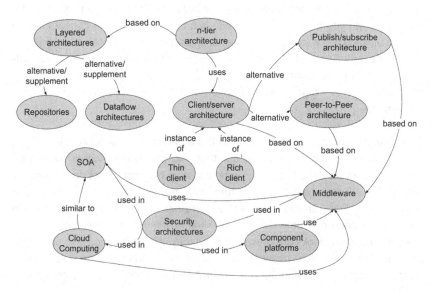

Figure 6.4-1: Overview of basic architectures

6.4.1 Layered Architectures

Layers pattern

One fundamental question about structuring architectures that affects both functional and non-functional requirements is how to divide a system into groups of similar functions or responsibilities. The Layers pattern [Buschmann et al. 1996] and the Layers style [Shaw and Garlan 1996] describe a typical solution.

You apply layers in situations where a group of building blocks is dependent on another group of building blocks in order to provide their function, and this group is in turn dependent on another group of building blocks, etc. The Layers pattern states that every layer groups a number of building blocks and the layer above this group provides services through interfaces. In every layer the building blocks of that layer can interact freely. Between two layers, communication may only take place via the specified interfaces. Generally speaking, you should not bridge layers. This means that layer "n" only calls the services of layer "n-1" but not those of "n-2."

The main aims of creating layers are to increase the modifiability of the system, to design the system so that it is portable, and/or to increase the reusability of the layers.

Figure 6.4-2 shows a schematic example of a layered architecture.

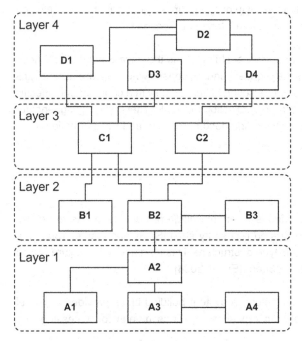

Figure 6.4-2: *Example of a layered architecture. [Avgeriou and Zdun 2005]*

6.4.2 Dataflow Architectures

Another fundamental type of structuring is along the dataflows of an architecture. This type of architecture is particularly useful if you can split a complex task into a series of simple tasks and then map it as a combination of independent calls. It is difficult to achieve this with a monolithic building block because it would quickly become overcomplicated and thus modifiability and reusability would suffer.

Batch sequential style

One solution is the Batch sequential style [Shaw and Garlan 1996]. Here you split a task into partial steps and then implement them as separate and independent building blocks. Every partial step runs to completion and then calls the next step in a sequence of steps. In every step the data is used for calculations and the results data is forwarded to the next step as a whole.

Pipes and filters pattern/style

Batch sequential is the basis for simple dataflow architectures. Sometimes there is an additional requirement for streams of data to be provided. Different clients also require different combinations of processing steps. In this case it makes sense to use the Pipes and filters pattern [Buschmann et al. 1996] or the Pipes and filters style [Shaw and Garlan 1996]. Here too, you split a task into sequential partial steps and implement them in separate building blocks (the filters). Filters have a number of input and output interfaces that you can use to combine the filters flexibly using so-called pipes. Each pipe realizes a datastream between two filters. Filters consume and deliver data incrementally. This means that different filters can potentially work on tasks in parallel. Pipes act as data buffers between filters. For more details on Pipes and filters, see Section 6.3.

Example: Servlet filter

One example of a Pipes and filters architecture is the Java Servlet filter. These filters allow you to access the requests and responses when you are accessing a web resource. You can configure several filters flexibly in a chain for one specific web resource. Examples for the application of Servlet filters are logging, encryption and decryption, compression and decompression, and transformation (e.g., from XML using XSLT).

6.4.3 Repositories

Shared repository style

The main task of repositories is to enable different building blocks to access data simultaneously. The Shared repository style [Shaw and Garlan 1996] is a fundamental example of this type of structure. This fundamental structure is also described in the Repository pattern [Evans 2004].

In a shared repository architecture, a system building block provides a central data storage unit. The shared repository provides means for accessing and changing the data, for example, an API or a query language. It must ensure efficient access to the data for clients, be scalable, and guarantee the consistency of the data. For example, the repository can offer suitable locking functions or transaction mechanisms to exclude the data being changed by two clients simultaneously. Other functions, such as security functions, can also be offered.

Figure 6.4-3 shows a schematic example of a repository architecture.

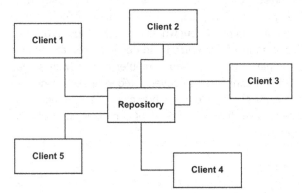

Figure 6.4-3: *Example of a repository architecture. [Avgeriou and Zdun 2005]*

A simple example of a repository architecture is a metadata repository for an enterprise application integration (EAI) solution. EAI solutions often require data transformations that are performed by transformation tools (also referred to as mapping). The different distributed building blocks of the EAI architecture require uniform and consistent information about the data sources and data destinations of a transformation, the transformation rules, and the dataflow rules. It must also be possible to change this information and these rules concurrently. You can solve this by using a central metadata repository that can be accessed by all building blocks of the EAI architecture and that provides services, such as locking for concurrent changes.

Example: EAI metadata repository

6.4.4 Client/Server Architecture

The client/server model, also documented as an architecture style (see [Shaw and Garlan 1996]), has a significant importance in modern software architecture. Here the user operates application programs (clients) on his or her computer and these programs access the resources of the server. The resources are managed, shared, and made available centrally. As you can see in Figure 6.4-4, the client/server model is based on a simple request-response schema. This means that files no longer have to be transferred as a whole—requests can be placed specifically. For example, the server often accesses a (relational) database and executes a query specified in the client's request.

Client/server model

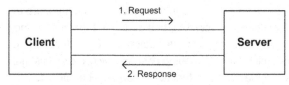

Figure 6.4-4: *Client/server model*

Note that you also have to consider and make decisions about centralization versus decentralization in a "larger" or "smaller" context. For example, if the system building blocks are not individual computers but whole networks, there are similar considerations and mostly a mix of centralized and decentralized elements. Figure 6.4-5 shows an example of a centralized computer center (with some central servers Z1 ... Z3) that is connected to several decentralized branches and that offers centralized server services to these branches. Each branch has one or more centralized servers. In turn, the individual computer connections realize the client/server model.

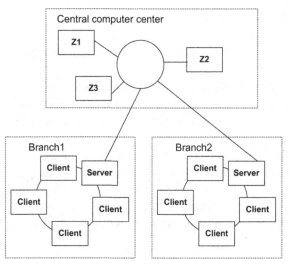

Figure 6.4-5: *Example of a computer network*

6.4.5 n-Tier Architecture

Two-tier architecture

A tier is a means for structuring the distribution of software building blocks on hardware building blocks. A tier contains cohesive system building blocks (software and hardware building blocks) that are connected via a network. The classic client/server model, for example, is based on a two-tier architecture: the user interface is usually located on the user's PC and the database management is on a more powerful computer that serves several clients. The calculations and the process control are thus split between the client and the server. For example, the database server provides stored procedures and database triggers for executing calculations on the database. Of course, there are also two-tier architectures (and general n-tier architectures) that do not use a database, but we use this typical example here for illustration.

Two-tier architectures work well up to a certain number of clients working simultaneously on the database. However, with a very high number of users, the performance decreases quickly. There is also a dependency to the manufacturer of the database: since the database procedures are proprietary and dependent on the manufacturer, changing the database usually involves considerable effort and costs.

Three-tier architectures resolve this problem by introducing an intermediate tier between the client and the database server. The intermediate tier takes over tasks such as queuing, scheduling of requests, handling requests according to priority, and so on. Central tasks of the application logic are also implemented here. There are a number of standard solutions that realize this tier, such as transaction processing monitors, messaging servers, application servers, and others. The additional tier improves performance in the case of a larger number of clients and increases the flexibility. Figure 6.4-6 shows a typical three-tier architecture.

Three-tier architectures

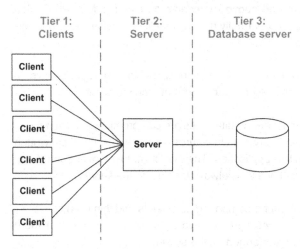

Figure 6.4-6: Three-tier architecture

Two-tier architectures and three-tier architectures are special cases of n-tier architectures. Sometimes architectures have more than two or three tiers. This is often because of high loads, security requirements, reliability requirements, or similar requirements for specific quality attributes of the architecture. For example, you can create the server in the intermediate tier redundantly to achieve higher performance, reliability, or load balancing. To do this, you have to insert an additional instance that takes over the distribution of requests to the redundant architecture, thus creating a four-tier architecture. You can also create the data-

n-tier architectures

base redundantly on the data tier. You use this type of architecture in particular if a distributed architecture has particularly high requirements for load figures, availability, or reliability. Another possible use case for n-tier architectures is that an entire application should run on different, dedicated hardware building blocks. For further discussion of this topic, see [Dyson and Longshaw 2004], where this type of architecture is covered in detail.

Connecting multiple three-tier architectures also leads to n-tier architectures with higher numbers. A server is often a three-tier architecture client of another server in another three-tier architecture. From the point of view of the original client, the entire architecture is then a four-tier architecture.

6.4.6 Rich Client versus Thin Client

Rich client and thin client

A central question in the design of a client/server architecture is how to split up the functionality between the client and the server. This question is known as the decision between a rich client and a thin client.

The mainframe model outlined above represents an extreme form of the thin client: the terminal as client has virtually no functionality. All calculations are performed on the mainframe.

The introduction of PCs and the file sharing concept led to a strong emphasis on the rich client: almost all calculations were performed on the client.

The client/server model and n-tier architectures are compromises between these two extremes. The first client/server architectures usually had a rich client written specifically for the respective application. The rich client takes over some functionality, but part of the functionality is always located on the server.

Weighing up: Rich client or thin client

There are a number of criteria for comparing rich clients and thin clients:
> A thin client generally places a greater load on the *server resources* as more calculations have to be performed on the server.
> The *network load* is a further important criterion, as is the related *client performance*. With every network request you have to wait considerably longer than for a local request. Therefore, the type and quantity of data to be transferred is important in deciding which model is more suitable with regard to network load and performance.
> With thin clients, you are generally more dependent on the *network operability*. In contrast, with rich clients it is usually easier to provide a local working environment. Therefore, rich clients are often more suitable for laptops for

field employees, for example. However, the disadvantage here is that under some circumstances, the data has to be replicated and synchronized.

> Last but not least, *client maintenance and delivery* are important topics: central software building blocks can be replaced on the server to which the developers have direct access. In contrast, to update the client, you may have to access a number of workplace computers, which means a considerably higher effort.

As a result of the last point in particular, the success of the World Wide Web meant that in many cases, the web browser was used as a thin client solution. An *application server* contains the complete application logic and the users use only a standard browser to access the applications. This has the advantage that you have very few clients to maintain. The disadvantage of this solution is that you are restricted to the functionality of the browser—in particular the restricted user interface—and therefore have to send every request via the network. This means that the work is difficult without network access. One consequence is also that the performance of the application tends to be low.

Web browser as thin client and application server

A more recent trend is the return to rich clients because the thin client technologies based on browsers do not satisfy all requirements. An important driving factor here is the so-called rich client platforms, such as Eclipse [Eclipse 2010a]. They offer automatic delivery and updates of clients in a standard environment but are equally as good in the user environment of a classic desktop application.

Rich client platforms

Web 2.0 or Ajax represent a middle course between the two alternatives. Ajax is the option of performing asynchronous queries with Javascript and thus reloading and changing content without the user having to switch web page. Parts of the tasks are performed in the browser, but the scripts that implement these tasks are provided by the server. The term "Web 2.0" refers less to specific technologies than to specific types of web applications in which users create and edit content themselves, for example, with Ajax or similar technologies. These web applications are often social software that allows users to network with one another.

Alternative: Web 2.0/ Ajax

6.4.7 Peer-To-Peer Architecture

Client/server is an architecture style that is a specialization of the general explicit invocation style [Shaw and Garlan 1996]. This means that the client communicates with the server via direct, explicit calls and receives responses to these calls from the server. One alternative is the peer-to-peer style [Shaw and Garlan 1996], which also specializes explicit invocation but focuses on direct communication between clients rather than communication via a central service.

Peer-to-peer style

P2P model

Peer-to-peer (P2P) uses a series of equal peers. In the pure P2P architecture structure there is no central server. Every peer can offer and consume services in the network. The entire status of the system is spread over the peers. Internally, P2P systems are realized partly with standard middleware, but the user of a P2P system is not aware of this.

In the P2P architecture, you can add or remove a service at any time. Clients must therefore find out which services are currently available before using a service.

Not all P2P systems are "pure" P2P systems. Most systems are hybrids and use central servers for certain services, for example, as points of access into the network.

6.4.8 Publish/Subscribe Architecture

Publish/subscribe style and pattern

Publish/subscribe is a pattern [Buschmann et al. 1996] or style [Shaw and Garlan 1996] and represents an alternative to client/server and peer-to-peer. In contrast to client/server and peer-to-peer, publish/subscribe represents a form of the implicit invocation style [Shaw and Garlan 1996] rather than being based on the explicit invocation style [Shaw and Garlan 1996]. This means that calls are not sent directly between the communication participants; events are forwarded via an intermediary.

Publish/subscribe is dedicated to the problem that a series of clients has to be informed about runtime events. These events have a different nature to the direct, explicit invocations found in client/server and peer-to-peer: sometimes a series of clients must be informed actively about an event; in other cases, only a specific client is interested in the event. In contrast to the explicit invocation style, the producer and consumer of an event must be decoupled, for example, to ensure separate modifiability or so that a defined time can pass between the occurrence and the handling of the event.

Publish/subscribe enables the event consumer to register for specific event types. When such an event takes place, the event producer informs all registered consumers—for example, using a publish/subscribe system. The publish/subscribe system therefore decouples the producer and consumer of events.

6.4.9 Middleware

Once you have decided on one of the above-mentioned architecture alternatives (client/server, peer-to-peer, or publish/subscribe), you have to decide on the type of connection for the system building blocks. The most important architecture structures in this area are different middleware-based architectures. Below we will discuss communication middleware—referred to here as "middleware." (There are other forms of middleware, but we will not look at these in detail here.)

Middleware is a platform that offers applications services for all aspects of the distribution, such as distributed calls, efficient access to the network, transactions, and much more. The book *Distributed Systems* by Tanenbaum and van Steen [Tanenbaum and van Steen 2003] offers a general introduction to the topic "distributed systems." The information presented below is based on the introduction in the book *Remoting Patterns* [Völter et al. 2004], which introduces a pattern language for OO-RPC middleware systems that builds on the broker pattern [Buschmann et al. 1996] used as an example above (see Section 6.3). As a pattern, broker generally represents the architectural basis for most common middleware systems.

Architecture for distributed systems

Distributed systems are used in various areas of application. Many of the largest and most complex systems used today are distributed systems. Examples are Internet systems, telecommunications networks, business-to-business applications (B2B), international finance transactions, embedded systems, and many more.

In addition to distributed problems, such as the collaboration of spatially distributed partners via the network, there are many other reasons for selecting distributed architectures. For example, the performance and scalability of a distributed system can be considerably better than with a non-distributed system. A distributed system can therefore manage scenarios that involve system loads so high that an individual computer can no longer manage them cost-effectively. Alternatively, the error tolerance of the system can increase as a result of distribution: many error tolerance procedures are based on the physical redundancy of hardware units such as computers or processors—which in turn entails a distributed architecture.

However, compared to non-distributed systems, you have a series of "new" challenges to overcome if you give a system a distributed architecture. Important challenges are:

> *Network latency:* A distributed call requires considerably more time than a local call.
> *Predictability:* As a result of the latency and the possible failure of the network, it is also much more difficult to predict call times. Therefore, in distributed architectures that require real time behavior, it is a major challenge to guarantee this.

Challenges in distributed systems

> *Concurrency:* In contrast to single-processor systems, distributed systems have real concurrency. Therefore, you have to consider resulting problems such as non-determinism and deadlocks as early as the planning stage for a distributed architecture.

> *Scalability:* As a result of distribution, in many systems it is more difficult to predict when clients access the system and how many. Therefore, in distributed systems, you will tend to have to deal more with potential high load situations and ensure even more that the entire system is scalable.

> *Partial system failure:* Since several hardware and software elements are used together in a distributed system, you may face situations in which parts of the system fail but other parts continue to work. In these cases, the parts of the system that are still working can try to reconfigure the system such that it continues to work despite the partial system failure—this is, however, no trivial matter (see [Tanenbaum and van Steen 2003]).

Communication middleware

You could develop distributed systems based directly on the network APIs of the operating system—for example, with the TCP/IP protocols. However, the developer would then have to deal with all of the challenges detailed above himself. He would then probably lose sight of his actual task very quickly—to develop a functional, distributed system. Furthermore, good solutions for the above-mentioned challenges would probably not be reused.

A communication middleware dedicates itself to these problems. Its task is to take over the communication tasks transparently for the developer and to hide the complexity and heterogeneity of the underlying platform.

Figure 6.4-7 shows the structure of a middleware. The middleware is an additional software tier that sits between the distributed application and the APIs of the operating system. Clients and server applications usually must not bypass this tier to execute services of lower tiers directly—thus the middleware achieves transparency of the distribution tasks from the application view.

However, the middleware only makes the distribution as transparent as possible. Developers and architects must always bear the distribution aspect in mind because the application must often handle, for example, errors caused by a partial system failure of the network or a server directly. In the example "server failure," the client could contact a different server or simply forward an error message. The application logic of the client determines what should be done and therefore the middleware cannot take over this task transparently. It is the task of the middleware to return qualified error messages to the client or to enable the server to do this.

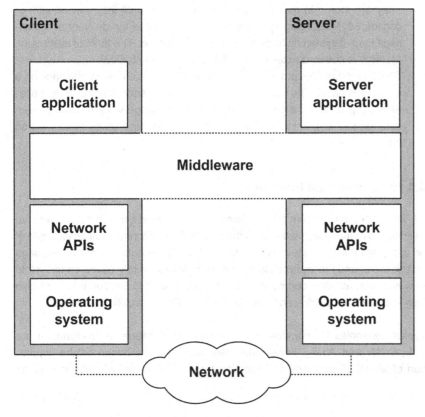

Figure 6.4-7: Schematic representation of a middleware architecture

A number of distribution styles are used in middleware systems today. From an historical point of view, the distributed calculation is based on simple *file transfer* (see the file sharing discussion above). This is now out of date for many of today's systems with high system loads since it leads to high latency and high resource usage. Most modern middleware systems are based on one or more of the following distribution styles [Völter et al. 2004]:

> *Remote procedure call (RPC) systems* use the known and for many developers familiar procedure abstraction in a distributed environment. A distributed procedure call can be executed very similarly to a local procedure call and the RPC middleware forwards it transparently from the client to the server. Several RPC systems support object-oriented abstractions—so-called OO-RPC systems. [Völter et al. 2004] covers the OO-RPC system in detail.

> *Messaging systems* send messages asynchronously (or also synchronously as an option) from a sender to one or more recipient systems. There are various message types, such as requests, responses, error messages, etc.

Distribution styles

They are stored in message queues temporarily until they can be sent or consumed. Messaging systems can thus guarantee the delivery of a message even if system failures occur from time to time. The topic of messaging systems is covered extensively in [Hohpe and Woolf 2003].

> *Shared repositories* provide different clients with a common dataspace on a distributed basis. The clients have read and write access to this dataspace.
> *Streaming systems* allow continuous data exchange via a datastream—in contrast to the discrete exchange of data in the three styles mentioned so far.

6.4.10 Component Platforms

Component platforms in the enterprise environment

We introduced component architectures as a concept in Section 6.2.3. Here we will discuss component platforms in the enterprise environment as an example of an important basic architecture. [Völter et al. 2002] contains a pattern language on this topic, and the information presented below is loosely based on this. Note however, that all other component approaches named in Section 6.2.3 are also very important in practice and belong to your software architect's "toolbox."

Typical examples for component platforms in the enterprise environment are JEE, CCM, and .NET. These component platforms are based on the separation of technical concerns and functional concerns for an information system.

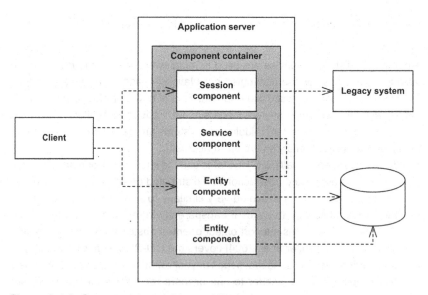

Figure 6.4-8: *Component container architecture*

Examples of technical concerns in the enterprise environment are distribution, security, persistence, transactions, concurrency, and resource management. In other environments, such as embedded systems, other technical concerns may be important. The component container—the central building block of the component platform—takes over the technical concerns automatically. This architecture is reflected in Figure 6.4-8.

Types of components

The functional requirements a component-based system must satisfy are realized through the components. In the component approaches mentioned, there is a differentiation between the different types of components that fulfill diverse tasks and have different lifetimes (the container also manages these lifetimes):

> *Entity components* represent persistent data. The container manages the persistence automatically. Entity components usually exist from the start of the application to its termination.
> *Session components* can hold a status during a user session. This means that their lifetime generally corresponds to a user session.
> *Service components* provide services that can be processed within a single call. Their lifetime thus corresponds to exactly one call.

Black box reuse

In contrast to object-oriented approaches, component-based systems use exclusively black box reuse based on the component interface. This means that the interaction between the components is realized by well-defined component interfaces and delegation to other components, without being dependent on concrete implementations of these components. You can therefore develop the implementations of the components further independently of one another and the implementations can support different versions of a component in parallel.

Components and middleware

Component platforms usually support a number of middleware systems for distributed communication, such as CORBA, RMI, or .NET. Many component platforms are integrated in existing application servers.

Pooling and passivation

In many situations, not all instances of a component can be held actively in the memory of the server since this would lead to resource problems. The container can assign any number of logical instances sequentially to a physical instance (so-called pooling of resources). It can also remove component instances temporarily not required from the memory and buffer them in a database. This is known as passivation. The component instances are reactivated automatically when they are required again. In order for this to work, the container must be able to control the lifecycle of the component instances. The components therefore provide so-called lifecycle operations, such as *activate, destroy, passivate,* etc.

For a deeper understanding of component platforms, we recommend the book *Server Component Patterns* [Völter et al. 2002].

6.4.11 Service-Oriented Architectures

Service-oriented architectures (SOA) and services

Service-oriented architectures (SOAs) are a basic architecture that represents the technically functional interfaces of software building blocks as reusable, distributed, loosely coupled, and standardized accessible services (see [Zdun et al. 2006] and [Zdun and Hendrich 2006]).

SOA key concepts

Figure 6.4-9 provides an overview of the key concepts of service-oriented architectures.

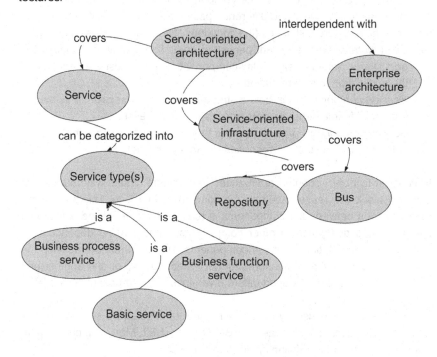

Figure 6.4-9: *Concept overview for service-oriented architectures*

In an SOA, services are generally distinguished by the following properties:

Properties of services

> Services generally have a lower level of detail than component interfaces and are structured more strongly than components with regard to their business relevance (see also component architectures in Section 6.4.10).

> Services communicate in a technology-independent and standardized way with synchronous or asynchronous messages.

> Services often permit anonymous use. That is, you do not know who is using the service. The service works as if it did not know its client. In other words: the client and the service are loosely coupled.

> To a certain degree, services are self-descriptive. This feature is frequently realized using metadata whose properties are determined using a lookup service.

> Services are ideally idempotent, without status, and completed transactionally. Idempotent generally describes operations that always lead to the same results, irrespective of how often they are repeated with the same data. Expressed mathematically: $an = a, n > 0$.

> Services consist of the service interface and the service implementation. The service interface has the character of a contract (see also *design by contract* in Section 6.1.6) and connects service consumers to service providers (see the architecture principle of loose coupling in Section 6.1.1). The service implementation is not part of the contract and is interchangeable when in keeping with interface commitments.

Figure 6.4-10 shows the structural key abstractions of an SOA. The process topological view used there underlines the intermediate character that helps the SOA systems to achieve loose coupling. The service consumer does not ask for a specific service from the service provider. The bus and repository building blocks are responsible for the communication performance when the service is called and for reporting the results, even though you could realize a simple SOA without this. The repository building block registers the service provider and supports complex searches for this service provider. The bus building block supports the reporting of messages and thus switches between all other building blocks of an SOA. Using the SOA approach enables you to detach non-functional aspects from the service consumer and provider. Examples of such non-functional aspects are security, logging, transformation of messages, and content-based forwarding of messages. The bus and repository thus offer a configurable access to the above-mentioned aspects. This enables you to implement very elegant fundamental architecture principles, for example, design for change as in Section 6.1.3, or separation of concerns as in Section 6.1.4. You can therefore separate the security requirement from the technical building blocks and make it accessible on the bus and repository basis (in a way that it can be configured).

Four key abstractions of an SOA

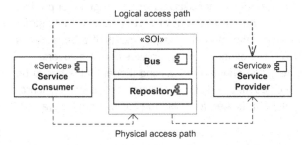

Figure 6.4-10: Key abstractions of a service-oriented architecture

SOA compared to SOI

An SOA focuses mainly on the level of the technical architecture of an application (see also Section 3.2). However, the SOA approach suggests the use of intermediary middleware for the bus and repository building blocks. Various terms are used today for middleware that is specially tailored to the requirements of SOA solutions. A more product-independent term is service-oriented infrastructure (SOI). Another term used very often, with almost the same meaning, is enterprise service bus (ESB).

With reference to the key abstractions of an SOA depicted in Figure 6.4-10, an SOI is restricted to the bus and repository building blocks. In the meantime however, a correspondingly enhanced SOI includes further building blocks, such as a process engine. From a technical point of view, you can realize a basic SOA based on component platforms such as CORBA, RMI, or .NET, which possess all rudimentary bus and repository building blocks. However, special service-oriented infrastructures offer functions that exceed the capabilities of the aforementioned component platforms:

> The creation of new, more complex services through orchestration. Complex services arise based on simpler services, whereby the execution of the complex service is by means of an interpreter or conductor. An important standard for the orchestration of web services is the Business Process Execution Language (BPEL). This capability is realized by process engines.

> Support from Internet standards such as web services, SOAP, and XML. You use these standards to implement remote service calls with regard to interface abstraction, call log, and format description.

> Embedding and support from enterprise application integration (EAI).

> Injection points for aspects such as security, content-based message forwarding, or message filtering. See also Section 6.2.7.

> Building blocks for implementing SOA governance, service management, and service versioning.

> Business activity monitoring (BAM) building blocks to support continual process analysis and optimization.

Enterprise service bus (ESB)

Enterprise service bus (ESB) is a product category that has developed in the industry for broad areas of service-oriented infrastructures. Although other product categories can be classified in the environment of service-oriented infrastructures, a considerable proportion of the integration requirements of larger systems are implemented using ESBs. The spectrum of capabilities of ESBs covers:

> A results-driven and message-oriented processing model that is based on document standards such as XML and supports synchronous and asynchronous communication. An ESB is therefore also the basis of an EDA (event-driven architecture) .

> Content-based message forwarding and filter functions that ensure that messages always reach the correct recipient. See also Message-Oriented Middleware in Section 6.7.1.3.
> Transformation functionalities that support changing the format and content of messages.
> A number of interfaces for common middleware systems, databases, and standard applications. ESBs frequently offer converters or adapters that support mapping between standard interfaces.

An ESB is managed on a distributed basis and is not based on a central control. However, the ESBs of different manufacturers are often realized in very different ways technically. The basis of the common ESBs today is mostly coupled to the product history of the respective manufacturer. However, the product approaches known today can be assigned to one of the following categories:
> Application-server based ESBs
> ESBs based on EAI frameworks or message-oriented middleware (see Message-Oriented Middleware in Section 6.7.1.3)
> ESBs based on XML appliances. An XML appliance is a separate computer system that can exchange XML-based messages with other systems, whereby these messages are forwarded in particular content-based, securely, and efficiently.

ESB implementations

Beyond their implementation, concrete ESBs can be very different with regard to their functionality and their operating characteristics (e.g., economic usability or operational security). For manufacturers that already have an extensive middleware range, ESB-type products complete the corresponding middleware packages.

The horizontal structure of an SOA discussed up to this point is primarily a runtime consideration of the SOA architecture approach. Service-oriented infrastructures are important in this consideration. However, SOAs also have a deeper vertical structure. An SOA frequently covers several tiers. As the example in Figure 6.4-11 shows, these levels can be different with regard to granularity, freedom from functional contexts, number of relationships to other services, or also with regard to the average frequency of change of the respective services.

Vertical levels of an SOA

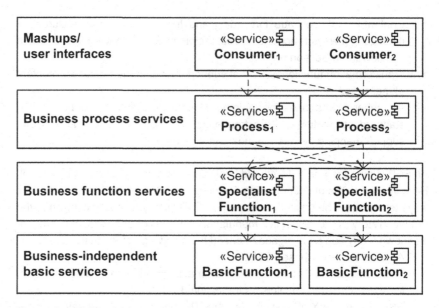

Figure 6.4-11: *Vertical structure of an SOA*

Non-functional requirements placed on an SOA or individual services, such as reusability, must therefore be assessed based on the level. This makes it easier to reuse business-independent basic services in different business contexts. For a business process service, however, reusability will be much more difficult to achieve.

SOA and enterprise architecture

The SOA approach is increasingly replacing the "application" concept in favor of the "service" concept. This is primarily because services should be much more finely grained and should be able to exist independently of the business context. This is good and desired and increases the possibility of reusing a corresponding service more easily. However, at the same time, this demand increases the complexity of an SOA. A service that was previously only used and only existed as part of an individual application should now be capable of being used outside the boundaries of this application. Applications that accommodated such services previously, however, were never just soulless function containers—they always restricted the room for interpretation to which embedded services related as well. A business function could relate simple questions such as "What is a product?" or "What does the concept 'customer' mean to me?" to the restricted room for interpretation in which it existed. Note here that it is difficult to achieve integration at a high semantic level, which means that you have to integrate heterogeneous "customer concepts" later. If, in the SOA sense, you start to place such a business function alone and remove it from the context of closed applications, the room for interpretation expands significantly—in many cases on a large scale. For example, it stretches to the whole department, the area, the enterprise, or a partner network under consideration. If terms such as "customer" or "product" previously had to be explained in the context of individual applications, you now have to do this for the extended scope. Since a cross-system understanding of basic concepts is the responsibility of enterprise architecture, the success of a comprehensive SOA initiative created is directly linked to the enterprise architecture topic (see also Enterprise Architecture in Section 3.2).

Up to this point we have investigated the topology and non-functional aspects of SOA. One of the greatest challenges for you as an architect, however, is the relevant specialist or functional decomposition of the problem. For example, you must decide how to split the entire solution space of processes and applications into relevant part solutions or services. The optimization goal that you will often follow in your decomposition approach is to be able to react to future changes in the specification easily and with little effort (see also *design for change* in Section 6.1.3). However, you could also ask yourself how you should design a specific service interface to achieve high reusability for this service. You share the responsibility for answering such questions appropriately to the problem with the experts from the relevant business domains. The quality of any given SOA design, more than with other basic architectures, depends on the functional approach, understanding, and experience of the experts involved.

SOA model development

We can generally identify the following procedures for modeling the solution space:

> *Top-down approach:* In the top-down approach, you start with given processes and identify the functional software building blocks necessary to realize these processes.
> *Bottom-up approach:* In the bottom-up approach, you start with the number of software building blocks already available and try to map these into new application contexts.
> Finally, the *meet-in-the-middle* approach connects the top-down approach to the bottom-up approach. From the top down you determine the functional requirements. From the bottom up you take stock of existing services. Based on this information, you can determine missing functions and plan their realization. This procedure is explained in detail in the Business-Driven Service pattern [Zdun and Hendrich 2006].

A typical situation in which an SOA can be used meaningfully is the fusion of two enterprises. These situations frequently involve different infrastructures, programming languages, component platforms, middleware systems, etc. In the en-

Usage scenarios of an SOA

terprises concerned, a number of business processes have often already been defined and implemented. Although the heterogeneity will tend to increase at infrastructure level, the business processes of the enterprises concerned will usually overlap considerably. All of these software building blocks have to somehow be integrated, sorted out, or replaced. Such heterogeneous situations at technical and functional levels are not restricted to enterprise fusions: there are many examples in which this form of functional overlapping or infrastructural heterogeneity can already be observed between individual departments of one and the same enterprise. As long as the departments have nothing to do with one another, this is not a serious problem. However, if the business fields, business constraints, or legal constraints suddenly change and a tight networking of the departments mentioned is regarded as critical for business, then this situation is hardly different to a situation with fusions.

Further examples in which SOAs can be used meaningfully:
>   Development of a mashup based on web services to realize a requirement in an enterprise quickly.
>   Reuse of a currency conversion service implemented in an enterprise. This scenario reduces redundancies as well as implementation, test, and maintenance costs.
>   Making the functionality of a legacy system (e.g., AS 400) accessible via web services to protect investments made.
>   Realization of the functional connection to a business partner via an agreed service interface. This approach allows the enforcement of rules directly on the call path and thus outside of the business solutions involved in the enterprise.

6.4.12 Security Architectures

Security as a distributed aspect

Before considering the topic of security architectures in more depth, it is important to understand that security is a so-called crosscutting concern. From the view of a software architect [Schumacher et al. 2005], this means that the security architecture of an application is not completely absorbed in the software architecture itself. The security aspect is in fact a high-grade distributed aspect. It is realized across several system building blocks that cannot be directly attributed to the software architecture of applications under consideration. Some examples of such system building blocks are firewalls, public key infrastructures (PKI), reverse proxies, web access management solutions (WAM), and directory services.

The term "security architecture" thus refers to:
>   An application to be protected or made secure.

> Further system building blocks that do not belong to the application under consideration and are therefore assigned to the underlying security infrastructure.

Figure 6.4-12 provides an overview of the key concepts in the area of security architectures.

Key concepts of security architectures

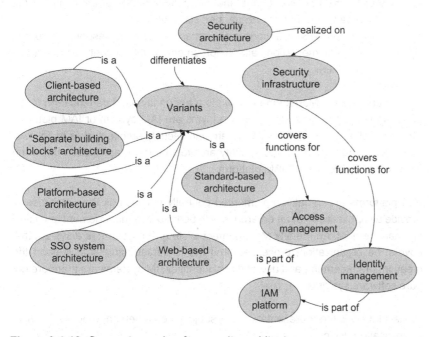

Figure 6.4-12: Concept overview for security architectures

Before you can design a comprehensive security architecture for an application, certain prerequisites must be fulfilled. The quality and completeness with which you can design a security architecture at application level depends heavily on the scope and extent to which the following prerequisites are met:

Prerequisites for security architectures

> Existence of security systems at all network levels, including operating systems
> Systems for user and identity management
> Systems for authentication
> Systems for authorization management
> Systems for privacy
> Systems for non-repudiation
> Systems for operation management and threat detection

In addition to the primary technical prerequisites, there are further organizational constraints that a security architecture must refer to:

> Information and protection class assignment in the enterprise. These assignments are made to formulate the protection requirement for information, data, and documents categorically and be able to enforce it in the IT systems.

> Guidelines for handling goods and information worthy of protection at the levels department, enterprise, partner, state, etc.

> Organizations and institutions in the enterprise that are responsible for the planning, implementation, and enforcement of the security architectures considered here.

Identity and Access Management (IAM)

Identity and Access Management (IAM) is a frequently used generic term for all of the above capabilities. Common synonyms are IAM system or IAM platform. The connection between the IAM system and security architecture is as follows: you design and implement the security architecture of an application based on the security systems of an IAM platform.

IAM platforms

IAM platforms are usually implemented centrally and across the enterprise to provide all applications of an enterprise with both access management and identity management. An Identity Management system (IM system) is a system that covers the organization, processes, and the IT infrastructure that support the creation, management, and use of digital identities. IM systems are therefore not pure software systems.

Digital identity

Digital identity is the representation of a subject, i.e., a person, process, service, or application using:

> Unique ID (e.g., artificial or derived key),
> One or more credentials (e.g., user name and password), and
> Further attributes (e.g., e-mail address, age, position)

Access Management (AM)

Access Management systems (AM systems) are systems that provide the applications supported with functions for identity verification (authentication) and access and authorization control.

Link between personnel systems and IAM platforms

Personnel management systems and processes are mostly realized directly based on IAM platforms. This means there is a very close link (at least for the IM area) between personnel management systems and security systems.

IAM goals

The goal of IAM systems is to give the correct people, groups, and applications timely access to the correct enterprise functions. Furthermore, the aim is to do this in a user-friendly, efficient, secure, and comprehensible way. IAM systems are thus not exclusively about increasing security for applications but rather also about designing basic access rules efficiently. Therefore, functions such as single sign-on (SSO), as well as role and group management, also belong to the area of IAM systems. In enterprises, IAM systems are motivated not only by security arguments but above all by the reduction of costs and redundancies. It is therefore better to integrate individual applications with an enterprise-wide and central user management than to provide a separate user management function for every enterprise system. One example for the reduction of costs is the introduction of a single sign-on solution. This ensures a big reduction in the number of support requests submitted to help desks and therefore reduces costs further.

The examples already show that applications with an enterprise-wide IAM platform must be integrated before the improvements described can be achieved. Security architects are responsible for implementing this integration.

Application integration with IAM platform

The most important performance characteristics or functions of security architectures are:

Performance characteristics of security architectures

> *Privacy:* This means that messages that are exchanged between two system building blocks cannot be read or understood on the communication path itself. It is achieved by encrypting the message before sending it and decrypting it directly before further processing on the part of the receiving system building block.

> *Integrity:* This requires that it must not be possible to change messages on the communication path. The recipient has the guarantee that no unauthorized third party has changed the message while it was en route and then forwarded it. Integrity is usually realized through hashing procedures. Here, a hash value is calculated for the original message and sent with the message itself. The recipient calculates a comparative value based on the message received and then compares both hash values. If they match, everything is correct and proper. A difference in the values means that integrity has been breached.

> *Authentication:* The process of verifying identity. A user uses credentials to prove to the authentication function that he or she is who they claim to be. A widespread type of credential is the combination of user name and password.

> *Authorization:* The process of access control by means of a corresponding system building block. The identification of a user or system is the necessary prerequisite for the authorization step. The access control system can thus deny an identified user the execution of a function but simultaneously permit the user to read a value table.

> *Non-repudiation:* The ability to prove security-related events beyond doubt, i.e., in a court of law if necessary. This performance characteristic is fre-

quently realized using special access-protected journals, and in connection with corresponding transactions, sometimes also through digital signatures.

> *Intrusion protection:* The set of all measures that guarantee operating integrity and vitality. This includes providing an effective defense against attacks such as denial-of-service (DoS) attacks.

Further performance characteristics, which in part can be derived from the characteristics named above, are:
> Detection of security gaps and incidents
> Development and enforcement of security guidelines
> Single sign-on
> Role-based and group-based access models

Architecture approaches for security architectures

You can implement even a comparatively simple performance characteristic such as authentication in many different ways. For example, an application could save the IDs and passwords for all users in a separate database. The application could then use a dialog to request these two values from a user logging on in order to compare them with the entries in the database. If a corresponding entry exists, this means that the user was able to prove his or her identity. If this is not the case, the application would deny the user access.

In a completely different example, an application would have been able to delegate the authentication step to a central directory service instead of implementing it itself.

Below we will explain three of the most common types of security architecture today. Each type described covers all security performance characteristics—privacy, integrity, authentication, and authorization—but to a different degree.

Security architecture based on separate system building blocks

Figure 6.4-13 shows security architectures that are based on separate system building blocks. In this approach, all major security functions themselves are implemented. The authentication function is programmed in a method that performs a value check on the separate user database. The authorization function is implemented by reading role information for the identified users from a separate privilege database. Privacy is achieved by checking the access to the data systems and encrypting the data transport paths themselves. This type of security architecture is still very widespread. Many standard systems even implement their security architecture based on separate system building blocks. This is because they cannot assume that the required system building blocks are offered standardized and centralized in all target environments. However, security architectures of this type have many disadvantages. It is often difficult to integrate them with existing IAM systems. Often, the only integration option is to provision data from IAM systems in corresponding applications, which does, however, lead to tight coupling (see also loose coupling in Section 6.1.1). Even self-implemented encryption procedures rarely satisfy modern requirements. Here provisioning refers to the automation of all processes with regard to the creation, management, deactivation, and deletion of digital identities as well as their attributes and authorizations.

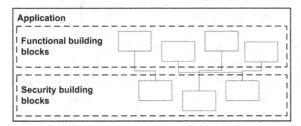

Figure 6.4-13: Security architectures based on separate security building blocks

Figure 6.4-14 shows an architecture that is based on standard services. This security architecture represents an improvement compared to the completely proprietary security architectures. Examples of this type of standard services are LDAP directory services or public key infrastructures (PKI). The advantage of security architectures based on standard services is that you can replace security-related system building blocks without having to adjust the application itself. This means that you can replace the implementation of an LDAP directory service that implements the authentication function at any time without having to adjust the application. One disadvantage is that, as before, you have to link security-relevant information at the application level. If, for example, user information is read from an LDAP directory, but data that describes the access authorization situation is read from a privilege database, then you have to link these two items of information at the level of the application.

Security architectures based on standard services

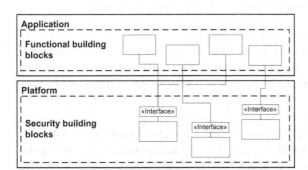

Figure 6.4-14: Security architectures based on standard services

**Security
architectures based
on component
platforms**

Security architectures that are based on component platforms overcome the disadvantages of the two categories previously discussed. As Figure 6.4-15 shows, component platforms define the supported applications compared to separate standards that bundle security functionality at a higher level of abstraction and integration. For example, they link authentication and authorization functionality. They themselves are based on standard services. This means that you can adjust their implementation without this having any effect on applications operated. One example of a corresponding component platform is JEE. The JEE server provides its applications with standardized (e.g., JAAS-API) security functions (e.g., authentication and authorization) and allows you to integrate security building blocks that lie outside the JEE server. One example is the connection of an external directory service based on JAAS-SPI. Component platforms also support the whole range of security functions of built-in user management and role management. They do this through the support of various authentication methods right up to encryption and signature functions. CORBA or the .NET platform from Microsoft are further examples of component platforms that define their own security standards.

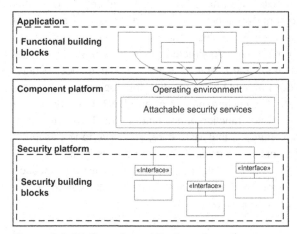

Figure 6.4-15: *Security architectures based on component platforms*

**Further security
architecture
approaches**

In addition to the approaches detailed above, there are a number of other security architecture approaches today. We will however only explain client-side architectures, web-centric architectures, and single sign-on architectures here in more detail.

**Client-side security
architectures**

The central element of client-side security architectures (see Figure 6.4-16) is a software building block that is installed on the user's end device (e.g., laptop) and that manages the access data for all registered applications. This building block activates itself when a user accesses a recognized application and it first and foremost takes over (virtually "from outside") the authentication of this user. Client-side security architectures are easy to implement and completely non-invasive. They simulate the user to all registered applications. Their biggest disadvantage is that their performance is restricted to authentications in which there is a real dialog with an end user. They do not cover situations in which a software building block has to authenticate itself to another software building block. Client-side architectures may be suitable for many software architectures from thin clients to rich clients, but they are limited by complex authentication processes. They also do not help to free applications from the burden of user management by, for example, centralizing this function.

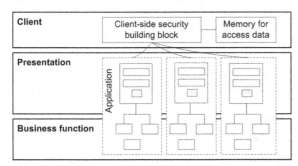

Figure 6.4-16: *Client-side security architectures*

Web-centric security architectures, also known as reverse proxy architectures and shown in Figure 6.4-17, are restricted to web applications. A web building block (reverse proxy) protects static and dynamic web applications. From the view of the software architect, their advantage lies in the fact that authentication, authorization, and the security session migrate to the system perimeter and no longer have to be programmed in the application itself. Web-centric security architectures can support open token standards as well as introduce token formats themselves. Applications are either directly integrated with the web-centric security building block or are operated on a component platform that has been integrated.

Web-centric security architectures

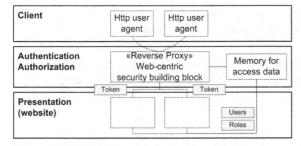

Figure 6.4-17: *Web-centric security architectures*

Single sign-on architectures

Single sign-on building blocks, as shown in Figure 6.4-18, are system building blocks at the security infrastructure level. They take over authentication, session management, and token management and verification. Ideally, the authentication step is part of the first system logon (e.g., logon to the operating system). As soon as the user has successfully logged on, the single sign-on building block creates a security session and issues the user with a key (token) that represents this session. From now on, the user no longer has to log on individually to applications that accept this key. The advantage and disadvantage of single sign-on architectures is their deep integration with corresponding applications.

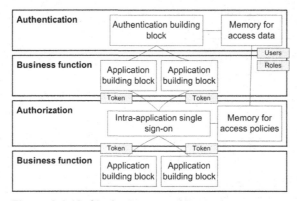

Figure 6.4-18: Single sign-on architectures

6.4.13 Cloud Computing Architectures

Cloud computing introduction

Cloud computing refers more to a set of characteristics that all IT systems implementing a cloud model share rather than a specific architecture. Furthermore, cloud computing is a rather orthogonal element to many of today's IT related themes. The most unique feature that the concept of cloud computing encompasses is its focus on all aspects of an IT system's operating model. Cloud computing has received a lot of attention for its promise to increase the transparency of IT services towards their actual consumers. In this section we will look at:

> Cornerstone elements of cloud computing
> Different types of clouds
> Cloud computing benefits and challenges
> Three distinct cloud computing adoption scenarios

Cloud computing definition

Most definitions of cloud computing are based on the set of key characteristics below. Any IT system that claims to meet the cloud criterion must at least encompass the following attributes:

> It provides on-demand network access to a pool of configurable computing resources that are often shared amongst clients.
> Here, the term computing resource spans a broad range of IT services such as networks, servers, storage, applications, development tools.
> The provision of computing resources requires no or only minimal management effort and service provider involvement.
> It offers an elastic and scalable form of coping with both increasing as well as decreasing demand for computing.
> It provides a consumption-based pricing model by leveraging a metering capability at some level of abstraction.

A widely used definition of cloud computing comes from the National Institute of Standards and Technology [NIST 2009]:

Definition: Cloud computing according to NIST

Cloud computing is a model for enabling convenient, on-demand network access to a shared pool of configurable computing resources (e.g., networks, servers, storage, applications, and services) that can be rapidly provisioned and released with minimal management effort or service provider interaction.

Beyond the core set of cloud computing attributes there is an extended list of characteristics that are often referred to in the broader cloud computing context. In the following paragraphs we will elaborate on four cloud computing distinctions:

Cloud computing categories

> Types of services (e.g., SaaS, Paas, and IaaS)
> Deployment models (e.g., private cloud, public cloud, and hybrid cloud)
> Locality aspects (e.g., internal and external clouds)
> Cloud adoption scenarios

Figure 6.4-19 provides an overview of the key concepts in the area of cloud computing architectures.

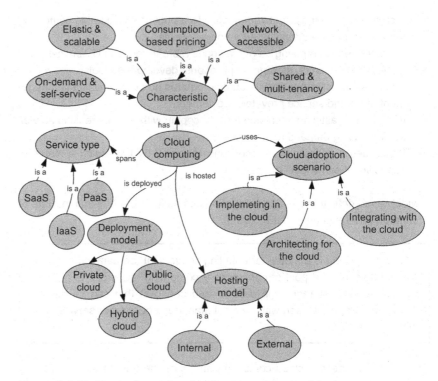

Figure 6.4-19: Concept overview for cloud computing architectures

Service types that clouds offer

SaaS, PaaS, and IaaS—the three types of services named above—are only the tip of the iceberg, as you can see in Figure 6.4-20.

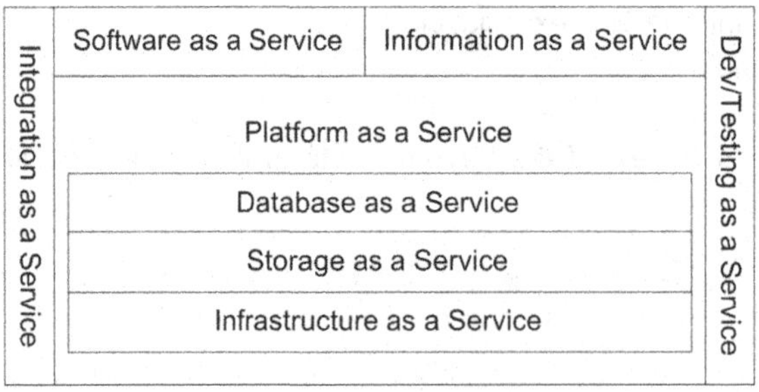

Integration as a Service	Software as a Service	Information as a Service	DevTesting as a Service
	Platform as a Service		
	Database as a Service		
	Storage as a Service		
	Infrastructure as a Service		

Figure 6.4-20: Cloud computing service types

SaaS, PaaS, and IaaS can be considered super categories of a much broader and deeper service type taxonomy that the cloud computing world now distinguishes:

> Software as a Service (SaaS) is a very broad category of services whose only common feature is that the actual software is delivered via the web

and usually accessed through a web browser by an end user. Examples of software offerings that already exist in the cloud are e-mail, calendar, document sharing, or web conferencing. Other examples in the area of business domain-specific software are customer relationship management (CRM) or enterprise resource planning (ERP) types of applications.

> Information as a Service (INFaaS) refers to the consumption of information, situated anywhere in the cloud, through a well-defined information interface.
> Platform as a Service (PaaS) offers readily integrated and coherently set-up application and development platforms. Examples of PaaS offerings are pre-fabricated JEE or .Net environments.
> Integration as a Service (INTaaS) refers to cloud-based offers encapsulating complete integration stacks that support interfacing with applications, semantic mediation, and flow control functionality.
> Infrastructure as a Service (i.e., IaaS) primarily relates to services of the type computing power, such as servers and server farms. Beyond this specific use, the term is also often used as an umbrella term to refer to the remaining set of service types in this list (i.e., STaaS and DaaS).
> Storage as a Service (STaaS) offers storage and disk systems on demand.
> Database as a Service (DaaS) provides higher abstraction level access to persistence systems than StaaS usually does.

Deployment types are yet another important dimension if you want to understand all of the different flavors of cloud computing offerings available today. The three predominant categories here are:

Different approaches to deploying a cloud

> Private clouds, where all cloud services are provided solely for one organization or enterprise. Public clouds, where all cloud services are made available to the general public or at least a broader group of individual clients (so-called community clouds)—typically by an organization selling cloud services.
> Hybrid clouds, where the hybrid cloud is a composition of two or more clouds—private or public—that remain unique entities.

Another distinction that will continue to be an important criterion to consider in the cloud computing domain is hosting. Here we can distinguish between the following:

Clouds and the hosting criterion

> Internal clouds are an IT capability offered as a service and hosted by an enterprise's own IT organization.
> External clouds can be—similar to internal clouds—public or private. However, an external cloud is an offering hosted by an IT organization that is external to the organization or enterprise consuming this cloud's services.

Figure 6.4-21 summarizes fundamental cloud computing characteristics and provides an overview of the key dimensions to consider.

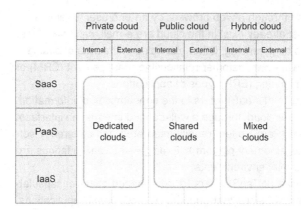

	Private cloud		Public cloud		Hybrid cloud	
	Internal	External	Internal	External	Internal	External
SaaS	Dedicated clouds		Shared clouds		Mixed clouds	
PaaS						
IaaS						

Figure 6.4-21: A cloud computing taxonomy

So far we have only looked at general cloud computing characteristics and a high-level taxonomy to distinguish between the multitude of cloud computing offerings available.

Cloud adoption scenarios

Another important distinction is the different architecture adoption scenarios that you can take:

> Implementing in the cloud: In this scenario you use cloud services (e.g., development and test environments) to ease development and test efforts.

> Integrating with the cloud: In this scenario you integrate your IT system with existing cloud services, for example, a cloud storage service.

> Architecting for the cloud: In this scenario you design, build, and provide IT systems that are cloud services themselves.

Before we move on to elaborating on the various adoption scenarios of cloud computing, we will provide a brief overview of the benefits that IT managers, sourcing departments, architects, and end users associate with cloud-based services. However, everything comes at a price—even here. Cloud computing also imposes a set of significant challenges on all of the above-mentioned parties. Below we outline both sides of the cloud computing coin—its benefits as well as some of its challenges.

Cloud computing benefits

Benefits associated with cloud computing are:

> Shared costs: In the past, each application was supported by a dedicated physical node. This was the most reliable way to insulate an application from being negatively impacted by others. Today, virtualization technology allows us to effectively isolate applications even though they all are hosted in parallel on a single physical node. This allows cloud vendors to share hardware costs across multiple clients. For applications that are capable of

6 | Architecture Means (WITH WHAT)

multi-tenancy, cost sharing can be taken even one step further up to the application layers—thus up to respective SaaS offerings.

> Variable instead of fixed costs: From an enterprise's perspective, most IT-related costs are fixed for one year. Examples are fixed number of operators, fixed number of licenses, dedicated computers, or leased network links. The cloud computing paradigm allows these costs to become variable and consumption-based.

> OPEX over CAPEX: Another financial benefit is that a cloud's "pay as you go" model promotes an operational expenditure (i.e., OPEX) schema over a capital expenditure (CAPEX) schema. In most enterprises OPEX-related request processes are significantly faster than CAPEX-related ones, which increases the throughputs of financial departments as well as relevant workloads.

> Time-to-value: The most important of all cost arguments is probably that you can use a readily available cloud solution, be this an application, infrastructure, or platform, immediately whereas the on-premise creation of a similar solution would last significantly longer. Time-to-value is therefore the most convincing factor for an ROI-focused IT management.

> Scalability: Beyond financial arguments, scalability is the key criterion for rationalizing cloud-based solution approaches. Since it can be very difficult to predict future capacity requirements, overly scalable solutions that are capable of serving request troughs as well as the highest request peaks can quickly become a competitive advantage in today's fast growing businesses.

> Opaque operations: Setting up and running an operational environment that is sufficiently staffed, highly available, scalable, capable of recovering from disaster, monitored, secure, configurable and adaptable to specific customers' needs, as well as surrounded by self-service provisioning processes, is a very complex and expensive undertaking. Clouds make most if not all of these operational duties opaque to their respective clients.

> Additional benefits include the simplification and increase of access to IT services for mobile workforces, a clear push for extreme standardization, as well as higher added value due to the fact that many clouds offer clients the opportunity to participate in extending the cloud—thus making it more useful for themselves but also for other clients.

As stated above, the benefits come at a price. The most important challenges that you should be prepared to cope with in the context of cloud computing are:

Cloud computing challenges

> Availability and vendor lock-in: The most significant challenge of clouds is probably that a cloud vendor can disappear from the Internet overnight and take your cloud-based solutions with him. The more standardized the services that you consumed as a client were, the easier it will be for you to find another vendor offering a similar service. However, the more you use cloud

services from the application layers (i.e., SaaS), the more difficult it will be for you to find a comparable offering, since semantic coupling is usually a lot higher further up the abstraction stack. Therefore, companies striving to adopt cloud computing should include the maturity of the cloud provider as a crucial element of their due diligence.

> Privacy and legislation: Many enterprises have already moved some of their data off premise in the past, for example, in the context of data center outsourcing endeavors. However, moving data into a cloud without knowing where this data will actually reside (i.e., in which country) is still not an option in a lot of industries today. For example, there are legal regulations in some countries prohibiting certain data from leaving the country.

> Security: Security measures established in the past to secure the perimeters of the physical computing environments of our corporations do not work well any more with virtualized, shippable, cloneable, and configurable applications, computers, networks, and persistence systems. If I can provision and de-provision a new computer in seconds, bring it to service and take it out of service based on demand, when do I scan this computer for viruses, patch the virtual OS, or inventorize its installed base? Security means that cope with the transiency and speed at which cloud-based solutions change their shape and appearance need to be completely different to traditional means.

> Users, identities, privileges: Cloud computing also poses completely new requirements on identity and access management. In the same way as the enterprise's own solutions grant or deny their users access to information, cloud-based solutions also have to work from a clearly defined user base. For hybrid clouds this means that these solutions need to cope with harmonized and aligned user base supersets of the individual clouds. All of this requires that enterprises have clear user models both within and beyond the enterprise and this is not an easy challenge to deal with at all.

> Customization: Cloud offerings are similar to non-cloud solutions in that they are designed generically for a mass market but offer customization means so that clients can adjust them to their specific needs. For cloud vendors this means that they have to extend their multi-tenancy model to also include client-specific configurations and customizations. This usually makes architectures of cloud solutions significantly more complex. Beyond these structural extensions that cloud vendors need to cater for, there are different approaches for offering customization hooks to their client base. Examples are property pages and script languages, as well as compiled modules that can be registered with the cloud's own compile base. The specific options a vendor offers around a cloud depend heavily on the complexity level of required customizations as well as on customization skills available at clients.

> Integration: Last but not least we will expand on the challenges that arise from integration needs clients have around clouds. It is quite common to see an SaaS solution insulated from an on-premise IT solution even though

both need to support one and the same business process. This means, for example, that users of this business process have to revalidate and re-enter data manually. System level integration between an SaaS and an internal IT solution may remove or lower this burden on end users. However, system level integrations in a cloud context come at a higher price than integration between non-cloud solutions do, but this is not limited to the aspects listed above (e.g., security, availability, users, and privileges). IT providers have identified the integration challenge and provide both software and hardware specifically for cloud integration (e.g., IBM WebSphere Cast Iron).

Cloud computing and cloud computing architectures are means that you can apply in three main scenarios. In the first scenario you use cloud computing to ease development and test efforts. In the second scenario you integrate your IT system with existing cloud services, and in the third scenario, you design and build services that the cloud provides yourself.

Cloud adoption scenarios

As an architect you can consider cloud computing as an important means for accelerating your development and testing efforts. Nowadays, cloud providers, e.g., Amazon, Microsoft, Oracle, and IBM, offer cloud environments that allow you to use development and test environments from the cloud quickly and agilely. Such offerings reduce the overall costs of labor and capital and reduce the risk of misconfigured environments since they are provided in an automated fashion based on standardized images. An image is a standardized configuration of a software building block that the cloud management environment can provide in an automated fashion. For example, standardized application or database servers can be provided immediately based on defined images. This also increases the overall architectural compliance as standardized images can enforce architectural principles and guidelines. However, the creation of images that adhere to actual project standards takes time and effort. Therefore, you should plan your development and test environment early, define the standards, and create the environment images based on your defined standards. Besides using cloud computing for development and test environments, moving the integrated development environment (IDE) to the cloud may also be an attractive option to pursue. Instead of having to install your favorite IDE on each and every developer's workstation and letting each developer configure his installation to match project standards, developers can log on to the cloud and use the preconfigured IDE. This type of approach is particularly worthwhile if you have a large project team spread across the globe. Thus cloud computing is an essential means that can support you in implementing the architecture (see Section 8.6).

Implementing in the cloud

As more and more companies adopt cloud computing as part of their IT sourcing strategy, more and more IT systems will run in the cloud. IT systems may either use cloud computing services or may be cloud computing services themselves.

For example, the management information system presented in Chapter 8 may use a cloud storage service to persist its data or it may actually be designed as an SaaS offering itself, allowing multiple tenants to capture, analyze, and report relevant management information. This means that the architecture of your IT system must take account of cloud computing characteristics.

Integrating with the cloud

If your IT system is not an SaaS offering itself but only uses cloud computing services, the functional architecture is not affected. However, the technical architecture needs to consider the fact that the IT system is going to use cloud computing services. The APIs of the various cloud computing providers are still proprietary. This means that your architecture should contain specific integration building blocks (see Section 8.5). These building blocks abstract from the proprietary API of the cloud provider and provide the required functionality via well-defined and cloud provider-independent interfaces. Many cloud computing providers have identified the need for standardizing cloud computing APIs and have thus signed the Open Cloud Manifesto [OCM 2010].

Architecting for the cloud

If you are tasked with the design and development of a real SaaS offering, you will have to design both your functional and your technical architecture for this purpose.

For example, the IT system will require functionality in addition to the primary business logic (e.g., customer relationship management) such as
> Ordering
> Provisioning
> Metering
> Billing
> Accounting

This functionality is required to manage orders for your service, provide the service, as well as meter, bill, and account for tenants' use of your service.

Furthermore, your IT system must support multiple tenants, should allow for easy integration, should not be bound to specific hardware, and should allow for self-service to name just a few additional requirements.

These requirements impact not only the technical but also the functional architecture of your IT system. For example, you may identify a functional building block responsible for satisfying the metering requirements. Moreover, the technical architecture must support the multi-tenancy requirement. This requirement cannot be assigned to a single building block. Instead, your overall architecture must allow for multiple tenants to use your IT system at the same time without interfering with each other. For example, company A and company B may use your CRM SaaS offering but must not see each other's CRM data. Such requirements not only affect the identification of required building blocks but also impact the programming model required to implement the functionality. For example, developers may not store the tenant-specific state in global variables as this would compromise the multi-tenancy capability.

Cloud computing reference architectures can help you design your own architecture by identifying the required building blocks from a functional as well as technical perspective and defining the relationships among those building blocks (see Section 6.5). If actual implementations of the reference architecture are available, the implementation of your IT system can even be accelerated. Cloud computing reference architectures are similar to reference architectures of the telecommunications industry, since operation support systems (OSS) and business support systems (BSS) are required to provide the functionality of a fully fledged cloud computing offering/platform. Figure 6.4-22 depicts a cloud computing reference architecture illustrating the major building blocks required.

Cloud computing reference architectures

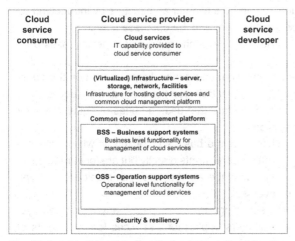

Figure 6.4-22: Cloud computing reference architecture. (Following [IBM 2011])

Due to the importance of cloud computing, we anticipate that more and more specific architecture means such as styles, patterns, and reference architectures will be defined, enabling you to define your own cloud computing IT system based on industry best practices and proven experience.

6.4.14 Summary

Summary: Basic architectures

> There are fundamental basic architectures that are used in many systems.
> One fundamental question is the comparison of centralization to decentralization. Here you often have to find a compromise. However, in considering an entire system at physical and logical level, centralization and decentralization do not exclude each other—you can often use them in combination to take advantage of synergy effects.
> Layered architectures enable you to structure architectures by arranging building blocks in layers where every layer provides the layer above with services through interfaces.
> Dataflow architectures structure an architecture along the dataflows. They are particularly useful if you can split a complex task into a series of simple tasks and then map it as a combination of independent calls.
> In a shared repository architecture, a system building block provides a central data storage unit.
> The classic client/server model is based on a two-tier architecture.
> Three-tier architectures expand the two-tier architecture by introducing an intermediate tier between the client and the database server.
> Two-tier architectures and three-tier architectures are special cases of n-tier architectures.
> The decision between a rich client and a thin client is based on the question of how to split the functionality between the client and the server.
> Peer-to-peer is a basic architecture that uses a series of equal peers for (distributed) communication.
> A publish/subscribe architecture is a basic architecture in which calls are not sent to the communication participants directly but are forwarded by an intermediary. In a publish/subscribe architecture, communication is typically via asynchronous events.
> Middleware is a central technology for connecting many distributed systems. It is a platform that offers applications services for all aspects of the distribution, such as distributed calls, efficient access to the network, transactions, and much more.
> Component platforms are based on the separation of technical concerns and functional requirements. A container takes over the technical concerns automatically. Examples of technical concerns in the enterprise environment are distribution, security, persistence, transactions, concurrency, and resource management.
> Service-oriented architectures (SOA) are a basic architecture that represents the functional interfaces of software building blocks as reusable, distributed, loosely coupled, services that are accessible as standard.
> Security architectures refer to an application that is to be protected and an underlying security infrastructure.

> Cloud computing refers more to a set of characteristics that all IT systems implementing a cloud model share rather than a specific architecture. The typical service offerings distinguished today are Infrastructure as a Service (IaaS), Platform as a Service (PaaS), and Software as a Service (SaaS) and these are the most common types of services provided via a cloud.

6.5 Reference Architectures

In the previous sections we presented important architecture design means—such as architecture principles, tactics, styles, and patterns—that form the basis for successful architectures. We also discussed the application of these means in common basic architectures. They represent solutions for general architecture requirements or rather, qualities. However, IT systems are not assessed primarily on the basis of their architectural elegance. They must satisfy functional requirements and offer a concrete benefit for the customer. This presents you with a great challenge. On one hand you have to be an expert in basic architecture questions, but on the other hand, you also have to know the special characteristics and needs of different industries and take account of these in the architecture design. You can only create IT solutions that support business strategies and that can differentiate you from competitors when you consolidate general architecture expertise and industry-specific knowledge. The industry-specific knowledge is not restricted to business models and processes and IT support for these: it extends to IT system landscapes valid for an industry and the requirements of these landscapes. To act successfully as an architect in different industries, you need means that unite the knowledge and experience of the general architecture disciplines with those of the concrete industries.

Figure 6.5-1 illustrates that reference architectures combine both general architecture knowledge, such as patterns and architecture concepts, as well as concepts and knowledge of the domains.

Different aspects and requirements

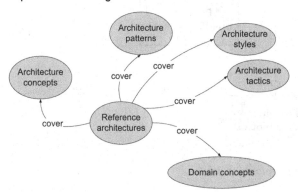

Figure 6.5-1: Overview of reference architectures

6.5.1 Definition and Elements

Definition: Reference architectures

Reference architectures combine general architecture knowledge and general experience with specific requirements for a coherent architectural solution for a specific problem domain. They document the structures of the system, the main system building blocks, their responsibilities, and their interactions

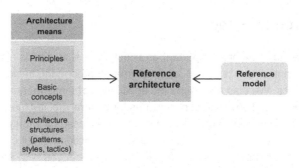

Figure 6.5-2: *Elements of a reference architecture*

Elements

As you can see from Figure 6.5-2, reference architectures are created on one hand based on proven architecture means, and on the other hand, based on specific requirements in the form of desired functionality expressed in a reference model.

Reference models

A reference model contains the specific characteristics of the problem domain addressed. The functionality is divided up into dedicated function building blocks. A reference model documents these building blocks and the information flows between them [Bass et al. 2003]. Figure 6.5-3 shows an example of the structure of a reference model.

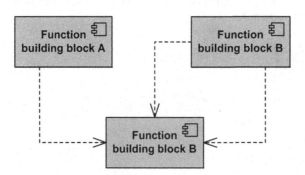

Figure 6.5-3: *Structure of a reference model*

By interacting, the conceptual function building blocks fulfill the requirements of the problem domain. A reference model does not yet state how an IT system under construction fulfills this functionality. The reference architecture takes over this task by describing how the function building blocks are distributed to system building blocks. It also explains their responsibilities and their interaction [Hofmeister et al. 1999].

mid**Reference architectures as copies of reference models**

6.5.2 Use and Advantages of Reference Architectures

When designing an architecture, you use reference architectures and convert them into concrete architectures. Here you have to weigh up which parts of a reference architecture you need for the problem in question. Reference architectures are often very extensive. Therefore, a direct copy generally does not make sense. Instead, you should always only implement those elements that you really need to reduce the complexity of the architecture you are designing (see Figure 6.5-4).

Use of reference architectures

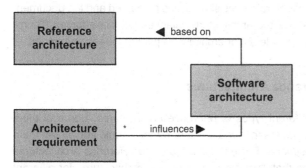

Figure 6.5-4: Use of reference architectures

The use of reference architectures brings the following advantages:

> You can build on the knowledge and experience of other people who have contributed to the design of the reference architecture.
> A reference architecture reduces the risk of designing a non-viable architecture.
> Using a reference architecture leads to an increase in quality for the architecture you are designing since it is based on a proven architecture means.
> A reference architecture reduces the cost of the architecture design because it already contains important findings from the area of the problem domain analysis and therefore reduces the effort for this activity.
> The use of a reference architecture allows you to develop an IT system more quickly and gives you a better time-to-market.

Advantages of reference architectures

6.5.3 Requirements Placed on Reference Architectures

Requirements placed on good reference architectures

In order to offer real advantages in architecture design, good reference architectures must have the following features:

> They must be based on proven principles, patterns, styles, and tactics.

> They must have been used successfully. Reference architectures only prove how good they are in practice when they are used successfully. Before you decide on a reference architecture, you should therefore always ensure that it has already been used in a similar context.

> They must be adaptable to concrete needs. As already stated, reference architectures can be very extensive. It must therefore be possible to design the concrete architecture based on the reference architecture and to expand it step-by-step when new requirements arise.

> They must be documented extensively. You can only use a reference architecture successfully if you have access to meaningful documentation. This documentation should clearly show which architecture means have been applied and how the *reference model* has been mapped to the reference architecture. The architectural forces should also be named and the documentation should show how the architecture balances out these forces. Therefore, a documentation style as for architecture patterns is recommended.

6.5.4 Types of Reference Architectures

Platform-related reference architectures

In practice there are different types of reference architectures. Some of them are like standards. This means that you must, or rather, should implement them exactly as they are described. For example, there are reference architectures for component platforms that illustrate how to realize architectures for different problems based on the platform. Known representatives of this type are JEE BluePrints from Sun Microsystems for the JEE platform [Oracle 2011a]. The realization of a service-oriented architecture or the development of a web-based shopping solution are examples of such reference architectures. The focus of these architectures is on the correct use of the underlying platform. A reference architecture in this category covers not only conceptual artefacts, such as architecture diagrams, but also concrete implementations in the form of source text or ready-to-run building blocks.

Industry-specific reference architectures

There are also extensive, industry-specific reference architectures tailored to the concrete needs of enterprises. Many IT service providers and consultants offer, for example, reference architectures for the telecommunications, air travel, bank, or insurance industries to name just a few. Their underlying reference models cover function building blocks and information flows that usually enable support for all important business processes in an enterprise. Furthermore, these reference architectures show how the function building blocks are mapped to concrete, commercial software products. The individual development is normally restricted to the adjustment and integration of the products in the IT system landscape of the customer. NGOSS and OSS/J are examples of such reference architectures (see Section 6.5.5).

Between the platform-specific and industry-specific reference architectures are reference architectures that are concerned with a topic relevant in different industries, for example, Supply Chain Management (SCM) and Customer Relationship Management (CRM).

Cross-industry reference architectures

A special form of reference architecture is a product line architecture. It defines the common architecture of several similar software products [Hofmeister et al. 1999]. This form of reference architecture covers the common system building blocks, their responsibilities, and their cooperation. Product line architectures are designed with the aim of designing products more cost-effectively by having them share a common architecture and under some circumstances, they can even reuse prefabricated ready-to-run software building blocks.

Product line architectures

6.5.5 Example of a Reference Architecture

The *New Generation Operations Systems and Software (NGOSS) initiative* from TeleManagement Forum defines a comprehensive reference architecture tailored to the telecommunications industry [TMF 2004a].

Example of an industry-related reference architecture

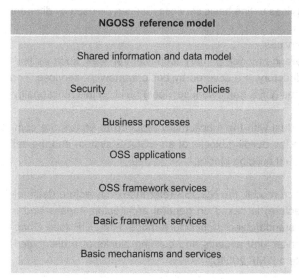

Figure 6.5-5: Overview of the NGOSS reference model

NGOSS reference model	This reference architecture is based on the reference model [TMF 2004b] presented in Figure 6.5-5 and explained below:

> *Shared information and data model (SID):*
> The shared information and data model is a standardized model from the telecommunications domain. It defines the standard abstractions, such as customer, order, and network service. The model also makes clear statements about the meaning of the abstractions, their behavior, and their collaboration.

> *Security:*
> This function building block defines the security mechanisms and policies. These are based on the Information Security Management Standard [ISO17799 2001].

> *Policies:*
> NGOSS recommends the use of policy-based management (PBM). PBM is based on rules that define how to handle building blocks. The system evaluates and applies these rules at runtime.

> *Business processes:*
> This part of the NGOSS reference model contains standardized business processes and activities for the telecommunications domain. These are summarized in the Enhanced Telecom Operations map (eTOM).

> *OSS applications:*
> Business-related functionality to be supported by an NGOSS-conform IT system is grouped in this part of the NGOSS reference model. In this context, OSS stands for Operations Support System. For more detailed information on this topic, see [Terplan 2001].

> *OSS framework services:*
> OSS framework services define basic services that can be used by different OSS applications.

> *Basic framework services:*
> In the NGOSS reference model, primary technical services, such as finding a service in a directory, are covered by basic framework services. The higher quality services (OSS framework services) build on this functionality.

> *Basic mechanisms:*
> Basic mechanisms deal with the functionality required to enable the communication between the building blocks of an NGOSS system and the call of services of individual building blocks.

NGOSS and RM-ODP   In addition to the reference model, the NGOSS reference architecture (technology-independent architecture) is based on general architecture means and is therefore based on the standardized architecture model RM-ODP (see Chapter 4). It defines the architectural aspects and building blocks of a distributed, NGOSS-conform IT system [TMF 2004b].

However, TeleManagement Forum does not offer a concrete implementation of its reference architecture. Software manufacturers and IT service providers use the reference architecture to realize concrete solutions. TeleManagement Forum provides the option of certifying these solutions. This is an advantage for customers since they can rely on the TMF seal of quality when selecting NGOSS implementations.

NGOSS implementations

The NGOSS reference architecture is a technology-independent architecture. You have to map it to concrete component platforms for the respective use case. Therefore, leading manufacturers launched the OSS for Java (OSS/J) initiative as part of the Java Community Process (JCP) for the JEE platform. The initiative implements the NGOSS reference architecture based on JEE [OSSJ 2004].

OSS/J as NGOSS implementation

The aim of the OSS/J initiative is to offer software building blocks or rather, products, based on OSS/J for the telecommunications domain. This means that you can combine products from different manufacturers to form a comprehensive telecommunications solution by considerably reducing the integration costs.

Aim of OSS/J

To do this, the OSS/J initiative defines different application programming interfaces (API) based on eTOM from NGOSS. The API specifications reflect on one hand the required functionality and on the other, the architecturally significant system building blocks. Table 6.5-1 gives an overview of the APIs.

Parts of OSS/J

Table 6.5-1: Overview of OSS/J APIs

Java API	Description
OSS Common API	This API contains basic communication mechanisms and design guidelines that all other APIs must satisfy.
OSS Service Activation API	In a telecommunications architecture, it must be possible to activate services (e.g., SMS) for a customer automatically after a contract has been signed. To do this, the Service Activation API creates the required functionality and models the relevant building blocks.
OSS Quality of Service API	The Quality of Service API defines the functionality and building blocks for monitoring and determining the quality of the telecommunications services. For example, it is important to determine whether the bandwidth available in a network drops below a specific value.
OSS Trouble Ticket API	The Trouble Ticket API is used to manage error tickets. It covers the required functionality and building blocks in the area of error management and tracking.
OSS IP Billing API	Customers must be billed for the use of telecommunications services. Therefore, you need building blocks that take over the billing. The IP Billing API is dedicated to these building blocks and their functionality by defining their required characteristics.

Java API	Description
OSS Inventory API	A telecommunications architecture consists of different network building blocks such as servers, routers, and switches. Inventorizing these parts and being able to call up their location quickly, for example, in the case of an error, are important requirements of telecommunications providers. Therefore, it must be possible to run inventories. The Inventory API models the relevant functionality and required building blocks.
OSS Service Quality Management API	This API is dedicated to the required functionality for determining the quality of a telecommunications service and demonstrates the building blocks required.

Responsibilities

As a whole, the OSS/J APIs model the required functionality of a telecommunications architecture. The Common API mainly addresses the OSS framework services of the NGOSS reference model. In contrast, the other APIs are dedicated to the functionality modeled by the OSS applications and the building blocks. In OSS/J, the JEE platform assumes the task of the basic framework services and the basic mechanisms and services. The use of JEE as an architecture platform has the great advantage that you can rely on a proven platform that offers important basic services such as scalability and transaction control.

OSS/J architecture example

Figure 6.5-6 shows an example of a simple architecture based on OSS/J.

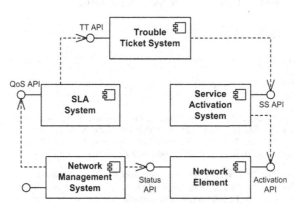

Figure 6.5-6: A simple OSS/J-based architecture

The architecture shown is based on the use of the standardized OSS/J APIs for integrating different subsystems of a telecommunications system. Since the systems required offer corresponding interfaces, the systems can communicate with one another without having to access system-specific interfaces. This reduces the integration effort considerably.

In the underlying scenario a network management system monitors network elements. As soon as an error is detected in a network element, the network management system forwards a corresponding message to the SLA system. The message complies with a format defined by the OSS/J initiative. The SLA system checks whether the defined service level agreements have been violated. If this is the case, the SLA system requests that the Trouble Ticket system creates a corresponding Trouble Ticket. As soon as the error in the network element has been corrected by a technician, the Trouble Ticket is closed and an OSS/J confirm service activation request is sent to the Service Activation system. This reactivates the corresponding network element.

In a simplified way, this example shows which types of systems are required to realize this scenario. It also illustrates the structure of a corresponding telecommunications architecture as well as the responsibilities and interaction of the subsystems.

6.5.6 Summary

> Reference architectures combine general architecture knowledge and general experience with specific requirements for a coherent architectural solution for a specific problem domain.
> Reference architectures are created based on proven architecture means (e.g., principles, patterns, styles, and tactics), as well as on specific requirements in the form of desired functionality expressed in a reference model.
> A reference model contains the specific characteristics of the problem domain addressed.
> The selection of a reference architecture as an architecture design means offers great advantages as you can build on the knowledge and experience of other people who have contributed to the design of the reference architecture.
> In practice there are different types of reference architectures: platform-related reference architectures, industry-specific reference architectures, cross-industry reference architectures.
> A product line architecture is a special form of reference architecture. It defines the common architecture of several similar software products.
> The New Generation Operations Systems and Software (NGOSS) initiative from TeleManagement Forum defines a comprehensive reference architecture tailored to the telecommunications industry.

Summary: Reference architectures

6.6 Architecture Modeling Means

Modeling as a fixed part of modern software development

From the very beginning, software development has been accompanied by constant innovations with regard to new concepts of abstraction. As an abstraction concept, modeling now has a fixed place in modern software development. With regard to software architectures, modeling is used as a means for documentation, specification, communication, analysis, and validation of architectures, to some extent also to support automatic code generation. We explained this last aspect in the context of architecture-centric MDSD (see Section 6.2.6).

Structure of this section

At the beginning of this section, we will introduce and explain important modeling terms and concepts in the context of software development. Later on in the section, we will address modeling languages that you should use in architecture modeling. We will consider three important means with regard to their options for modeling architecture precisely: Unified Modeling Language (UML), domain-specific languages (DSL), and a special language family of DSLs, the architecture description languages (ADL). This list is not exhaustive. There are further options, for example, entity relationship diagrams or notations from the environment of structured analysis/design (SA/D), which you can also use to formally record and document at least some aspects of an architecture. Figure 6.6-1 gives an overview of the concepts and architecture modeling means presented in this section.

Architecture model is not a method

Note that an architecture specification in the form of a model is not a method in the sense of a method model (see Section 6.6.5). A method defines concrete procedure instructions (contents) and a development process. Combined, these specify *what* has to be done, and *how* and *when* it has to be done. A method thus specifies an ordered framework of the models, for example, the architecture model, that you create during the lifecycle of a project. However, modeling is a suitable means if you want to formulate the method precisely. A corresponding metamodel is covered in Section 6.6.5.

6.6.1 Basic Concepts of Modeling

Definition: Model concept according to Stachowiak

There are a number of different definitions of the model concept in literature. Amongst other reasons, this is because the use of models has established itself in the most varied engineering disciplines and fields of science. For a generally recognized and cross-domain definition of the model concept we can refer to [Stachowiak 1973]:

> *Reproduction.* A model is always a reproduction of something, a natural or a synthetic original, which can be a model itself.

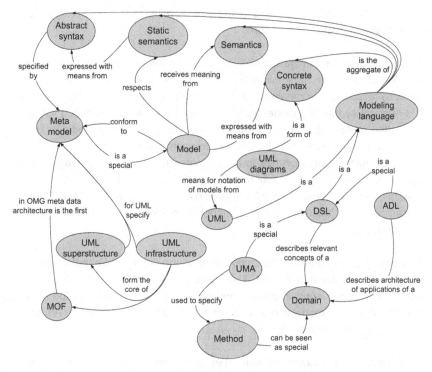

Figure 6.6-1: Basic concepts of modeling and architecture modeling means—overview

> *Abbreviation.* A model does not reproduce all attributes of the original, only those that appear relevant to the model creator or the model user.
> *Pragmatism.* Pragmatism means "orientation around usefulness." A model is not assigned to an original for its own sake. The assignment to the original is affected by the questions: Who is the model for? What is the model for? Why has the model been created? A model is used by the model creator or the model user in place of an original for a certain period of time to serve a certain purpose. The model is therefore interpreted.

Models are thus an abstraction of the original because they do not consider all details, only those that are useful to the stakeholder of the model for his or her purposes.

In this book, we will look at models in the context of the design of object-oriented software systems. In software development too, a model is considered to be the abstract reproduction of an original. This section introduces the most important

Models in software development

terms in the context of modeling in software development and develops a conceptual superstructure for the topic.

Metamodeling

The basis for any automated processing of model data is the definition of a model in a formal language. In software development, a special type of modeling has evolved to satisfy this requirement. Here, model types (or to be more precise, the abstract syntax of a model type, see below) are usually described via models called *metamodels*. The operation of constructing such a model is known as *metamodeling*. Metamodeling thus represents a special case in modeling. A notion of object orientation has thus permeated the formalism or language usage of metamodeling. This notion is that a metamodel specifies types that you instantiate in the model. A model is thus also known as an *instance* of the related metamodel. The language usage "a model is conform to its metamodel" is also common.

Modeling layers

The cascade of sequential abstraction through the creation of a metamodel can potentially continue unrestricted. The hierarchy of models created opens up a series of *modeling layers* into which you can classify the respective models. You can only classify a model into a concrete modeling layer uniquely with reference to a specific *model hierarchy*.

Four-layer modeling architectures

In practice, the concept of *four-layer modeling architecture* has is well-established. The individual modeling layers are referred to mostly with M0 to M3, as in this book. The model located at M3 closes the model hierarchy in an upwards direction. From a conceptual point of view, this conforms to a metamodel of a layer M4, which in turn is isomorphic to the model defined at layer M3. In this context, an isomorphic mapping is the reversible, unique (bijective) mapping of the model elements of one model to elements of the other model with the same meaning. With the four-layer modeling architecture from OMG, Section 6.6.2 presents a concrete modeling architecture for a family of modeling languages.

Modeling languages

Due to the fact that it defines a (usually infinite) number of valid instances, a metamodel can also be understood as a means for describing a *modeling language*. It is usually only the abstract syntax of the specified modeling language that is defined exactly in a formal manner. Therefore, the terms "metamodel" and "abstract syntax" are often used synonymously. Since the semantics of a modeling language are frequently defined informally in the form of natural language, in this case we also refer to semi-formal languages.

Whilst the *abstract syntax* only describes the structure of a modeling language, the *concrete syntax* provides an instrument for the textual or graphical notation of models. To explain this we will use an analogy to classic programming languages. Here the concrete syntax defines which entries a parser accepts for this language. The abstract syntax merely specifies what the structure of the language looks like. There are no details, for example, of how key words are written. The abstract syntax is mostly specified by a metamodel.

Abstract and concrete syntax

The *static semantics* of a language define the well-formedness criteria that its syntax cannot define. Without going into the precise theoretical background, here we will use an illustrative example from the world of classic programming languages: some languages have the rule that variables have to be declared before values can be assigned to them. With regard to the individual phases of a compiler, the parser would not be able to recognize a violation of this rule. Initially the compiler's static analysis would fail. In the context of modeling languages, the static semantics are mostly defined by a series of constraints. Constraints always refer to dedicated model elements as the context. Typical constraints are, for example, the constraint of the value range of attributes of a model element or the constraint of the relationships between model elements.

Static semantics

In addition to the abstract and concrete syntax, as well as the static semantics, every language must also have *semantics* that precisely define the meaning of the model. In the case of UML, the semantics of the model elements are described informally in the UML superstructure (see Section 6.6.2) through natural language English explanations as part of the definition of the abstract syntax. In the case of MDSD (see Section 6.2.6), we also refer to a translational definition of the semantics. This means that the models are mapped on another well-known language (often a 3GL language) using transformations. These mapping rules thus define the meaning of the modeling language used.

Semantics

6.6.2 Unified Modeling Language

The *Unified Modeling Language* (UML) arose at the end of the 1990s as a result of the merging of different notations by Rumbaugh, Booch, and Jacobson. The great success of UML brought an end to the Babylonian language confusion in the notations in the object-oriented community (see Table 6.6-1).

One of the most important standard modeling languages

Table 6.6-1: From notations Babylon to UML

Period	Notation	Comment
2005	UML 2.0	Revised metamodel
2001	UML 1.4	Market dominance achieved
1999	UML 1.3	XML Metadata Interchange (XMI)
1998	UML 1.2	OMG takes charge
1997	UML 1.0	Object Constraint Language (OCL)
1996	Unified Modeling Language (UML) 0.9	Unified Method and OOSE
1995	Unified Method	OMT and OOD
1992	OOD and OOSE	Booch and Jacobson
1991	OMT	Rumbaugh
1987–1998	OMT, OOD, OOSE, OOSA, and many more	Notations Babylon

Under the care of the Object Management Group (OMG), UML has now become one of the most important standards in software development. In this book we refer to UML in version 2.0. It is supported by almost all development tools. Before we look at the different types of diagrams, we will first outline the embedding and integration of UML in the OMG modeling architecture and place them in the context of the concepts presented in Section 6.2.1.

The Meta-Object Facility

Facility The *Meta-Object Facility* (MOF) [OMG 2010b] is the basis of the OMG modeling architecture. The MOF specification defines an abstract syntax and a framework for the construction and handling of technology-independent metamodels, referred to as MOF-based metamodels. In addition to further OMG standards, such as the *Common Warehouse Metamodel* (CWM) [OMG 2003], the UML metamodel can also be classified with the MOF-based metamodels. MOF is based on the concept of a four-layer modeling architecture presented in Section 6.6.1.

The four-layer modeling architecture of the OMG

Figure 6.6-2 shows the four-layer OMG modeling architecture. The left column uses the OMG standardized naming for the model levels. The middle column lists concrete models at each layer. For illustration purposes, here we also show a comparison to a known language architecture. The right column therefore assigns terms from the Java programming language to the corresponding layers.

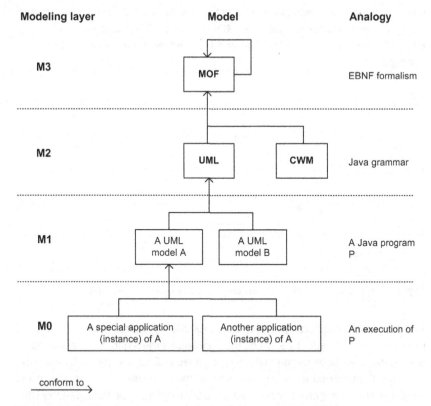

Modeling layer	Model	Analogy
M3	MOF	EBNF formalism
M2	UML CWM	Java grammar
M1	A UML model A A UML model B	A Java program P
M0	A special application (instance) of A Another application (instance) of A	An execution of P

conform to

Figure 6.6-2: The four-layer modeling architecture of the OMG

The specification of UML 2.0 has a much more modular structure than previous versions. To reuse defined packages and their elements, UML 2.0 specifies the *Package Merge Algorithm* [Zito et al. 2006], a complex transformation guideline for merging two packages. One central new feature of UML 2.0 in comparison to its predecessor version is the separation of the UML specification into infrastructure and superstructure. This separation enables you to reuse (using package merge) the infrastructure as a basis for other metamodels.

Modular structure of the UML 2.0 specification

The *Core* package specified by the UML *Infrastructure specification* [OMG 2007b] is the language core of UML. It was designed in such general and reusable terms that it can also be used as the core of other language definitions. Figure 6.6-3 shows the use of the *Core* package both as a basis for the MOF specification and as a basis for the UML and CWM specification (*Common Warehouse Metamodel*) [OMG 2003]. Together with the *Profiles* package, also defined by the infrastructure, it forms the *Infrastructure Library* (IL). Note that you can

The UML infrastructure

use the IL in different modeling layers of the modeling architecture. The inclusion of the norming process for UML and MOF in version 2.0 thus follows the goal of completely uniting the core of UML and MOF based on a uniform set of basic concepts.

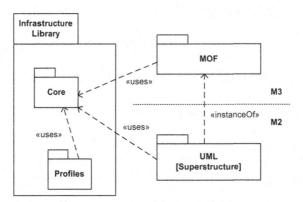

Figure 6.6-3: Usage of the Infrastructure Library in MOF and UML

The UML superstructure

The *UML Superstructure specification* [OMG 2007a] is also based on the *Core* package of the infrastructure. Using the package merge algorithm, the sub-packages defined in *Core* merge with the packages defined by the superstructure. They are then refined to receive the special model elements that make up the language definition generally referred to as UML metamodel. Note that the UML superstructure only specifies the abstract syntax of the language. For notation, referred to as concrete syntax in Section 6.6.1, there are both graphical and textual variants that in turn are defined in separate specifications. One textual representation option is the *XMI Standard* [OMG 2007c]. The diagram types described later in this section are a graphical notation variant.

Adapting UML to specific application domains

The UML language constructs are designed very generically. Within domain-specific languages (see Section 6.6.3), modeling languages adapted to a specific application domain and reflecting the concepts of a specific domain as precisely as possible are often required. One option for realizing such a language is to adapt UML. We will outline the two basic options for adapting UML to specific usage purposes below.

Extension of the UML metamodel

One option for extending UML is a real extension of the UML metamodel. Here, you use the language means of the next higher metalevel for modeling, in this case MOF. By instantiating elements specified by MOF, you can define completely new model elements and also refine existing elements of the UML metamodel (using specialization). Note that the instantiation of MOF elements is in no way restricted only to the instantiation of the MOF metaclass *Class*—you can use all language means used to extend the UML metamodel. Due to the far-reaching effects on the metamodel, this form of extension of the language scope is referred to as a *heavyweight extension*.

With the definition of UML 2.0, the *stereotype mechanism* of the predecessor version was extended to a more extensive *profile mechanism*. Figure 6.6-4 provides a simplified illustration of the relevant section of the UML Superstructure [OMG 2007a].

Profile mechanism of UML 2.0

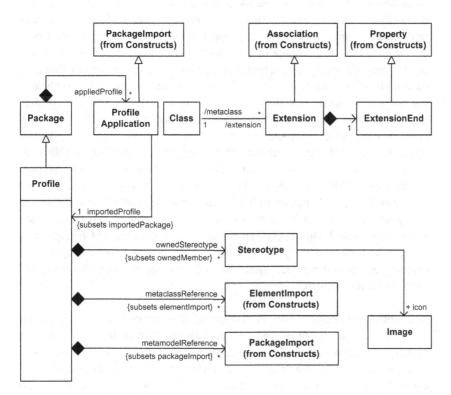

Figure 6.6-4: *Profile mechanism of UML 2.0: Relevant section of the UML Superstructure. [OMG 2007a]*

The core of the profile mechanism is the *Extension* (see Figure 6.6-4). This special association defines the metaclass that is extended through the stereotype specified as part of a profile definition. Profiles are special packages. You can profile a package by applying a *ProfileApplication*, a specialization of *PackageImport*. This means that you can use the stereotype defined by a profile within the profiled package. A *Stereotype* can have attributes referred to as *tagged values*. The only other language means available to the definition of profiles is the specification of constraints (see Section 6.6.1) for the new stereotype defined. In addition to the heavyweight extension of the metamodel presented above, the UML profile mechanism therefore also allows the addition of existing modeling concepts without any intervention in the metamodel. UML profiles are therefore referred to as *lightweight extensions*.

Each of the two extension mechanisms presented have their own specific advantages and disadvantages that we will outline below. The goal of extending UML is always to create models conform to the extended metamodel. The functional requirement of specifying profiles and applying them to concrete models is realized in most UML tools. Many UML tools also offer the option for verifying constraints specified by an applied profile. If the purpose of an extension of the UML metamodel is only the introduction of new terms (in the form of stereotypes), the profile mechanism is a suitable means. However, the power of expression of profiles, when compared to heavyweight extensions of the UML metamodel or the definition of an independent metamodel based on MOF, is very restricted. Many facts can only be formulated with difficulty and using complex, difficult to understand constraints. Here the use of so-called *metacase tools* is recommended, for example MetaEdit+ [MetaEdit 2010]. Metacase tools allow you to define your own metamodels based on a dedicated metametamodel. To a certain extent, you can assign a separate representation to every language element of the metamodel created. That is, you can define the concrete syntax of the language. This can be both graphically oriented and textually oriented. In the first case, for example, you assign graphical symbols to the language elements; in the second case, dedicated keywords.

One model, different views

The central philosophy of UML is "one model, different views." This means that with UML, you can partly visualize different aspects of a system with a number of different diagram types. Table 6.6-2 gives a short overview of the diagrams (UML views) of UML. The focus is on aspects important for architecture modeling, whereby there is a differentiation between static and dynamic aspects of the architecture. For a comprehensive overview with details of all notation elements and the specific UML terms, see [Booch et al. 2005].

Table 6.6-2: *Architectural meaning of the UML diagrams*

Diagram	Shows	Static/dynamic
Activity diagram	Steps that run within a system to fulfill a specific task. With specification of the building blocks involved	Dynamic
Use case diagram	Use cases of a planned or existing system and the parties involved	Dynamic
Interaction overview diagram	The interactions that run between building blocks and when they run	Dynamic
Class diagram/component diagram	Interfaces and relationships of building blocks	Static
Communication diagram	Building blocks that collaborate or communicate	Dynamic
Composite structure diagram	Building blocks with regard to their interfaces and relationships as well as their internal workings	Static
Object diagram	Internal structure of a building block at a specific point at runtime	Static
Package diagram	Logical grouping of cohesive building blocks.	Static
Sequence diagram	Communication processes between building blocks	Dynamic
Timing diagram	States of building blocks dependent on the time	Dynamic
Deployment diagram	Physical deployment of building blocks at runtime	Static
State machine diagram	States of a building block and events that cause these states	Dynamic

Table 6.6-3 shows how you can use UML to represent static and dynamic aspects of architecture views (see Section 4.2). It details which diagrams you should ideally use for the respective architecture views of the common architecture view model from Section 4.2.

Figure 6.6-5 shows an example of a static UML diagram. It shows the logical view (see Section 4.2) of a multi-layered architecture. The diagram shows the main building blocks of an online ordering system together with its dependencies and relations. The architecture patterns Front Controller, Business Delegate, and Data Access Object [Alur et al. 2003] are used. Model elements that realize the corresponding roles of the patterns named are indicated by special stereotypes, which in an ideal case, are defined by a profile. In this example, the focus is on

Example of a logical architecture view

Table 6.6-3: *Representation of architecture views with UML*

Architecture view	UML diagram
Requirements view	Activity diagram Use case diagram Class diagram Package diagram Sequence diagram State machine diagram
Logical view	Activity diagram Class diagram Component diagram Composite structure diagram Package diagram Sequence diagram State machine diagram
Data view	Class diagram Component diagram Package diagram
Implementation view	Class diagram Component diagram Package diagram Sequence diagram Deployment diagram State machine diagram
Process view	Activity diagram Communication diagram Interaction overview diagram Sequence diagram Timing diagram
Deployment view	Component diagram Package diagram Sequence diagram Deployment diagram State machine diagram

the building blocks and their relationships. Stereotypical dependency relationships are used for notation, namely "uses" and "delegates". To address the interfaces, you would usually create further diagrams that, with the help of further notation elements (e.g., interface class or component), would represent the building blocks in more detail. A diagram should not represent too many aspects at once.

This ensures that the power of expression of a diagram on specific points is not lost in a sea of different aspects.

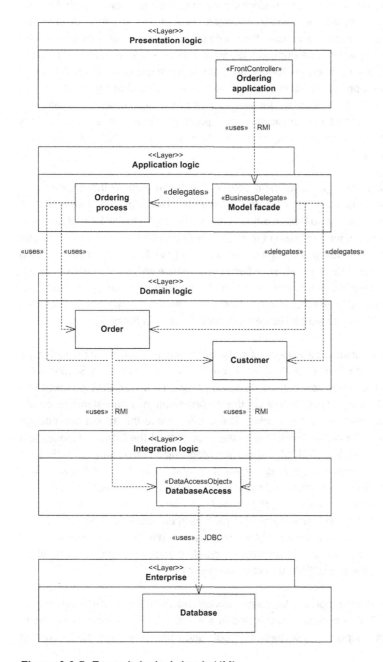

Figure 6.6-5: Example logical view in UML

6.6.3 Domain-Specific Languages

Domains and domain-specific languages

In this context, a *domain* is a restricted area of interest or knowledge that can be both functionally and technically motivated. Typical domains are, for example, embedded systems, insurances, financial service systems, but also software architectures. The aim of a domain-specific language is to formally cover relevant properties for a respective domain and map them in the form of a suitable language. The opposite of domain-specific languages (DSLs) are general purpose languages (GPL). These are languages that are designed so generically that they can be used for all applications and problems. Typical examples of GPLs are known 3GL programming languages such as Java or UML, as covered in Section 6.6.2.

Domain analysis and formalization of domain knowledge

The starting point for designing a DSL is the identification of the relevant concepts of a domain as part of the *domain analysis*. The formation of an extensive concept is usually a suitable starting point, for example, in the form of an ontology. One option for formalizing the knowledge provided by the domain analysis is to define a modeling language embedded in a (usually four-layered) modeling architecture. A DSL is usually specified in accordance with the considerations detailed in Section 6.6.1, so in the definition of a metamodel (layer M2) conform to a metametamodel (layer M3). On this basis, you can then define concrete models (layer M1) that represent instances of a specific domain (layer M0).

Excursion: Specification of DSLs in practice

In a brief excursion, we will look at some of the existing options for specifying a DSL in practice. We have already presented two such options in Section 6.6.2 with the UML extension options discussed there. However, their practical use is dependent to a large extent on the implementation of the standard by the UML tools available on the market. These often place the aspect of language extension in the background. Due to the popularity of the Eclipse development environment [Eclipse 2010a], the *Eclipse Modeling Framework* (EMF) [Eclipse 2010b] is becoming increasingly interesting and important. It follows various OMG specifications of MOF and UML. EMF is a Java-based realization of a four-layered modeling architecture. The *Ecore Model* can be seen as an equivalent to MOF that closes the hierarchy of EMF models in an upwards direction and thus represents the metametamodel of the modeling architecture. Furthermore, EMF offers generic editors and generators for creating and processing models, which also makes the use of EMF attractive in practice.

DSLs as a means for formalizing architecture knowledge

The term "domain-specific language" is very broad. In the MDSD context (see Section 6.2.6), the models formulated in a specific DSL are mostly reduced to the aspect of inputs for transformation tools and code generators. Note here that code generation in no way represents the only use case of a formalization of domain-relevant concepts. In the context of domain architecture, the formal recording of an architecture is therefore a suitable means if you want to "standardize" an architecture, for example, as part of a large project. The benefits extend from a precise means of documentation to the basis for the design of a product line of a system family based on this architecture (see Section 6.2.6). An architecture documented purely informally is not sufficient for this purpose, since the required precision is missing.

An architecture metamodel formally defines the building blocks that make up an architecture, their relationships to one another, and possible constraints that define when a system has a valid architecture and when it does not. A concrete architecture is therefore specified by instances of an architecture metamodel.

Architecture metamodel

In this example, the means for describing the metamodel is UML, or more precisely, the UML's notation. The use of the graphical notation of UML for specifying a metamodel has already been used as part of the introduction of MOF. The *Object Constraint Language* [OMG 2010a] is also often used to precisely formulate the constraints specified in this example in the form of simple notes. At this point we should highlight again the big difference between DSLs and UML. UML is not specialized to specific domains and you can therefore use it for a broad range of areas, in contrast to DSLs. The price for this flexibility is a loss of precision. Compared with DSLs, UML also has restricted analysis and simulation options as well as possible misunderstandings with regard to the semantics of a model.

Reference to UML

Describing the architecture of a system using a DSL suitable for the architecture has some advantages. For example, the communication across the system or architecture is clearer because the concepts are clearly defined. Ultimately, an architecture metamodel is a type of structured glossary that represents an important part of an architecture documentation. The requirement to create an architecture metamodel helps you to achieve clarity about the architecture—the formalization forces this. The approach is also appropriate for a technology-free architecture definition. It avoids defining realization technologies too early. The procedure also paves the way for automation in software development (see Section 6.2.6).

Consequences

6.6.4 Architecture Description Languages

Architecture Description Languages (ADLs) [Shaw and Garlan 1994] are a special case of a technically motivated domain-specific language. The domain here

Precise representation of architecture

is *software architecture*. ADLs therefore specialize in the precise representation of architectures even before a system is implemented [Shaw et al. 1995]. They thus support architecture-based software development. With ADLs and corresponding tools, you can design, analyze, and simulate an architecture. In particular, you can determine whether the architecture meets the existing requirements in such an early phase. With ADLs you try to increase the extent to which architectures can be understood and reused and to achieve better analysis options in this area [Shaw et al. 1995]. ADLs are distinguished by [Opengroup 1999]:

> A formal representation of architecture using textual and graphical notations at a very high level of abstraction.
> Legibility for man and machine.
> Analysis options for various architecture aspects such as completeness, consistency, performance, etc.
> Partial support for automatic code generation.

ADLs are not yet in widespread commercial use

ADLs are still in the development stage and far away from being standardized. This is shown by the following points [Opengroup 1999]:

> There is no common agreement on which architecture aspects ADLs should document and which ADLs are most suitable for specific problems.
> There is no clear distinction from other means such as formal specifications or simulation languages [Medvidovic and Taylor 2000].
> There is no *one* standard ADL, rather a series of ADLs that are concerned with different architecture aspects and domains.
> The different ADLs each have very different structures and the power of their analysis or simulation tools is also very different.
> ADLs are still a research topic at universities and are only rarely used commercially. They tend to be geared towards academic purposes with no reference to commercial use.
> The notations of the different ADLs are difficult to process and are not supported by commercial development tools.
> ADLs specialize primarily vertically in the analysis of specific architecture aspects.
> Some ADLs can be directly translated into code—for others the implementation of the specified architecture is still open.

In the course of this section we will discuss the common characteristics of ADLs. Following [Medvidovic and Taylor 2000, ADML 2002], Table 6.6-4 gives an overview of existing ADLs and their principle uses.

Table 6.6-4: *Overview of ADLs*

ADL	Description
ACME	Developed (as a number of other ADLs) at the Carnegie Mellon University (CMU) as part of the ABLE project (Architecture Based Languages and Environment) [ABLE 2009]. Focuses on static architecture aspects and tool-supported interchangeability of architecture documentation between different ADLs. Can be used as the basis for new tools of this type
ADML	Developed by The Open Group. Based on ACME and introduces an XML-based and therefore standardized form of representation
Aesop	Developed at CMU. Support for hierarchy-based architecture styles in the specification of architectures
C2 SADL	Developed at the University of California. Development of architectures for distributed and dynamic systems
Darwin	Similar direction to C2, but with a stricter formalism in the description of dynamic aspects
Koala	Developed by Philips. Development of product line architectures for the embedded area
MetaH	Developed in Honeywell Labs. Development of architectures for the navigation systems domain
Rapide	Developed at the University of Stanford. Modeling and simulation of the dynamic behavior of distributed, object-oriented systems
SADL	Developed at the System Design Laboratory of SRI. Definition and formal analysis of architectural hierarchies
UniCon	Developed at CMU. Generation of connectors for existing components using widespread interaction protocols
Weaves	Development of architectures for systems with realtime processing of large data volumes
Wright	Developed at CMU. Support in the area of connectors. Specification and analysis of protocols

What all ADLs have in common is that they focus on component-based architectures and at the core, are concerned with the architecture aspects illustrated in Figure 6.6-6 [Medvidovic and Rosenblum 1997, Garlan et al. 2000]:

Specification of components and connectors

> *Components:* The definition of a component contains the syntactic and semantic specification of functional and non-functional aspects of a building block using interfaces. Both the interfaces exported by a component and the imported interfaces required are described. The data and data integrity of components are also described. The understanding of a component here is based largely on the definition introduced in Section 6.2.3.
> *Connectors:* Components communicate with one another using connectors that define how and according to which rules components interact with one

another. Connectors can represent various communication technologies (e.g., RPC, HTTP, or Unix Pipes).

> *Architecture configuration:* The architecture configuration describes the architectural structure by defining which components are connected via connectors and how they are connected.

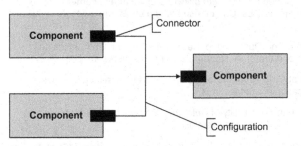

Figure 6.6-6: *ADL core concepts*

Component diagrams of UML 2.0

With regard to the component diagrams of UML in version 2.0, we can observe a merging with concepts of ADLs. Therefore, as a pure documentation means, in practice UML is generally preferred over ADLs. However, ADLs support a series of static (at compile time) and dynamic (at runtime) analyses. The objects of such analyses can be, for example:

> Compatibility (typing, syntax, and behavior) of the interfaces of components of a configuration.
> Degree of fulfillment of specified restrictions.
> Performance, security, stability, and reliability aspects of the architecture.
> Compliance with architecture guidelines.

Example architecture configuration

Figure 6.6-7 shows the architecture configuration of a very simple client/server example, presented in a box and line diagram. The component *Customer* uses the component *Database access* via an RPC connector.

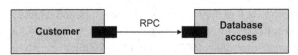

Figure 6.6-7: *Simple client/server example with ADL*

The following example code shows the formal definition of the architecture configuration presented above in the ADL ACME [Garlan et al. 2000]. The prerequisite is that the components and RPC connector used here have already been defined formally at another point. Firstly two components (*Customer* and *Database access*) are declared. The component Customer (client) receives a *send request* port and the component Database access (server) receives a *receive request* port. Then a connector (*RPC*) with the roles *caller* and *callee* is declared.

Finally, the two components are connected (attachments) via the connector by associating the ports with the corresponding roles of the connector.

```
System ExampleSystem = {
    Component customer = {Port send-request}
    Component databaseAccess = {Port receive-request}
    Connector rpc = {Roles {caller, callee}}
    Attachments : {
            customer.send-request to rpc.caller;
            databaseAccess.receive-request to rpc.callee
        }
}
```

ADLs define a metamodel that you can use for architectures generally and provide means for modeling an architecture. As always, if you look for a generic solution to a problem, the solution is usually rather unspecific. ADLs are therefore rarely used in practice. There is a recognizable trend that ADLs are becoming increasingly specific for certain domains. Examples are the EAST ADL for describing the architecture of software on (vehicle) control units [EAST 2005] or the EDOC profile for distributed enterprise applications [OMG 2005].

Trend towards convergence with DSLs

6.6.5 Unified Method Architecture

The development and introduction of software systems covers typical core disciplines (requirements engineering, analysis, design, implementation, and test), (architecture) activities, (architecture) actions, as well as a series of overarching tasks that can be found completely in almost every software project (see Section 8.1). A structured and planned procedure is essential, particularly in larger projects.

Motivation

The structuring of the procedure addresses two central topics, called *development process* and *method content* (or in abbreviated form *process* and *content*) in the context of OMG [OMG 2008c]. Method content is a defined procedure for executing specific activities. It can thus be regarded as a "recipe" or "procedure guide." Method content reflects the „best practices" gained from experience for a specific activity, for example, the creation of a use case model, and provides them in the form of a procedure guide. In contrast, a development process structures individual disciplines and activities and places them in relationship to one another. In particular, the development process thus defines a chronological sequence and refers to the lifecycle of a project. We will illustrate the conceptual separation of content and process using an example. The above-mentioned example activity of creating a use case model will be part of the development process in a number of projects executed both according to the waterfall model and

Conceptual separation of content and development process

projects executed iteratively. With regard to the method applied, i.e., the content applied, the activity will only be marginally different, if at all. The difference is that in projects executed according to the waterfall model, this activity typically happens once during the analysis phase; in projects executed iteratively, the use case model to be created is refined repeatedly and step-by-step in the course of different phases.

Method

In the context of OMG, a *method* is the aggregate of content and process. There are a series of commercial and open methods, such as the Rational Unified Process [Kruchten 2000], the V-Modell 97, the V-Modell XT [V-Modell XT 2009], or the Open Unified Process [Eclipse 2010c]. In these examples the time structuring aspect of the method, i.e., the process, is more strongly accentuated than the method content.

Method metamodel

The generally prescriptive description of a method maps from an original (the actual method applied), abstracts from irrelevant details, and is subject to a certain pragmatism. It can therefore also be perceived as a model, referred to as method model below (see Section 6.6.1). If we consider the basic concepts of model creation introduced in Section 6.6.1 again, here we arrive at the concept of the *method metamodel*. A method metamodel defines general terminology and semantics for describing concrete methods. For a long time, method metamodels existed only in the minds of the process engineers or in the form of a hard-coded implementation in mostly proprietary tools. However, in order to be able to guarantee interoperability between different method models, a standardized method metamodel and thus embedding in an existing modeling architecture (see Section 6.6.1) is necessary. Figure 6.6-8 shows the classification of the concepts introduced in this section in the OMG modeling architecture (see Section 6.6.2). We will look at the example method metamodels (UMA and SPEM) shown in Figure 6.6-8 later on in this section.

Historical development of the SPEM and UMA specifications

As far back as 2002, OMG tried to standardize a method metamodel with the specification of the *Software Process Engineering Metamodel* (SPEM) [OMG 2008c]. In versions 1.x, SPEM was specified as both an independent metamodel based on the UML superstructure and as a UML profile (see Section 6.6.2). The underlying basis in both cases was UML version 1.4. SPEM version 1.x was, however, largely unaccepted, meaning that only a few, mainly commercial, implementations were produced. Since UML 2 has increasingly established itself, the desire to use the new features of UML 2 for SPEM as well was quickly recognized. The *Unified Method Architecture* (UMA) [Haumer 2005], a standardized method metamodel from IBM, addresses some of the weaknesses of SPEM in versions 1.x. Just like the adaptation to UML 2, it also influences the SPEM 2.0 specification decisively [OMG 2008c]. UMA is implemented as part of the freely available *Eclipse Process Framework (EPF)* [Eclipse 2010c] and the *Rational Method Composer (RMC)*, a commercial tool from IBM. EPF and RMC provide

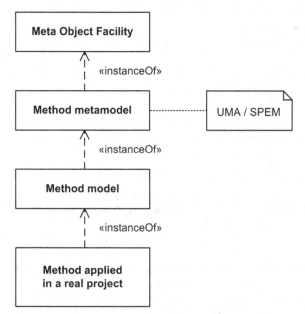

Figure 6.6-8: Classification of method model and method metamodel in the OMG modeling architecture

the functionality for modeling concrete methods based on UMA. You can then export these methods in various output formats (for example, HTML) and provide them to the development team. In this context therefore, you use method metamodels as documentation means.

SPEM and UMA can be considered as special DSLs (see Section 6.6.3). The language constructs of these DSLs stem from the functional domain "Methods for developing software systems." Later in this section we will briefly present the implementation of the domain-specific language constructs as heavyweight extension of the UML metamodel (see Section 6.6.2) using a few selected elements of UMA.

SPEM and UMA as special DSLs

The basic philosophy of a separation of method content and development process is also reflected in UMA. A model element is therefore either a building block for modeling method content or a means in the specification of processes or process building blocks. The only exception is the element *Guidance*, which enables the formulation of support and guidelines. These can be used in the method context and in the process context. The distinction of the language constructs of UMA as method or process building blocks is realized via the object-oriented concept of generalization. *MethodElement* or *ProcessElement* are thus the root elements of the inheritance hierarchies shown in Figures 6.6-9 and 6.6-10.

Separation of method content and development process in UMA

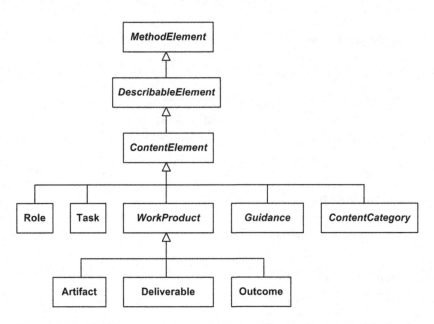

Figure 6.6-9: UMA language constructs for modeling method content (extract)

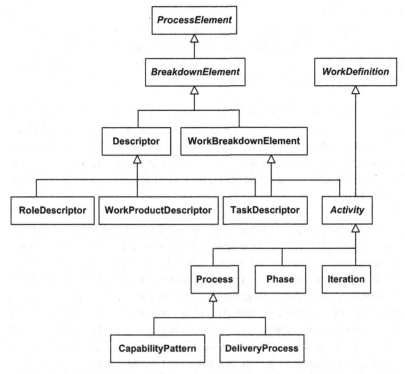

Figure 6.6-10: UMA language constructs for modeling development processes (extract)

Method content enables you to model procedure guides for realizing specific development goals. Figure 6.6-11 expresses the central relationships between the three language constructs *Role*, *Task*, and *WorkProduct* for the definition of a method. These three language constructs form the core concept of a method specification.

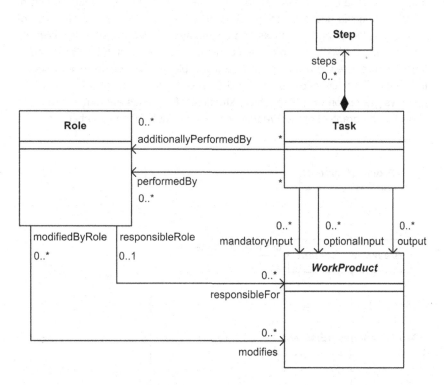

Figure 6.6-11: *Relationships between the UMA language constructs Role, Task, and WorkProduct*

A *Task* defines work to be performed by a specific *Role*. A task has a performing role (*performedBy*) as well as any number of additional processing roles (*additionallyPerformedBy*). You can assign input and output *WorkProducts* to a task. They are classified as optional (*optionalInput*) or necessary (*mandatoryInput*). Every task has a clearly defined goal and provides a step-by-step instruction in the form of all *steps* necessary for achieving the goal. A *WorkProduct* represents an abstraction of those elements that are created, required, or modified by tasks. Since project participants perform tasks in a specific role (naturally, one project participant can take on several roles), roles use work products to perform their tasks or create them during a task. UMA also assigns a responsible role to every work product.

Hierarchical structure of project activities

You can use activities and process building blocks to structure contents and place them in relationship to one another. Activities and process building blocks define when the basic tasks defined as content are to be performed as part of a project-specific development process. In UMA, the hierarchical structure of all work packages and sub-tasks of a project are referred to as the *WorkBreakdownStructure* (WBS). In the context of project management, the WBS is sometimes also referred to as the project structure plan (PSP). Figure 6.6-12 shows the core of the relevant extract of the UMA specification with regard to the WBS. It shows the option of a hierarchical structure of activities and subclasses (not shown in the graphic) of the *BreakdownElement* class defined as abstract.

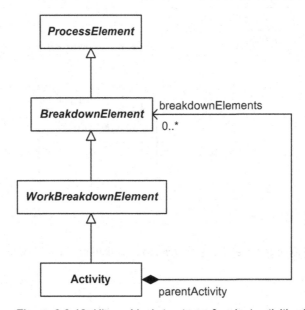

Figure 6.6-12: Hierarchical structure of project activities in UMA

You integrate content into the WBS using *descriptors*. Figure 6.6-13 shows this using the example of the method element *Task*. The indirection introduced by the descriptor concept enables you to adapt method content to special activities individually, for example, via the selection of the steps to be performed in a specific context.

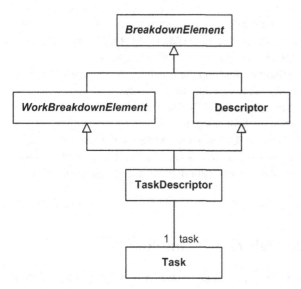

Figure 6.6-13: Integration of method content using the Task example

6.6.6 Summary

> A modeling language is the aggregation of concrete syntax, abstract syntax, and static and dynamic semantics. The abstract syntax is mostly specified by a metamodel. The terms "well-formedness criteria" and "constraints" are also used as synonyms for static semantics.

> Models are noted in a concrete syntax, are given meaning by the semantics of the modeling language, respect the well-formedness criteria, and conform to a dedicated metamodel.

> A metamodel is a special model for defining the abstract syntax of a modeling language. In particular, you specify the types of model elements as well as their possible relationships to one another. Models are also known as instances of the related metamodel.

> The cascade of sequential abstraction through the creation of a metamodel opens up a hierarchy of modeling layers and is referred to as modeling architecture.

> Four-layered modeling architectures are well-established in software development. The most prominent representative is the OMG modeling architecture with MOF as the uppermost metamodel, in this case also referred to as metametamodel.

> UML is a special modeling language. The UML infrastructure is the core of MOF and the UML superstructure. The UML superstructure specifies the UML metamodel. UML diagrams are an option for the notation of UML models.

**Summary:
Architecture
modeling means**

> Using the UML profile mechanism or a real metamodel extension, you can adapt and extend the language scope of UML to meet specific needs.
> Like UML, domain-specific languages (DSLs) are special modeling languages. You can use them to describe the relevant concepts of a specific functionally or technically motivated domain precisely.
> Architecture description languages (ADLs) are special DSLs used to describe the architecture of applications precisely.
> Unified Method Architecture (UMA) is a special DSL and is used to specify methods. In this book, analogous to the OMG terminology, methods are considered as the aggregation of method content and development process.

6.7 Architecturally Relevant Technologies

Overview

This section covers some categories of technologies that are used in modern software architectures and therefore belong to your software architect's "toolbox." In detail we will discuss communication middleware systems, databases and persistence of business objects, data exchange and data transformation with XML, web application servers, component platforms, and web services. Figure 6.7-1 gives an overview of the technologies covered.

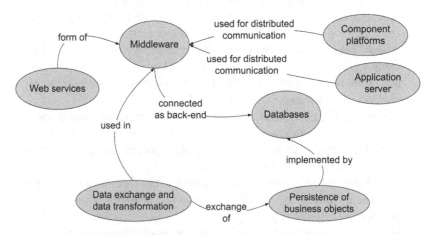

Figure 6.7-1: Overview of architecturally relevant technologies

The technologies specified provide a "general" infrastructure in many software architectures. Of course, this is still only a small selection of technologies. There are many basic technologies that are very important for many architectures but including them would exceed the scope of this section: for example, compilers or virtual machines. There are also many specific technologies, for example, content management systems or enterprise resource planning systems (ERP).

6.7.1 Middleware Systems

We have already addressed middleware as a basic architecture in Section 6.4. We will now discuss some examples of important middleware systems in more detail. They are: transaction processing monitors, RPC and OO-RPC systems, and message-oriented middleware. We will also give a brief overview of other systems. Later on we will discuss web services. These are a special case because although they realize middleware basic architecture, they also support the more extensive SOA basic architecture.

6.7.1.1 Transaction Processing Monitors

Transaction processing monitors (TP monitors) are one of the oldest forms of middleware. They provide an infrastructure for developing, running, and controlling distributed transactions.

Transaction processing monitors can efficiently map a number of client requests on servers or databases. Many of them support a series of communication styles, such as RPC, publish/subscribe, and message queues.

The concept of the transaction was developed in the database environment. Transactions should usually have a set of properties (so-called ACID properties):

ACID properties

> *Atomicity:* A transaction is treated as an inseparable unit and is either processed completely or not at all.
> *Consistency:* When a transaction finishes, the system must be in a consistent state.
> *Isolation:* The behavior of a transaction must not be influenced by other transactions.
> *Durability:* Once a transaction has been completed, changes are permanent or persistent—they can thus even survive the system crashing.

A distributed transaction covers more than one distributed resource. RPC treats all calls as if they were independent of one another. In contrast, transaction processing monitors allow the user to group a series of calls in one transaction. You can also realize distributed transactions through a two-phase commit protocol (2PC, see also [Gray 1978]). This protocol guarantees the ACID properties for a transaction and supports the distributed synchronization of several transaction resources.

Two-phase commit

Transaction processing monitors: Products	One of the first transaction processing monitors was the Customer and Control System (CICS) from IBM [IBM 2003]. It was developed in the late 1960s and is still used today. Other known commercial transaction processing monitors are Tuxedo from Oracle [Oracle 2011d] and the Microsoft Transaction Server (MTS), which is now integrated into the Microsoft COM+ Component Services [Microsoft 2010].

6.7.1.2 RPC and OO-RPC Middleware

RPC/OO-RPC middleware systems	RPC and OO-RPC middleware systems use the RPC distribution style described above to call procedures or methods (hereinafter referred to uniformly as "operations") in a distributed way. Distributed calls should, as far as possible—but not further—look like local operation calls. Internally, RPC and OO-RPC systems are realized in a very similar way. The main difference is that OO-RPC also supports object-oriented abstractions, in particular such as object identity, but also class and inheritance relationships.

RPC implements the client/server model as follows: clients call operations; servers accept operation calls. The server provides a set of operations that the client can call distributed.

From the client view, RPC operations look identical to local operations: they also have an operation name, parameters, and a return type. One considerable difference is that there can be additional error messages, for example, because the network fails, or the server has not implemented a called operation. The client must be informed of these errors—that is, the client must be able to process them.

Synchronous and asynchronous RPC	In a typical case, the client process is blocked until the response to the operation call has been returned by the server. This synchronous type of RPC is the standard case in most RPC systems. Some RPC systems also support asynchronous RPC. In this case, the client does not block and continues its work immediately after the request. Usually there are different types of asynchronous operations—including those that return a result and those that do not (so-called one-way operations).

Procedural RPC systems	Early, popular RPC systems are the Distributed Computing Environment (DCE) [OSF 1991] and Sun RPC [Sun 1988]. These already implement the typically simple way of calling RPC operations: the server registers a procedure as a so-called endpoint in the server application and registers this service in a directory server—which may run on a different computer. The client can now find this service using the directory server. In the future the client uses the endpoint to actually call the distributed procedure.

DCE primarily arose as a procedural RPC. It does have an enhancement to support distributed objects though. Today, however, there are many OO-RPC middleware systems that have been designed specifically for this purpose. Examples are:

> Common Object Request Broker Architecture (CORBA) [OMG 2008a]
> Microsoft's .NET Remoting [Microsoft 2009]
> Various web service frameworks (see the section on web services below)
> Microsoft's DCOM [Grimes 1997]
> Sun's Java RMI [Grosso 2001]

For a deeper understanding of this type of middleware system, we recommend the book *Remoting Patterns* [Völter et al. 2004]. It discusses the fundamental design and architecture patterns of RPC and OO-RPC middleware systems.

6.7.1.3 Message-Oriented Middleware

Message-oriented middleware (MOM) systems use the message metaphor to realize asynchronous, distributed communication. Neither the client nor the server send or receive requests, responses, or other message types directly. Instead, they place them in, or expect them from, message queues. This means that instead of blocking, in the standard case the clients continue their work immediately after sending a message.

Results are either:

> Returned by a *callback* (an operation called asynchronously as an event), or
> Obtained by the client by means of request to the message queue (so-called "polling").
> Both variants are asynchronous. It is therefore essential that the client can assign a specific response to a previous request, since the responses do not necessarily arrive in the same order in which the requests were sent. Responses are usually assigned to requests by means of a unique identifier that is sent with the request and that is returned with the response (a so-called "correlation identifier" [Hohpe and Woolf 2003]).

MOM systems typically support several message channels as a connection between specific senders and specific receivers. Each of these channels has its own send and receive message queues. Client and server applications typically do not interact directly with message queues or message channels. Instead, they use so-called endpoints as abstractions—these take over all interaction with the MOM system.

OO-RPC middleware systems

Messages and message queues

Asynchronous results

Characteristic functionalities and properties of MOM

MOM systems also have some distinguishing properties. Typically, these are:

> Messages are reliably transmitted. This means that a temporary breakdown in system resources, such as the network or the server, can be tolerated.
> The sequence of delivery and receipt of messages can be guaranteed.
> If a message still cannot be delivered after a long time, it can be removed from the MOM system automatically if you set an expiration time.
> The MOM system automatically recognizes and processes messages sent twice erroneously.

MOM: Products

The MOM concepts are implemented in a series of middleware systems. Examples are IBM WebSphere MQ (previously MQ Series) [IBM 2004], JMS [Oracle 2011b], Microsoft MSMQ [Microsoft 2011], and TIBCO Enterprise Message Service [TIBCO 2011].

For a deeper understanding of MOM systems, we recommend the book *Enterprise Integration Patterns* [Hohpe and Woolf 2003].

6.7.1.4 Further Middleware Systems

The three types of middleware systems discussed in more detail (transaction processing monitors, RPC systems, and MOM systems) are relatively widespread today and are commercially accepted. However, there are a number of other middleware systems that are also frequently used or are still being developed. We will give a brief overview of these systems here (for a more in-depth discussion, see the book *Remoting Patterns* [Völter et al. 2004]):

> *Peer-to-peer* systems (P2P) are different to other distributed architectures in that they are not based on the client/server style or n-tier architecture style. In contrast, they are based on a network of equal peers that communicate with one another and coordinate each other. Internally, many P2P systems are realized with distributed objects. Examples of P2P systems and projects are: Napster [Roxio 2003], SETI@home [Anderson et al. 2002], and JXTA [Sun 2003].
> Closely related to P2P systems are *spontaneous networks*. They allow you to offer and remove any services in the network at any time. You can use spontaneous networks as an infrastructure to implement a P2P network. One example of a spontaneous network is Jini [Jini 2007].
> The aim of *Grid Computing* [Foster et al. 2001] is to use distributed resources, such as computer performance, information, or memory together. A network of connected computers is merged to one system.
> *Mobile Code* [Fugetta et al. 1998] is different to other middleware approaches in that it sends not only requests and results—i.e., data—but also code. Code can thus be provided by the client and executed in the local context of the server. This has the advantage, for example, that clients can influence

the calculation guidelines but the data for a calculation still does not have to be sent completely via the network.

6.7.2 Databases and Persistence of Business Objects

Databases are often an important part of the software architecture. Our aim here is not to provide an introduction to databases but to give an overview of the architecture requirements of persistent data management. We will therefore discuss the typical problems and technological solution options when using database technologies to manage business objects persistently. In general, persistence means that you transfer data from volatile storage (often also denoted as transient storage or representation), such as the main memory (RAM), to permanent storage media, such as hard drives or optical storage media. The aim of this is to store business data "securely" and, if necessary, update it for changes accordingly.

Persistence requirement

Another important problem that leads to persistent data management is that the memory requirements of many programs considerably exceed the main memory available. In general we can say that the slower a memory is, the cheaper it is. You therefore try, as far as possible, to replace expensive main memory with cheaper storage options, such as hard drives, optical storage media, or tape storage. The persistent storage of business objects is usually based on a database, i.e., storage on hard drives. However, there are also other forms of "secure" storage of business data. For example, for large volumes of data, optical storage media with so-called "jukeboxes" are used. Today these allow access to an almost unlimited volume of data, but they are considerably slower than hard drives.

In addition to the basic persistence requirement that a database must satisfy— i.e., its main functionality—there are a number of other requirements that can be placed on the database or the database management system:

Further requirements

> In many systems a number of requests can be submitted to a database at the same time. Therefore, good *performance* and *scalability* are necessary.
> Since the database is a central part of the IT architecture, high *availability* is also an important point.
> The database should support transactions. Here we differentiate between short-running transactions, such as a series of requests, and long-running transactions, such as a workflow with human interactions. In long-running transactions, the above-mentioned ACID properties can sometimes be difficult to maintain. Therefore, these have to be supported specially, i.e., generally not only by the database but also by application logic.

> A database should support the *security* of the data and be able to manage different security rights, for example, with a user and/or role concept.
> The *simplicity* of the access to the data is important in order to be able to understand the data models and access the data easily. In particular, this also means that it must be possible to map the data models and access structures on the application architecture easily.
> The database should provide a maintenance interface for the *administration* and *control* of the database.

Structural break between database and object-oriented application

Another problem is that in many projects today, development is on an object-oriented basis but the predominant databases are based on relational data models. In other words, you have to decide whether you want to use the more usual relational database management system (RDBMS) or, as a result of the object-oriented nature of the application, you want to use an object-oriented database management system (OODBMS). Note that this problem occurs not only with object orientation but also with other programming paradigms, such as procedural programming, logical programming, or aspect orientation. For each programming paradigm, you have to think about how to map the data to the database in a meaningful way. The following are examples of options that are always possible:
> The database is capable of mapping data abstractions and relationships of the programming paradigm itself.
> The database supports abstractions other than the programming paradigm. This situation is known as a *structural break* that you have to react to. This means that you have to consider how you can map the application model to the database model.

Now we will look at the solution options for the example of persistence of object-oriented business objects more precisely. If you store object-oriented business objects, you generally want to map their properties, such as object relationships, object identity, class relationships, inheritance, polymorphism, etc., to the storage in the database. Here an OODBMS offers the advantage that it already maps object-oriented properties. This means that mapping the object-oriented models in the programming language is very simple. However, the serious disadvantage of OODBMS systems is that they are used considerably less often than relational database systems. Since databases are mostly extremely important for enterprises, in many projects the risk of selecting an OODBMS system is considered to be too great.

Object-relational mapping

In contrast, storing business objects in relational databases often leads to the above-mentioned structural break: the relations in tables and relationships are mapped using foreign keys. This model must be mapped to the object-oriented model with its relationships, hierarchies, and identities. This mapping is not unique and there is therefore a whole series of approaches for object-relational mapping [Keller 1997].

One simple approach is to embed the SQL code for the access to the database in the application logic. However, this has serious disadvantages: you have to change the application logic code for even simple data changes. The aspect "persistence" is distributed across the whole program meaning that central changes are difficult. Therefore, it is generally recommended that you introduce at least separate "data classes"—their task is to handle database accesses and they are independent of the application logic.

However, a lot of tasks for database access are recurring. To overcome this situation, a separate database access layer is frequently introduced. This encapsulates all requests to a database and cannot be circumvented. It is where object-relational mapping takes place. The database access layer often consists of two layers itself [Keller and Coldewey 1998] (see Figure 6.7-2): a logical access layer provides a stable interface for the application layer; a physical access layer below that establishes the actual access to the database and you can, for example, modify it for performance reasons or for changes to the database version.

Database access

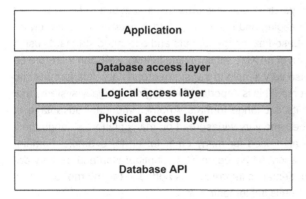

Figure 6.7-2: Database access layer. [Keller and Coldewey 1998]

Many languages have standard libraries for the database access. Java, for example, has JDBC (Java Database Connectivity)—a library for access to relational databases. In general, JDBC offers functions for establishing the connection to a database, the use of SQL instructions for so-called CRUD operations (create, read, update, delete), and the evaluation of the results. An advantage of this type of standard library is, at least primarily, the independence from the database implementation. However, the database programming is still at a very low level here, and developers need to have precise knowledge of SQL and have to resolve all technical details of the persistence.

Standard libraries for database access

Object-relational mapping

Many languages also have more extensive standard libraries that enable transparent persistence of the objects. This functionality is known as object-relational mapping (ORM). It means that the developer only has to configure the persistence (which objects have to be kept persistent, where the data is stored, etc.) and all other persistence tasks are taken over automatically. Examples in Java are the Java Persistence API (JPA) in EJB 3, Hibernate, and Java Data Objects (JDO).

6.7.3 XML and Other X Standards

Transformation

The smooth exchange of structured data and the transformation of this data are of enormous importance for many information systems.

XML

With the appearance of the Internet, the description, exchange, and processing of structured data was carried out more and more based on web protocols. HTML—the language with which web pages are described in WWW—is, however, not suitable for representing structured data. Therefore, the eXtensible Markup Language (XML) [Bray et al. 1998] was developed with the aim of providing a flexible, extensible, and simple standard for structured data exchange on the Internet. XML allows you to describe information in a structured way. It is not a standard itself for exchanging and processing data in enterprises. It merely allows you to define XML-based exchange formats and exchange standards using a document type definition or an XML schema (see below). XML can therefore be extended flexibly. It is also very simple to transform proprietary data formats into XML formats and vice versa. This is important for integrating legacy systems that often use proprietary data exchange formats. Another important advantage of XML is that it has now become very widespread on many platforms, languages, and systems. It is now also used for many other tasks: for example, domain-specific languages are described based on XML, configuration and delivery descriptors are formulated, semantic information is added to the Internet based on XHTML, object serialization is implemented, etc.

DTD

You can use a document type definition (DTD) to specify the structure of XML documents. DTDs are easy to understand and validators for DTDs are widespread and efficient. However, DTDs have some disadvantages: in particular they are not XML documents themselves and therefore you cannot edit them using XML tools. The possibilities for data specification are also limited: for example, you have no built-in language means for specifying data types.

XML schema

The XML schema standard [W3C 2004] aims to solve these problems. Every schema is a valid XML document and XML schemas allow typed data based on primitive and self-defined data types.

The definition of the data formats—in DTDs or schemas—is particularly important for complex applications.

Beyond these basic elements of the XML language there are many other standards that complete XML in different areas. We will list a few central standards that are generally important briefly here:

Further XML standards

> XML namespaces are used to differentiate between names in different contexts. This allows the developer to select the name without naming conflicts occurring in the case of common use of two documents developed independently of one another (because both documents specify their names uniquely in the context of their namespace).
> XHTML is an XML variant of HTML. It has the same presentation-oriented properties as HTML, but in the XML sense is well-formed (for example, every opening tag must also have a closing counterpart).
> XLink is a linking mechanism for XML documents. Its links far exceed the links known from HTML. For example, you can link to a number of documents and specify traversals.
> XPath is a language for localizing and extracting information within an XML document.
> XSLT allows you to generate any documents from XML documents. It is used most frequently in practice to transform XML documents. In XSLT, XPath is used to specify XML structures.
> XQuery is an SQL-like query language for queries to XML documents.
> The Resource Description Framework (RDF) is an XML language that allows you to specify metadata via web resources. Under some circumstances this metadata can be described in an ontology language.

This is just a small extract of the multitude of XML standards. As well as these general standards, there are many more domain-specific or industry-specific XML languages.

In addition to the XML languages, there are many standards, de facto standards, and APIs for processing XML, such as:

XML processing: APIs and standards

> SAX—a programmatic API for processing XML
> DOM—a document tree-based API for processing XML
> Redland—an API for access to RDF data

We explained XML here as an example of a standard for the definition of data exchange languages due to the fact that it is very widespread. There are many other languages and formats. It often makes sense to use XML. The central advantages are that XML is simple, flexible, and extensible. However, there are also some disadvantages. As a result of its properties, XML needs quite a lot of

XML: Advantages and disadvantages

memory space (or bandwidth for data exchange). This is because it uses meaningful tags and mostly a presentation that can be read directly by human beings. In some cases, the string processing during parsing and interpretation of XML can also lead to performance problems. Furthermore, XML itself is very simple, but some XML standards are already very complex. These reasons might indicate that a proprietary format is more suitable for certain tasks than XML. The migration to XML, particularly in legacy applications, can cause considerable costs.

6.7.4 Dynamic Web Pages and Web Application Servers

Dynamic web pages

Today, almost all (larger) websites require web pages to be created dynamically. This means that data is created dynamically or retrieved in a web request by a back-end, such as a database or legacy application. These results are then formatted with HTML and then delivered. Using web requests (for example, triggered by clicking a link in the browser) or HTML forms, you can change the data in a back-end from a browser. These changes must be written back to the back-end.

Web application server

To enable such dynamic interactions in the web, there must be a program behind the web page that creates the page dynamically from the current data of the back-end, and, if necessary, performs changes to the back-end. A web server that enables this is known as a web application server.

Technologies and architectures for server-side program modules

There are a number of technologies and architectures that you can use to integrate server-side programs in a web server architecture. These have various advantages and disadvantages:

> The *CGI interface* (Common Gateway Interface) is one of the earliest technologies still used that is supported by practically every web server. When a web request comes in, a process that executes a "little program" is started dynamically. Scripting languages such as Perl or Tcl are often used to do this, but you can use any programming language. The program receives the request parameters via environment variables. The new process for every request can however lead to performance problems and high resource consumption. *Fast CGI* is a CGI extension that uses multi-threading to avoid this problem. However, there is still the general problem of CGI that "larger" interactions, such as a complete business transaction, are mapped using many small programs that are not connected to one another. This means that complex CGI architectures are difficult to understand and maintain.

> There is a series of *template languages* that embed program text in HTML pages and allow it to be replaced by the application server dynamically. Examples are PHP, ColdFusion, Active Server Pages (ASP), and Java Server Pages (JSP). In these languages the code consists of normal HTML code

with code in the respective template language embedded in specific areas that are often indicated by pre-defined start and end characters such as "<% ...%>". All approaches named offer wide support, good performance, comfortable libraries, a good database connection, and are relatively easy to learn. However, these approaches sometimes have one or more of the following difficulties, particularly for complex projects. For example, simple means for communicating with other applications are missing. Program logic in the respective template language can also often not be used for other purposes. The individual pages remain relatively loosely coupled and are therefore—just like with CGI—driven only by requests.

> Some of the disadvantages of template languages are solved by *application servers*, such as Apache Tomcat, JBoss, BEA WebLogic, or IBM WebSphere. These are often part of larger standard architectures, for example, Microsoft's .NET or JEE. Application servers are professional complete systems that typically offer a server-side component model, transaction management, scaling, load balancing, security mechanisms, fail-over, and integration with other middleware and web services.

> *Web content management* and *community systems*, such as Zope or Open ACS, are based on web application servers and also offer many extension modules, for example, for community functions, forums, Wikis, collaboration in virtual groups, etc.

> Agile web frameworks are web frameworks in dynamic programming languages, such as Ruby on Rails, Seaside, Mason, or Grails. They are referred to as "agile" because they have been designed in order to support principles such as "Don't Repeat Yourself" (DRY) and "Convention over Configuration." This means that these frameworks support agile software development by placing programming conventions above the application configuration and thus allow fast implementation of requirements.

For information about patterns underlying these technologies we recommend the pattern language on the topic of generation and conversion of contents in the web, see [Vogel and Zdun 2002].

6.7.5 Component Platforms

In this section we will present some known platforms that implement the component platform basic architecture from architectural viewpoints.

Component platforms

6.7.5.1 *Java Enterprise Edition (JEE)*

Java Enterprise Edition (JEE) is a component platform based on Java technology in the Java programming language. This component platform is thus plat-

JEE

form-independent. The manufacturer-independence is limited, as the platform is based on specifications from Oracle. JEE is firstly a collection of specifications for the building blocks of a component platform. If you want to use JEE, you have to select a product (container and services) from a number of JEE implementations from different manufacturers (commercial or open source). Depending on the orientation of the product, only certain parts of the JEE specifications are implemented. There can also be proprietary extensions that lead to a close manufacturer lock-in. You have to consider all of this when making a selection from an architecture view. The implementations that you finally decide on depend above all on your requirements and your budget.

JEE restricts architectural freedom

One concern for the architecture of a system is that JEE involves numerous interfaces that have to be satisfied and you have to extensively configure JEE components via XML configuration files (so-called deployment descriptors) for the purposes of delivery. You also have to configure the container. JEE implements many of the concepts described in the previous sections. These concepts should also be applied if you use JEE. This means that you must use JEE quite specifically in an architectural framework and not just in its "raw" form. This is important on one hand because JEE gives rise to architectural constraints, and on the other hand, an improper use of JEE can lead to critical problems for a system (e.g., bad performance). We strongly recommend using proven JEE design technologies in this context as they are explained, for example, in [Alur et al. 2003]. We will now give an overview of the central parts of JEE. Figure 6.7-3 shows an overview of the JEE component platform. For detailed descriptions and further literature recommendations, see [Oracle 2011c].

> Java *Servlets/Java Server Pages (JSP)/Java Server Faces (JSF):* These building blocks are responsible for communication between the browser as client and the model layer in JEE-based web applications. They are located in the presentation layer.

> *Enterprise JavaBeans (EJB):* These building blocks represent the actual model components and are therefore located in the model layer. They exist in the forms Entity Bean (entity component), Session Bean (session component), and Message-Driven Bean (message component).

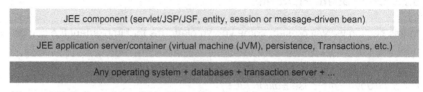

Figure 6.7-3: Overview of the JEE component platform

6.7.5.2   Microsoft .NET

From a conceptual point of view, Microsoft's component platform .NET is very **.NET vs. JEE**
similar to JEE. For example, it also has a virtual machine, the Common Language Runtime (CLR). However, there are a number of important differences in
the implementation of the concepts. .NET supports different programming languages (VB, C++, etc.), whereby only C# as the actual .NET programming language supports the component capability of .NET to its full extent. .NET is more
data-oriented than object-oriented. This means that the object-oriented design is
strongly driven by data structures.

This fact is also shown in the implementation of the component approach. In the
stricter sense, .NET only has entity components as components. However, the
most serious differences to JEE are that .NET, although basically available in
platform-independent form, is only available for the Windows platform in a usable
form and there is a very strict manufacturer lock-in because there is only one
significant manufacturer, namely Microsoft.

The close integration with the operating system means that in comparison to
JEE, the integration of the different building blocks of this infrastructure is better
overall. We can conclude that the architectural situation is very similar to JEE,
but extended by the platform aspect. For more details about .NET, see [Microsoft
2009]. The main differences between and common features of JEE and .NET are
visible if you compare Figure 6.7-4 with Figure 6.7-3.

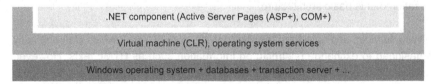

Figure 6.7-4: Overview of the .NET component platform

6.7.5.3   CORBA Component Model (CCM)

Since version 3.0, the CORBA Component Model (CCM) is part of the Common **CCM**
Object Request Broker Architecture (CORBA). It is the specification of a model
for distributed components of the model layer and its containers. CCM is independent of any programming language or platform. With some limitations, JEE
and .NET are CCM implementations. With the exception of a few Open Source
products, up until now there has been no complete implementation. OMG now
uses JEE more than component technology. In addition to the component types
described above, CCM also has the process components. These correspond to

a business transaction and can be used persistently as well as by several clients. You can define the following interfaces for a CCM component:

> *Facets:* Services that the component offers externally.
> *Receptacles:* Services that the component requires from other components.

Figure 6.7-5 shows an overview of CCM. For more information about CCM, see [OMG 2006].

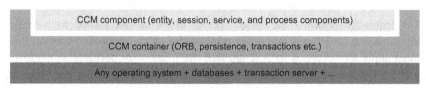

Figure 6.7-5: *Overview of the CCM component platform*

6.7.6 Web Services

Web services

Here we will briefly discuss web services specifically as a middleware architecture that implements the SOA basic architecture and that heavily uses the previously described XML and Internet standards. SOA describes a general basic architecture for loosely coupled interaction between different distributed software applications. In contrast, *web services* represent a possible (standardized) realization of this basic architecture.

Web services: Origin

Web services originate from the World Wide Web (WWW), which was originally designed to exchange unstructured information such as HTML texts. However, interactions between programs have become increasingly important, for example, in the area of e-commerce or EDI. XML [Bray et al. 1998] and standards based on XML are used here in particular. The XML RPC specification [Winer 1999] represents a first standard for RPC communication via XML.

Web service protocols

Web services today are based on a layered architecture made up of several standardized protocols:

> SOAP [Box et al. 2000] is an XML-based message exchange protocol that has quickly become a de facto standard for web services. It is the—clearly extended—successor to the XML RPC specification.
> An alternative to SOAP is REST (Representational State Transfer). It is not a standard but an architecture style that is based on existing web standards such as HTTP and URI. With REST-conform web services, the interaction between client and server is processed using the standardized interface

defined by HTTP. The concrete data exchange takes place via user-defined XML formats.

> WSDL [Christensen et al. 2001] plays an important role in web service architectures. It is an interface description language that is understood by both the senders and recipients of the messages. WSDL is therefore very important for interoperability in heterogeneous systems, for example, if different web service systems are to interoperate. WSDL is also based on XML.

> Web services do not need a special communication protocol. You can use HTTP or other protocols such as SMTP, FTP, JMS, IIOP, or other protocols, for example. HTTP is supported as standard protocol in most web service systems today and you can generally use a number of other protocols as plug-ins.

> UDDI is a standard for a lookup service [OASIS 2002]. It allows you to find web services and their WSDL description based on properties. However, so far, UDDI has not really established itself commercially and many other—in part, proprietary—lookup services are used.

> There are some standards for composing web services. One important category of these standards describes the orchestration of web services through business process models that are processed in a process engine. The activities of the processes (i.e., the process steps) call the web services or receive their results. The most important standard in this area is currently the Business Process Execution Language for Web Services (BPEL4WS) [Andrews et al. 2003], an XML-based workflow definition language that allows you to describe business processes.

In addition to these standards, there are a number of other web service standards, for example, in the area of security and long-running business transactions.

6.7.7 Summary

> There are architecturally relevant technologies that provide a major infrastructure in many software architectures.
> Communication middleware is a central technology for many distributed systems.
> Main middleware systems are transaction processing monitors, RPC and OO-RPC middleware, and message-oriented middleware.
> A structural break is an important architectural problem that designates the break between two paradigms. For example, in persistent data management, there is a structural break between the paradigms of relational database management systems and the application logic.

Summary: Architecturally relevant technologies

> Object-relational mapping enables the integration of an object-oriented application with the relational paradigm. ORM also offers a database access layer for relational databases and object-oriented application logic. Object-relational mappers, such as Hibernate, are an important technology in this area.

> Another important technology for persistent data management is standard libraries for database access, such as JDBC.

> The description, smooth exchange, and processing of structured data are enormously important for many information systems. One important example technology in this area is XML.

> XML enables you to describe the structure of information in a standard way, separating content and structure information. XML itself is not a standard for data exchange as such, but enables the definition of XML-based exchange formats and exchange standards.

> A web application server is a server for web applications that creates dynamic HTML pages and executes the application logic between the client (browser) and different backend systems, such as a database.

> A component platform is a runtime environment (container) for components. It is based on the separation of technical and functional concerns. The component platform takes over the technical concerns. Examples of technical concerns in the enterprise environment are distribution, security, persistence, transactions, concurrency, and resource management.

> Important component platforms are Java Enterprise Edition (JEE), Microsoft .NET, and the CORBA Component Model (CCM).

> Web services are a technology serving as enabler while implementing the SOA basic architecture and which focuses heavily on XML and Internet standards.

Further Reading

Further Reading: 6.1 Architecture Principles

Further reading:
Architecture
principles

[Alexander 1977]
Alexander, Christopher; Ishikawa, Sara; Silverstein, Murray; Jacobson, Max; Fiksdahl-King, Ingrid; Angel, Shlomo,*A Pattern Language*, Oxford University Press, 1977

[Buschmann et al. 1996]
Buschmann, Frank; Meunier, Regine; Rohnert, Hans; Sommerlad, Peter; Stal, Michael, *Pattern-Oriented Software Architecture Vol. 1, A System of Patterns*, John Wiley & Sons, New York, 1996

[Gamma et al. 1995]
Gamma, Erich; Helm, Richard; Johnson, Ralph; Vlissides, John, *Design Patterns - Elements of Reusable Object-Oriented Software*, Addison-Wesley, Reading, 1995

[Kiczales et al. 1997]
Kiczales, Gregor; Lamping, John; Mendhekar, Anurag; Maeda, Chris; Videira Lopes, Cristina; Loingtier, Jean-Marc; Irwin, John, *Aspect-Oriented Programming*, ECOOP 1997, 220-242, 1997

[Lieberherr and Holland 1989]
Lieberherr, Karl; Holland, Ian, *Assuring Good Style for Object-Oriented Programs*, IEEE Software, 38-48, September 1989

[Liskov 1988]
Liskov, B, *Data Abstraction and Hierarchy*, SIGPLAN Notices, 23(5), May 1988

[Martin 2000]
Martin, Robert C., *Design Principles and Design Patterns*, http://www.object-mentor.com/resources/articles/ Principles_and_Patterns.PDF, 2000

[Meyer 1997]
Meyer, Bertrand; *Object-Oriented Software Construction, second edition*, New Jersey, Prentice Hall, 1997

[Parnas 1994]
Parnas, David. L., *Software Aging*, In Proceedings of ICSE 1994, Sorrento, Italy, 1994

[Pree 1995]
Pree, W., *Design Patterns for Object-Oriented Software Development*, Addison-Wesley, 1995

[Tarr 2004]
Tarr, P., *Hyper/J*, http://www.research.ibm.com/hyperspace/HyperJ/HyperJ.htm, 2004

[Völter et al. 2004]
Völter, Markus; Kircher, Michael; Zdun, Uwe, *Remoting Patterns - Foundations of Enterprise, Internet, and Realtime Distributed Object Middleware*, John Wiley & Sons, 2004

[Yourdon and Constantine 1978]
Yourdon, E.; Constantine, L., *Structured Design: Fundamentals of a Discipline of Computer Programming and Design*, Prentice Hall, 1978

Further Reading: 6.2 Basic Architecture Concepts

Further reading: Basic programming paradigms

[Goedicke et al. 2000]
Goedicke, M.; Neumann, G.; Zdun, U., *Object system layer*, Proceedings of 5th European Conference on Pattern Languages of Programs (EuroPlop 2000), 397-410, Universitätsverlag Konstanz, Irsee, Germany, 2000

[Gamma et al. 1995]
Gamma, Erich; Helm, Richard; Johnson, Ralph; Vlissides, John, *Design Patterns - Elements of Reusable Object-Oriented Software*, Addison-Wesley, Reading, 1995

[Kiczales et al. 1991]
Kiczales, Gregor; des Rivieres, Jim; Bobrow, Daniel G., *The Art of the Metaobject Protocol*, MIT Press, 1991

[Kiczales et al. 1997]
Kiczales, Gregor; Lamping, John; Mendhekar, Anurag; Maeda, Chris; Videira Lopes, Cristina; Loingtier, Jean-Marc; Irwin, John, *Aspect-Oriented Programming*, ECOOP 1997, 220-242, 1997

[Szyperski 1998]
Szyperski, Clemens; *Component Software - Beyond Object-Oriented Programming*, Addison-Wesley, 1998

Further reading: Generative programming

[Czarnecki and Eisenecker 2000]
Czarnecki, Krysztof; Eisenecker, Ulrich W., *Generative Programming - Methods, Tools and Applications*, Addison-Wesley, 2000

Further reading: Model-driven software development

[OMG 2010c]
Object Management Group, *Model Driven Architecture*, http://www.omg.org/mda/, 2010

[Stahl and Völter 2006]
Stahl, Thomas; Völter, Markus, *Model-Driven Software Development*, Wiley, 2006

Further Reading: 6.3 Architecture Tactics, Styles, and Patterns

Further reading: requirement and analysis patterns

[Fowler 1996]
Fowler, Martin, *Analysis Patterns: Reusable Object Models*, Addison-Wesley, 1996

[Withall 2007]
Withall, Stephen, *Software Requirement Patterns*, Microsoft Press, 2007

[Bass et al. 2003]
Bass, Len; Clements, Paul; Kazman, Rick, *Software Architecture in Practice*, Second Edition, Addison-Wesley, New York, 2003

[Shaw and Garlan 1996]
Shaw, Mary; Garlan, David, *Software Architecture - Perspectives on an Emerging Discipline*, Prentice Hall, Upper Saddle River, N. J., 1996

[Buschmann et al. 1996]
Buschmann, Frank; Meunier, Regine; Rohnert, Hans; Sommerlad, Peter; Stal, Michael, *Pattern-Oriented Software Architecture Vol. 1, A System of Patterns*, John Wiley & Sons, New York, 1996

[Evans 2004]
Evans, Eric, *Domain-Driven Design - Tackling Complexity in the Heart of Software*, Addison-Wesley, Boston, 2004

Further reading:
Architecture tactics

Further reading:
Architecture styles

Further reading:
Architecture patterns

Further Reading: 6.4 Basic Architectures

[Avgeriou and Zdun 2005]
Avgeriou, Paris; Zdun, Uwe. *Architectural Patterns Revisited - A Pattern Language*. In Proceedings of 10th European Conference on Pattern Languages of Programs (EuroPlop 2005), Irsee, Germany, 2005

[Buschmann et al. 1996]
Buschmann, Frank; Meunier, Regine; Rohnert, Hans; Sommerlad, Peter; Stal, Michael, *Pattern-Oriented Software Architecture Vol. 1, A System of Patterns*, John Wiley & Sons, New York, 1996

[Dyson and Longshaw 2004]
Dyson, Paul; Longshaw, Andrew, *Architecting Enterprise Solutions*, Wiley, 2004

[Evans 2004]
Evans, Eric, *Domain-Driven Design - Tackling Complexity in the Heart of Software*, Addison-Wesley, Boston, 2004

[Hohpe and Woolf 2003]
Hohpe, Gregor; Woolf, Booby, *Enterprise Integration Patterns: Designing, Building, and Deploying Messaging Solutions*, Addison-Wesley, New York, 2003

Further reading:
Basic architectures

[Schumacher et al. 2005]
Schumacher, Markus, Fernandez, Eduardo, Hybertson, Duane, Buschmann, Frank, Sommerlad, Peter. *Security Patterns: Integrating Security and Systems Engineering*, John Wiley & Sons, 2005

[Shaw and Garlan 1996]
Shaw, Mary; Garlan, David, *Software Architecture - Perspectives on an Emerging Discipline*, Prentice Hall, Upper Saddle River, N. J., 1996

[Tanenbaum and van Steen 2003]
Tanenbaum, Andrew S.; van Steen, Maarten, *Distributed Systems*, Prentice Hall, New York, 2003

[Völter et al. 2002]
Völter, Markus; Schmid, Alexander; Wolf, Eberhard, *Server Component Patterns*, John Wiley & Sons, New York, 2002

[Völter et al. 2004]
Völter, Markus; Kircher, Michael; Zdun, Uwe, *Remoting Patterns - Foundations of Enterprise, Internet, and Realtime Distributed Object Middleware*, John Wiley & Sons, 2004

Further reading: Service-oriented architectures

[Zdun and Hendrich 2006]
Hendrich, C. Zdun, Uwe, *Patterns for Process-Oriented Integration in Service-Oriented Architectures*, Proceedings of 11th European Conference on Pattern Languages of Programs (EuroPLoP 2006), Irsee, Germany, 2006

[Zdun et al. 2006]
Zdun, U. Hendrich, C. van der Aalst, W.M.P. *A Survey of Patterns for Service-Oriented Architectures*, International Journal of Internet Protocol Technology, 1(3), Inderscience, 2006

Further reading: Cloud computing architectures

[IBM 2011]
IBM, Getting cloud computing right, http://public.dhe.ibm.com/common/ssi/ecm/en/ciw03078usen/CIW03078USEN. PDF, 2011

[NIST 2009]
National Institute of Standards and Technology, *The NIST Definition of Cloud Computing*, http://www.nist.gov/itl/cloud/upload/cloud-def-v15.pdf

Further Reading: 6.5 Reference Architectures

[Bass et al. 2003]
Bass, Len; Clements, Paul; Kazman, Rick, *Software Architecture in Practice*, Second Edition, Addison-Wesley, New York, 2003

[Hofmeister et al. 1999]
Hofmeister, Christine; Nord Robert; Soni Dilip, *Applied Software Architecture*, Addison-Wesley, New York, 1999

[ISO17799 2001]
International Organization for Standardization, *Information technology – Code of practice for information security management*, http://www.iso.org/iso/en/CatalogueDetailPage.CatalogueDetail?CSNUMBER=33441&ICS1=35&ICS2=40&ICS3=, 2001

[Oracle 2011a]
Oracle, *Java Blue Prints*, http://www.oracle.com/technetwork/java/blueprints-141945.html, 2011

[OSSJ 2004]
OSS through Java Initiative, http://www.ossj.org/, 2004

[Terplan 2001]
Terplan, Kornel, *OSS Essentials, Support System Solutions for Service Providers*, John Wiley & Sons, New York, 2001

[TMF 2004b]
TeleManagement Forum, *Next Generation Operations Support Systems Initiative (NGOSS)*, http://www.tmforum.org/browse.asp?catID=1911, 2004

Further Reading: 6.6 Architecture Modeling Means

[Booch et al. 2005]
Booch, Grady; Rumbaugh James; Jacobson, *The Unified Modeling Language*, Addison-Wesley, Amsterdam, 2005

[Shaw et al. 1995]
M. Shaw, R. DeLine, D.V. Klein et al., *Abstraction for Software Architecture and Tools to Support Them*, IEEE Transactions on Software Engineering, Vol. 21. No. 4., 1995

[Haumer 2005]
Haumer, Peter, *IBM Rational Method Composer: Part 1: Key concepts*, http://www.ibm.com/developerworks/rational/library/dec05/haumer/#notes, 2005

Further reading: Reference architectures

Further reading: Unified Modeling Language

Further reading: Architecture description languages

Further reading: Method metamodels

[OMG 2008c]
Object Management Group, *Software and Systems Process Engineering Metamodel Specification*, v2.0 (Beta 2), http://www.omg.org/spec/SPEM/2.0/, 2008

Further Reading: 6.7 Architecturally Relevant Technologies

Further reading: Middleware systems and remoting patterns

[Hohpe and Woolf 2003]
Hohpe, Gregor; Woolf, Booby, *Enterprise Integration Patterns: Designing, Building, and Deploying Messaging Solutions*, Addison-Wesley, New York, 2003

Further reading: Data persistency and data exchange

[Keller and Coldewey 1998]
Keller, Wolfgang; Coldewey, Jens, *Accessing Relational Databases: A Pattern Language*, In Martin, Robert; Riehle, Dirk; Buschmann, Frank (Eds.): Pattern Languages of Program Design 3, Addison-Wesley, 1998

[Völter et al. 2004]
Völter, Markus; Kircher, Michael; Zdun, Uwe, *Remoting Patterns - Foundations of Enterprise, Internet, and Realtime Distributed Object Middleware*, John Wiley & Sons, 2004

[Alur et al. 2003]
Alur, Deepak; Crupi, John; Malks, Dan, *Core J2EE Patterns*, Prentice Hall PTR, 2003

Further reading: Component platforms

[Bray et al. 1998]
Bray, T.; Paoli, J.; Sperberg-McQueen, C. M., *Extensible markup language (XML) 1.0*, http://www.w3.org/TR/1998/REC-xml-19980210, 1998

[OMG 2006]
Object Management Group, *CORBA Component Model*, v.4.0, http://www.omg.org/spec/CCM/4.0/, 2006

7 | Organizations and Individuals (WHO)

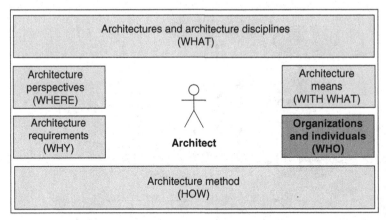

Figure 7-1: Positioning of the chapter in the architecture orientation framework

In this chapter we look at the *WHO dimension* of the architecture orientation framework more closely. We will show organizational and social influencing factors that affect the architecture of a system and that can influence the work of an architect. We will also provide basic knowledge about groups and their dynamics. In addition, we will define the role of the architect. Applying the knowledge contained within this dimension enables you to understand the relevance of the influencing factors mentioned, describe the role of an architect, consider the processes of group dynamics, and act accordingly.

Overview

Figure 7-2 shows the basic concepts covered in this chapter and visualizes how they connect.

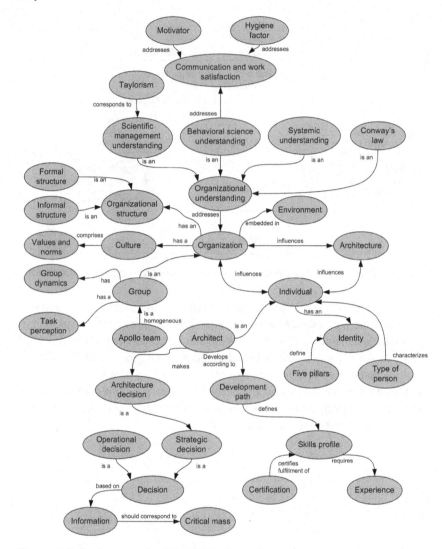

Figure 7-2: Basic concepts of the WHO dimension

7.1 General

Focusing on technical and architectural aspects is not enough

When you are designing an architecture, you have to take many influences and aspects into account. The most obvious are the consideration of the functional and non-functional requirements placed on the IT system that the architecture must satisfy. You can apply various architecture means to address these requirements (see Chapter 6). In addition to applying these means, you can view the so-lution to be created from different perspectives (see Chapter 4). You can also act according to a specific method to ensure a systematic and successful architecture design (see Chapter 8). In terms of the architecture definition introduced as part of the WHAT dimension (see Chapter 3), this covers all significant aspects required to perform an architectural activity. However, this alone is still not sufficient. You must also consider social and organizational influencing factors. This requires you to look at the bigger technological picture and have a basic understanding of organizations and individuals. Therefore, in this chapter, we will look at organiza-tions and individuals in general and show the interdependencies with architecture.

Architectures, or rather the IT systems based on them, are always designed by and for people. Furthermore, architectural activity is generally embedded within an organization, be that the enterprise for which the IT system is being designed or the project organization that consists of the persons involved. The organiza-tional term is therefore intentionally broad. It can refer to enterprises and project organizations. As shown in Figure 7.1-1, an architecture is therefore always inter-dependent with the organization in which it is designed and with the individuals involved in and affected by the architecture.

Architectures are created by and for people in organizations

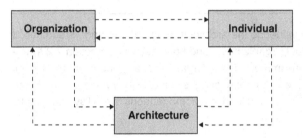

Figure 7.1-1: Interdependencies between the organization, the individual, and the architecture

An organization is distinguished by its culture and the related values and norms. These affect the architecture by defining the normative framework and thus the freedom of scope for the architecture design. This can be expressed by the spec-ification of very clear standards and guidelines and the organization rejecting, for example, new, unconventional approaches. As a consequence, an architecture that contradicts the values and norms of the organization runs the risk of failure even though it fulfills all functional and non-functional requirements. The culture of an organization also defines how people within the organization deal with one another and what expectations the organization has of them. This means that there are interdependencies between the organization and the single individual, which in turn affect the architecture. An organization therefore also affects the architecture as a discipline (see Chapter 3). An organization can consist of fur-ther sub-organizations with different cultures. An enterprise, as a high-level or-

Influences of the organizational culture

ganization, can thus consist of different departments or organizational units with their own cultures. This aspect is particularly relevant today, when enterprises are represented internationally, since organizations can cross different culture groups that have different values and norms.

Influences of the organizational structure

The structures of an organization also influence the architecture of an IT system. For example, if an enterprise has dedicated departments for developing different parts of an IT system, there is a risk that the overall architecture will reflect this organizational separation. This is because the organizational separation makes communication across department boundaries more difficult. Empirical studies show that it is precisely the integration to one overall system that places great challenges on organizationally separate project teams [Herbsleb and Grinter 1999]. The influence of organizational structures on the architecture of an IT system was recognized by Melvin Conway and has found its way into literature as Conway's law [Conway 1968]:

Conway's law

> Organizations that design systems are constrained to produce systems whose structures are copies of the communication structures of these organizations.

Organizations influence architecture

Organizations therefore influence the architecture. In order to understand this, it is important to know about organizations and how they work. Section 7.2 therefore looks at organizations in more detail. Organizational influences are of great importance above all in the age of offshoring, since only overarching, regular coordination and communication can lead to a homogeneous overall system [Curtis et al. 1988].

Influences of individuals

People vary in their strengths, weaknesses, desires, fears, and mentality. Through their individual properties they contribute to an IT system. They act in different roles, e.g., architect, designer, or developer, and fulfill the expectations placed on the roles in different ways. People can perform different roles simultaneously. Depending on his experience, an architect will design an architecture in one way or another. A designer will allow the architectural specifications to flow into his design according to his understanding and preferences, and a developer will implement these in his own special way. The individuality of each member of the project therefore influences the architecture, since every member fulfills his assigned roles in an individual way. People are unique and will always make very individual contributions. The different mentalities also influence the collaboration and communication between the members of the project. They have an indirect influence on the architecture, since important information may not be communicated or problems of understanding may not be voiced. This can mean that the architecture on paper is noticeably different to the architecture finally realized. It is also possible that the architectural specification is not accepted since its usefulness is not recognized or proposals from others are not accepted. In literature, this is often called the "Not-invented-here syndrome" [Cockburn 2002]. Sympathies and antipathies between people are also very important. If, for example, the collaboration between the architect and his team members is restricted due to personal differences, then not everyone in the team will be committed to the architecture and it will ultimately not be successful. This makes it indispensable that an architect is an expert not only in domain-specific and methodological areas, but also has social skills and a basic understanding of individuals. Section 7.3 looks at this understanding.

However, it is not only the organization and the individual that influence architecture. The architecture itself in turn affects the organization and the individual. An architecture defines the structures of an IT system by identifying its subsystems and building blocks. Each subsystem has dedicated responsibilities and there are dependencies between the subsystems. Each subsystem is usually developed further and implemented by different teams. The organization is therefore frequently structured around the architectural structures [Brooks 1995]. On one hand, the architecture therefore affects the organization. On the other hand, it also influences every individual team member, since each member is assigned specific roles. For example, the role of the designer, who structures the subsystem further, or the tester, who designs the test cases and scenarios for the subsystem.

Influences of architectures

7.2 Organizations

In the previous section we explained the reasons why organizations influence architecture. The following section conveys significant knowledge about understanding organizations. We will cover general topics from organization theory, and we will also look at these topics from the context of architecture. We will firstly introduce the topic in general, and then put it in context to architecture.

Objectives

An organization can be described according to the following definition [Kieser and Kubicek 1993]:

Definition: Organization

> An organization is a social entity that permanently follows an objective and has a formal structure that enables the activities of the member to be focused on the objective followed.

Over the course of time, different understandings and interpretations of organizations have evolved. We will discuss the significant basic understandings in more detail below. They are:
> Scientific management understanding
> Behavioral science understanding
> Systemic understanding

Different interpretation options

Scientific management understanding	The scientific management understanding has its roots in early industrialization. It is based on the principle of the perfect division of labor. The person as an individual is perceived as a production factor that can be planned, predicted, and controlled. Organizations shaped by this principle have rigid organization hierarchies. Communication takes place strictly via the hierarchy. This approach can lead to a strict delineation between the individual organizational units or teams. In its extreme form, there is a clear separation between planning and execution. F. W. Taylor can be seen as the father of this understanding [Taylor 1913]. The term *Taylorism* is therefore often used in this context.
Conway's law and Taylorism	If we recall Conway's law, it becomes evident why organizations that are built up on pure scientific management aspects develop IT systems that reflect their communication structures. The clear separation is present in the organization and there is no overarching understanding. If different teams are responsible for different subsystems of a system, for example, the architecture of the IT system will also display this structure. Based on this fact, as an architect you must be aware that significant architecture principles (see Chapter 6), such as separation of concerns, modularization, and information hiding, whilst important for the architecture of an IT system, should not be applied to the same extent to the organization that is realizing the IT system. Instead, important information must flow, communication must be made easier, and new forms of collaboration must be established, for example, through the use of collaboration tools such as Wikis, instant messaging systems, and team rooms.
Behavioral science understanding	The behavioral science understanding places the person at the center of the consideration by perceiving the person as a social being striving for recognition and appreciation rather than as a pure production factor. The strict division of labor thus becomes less important and the focus is on the creation of suitable working conditions that allow the person to develop. An important aspect here is the fostering of communication and increasing work satisfaction through appropriate motivation measures. In this context, Herzberg talks of motivators and hygiene factors [Herzberg 1966]. Motivators are, for example, work itself, responsibility, and recognition. These increase work satisfaction, but do not reduce work dissatisfaction. Work dissatisfaction is influenced by hygiene factors, such as the relationship to managers and peers as well as politics. If these factors are perceived as positive, they can reduce work dissatisfaction, but do not increase work satisfaction [Drumm 1995].
Behavioral science understanding and architecture	For the purposes of defining an architecture, from these findings we can see that, in order to minimize the work dissatisfaction, the principles and concepts of the architecture must be communicated to team members and suitable communication channels and means must be achieved. These can include joint standup

meetings, where problems and next steps are discussed [Beedle and Schwaber 2001], or the establishment of an instant messaging environment. However, this is not sufficient to increase work satisfaction. It is much more the case that each team member must be entrusted with activities with which they can identify themselves. In addition, they should be involved in the architecture design and encouraged to reflect in a solution-oriented way. Ultimately, architecture should be understood like a team sport. With this background, it also becomes obvious that a strict separation of roles, as given in Taylorism, does not make sense in realizing IT systems.

From a systemic point of view, an organization is nothing other than a system (see Section 3.3) and as such fulfills the classic properties of systems (see Figure 7.2-1).

Systemic understanding

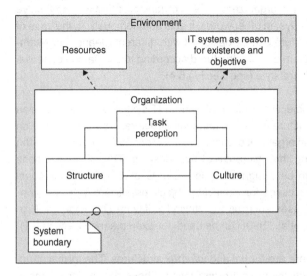

Figure 7.2-1: Organization as system (following [Steiger and Lippmann 2003]).

A system exists to achieve an *objective*. The realization of an IT system for the entry and automatic processing of orders is an example of a project organization objective.

Organizations have objectives

The environment, for example, the client of the IT system, sets the objective for the organization and thus provides its reason for existence. Furthermore, the environment provides the organization with *resources* to fulfill its *task*. These can be material things, such as rooms and tools, or immaterial things, such as information. People can also be made available to the organization until the objective is reached. They thus become part of the organization. Since an organization is

Organizations interact with their environment

embedded in its environment, the environment also specifies the *general conditions* within which the organization can act. An important aspect here is the *culture* of the environment and the related *values* and *norms*. These can include the way people deal with each other and concrete process specifications.

Environment and architecture

An enterprise can be the surrounding environment. As an architect, on one hand you are a member of the enterprise, and on the other, a member of the project organization. Depending on the culture, during the implementation of the architecture designed, you will be motivated to do some of the work yourself or to let your team members do the actual work.

Organizations have a task perception

An organization develops an individual understanding about how to achieve the objective given by the environment. This *task perception* is based on the experiences of the members of the organization. Each organization will therefore solve a given task in different ways. In other words, it acts autonomously. In the case of an IT system, an architecture can be designed with different means. For example, a data-centered system can be structured according to the Batch sequential style or the Pipes and filters style (see Section 6.4).

Organizations have structures

In order to achieve its objective, (e.g., realizing an IT system), the organization structures itself. The structure is on one hand the structural organization and on the other, the operational organization. The *structural organization* describes the positions to be filled and their hierarchical relationships. The job descriptions characterize the roles to be assigned within the organization. The *operational organization* defines processes for achieving objectives efficiently. In this context, development processes such as the Unified Software Development Process (USDP) [Jacobson et al. 1999] can be used, for example (see Section 8.1).

Formal and informal structures

Within organizations, there are *formal* and *informal* structures. The formal structures are given by the official project organization. These define, for example, that the communication with members of other sub-teams of a project must be via the team lead only. The informal structures circumvent these specifications and enable direct communication across organizational boundaries. These structures arise through relationships between people that go beyond the project organization. For example, people have already worked together in a previous project, or have the same hobby and play e.g., tennis together regularly. Studies indicate that it is these informal bridges that are essential for successfully achieving the organization's objective [Herbsleb and Grinter 1999].

Organizations have cultures

The task perception and the structures of the organization are based on the values and norms of the people involved. For example, if a project lead has a very authoritarian style of leadership, the organizational structure will be strictly hierarchical. There will be clear specifications about how tasks are to be fulfilled and understood. The same applies for the architect. If you trust the capabilities of your team members and allow them to participate in the design of the architecture, the organizational structures will be flatter and there will be a collective task perception. The particular values and norms of an organization are the *organizational culture*. The organizational culture also defines how the organization interacts with its environment. For example, it can define whether team members such as developers or testers may communicate with customers or not.

The structure, the task perception, and the culture of an organization are interrelated. They always describe the overall organization, but from different perspectives, and they influence each other. In complex organizations, cause and effect cannot be clearly separated [Steiger and Lippmann 2003].

Interdependencies between structure, task perception, and culture

In development projects and in IT generally, the influence of organizations on architectures is being increasingly taken into account. Over time, different organizational principles and patterns have developed for structuring and reflecting organizations. Alistair Cockburn, Jim Coplien, and Neil Harrison look at this set of topics in great detail [Cockburn 2002; Coplien and Harrison 2004]. Furthermore, in recent times, many agile software development and project management methods have emerged, such as Scrum, the Crystal family of methodologies, or Extreme Programming (XP) to name just a few [Fowler 2003]. All of these approaches are based on behavioral science understanding and systemic organizational understanding. They place the person at the center and consider him as a motivated individual. Furthermore, according to their understanding, organizations must be set up so that people feel good in them and can grow. Ultimately therefore, the objective of every organization must be to increase work satisfaction and reduce work dissatisfaction. The new methods also trust in the *self-organization* of organizations [Cunningham et al. 2001]. To satisfy all of these demands, it is important to have basic knowledge of individuals and self-organizing groups. On this basis, we will look at the person as an individual more closely in the next section. We will then cover groups as self-organizing entities in more detail.

Organizational understanding in IT

7.3 Individuals

Architectures are created by individuals. People have different character traits, strengths, weaknesses, preferences, and tendencies. Therefore, it is not enough to look at people as a pure production factor. Instead, you must perceive your team members as individuals and treat them accordingly. We therefore provide basic knowledge about individuals in this section.

Individuals shape architecture

To get an image of people and to understand them better, it is important to recognize that every person has their own identity. The identity can be seen as based on five major pillars. These pillars are presented in Table 7.3-1 [Petzold and Sieber 1993].

Five pillars of identity

Table 7.3-1: The five pillars of identity

Social network	Career and work	Physical state	Material Values	Values and norms
Family	Status	Health	Money	Religion
Friends	Activity	Age	Car	Politics
Neighbors	Responsibility	Nutrition	Clothes	Norms
Colleagues		Gender		Tradition
		Sexuality		

Each person's identity is defined by these pillars to different degrees. For one person career advancement is important, but for another unimportant. One person places great value on prestige, another is more interested in his family.

Types of people according to Belbin

Even though every person is unique, the types of people illustrated in Figure 7.3-1 can be distinguished [Belbin 1993]. This is just one possible theory, but one which illustrates the basic character traits of people well. Literature contains further approaches for interpreting people. For example, the approach developed by Myers and Briggs, which is based on the theories of C. G. Jung. It also outlines different types of people and shows which types can work together in a team. For more information, see [Briggs and Myers 1995].

Belbin identifies the types of people presented in Figure 7.3-1. It is important to know these basic types in order to understand the processes of group dynamics.

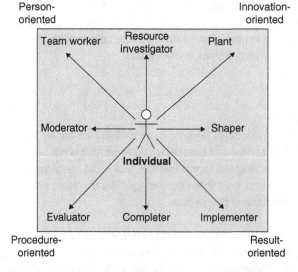

Figure 7.3-1: Types of people according to Belbin

The different types of people are described in Table 7.3-2.

Table 7.3-2: Description of types of people according to Belbin

Type	Description
Team worker	Based on their social nature, team workers have the ability to approach people and cultivate team spirit. In crisis situations they tend to be indecisive.
Resource investigator	Resource investigators seek out challenges and are extroverted and communicative. Their strengths lie in building up personal contacts and researching new topics. In contrast however, they tend to lose interest in a topic when it becomes routine.
Plant	Plants are people who take unconventional approaches and can contribute to solutions based on their knowledge and powers of imagination. However, they also tend to overlook regulations and have their head in the clouds.
Shaper	Shapers have a dynamic personality with a strong will and are capable of pushing through decisions. They are, however, excitable and have a tendency to provoke.
Implementer	Implementers are conscientious people who complete tasks thoroughly and carefully. They sometimes tend to be perfectionists and can allow themselves to be disturbed by trivialities.
Completer	Completers investigate content and are good at analyzing. However, they are not good at bringing in their own ideas and motivating other people.
Evaluator	Evaluators are disciplined and hard-working people who approach problem solutions pragmatically. They cannot, however, adapt to changing situations and accept unverified ideas.
Moderator	Moderators are self-confident people with few prejudices and a calm nature. They can integrate other people into the team activity easily and have a strong perception. However, they do not have the usual level of creativity.

People cannot be assigned to just one of the different types alone. Each person is too unique to allow this. However, tendencies are recognizable within each person. Since different individuals come together in each team, each architecture has a unique face. The composition of the team therefore says a lot about the success of a team (see Section 7.4).

Assignment is never unique

7.4 Individuals and Groups

In the development of an IT system, or rather the design of an architecture, different individuals come together for the duration of a project in order to achieve the objective together: the realization of the IT system. Individuals therefore join a group and take on different roles within the group as well as the tasks related to those roles (see Figure 7.4-1).

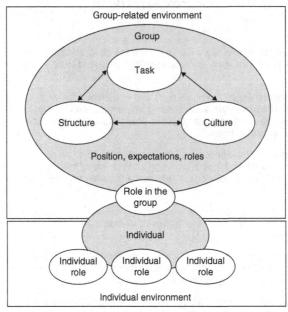

Figure 7.4-1: *The group as a system [Steiger and Lippmann 2003]*

Group as a special form of an organization

A group is a special form of an organization. It interacts with its environment, pursues a task, has a structure, and develops a culture (see Section 7.2). One important aspect is that each individual takes on one or more roles within the group. These can be the formal roles, such as architect, designer, or developer; they can also be informal roles, such as joker or scapegoat. A group defines its expectations of group members via these roles. Each person has their own role understanding and fulfills these expectations in their own way.

Individual environment

Furthermore, the person exists not only within the group, but also in his own individual environment. In this environment he takes on further roles not geared towards the objective of the group, for example, father, husband, or friend. People must therefore also satisfy the expectations of their individual environment. It is essential to realize that group members also have a life outside the group and must be granted enough freedom for this. Ultimately, this increases the probability of success of the group, since the people feel good within the group and do not feel under pressure. Edward Yourdon explicitly recommends to project leads that the individual environment of each team member must not be restricted [Yourdon 1997].

Experience shows that the type of group composition is significant for the group's success. Surprisingly, studies show that groups consisting of highly intelligent, analytical, and mentally strong people, so-called Apollo teams, generally produce worse results in the achievement of objectives than heterogeneous groups. One reason for the poor efficiency of Apollo teams is the desire of every member of the team to push their ideas through. Members of Apollo teams also pay less attention to the work and ideas of others [Belbin 1993]. Belbin names the following factors for well-functioning, successful teams:

> Groups are led by a good, cooperative moderator.
> As an absolute prerequisite for success, the group contains one or two plants.
> Team members are deployed in accordance with their capabilities.

Group composition and success

Groups should therefore have a heterogeneous group structure. This applies both for the character traits as well as the abilities and experience. To improve the understanding for the problem, Cockburn suggests, for example, composing teams from analysts, designers, and developers. This ensures that the business problem, for example, the evaluation of the creditworthiness of enterprises, is understood in the team just as well as the problems related to design and implementation [Cockburn 1996].

Heterogeneous group structure

In addition to a heterogeneous group composition, the identification with the group is also a critical success factor. When groups are established, and the individual group members know each other, they are capable of producing many times what an unestablished group can produce [Cockburn 2002]. This has to do with the fact that the group is already given, so has formed a structure or hierarchy, and does not need to find itself before dealing with achieving the group's objective.

Group identification and success

This process for forming groups is presented in Table 7.4-1. The model considers the entire life cycle of a group, from creation to recreation.

Group dynamics

Table 7.4-1: Group dynamics according to Tuckman [Stahl 2002]

Stage	Primary activity	Group performance	Means
Forming stage	Getting to know one another Assessing one another Classification	Separation	Conventions
Storming stage	Showing oneself Representing oneself Dispute	Amplification	Conflicts
Norming stage	Committing oneself Accepting Conciliation	Decision (selection)	Agreement
Performing stage	Participating Getting involved Collaboration	Confirmation (resta-bilization)	Cooperation
Adjourning stage	Balancing Reflecting Exchange of experi-ences	Change (variation)	Results

Forming stage

In the forming stage, the members of the group get to know each other and assess one another. Individual group members can be classified at this stage. The group also distinguishes itself from its environment. Treatment of one another is based on clear conventions. The group members are polite, pleasant, and accommodating. It is important that a leading role, for example, the architect, communicates the task and objectives of the group and lays down the organizational conditions. The group members must receive a clear picture of what is expected of them.

Storming stage

Based on the group understanding obtained in the forming stage, in the storming stage, each group member decides whether they want to stay in the group or not. Furthermore, each member tries to obtain an adequate position within the group. This can be different to the position or role envisaged. There is therefore an emphasis on differences of opinion, competitive behavior, and confrontations in this stage. These disputes must be permitted by the group leader in order to enable the group to find itself. However, the group leader should point out rules agreed in the forming stage and only permit confrontations within this framework.

The norming stage follows the storming stage. In this stage the group finds it-self. The members of the group identify themselves with the roles worked out and agree on rules for working together. The group develops an identity and a "we" feeling arises. From this point, tasks should be delegated to encourage the independence of the members of the group. This should be done based on the strengths and weaknesses of the individual members (see Section 7.3).

Norming stage

The performing stage is distinguished by the commitment of each team member. The team spirit that has developed results in goal-oriented, collaborative co-operation. At this point, the group has established itself and achieved its potential. In this stage, the independence of the group should be guaranteed and the group should be shielded from disruptive influences. However, this does not mean that information from outside that would, for example, show the group objective in a new light, should be blocked. In the development of an IT system, this can be new requirements, which of course must be considered.

Performing stage

After achieving the group objective, the adjourning stage reflects on the performance and experiences of the group. The group can also dissolve or set a new objective. Since the stages up to the performing stage can be very intensive and protracted for the group, retaining an established team and setting them a new objective is recommended.

Adjourning stage

The Tuckman stages described above are generally experienced several times before the group finds and establishes itself. This applies particularly to the first three stages of the model.

Spiral process flow

7.5 Architect as Central Role

As an architect you are involved in many tasks and communicate with different stakeholders. As a rule, you are involved as early as preliminary studies, for example, to verify whether an IT plan is feasible, through the analysis phase of a project, right up to the point when an IT system is put into operation. During this time you interact with many different roles, as shown in Figure 7.5-1.

Architect as central role

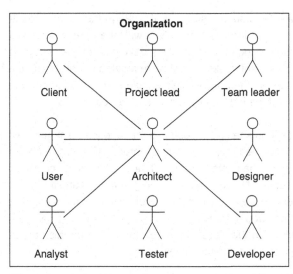

Figure 7.5-1: *Architect in the organizational social environment*

Architect as designer	As a result of this central nature, you are more than just a designer of an architecture, although this is one of your most important tasks. This is where you bring in all of your experience, identify the architecturally significant use cases, consider architecture principles, select appropriate architecture styles, and adapt proven reference architectures. However, these are just a few of your tasks.
Architect as problem solver	In designing the architecture, you act as a problem solver by creating the architectural basis for fulfilling functional and non-functional requirements.
Architect as decision maker	You answer architectural questions and make strategic decisions. You are expected to be capable of making decisions in uncertain situations.
Architect as visionary	You must also act as visionary for the architecture. You must never lose sight of the vision to be realized through the architecture. Rather, you must ensure that everyone involved always knows the basic principles of the architecture and acts accordingly. This applies to both the customer and the team.
Architect as communicator	You must also have extensive communicative skills. You must approach people proactively, convey information, and ensure that everyone involved has an adequate level of knowledge with regard to the architecture. To enable you to do this, you must be able to communicate your ideas and present them geared towards the target group.
Architect as listener	In addition to conveying information, you must of course be open to ideas and questions from others. You must therefore always listen actively, and, for exam-

ple, be responsive to suggestions from your team members. The team members are specialists in their area and can assess the usefulness of the architecture for their field. However, it is important not to lose sight of the overall view of the architecture. You must always assess the usefulness for the architecture as a whole.

In addition, it is your task to convince your team members of the selected architecture. You must therefore also see yourself as motivator. You should motivate in the spirit of the author Antoine de Saint-Exupéry:

Architect as motivator

> "If you want to build a ship, don't drum up people to collect wood and don't assign them tasks and work, but rather teach them to long for the endless immensity of the sea."

From De Saint-Exupéry's words, it becomes clear that the correct motivation can only be awakened if people work towards a goal with which they can identify themselves wholly and completely. For you, this means you have to get your team members on board. You can achieve this by delegating responsibilities and by considering ideas and suggestions from others. You should also communicate the usefulness and importance of each team member to them clearly to increase their satisfaction.

You are also the technical leader of an IT plan. You must therefore have leadership qualities. Some of these qualities, such as motivating the team, have already been mentioned explicitly. In exercising your leadership role, it is important to apply a leadership style suitable for the respective situation and the particular individual. For example, if team members are highly qualified and motivated, you should delegate tasks. A delegating leadership style is demonstrated through you outlining the problem and defining the boundaries within which team members have the freedom to make their own decisions. The team or the individual then makes decisions independently within their freedom to decide. In the case of team members who are highly motivated but lack sufficient experience, you should support them in making decisions. You can do this in your role as listener and by answering questions. The freedom to decide is given by the architecture, for example, through the definition of architecture principles and description of subsystems and their responsibilities, as well as the communication methods.

Architect as leader

However, you should not just design specifications—you should also be actively involved, since this makes a significant contribution to the success of the architecture. This enables you to assess immediately whether architectural ideas are realizable. It also increases the probability that the team members understand the architecture because there is direct communication between you, the designers, and the developers. Furthermore, it increases your acceptance by the team

Architect as practitioner

members, since direct collaboration breaks down social barriers [Ambler 2002]. You must therefore also always see yourself as a practitioner. The organizational pattern *ArchitectAlsoImplements* expresses this requirement [Coplien and Harrison 2004].

Architect as generalist

You must have a broad knowledge base that enables you to recognize and understand contexts, and derive consequences from them. With regard to the architecture disciplines presented in Chapter 3, this means that you have a general knowledge in the individual disciplines. You can therefore be considered a generalist who, for deeper questions and problems, accesses the specialist knowledge of your team members. However, in addition to these architecture-related fields of knowledge, you must also have considerable knowledge of the problem domain for which the IT system is being developed. This enables you to understand the wants and needs of the client and the user. You also need project management knowledge in order to design the project plan together with the project lead. Last but not least, you also need a well-founded knowledge in testing systems in order to coordinate the test plans and scenarios with testers.

Competencies of an architect

The knowledge and skills of an architect outlined above are very extensive, but important for success. Vitruvius reformulated the competencies of an architect as follows:

> The ideal architect should be a man of letters, a mathematician, familiar with historical studies, a diligent student of philosophy, acquainted with music, not ignorant of medicine, learned in the responses of juriconsults, familiar with astronomy and astronomical calculations.

This description expresses the broad knowledge basis expected of an architect, which stretches over technical, methodological, and social competencies.

Teams of architects

The tasks of an architect presented here are very extensive. The question is whether these tasks can be fulfilled by one person alone. Depending on their individual strengths and weaknesses, a person will be able to fulfill the tasks better or worse, and may be overstretched if they have to fulfill all tasks (see Section 7.3). This supports the need for establishing teams of architects, where the members of the team complement each other accordingly.

Dedicated development paths and requirement profiles

Some companies have formulated the competencies and skills expected of an architect specifically and developed dedicated requirements profiles for architects. One example is the Enterprise Architecture Skills Framework of The Open Group [Jones 2004]. In this framework, The Open Group differentiates between the following areas of knowledge:

> Generic skills—geared towards the social skills of architects and dealing with topics such as leadership and teamwork.
> Business skills and methods—communicating, for example, business processes and strategic planning.
> Enterprise architecture skills—conveying topics to do with enterprise architecture.
> Program or project management skills—promoting methodology skills within projects.
> IT general knowledge skills
> Technical IT skills—containing elementary topics such as software development and data modeling.
> Legal environment

A suitable development program is a useful basis for further development as an architect. However, architecture is always the result of experience. Therefore, you must be open to new experiences and recognize that you never stop learning. Every new architecture project is therefore an opportunity for further development and for increasing your wealth of experience.

Architecture requires experience

For some years now, various organizations and service providers, such as The Open Group, Oracle, Microsoft, SAP, etc. have been offering architecture certificates. These are increasingly recognized on the market as a record of achievement. However, as yet there is no *one* standardized manufacturer-independent and technology-independent and internationally recognized architecture certificate. As a result of the lack of orientation on the topic software architecture that often exists (see Chapter 1), there is no uniform perception about the career scenario of the software architect. This means that the content, structure, and scope of the certification programs are very different. The costs (from EUR 1,000 to over EUR 20,000) and time (from a few days up to several months) involved in obtaining an architecture certificate also vary greatly. Generally, the prerequisites for participating in certification programs are good knowledge of software engineering and sometimes extensive work experience (10 years and more). With some certification programs, there is also an admissions procedure to go through first. Final examinations can comprise multiple choice tests, interviews, and project examinations. Here we will take a brief look at the manufacturer-independent and technology-independent Open Group certifications. The Open Group differentiates three certification levels:

Certifications as record of achievement

> *Level 1: Certified IT Architect*
  A Level 1 certified IT architect can act as an architect under supervision. He has a broad range of required architecture knowledge.
> *Level 2: Master Certified IT Architect*

A Level 2 certified IT architect can act independently and take responsibility for the design of architectures.

> *Level 3: Distinguished Certified IT Architect*
Based on his broad and extensive architecture experience, a Level 3 certified IT architect has a considerable influence on his environment. He usually acts as Chief Architect, Enterprise Architect, or head of the IT architecture division of his enterprise.

The competency increases from Level 1 to Level 3. For more information see [Opengroup 2008b].

7.6 Summary

Summary: General

> Organizations, individuals, and architectures influence each other mutually.
> Conway's law states that organizations that design systems are constrained to produce systems whose structures are copies of the communication structures of these organizations.
> Architectures or rather the IT systems based on them are always designed by and for people.
> The architectural activity is always embedded within an organization, be that the enterprise for which the IT system is being designed or the project organization that consists of the persons involved.

Summary: Organizations

> An organization is a social entity that permanently follows an objective and has a formal structure that enables the activities of the member to be focused on the objective followed.
> In organization theory, there is a differentiation between scientific management understanding, behavioral science understanding, and systemic understanding.
> Scientific management understanding, also known as Taylorism, treats the individual as a production factor that can be planned, predicted, and controlled.
> Behavioral science understanding places the person at the center of the consideration by perceiving the person as a social being striving for recognition and appreciation rather than as a pure production factor.
> Systemic understanding considers the organization as a system that exists to achieve an objective, and which interacts with its environment. Orga-

nizations have an own task perception, an own culture, and formal and informal structures.

> Agile development processes are based on behavioral science understanding and systemic organizational understanding. They place the person at the center and consider him as a motivated individual.

Every person has their own identity. The identity is based on five major pillars: social network, career and work, physical state, material values, values and norms.

> Belbin differentiates between the following different types of people: Team worker, resource investigator, plant, shaper, implementer, completer, evaluator, and moderator.

> People cannot be assigned to just one of the different types of people alone. However, tendencies are recognizable within each person.

Summary: Individuals

> A group is a special form of an organization. It interacts with its environment, pursues a task, has a structure, and develops a culture.

> Belbin names the following factors for well-functioning, successful teams:

> The group is led by a good, cooperative moderator.

> As an absolute prerequisite for success, the group contains one or two plants.

> Team members are deployed in accordance with their capabilities.

> Groups should have a heterogeneous group structure. This applies both for the character traits as well as the abilities and experience.

> According to Tuckman, each group goes through the following stages: Forming, storming, norming, performing, adjourning.

> The Tuckman stages described are generally experienced multiple times before the group finds and establishes itself.

Summary: Individuals and groups

> As an architect you are involved as early as preliminary studies, for example, to verify whether an IT plan is feasible, through the analysis phase of a project, right up to the point when an IT system is put into operation.

> Architects act in different roles—for example, designer, problem solver, decision maker, visionary, communicator, listener, motivator, leader, practitioner, generalist.

> Teams of architects consist of members who complement each other mutually in order to realize the numerous architecture tasks ideally.

Summary: Architect as central role

> For some years now, various organizations and service providers, such as The Open Group, SUN, Microsoft, SAP, etc have been offering architecture certificates.
> The prerequisites for obtaining an architecture certificate are generally good knowledge of software engineering and sometimes extensive work experience (10 years and more).
> With some certification programs, there is also an admissions procedure to go through first.
> Final examinations of certification programs can comprise multiple choice tests, interviews, and project examinations.

Further Reading

Further reading: Social aspects of agile development

[Ambler 2002]
Ambler, Scott, *Agile Enterprise Architecture: Beyond Enterprise Data Modeling*, http://www.agiledata.org, 2002

[Cunningham et al. 2001]
Cunningham, Wart et al., *Manifesto for Agile Software Development*, http://agilemanifesto.org/, 2001

[Fowler 2003]
Fowler, Martin, *The New Methodology*, http://www.martinfowler.com/articles/newMethodology.html#N10233, 2003

Further reading: Influences of and on architecture

[Brooks 1995]
Brooks, F., *The Mythical Man-Month*, Addition Wesley, New York, 1995

[Cockburn 2002]
Cockburn, Alistair, *Agile Software Development*, Addison-Wesley, New York, 2002

[Conway 1968]
Conway, Melvin E., *How Do Committees Invent?*, Datamation magazine, F. D. Thompson Publications, Inc., April, 1968

[Curtis et al. 1988]
Curtis, B.; Krasner H.; Iscoe N., *A Field Study of the Software Design Process for Large Systems*, Communications of the ACM, Issue 31, Number 11, 1988

[Herbsleb and Grinter 1999]
Herbsleb, James D.; Grinter, Rebecca E., *Splitting the Organization and Integrating the Code: Conway's Law Revisited*, International Conference on Software Engineering, Los Angeles, 1999

[Beedle and Schwaber 2001]
Beedle, Mike; Schwaber, Ken, *Agile Software Development with Scrum*, Prentice-Hall, Upper Saddle River, NJ, 2001

[Cockburn 1996]
Cockburn, Alistair, *The Interaction of Social Issues and Software Architecture*, Communications of the ACM, Issue 39, Number 10, 1996

[Coplien and Harrison 2004]
Coplien, James O.; Harrison, Neil B., *Organizational Patterns of Agile Software Development*, Prentice Hall, Upper Saddle River, NJ, 2004

[Drumm 1995]
Drumm, Hans-Jürgen, *Personalwirtschaftslehre*, 3. neu bearbeitete und erweiterte Auflage, Springer-Verlag GmbH, Heidelberg, 1995 (available in German language only)

[Herzberg 1966]
Herzberg, Friedrich, *Work and the Nature of Man*, HarperCollins, 1966

[Jacobson et al. 1999]
Jacobson, Ivar; Booch Grady; Rumbaugh James, *The Unified Software Development Process*, Addison-Wesley, New York, 1999

[Kieser and Kubicek 1993]
Kieser, Alfred; Kubicek, Herbert, *Organisation*, Schäffer-Poeschel, 1993 (available in German language only)

[Petzold and Sieper 1993]
Petzold Hilarion G.; Sieper Johanna, *Integration und Kreation*, Junfermann, 1993 (available in German language only)

[Steiger and Lippmann 2003]
Steiger, Thomas; Lippmann, Erich (Hrsg.), *Handbuch angewandte Psychologie für Führungskräfte, Führungskompetenz und Führungswissen*, 2. Auflage, Springer, Berlin 2003 (available in German language only)

[Taylor 1913]
Taylor, F.W., *The principles of scientific management*, 1913

Further reading: Organizations

Further reading:
Groups and
individuals

[Belbin 1993]
Belbin, Meredith, *Team Roles at Work*, Butterworth-Heinemann, 1993

[Briggs and Myers 1995]
Briggs, Isabel; Peter B. Myers, *Gifts Differing: Understanding Personality Type*, Davies-Black Publishing, 1995

[Stahl 2002]
Stahl, Eberhard, *Dynamik in Gruppen*, BeltzPVU, 2002 (available in German language only)

[Yourdon 1997]
Yourdon, Edward, *Death March, The Complete Software Developer´s Guide to Surviving "Mission Impossible" Projects*, Prentice Hall, Upper Saddle River, N. J., 1997

Further reading:
Architect
certifications

[Jones 2004]
Jones, Judith, *Architecting the Enterprise, Developing Architecture Skills*, http://www.opengroup.org/architecture/0404brus/presents/jones/Developing_Architecture_Skills1.pdf, TOGAF, 2004

[Opengroup 2008b]
Opengroup, *IT Architect Certification Program* http://www.opengroup.org/itac/, 2008 [Petzold and Sieber 1993]

8 Architecture Method (HOW)

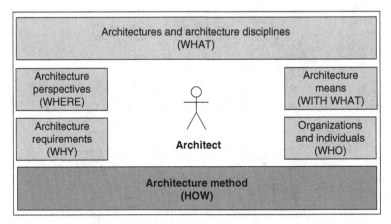

Figure 8-1: Positioning of the chapter in the architecture orientation framework

This chapter concentrates on the *HOW dimension* of the architecture orientation framework. Firstly we present knowledge about development processes that is relevant for you as an architect, before describing your individual activities during the creation of a system at a general level. We then make these activities more concrete using a real world example. This approach connects the architecture orientation framework to the contents of the previous chapters. It enables you to understand how to apply the information presented in the other chapters to a concrete problem (Figure 8-1).

Overview

Section 8.8 is based on the work by Prof. Dr. Uwe Zdun for the German Edition of this book.

Figure 8-2 shows the basic concepts covered in this chapter and visualizes how they relate to each other. Sections 8.1–8.7 discuss these concepts in detail.

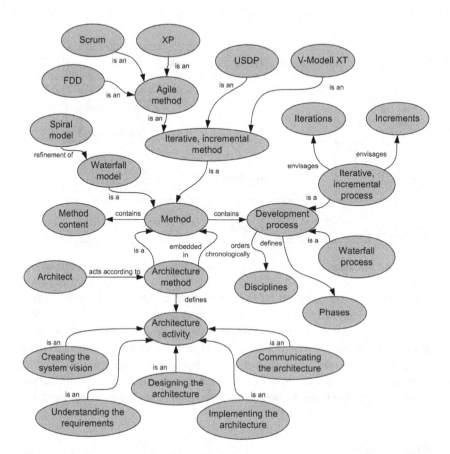

***Figure 8-2:** Basic concepts of the HOW dimension*

8.1 Architecture and Development Processes

The development of a software system only rarely follows the path you originally planned (see Figure 8.1-1). You may have to make changes even at the beginning of a project, for example, because important project team members with the required capabilities are not available. The project will continue to deviate from the planned path over the course of time and the end product will not match the original plan precisely. There can be various reasons for this. System requirements can change or important team members can leave the project. Learning effects (even for an architect) that arise during the course of the project and constraints can mean that the project needs to change course. As long as you can react to such changes, and still achieve the overall objective defined by the stakeholders, this is not a problem. The reaction to such changes can differ in quality depending on the method you select. As an architect you have to adapt your activities to the conditions. In the following section we will therefore briefly discuss the methods used most frequently in practice. Section 6.6.5 provides more detailed information.

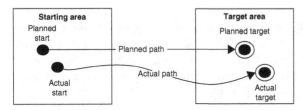

Figure 8.1-1: Planned development path vs. actual development path

The waterfall model was first discussed in an article in the 1970s [Royce 1970]. Its essence is the sequential and once-only processing of different software development disciplines (see Figure 8.1-2). A discipline is a set of related activities producing a set of deliverables required by the subsequent discipline. For example, the requirements gathering discipline deals with the gathering of the requirements and the creation of requirements specification deliverables, e.g., use case models. In the waterfall model, you execute the various disciplines, e.g., requirements gathering, analysis, design, and implementation one after the other. In other words, one discipline starts only once another discipline has been fully completed. This means that the deliverables of the respective disciplines must be complete and must contain no errors at the end of that particular discipline. Based on the requirements documented during requirements gathering, you create suitable analysis models. The design itself documents how the system should be realized during implementation. In this context, disciplines are often referred to as phases.

The waterfall model

Due to its simplicity (which is quite unlike reality), many people initially find the waterfall model very interesting. It is very easy to plan a development project using this approach: you can plan the beginning and the end of the different disciplines, and the specific point in time when people are required for individual activities (e.g., creating use cases, programming) [Cockburn 2002]. On the other hand, however, this approach contains many inherent risks for the planned project schedule: for example, feedback is collected from users of the system very late in the development process—specifically, during the test phase. This means

Advantages and disadvantages of the waterfall model

that you cannot react to errors in the system and to changed requirements. Furthermore, the deliverables you create (e.g., the design) will have gaps, be contradictory, or simply be defective. You cannot correct errors like this at short notice. It is often the case that the client only identifies or raises some requirements when the implementation phase starts (e.g., requirements for the user interface). If you use the waterfall model, you cannot take these late requirements into account appropriately. Furthermore, by definition, a sequential method takes longer than a non-sequential method since one discipline can only begin when the previous discipline is complete.

Waterfall model is rarely successful

Practice has shown that the waterfall approach is rarely successful [Parnas et al. 1986; Larman 2002; Cockburn 2002]. Despite this, many projects still apply it and thus fail. Even Royce was aware of and discussed the problems of a sequential method [Royce 1970]. The waterfall model can be viewed as an historical mistake [Oestereich and Weiss 2008].

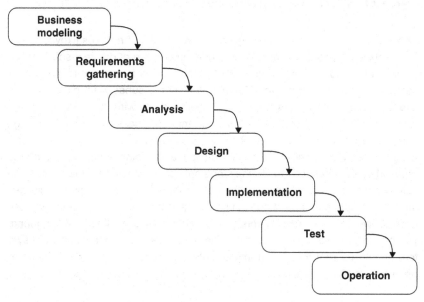

Figure 8.1-2: Example of the waterfall model

Architecture is not created in strict sequence

As the explanations clearly show, in an architecture method you cannot assume that you will design the architecture in detail first and then implement it. Doing this would mean that you could not adapt to changes to the requirements quickly enough. Furthermore, the architecture is validated too late in the development process. It is then very difficult to correct errors in the architecture and you can only do so with substantial effort and hence cost.

The spiral model is a refinement of the waterfall model that tries to resolve the weaknesses of the latter [Boehm 1998]. Instead of executing the specified disciplines sequentially just once, you subdivide a software development plan into several cycles and execute every discipline in every cycle. Each cycle ends with the stakeholders affected reviewing the deliverables: for example, users will test the system towards the end of a cycle. This review provides important information about the extent to which you have achieved the goals—information that you can then take into account in the next cycle. You thus create the deliverables, such as use case descriptions, UML components and sequence diagrams, or source code step-by-step. This reduces the risk that you might not achieve the goal at the end of a development project. An important part of the spiral model is the development of prototypes or simulations to assess alternatives and estimate risks. Prototypes in particular are a valuable tool for verifying or visualizing aspects of an architecture (see Sections 8.4 and 8.5).

The spiral model

Similarly to the spiral model, newer methods, such as Unified Software Development Process (USDP) [Jacobson et al. 1999], V-Modell XT [V-Modell XT 2009], Extreme Programming (XP) [Beck 2005], Feature Driven Development (FDD) [Parmer and Felsing 2002], and Scrum [Cohn 2010] also focus on a step-by-step development of software systems that runs through multiple cycles. In this context, the term "iterative, incremental development process" has become widespread. The entire development process is divided into individual, sequential development steps that build on one another, so-called iterations. What is special about this process is that all typical disciplines and activities of a software development take place within each iteration. This means that in each iteration, you analyze part of the overall task, create a design for what you have analyzed, and then implement the design. Thus, at the end of an iteration, you have moved one step further in the overall task and added another piece to the solution. Every one of these pieces that make up the solution is called an "increment," and represents a system with some parts that are already working. Thus you arrive at the final system, step-by-step and piece by piece—iteratively and incrementally.

Methods with an iterative, incremental development process

Of course, you must plan an iterative, incremental development process as precisely as a sequential one. It is particularly important to plan the iterations. Determine the number of iterations required, and then define the requirements to be realized in each of the respective iterations. As the architect, you must support the project lead in the planning in order to ensure that the architecturally significant requirements (see Section 8.4) are prioritized sensibly. The analysis of the requirements is one factor that determines the weighting of the individual requirements. For example, requirements with a great benefit for the user and/ or a high risk (e.g., time budget would be exceeded considerably or technical implementation is not possible without further effort) could receive a high weighting. In contrast, requirements with a low benefit and/or a low risk would receive

Iteration planning and requirements

a correspondingly lower weighting. During iteration planning, you distribute the individual requirements to the individual iterations based on their weighting: realize requirements with a high weighting early in the development process, i.e., in one of the first iterations; schedule requirements with a low weighting for later iterations. For more information about weighting requirements, see Section 8.4. However, the distribution of the requirements to individual iterations is not set in stone. During the individual iterations, you may change the weighting of individual requirements, new requirements may arise, and existing requirements may change. These changes mean that you have to adapt the initial iteration planning as well. This is where an iterative, incremental development process offers a decisive advantage: you can continuously adjust the development process and its results to the changing environment. However, this also means that you need a special method for your work. This chapter presents the essential method that you should be concerned with within a development process.

Resource planning and requirements

You must consider architecturally significant requirements in the effort estimation for resource planning (budget, time, people) as well as in the iteration planning in addition to the normal requirements. It is important that you are sufficiently involved in prioritizing and estimating the effort for requirements in order to support the project lead and domain experts—otherwise there is a risk that technical aspects do not receive sufficient attention or are estimated incorrectly (e.g., restricted possibilities of a framework with reference to the implementation of specific requirements). This can have negative consequences for the further project planning (e.g., implementation requires more people than planned).

Agile methods

We have already named some agile methods: XP, FDD, and Scrum. From an architectural view, what is relevant about agile methods is that they use exclusively an iterative, incremental development process and restrict the scope of the documentation or rather, question "superfluous" documentation [Cunningham et al. 2001]. For example, documentation should only cover existing, concrete requirements and not possible future ones. For you, the question is whether this also applies to the architecture documentation—or rather, how loosely must you define an architecture and how can you then make this explicit in an agile context? Opinions circulating in the XP community deem an architecture design unnecessary—although the issue is the subject of much controversy [Fowler 2004]. In general, we can say that the degree of the architecture design and the architecture documentation should fulfill the "sufficient-to-purpose" principle [Cockburn 2002; Fowler 2004]. Hence consider each specific situation individually. Ambler argues that you must pay sufficient attention to architecture even in agile methods. In the first iteration, it should be successful enough to serve as a vision and orientation for team members. You will adjust the architecture itself, and the documentation, as required over time in agile approaches [Ambler 2010].

Methods are templates that you have to adapt to concrete situations. For example, the project size is an indicator of how you should adapt a method in practice. Variants of USDP already exist for large and small projects. In addition to adapting methods, in large projects in particular, subprojects can use different methods suitable for their respective context (e.g., team members are very experienced, meaning that XP is suitable). However, this can also cause problems because inhomogeneous methods make coordination among the individual subprojects more difficult. You can also combine methods. Projects can base their concrete development process on USDP and XP, for example. USDP can define the general method, but you can also integrate best practices such as continuous integration and pair programming from Extreme Programming (XP) [Beck 2005] in the process. Here we should briefly mention the Software & Systems Process Engineering Meta Model (SPEM) from OMG [OMG 2008c] and the Eclipse Process Framework (EPF) [Eclipse 2010c]. SPEM is a metamodel for defining processes (see Section 6.6.5). With EPF, you can create, adapt, and combine processes based on the SPEM metamodel.

Methods can be adapted and combined

In this section we will take a closer look at USDP, frequently also referred to as UP (Unified Process). It is an example of an iterative, incremental development process [Jacobson et al. 1999]. One variant is the Rational Unified Process (RUP). Figure 8.1-3 shows the main elements of USDP.

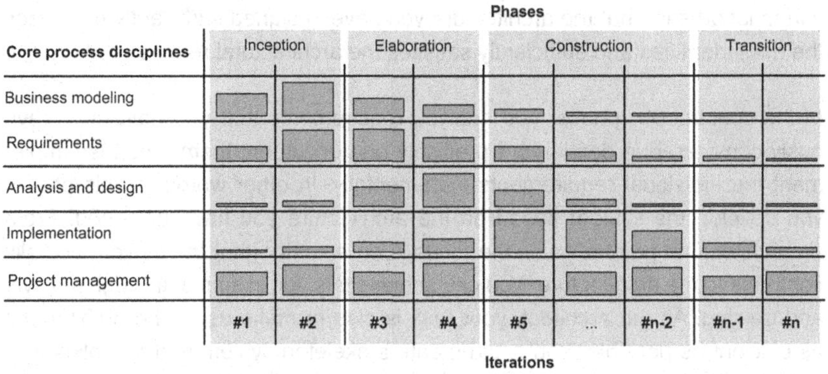

USDP as an example of an iterative, incremental development process

Figure 8.1-3: Elements of USDP

Figure 8.1-3 shows how an iterative, incremental development process is structured over time (phases and iterations) on the vertical axis, and over the core process disciplines on the horizontal axis. Only the core process disciplines most relevant for you as an architect are shown—USDP has further core process disciplines. For clarity, an iterative, incremental development process differentiates between specific phases (time sections) that run during the development of a system. Do not confuse these phases with the phases of the waterfall model. Each one can be made up of more or fewer iterations. The core process disciplines have a different weighting depending on the phase to which an iteration belongs. Figure 8.1-3 shows the weighting of the core disciplines at different times using different sized blocks at the intersections of the time and activity axes. However, it only shows the tendency in the weighting of the core process disciplines: in a concrete project, the absolute figures can be different. We will now briefly discuss the different phases.

Inception

In the inception phase, the focus is on the agreement of the stakeholders on the goals of the project. It is also important at this early stage to define the scope of the system to be realized. This includes defining the most important requirements and the acceptance criteria. You must also identify and assess risks. In this first phase you make initial decisions about the architecture and, if applicable, design an initial architecture to demonstrate feasibility and thus establish confidence in the planned project.

Elaboration

The elaboration phase is particularly challenging since here you must complete the architecture to such a degree that you have a stable architectural basis for the activities in the subsequent phases. In this phase you do the following: consider all architectural requirements, design the architecture, verify alternatives using architecture prototypes, and implement evolutionary architecture prototypes. An evolutionary architecture prototype is evolved over time in the actual IT system by adding more functionality incrementally. At the end of the elaboration phase, you must be sure that the architecture you have designed sufficiently minimizes the risks identified and sufficiently satisfies the architectural requirements.

Construction

In the construction phase, you analyze requirements that you have not previously considered in detail more precisely and document them. You also implement the individual requirements incrementally. In other words, in this phase, you develop the system based on the architecture you have designed. From an architectural point of view, the focus is on ensuring that the system actually conforms to the architecture. You can achieve this, for example, through reviews and training. As the architect, your task is also to make using the architecture as efficient as possible. You could create a skeleton system that complies with the architecture, for example (see Section 8.6). This would enable developers to concentrate on implementing the business logic and they would not have to deal with infrastructure-related logic.

Transition

In the subsequent transition phase, the focus is on ensuring that the system can be handed over to the end user. For example, errors are corrected, users are trained, the maintenance personnel are instructed, and the operating and installation documentation is created. As the architect you will frequently be involved in the error analysis and bug fixing. You will also be responsible for training the maintenance and operating personnel with regard to the architectural aspects.

Table 8.1-1 gives an overview of important relationships between the aspects of the architecture method described in Section 8.1 and the architectural topics discussed in Chapters 3–7.

Table 8.1-1: Overview of the connections between Section 8.1 and Chapters 3–7

Chapter/section number	Chapter/section heading	Reason for connection
3.2	From Classic Architecture to Software Architecture (WHAT)	Architectural activities and related decisions are influenced by the surrounding process
4	Architecture Perspectives (WHERE)	Activities and deliverables defined by processes are at different levels of abstraction and require the usage of different views
5	Architecture Requirements (WHY)	Processes must support the sufficient handling of architecturally significant requirements
6	Architecture Means (WITH WHAT)	Prozesses must ensure appropriate utilization of architecture means within architectural activities
7.1	General (WHO)	The architect acts in the context of an organization and his activities are therefore heavily influenced by this context. One important aspect is that organizations often define which kind of processes have to be applied by the different projects
7.2	Organizations (WHO)	Which development process is chosen also depends on the significant basic understandings of an organization. For example, scientific management understanding tends to prefer the waterfall model
7.3	Individuals (WHO)	The different identities individuals can have influence the way a process is executed and should be considered when choosing a process
7.4	Individuals and Groups (WHO)	Group dynamics and group composition influence the way a process is executed
7.5	Architect as Central Role (WHO)	Processes can be used to limit or to promote the architect's role

8.2 Overview of the Architecture Method

The previous chapters provided essential architectural knowledge that forms an important basis for you to practice successfully as an architect on a daily basis. However, this knowledge is worthless if you cannot use it consciously and purposefully. To do this, you have to develop an architectural awareness, think architecturally, and proceed architecturally so that the architectural knowledge discussed in the previous chapters actually brings useful benefits. But what is the best way to proceed? What are your important activities? How can you integrate the method into an existing software development process? And finally, what effect do other architecture dimensions (WHAT, WHERE, WHY, WITH WHAT, and WHO) have on the architectural activities? This section provides a brief overview of your activities as an architect. Sections 8.3–8.7 cover the individual activities in detail.

An architect needs a method

As explained in Chapter 3, software architecture covers not only the software structures of a system, but also the activities that lead to these structures. There are many architecture means for structuring (see Chapter 6). However, using them does not automatically lead to good architecture. It is therefore important to use a systematic architecture method as a basis when you are selecting the architecture means. Regardless of whether you develop the system based on the waterfall model or iteratively and incrementally, the challenge will always be to align your method to the definition of an architecture that fulfills both the functional and the non-functional requirements. As emphasized in Section 8.1, an iterative, incremental development process is preferred over a sequential process.

... and experience

However, applying an appropriate method is still no guarantee for a good architecture. As an architect you can allow yourself to be guided by a method. To create architecture, however, you will always have to use your own wealth of experience in addition to the generic help provided by a method. For example, you will have to adapt the recommendations of a method to the specific project situation based on your own experience.

The typical activities of an architect

What are the activities that make up an architecture method? Figure 8.2-1 visualizes the general architecture method using a UML activity diagram. We will explain the model later in this section before we analyze how it can be embedded in software development processes.

The activities presented in Figure 8.2-1 are based on the work of Bass et al. [Bass et al. 2003] and our own experiences. Bass et al. also introduce the activities "analyze and assess the architecture" and "ensure architectural conformity." In the method presented here, the architecture is assessed as part of the activity "designing the architecture." The activity "implementing the architecture" is devoted to the aspect of architectural conformity. The activities are independent of the concrete development process. However, with the exception of the activity "creating the system vision," you should always execute the activities iteratively and incrementally. Therefore, later in this chapter, we will look at the activities in the context of an iterative, incremental development process.

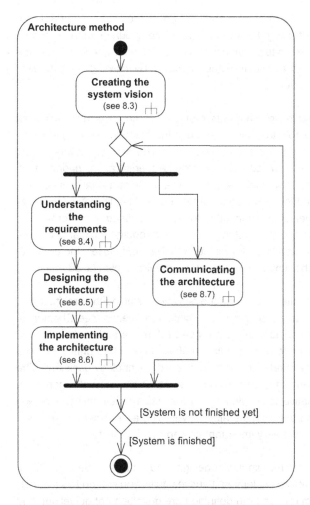

Figure 8.2-1: *Overview of the architecture method*

On one hand, a system vision evaluates the business usefulness of an initiative. For example, a system vision for replacing a host system that has grown over decades with a JEE-based system will contain clear statements about the desired and expected profitability. On the other hand, a system vision also defines the essential requirements for the future system. It is your responsibility as an architect to question these requirements critically with regard to their architectural feasibility in the overall or global IT context of an organization. You must also point out contradictory requirements and indicate alternatives. Therefore, it is essential that you participate in the creation of the system vision at this early stage. If you do not, there is a danger that a system vision will be unrealistic from an architectural point of view and the realization is therefore at a disadvantage

Creating the system vision

from the very beginning. As far as the architecture method is concerned, when executing the activity "creating the system vision," see yourself as an architectural consultant—your task is to position the system vision on viable architectural foundations. You can proceed with the other architectural activities once the system vision has been adopted.

Understanding the requirements

As explained in Chapter 5, requirements restrict your creative freedom as an architect. In order to be able to envision and use this freedom, you must understand both the stakeholders and the requirements. The activity "understanding the requirements" is therefore concerned with the identification, prioritization, and detailing of architecturally significant requirements. In particular, it is very important that you examine the non-functional requirements deliberately and thoroughly. These requirements are often either loosely formulated or not formulated at all. The more explicitly the architecturally significant requirements are detailed, the clearer your architectural freedom will be, and the more closely the architecture that you define in the next step will meet the requirements placed on it.

Designing the architecture

You create the actual architecture during the activity "designing the architecture." Here you can choose from a wide range of architecture means (see Chapter 6). For example, you may consider using a proven reference architecture, a tried and tested architecture pattern, or simple, timeless architecture principles. At a later point in time, you will make concrete platform or technology decisions. The architecture of the system is the sum of all decisions. There is usually more than one architecture alternative for implementing the given requirements. You will therefore have to decide between the alternatives. The assessment of architecture alternatives is therefore very important as part of this activity.

Implementing the architecture

An architecture should not remain just a design: you must also demonstrate it technologically and therefore implement it successfully. You can do this in different ways. The spectrum ranges from defining pure development guidelines and manual reviews to establishing an infrastructure that guides and supports the developers in implementing the system so that it conforms to the architecture. The implementation of the architecture is often neglected (see Chapter 7). This results in systems that follow the architecture only partially or not at all, and that do not satisfy architecturally significant requirements.

Communicating the architecture

As an architect you must not only design an architecture, you must also communicate it to the different stakeholders. The aim of the activity "communicating the architecture" is therefore to convey the best possible understanding of the architecture and the architecture decisions to the individual stakeholders (e.g., project leaders, developers, users, customers). In turn, this understanding is a good basis for the activities of the individual stakeholders. Here, communication comprises documenting an architecture and conveying it verbally based on or using the architecture documentation. You always communicate the architecture in parallel to the other activities. During the "understanding the requirements" activity, you will already be communicating with the stakeholders, for example, to point out contradictory requirements. In the "designing the architecture" activity, you will present your designs to stakeholders. During the implementation of the architecture, you will also run *source code reviews* to ensure architectural conformity. You will communicate with your developers and discuss the review results. And of course, communication also takes place during the creation of the system vision. However, the main part of the communication will take place during the development of a system.

After you have successfully created a vision for a system, and the actual software development project has begun, you will perform the other architectural activities over the entire software development process (see Figure 8.2-1). The focus shifts from "understanding the requirements" through "designing the architecture" to "implementing the architecture." "Communicating the architecture" does not become less important, however, since you must keep an architecture alive in the minds of the stakeholders.

An architect is involved over the entire software development cycle

An important result of the architectural activities is the creation of different architecture views as described in Chapter 4 [Rozanski and Woods 2005]. Table 8.2-1 shows the architecture views that you develop in the individual architectural activities.

Developing architecture views

Table 8.2-1: Architecture views and architectural activities

Architecture views	Architectural activities
Requirements view	> Creating the system vision > Understanding the requirements > Communicating the architecture
Logical view	> Creating the system vision > Designing the architecture > Communicating the architecture
Data view	> Designing the architecture > Communicating the architecture
Implementation view	> Implementing the architecture > Communicating the architecture
Deployment view	> Designing the architecture > Communicating the architecture
Process view	> Designing the architecture > Communicating the architecture

Architecture method activities in an iterative, incremental development process

You perform the architectural activities continuously in an iterative, incremental development process. In each iteration, the architectural work is made up of a combination of the activities. However, the ratio of the individual activities changes from iteration to iteration. In the initial phase, the main focus is on the activities "creating the system vision" and "understanding the requirements." During the development process, the focus then moves to the activities "designing the architecture," "implementing the architecture," and "communicating the architecture." The architectural activities thus fit into the structure of the surrounding iterative, incremental development process. This enables you to adapt the work in the individual architectural activities to the changing requirements, to the same extent as the development process is adapted.

Embedding architectural activities in development processes using the USDP example

The architectural activities can be embedded in the USDP disciplines. Figure 8.2-2 shows which architectural activities you take into account in each of the core process disciplines of an iterative, incremental development process using the example of USDP. You cannot always assign the activity to one core process discipline uniquely. However, this is not particularly significant as it is more important to perform the activities, regardless of the core process discipline in which they are to be embedded.

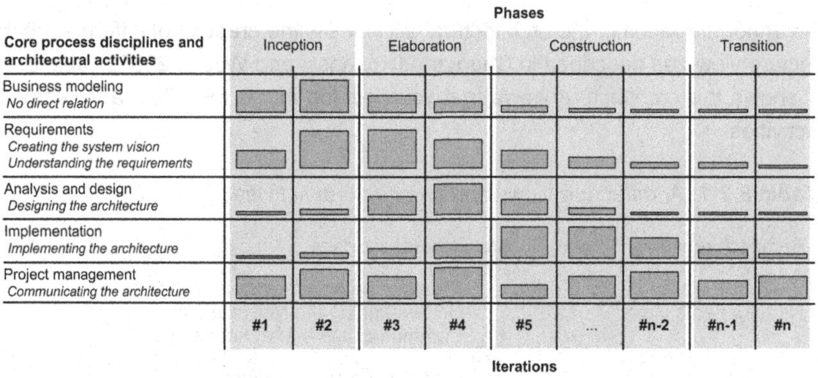

Figure 8.2-2: USDP core process disciplines and architectural activities

Do not architect in isolation, involve your team

An architecture is only successful if it is accepted by the team that has to realize and implement it. Furthermore, the stakeholders must also be informed and aware of the architectural decisions and the impact on them. Therefore, it is essential that you involve stakeholders in the definition of the architecture and that you communicate the architecture at an early stage (see Section 8.7). You will not be able to cover each and every aspect yourself. You will need the insights and experience of the experts in your team (e.g. security, usability, or integration experts and developers). Involving your team in the architecture activities will not only improve the acceptance of the architecture but will also make it sounder.

Although we are focusing on the architect and describe the architectural activities from an architect's perspective, you need to be aware that you are part of a team and that organizational and social aspects apply (see Chapter 7).

You also need to support your project manager from an architecture perspective. For example, you will need to identify the skills required and participate in the selection of appropriate practitioners (see Section 8.7). Furthermore, you will have to work together with the project manager to create a project plan based on the effort you have estimated. Often an architect is also considered a technical project manager.

Architect and project management

We will now look at the architecture method using a concrete real world example. We can use the Management Information System (MIS) presented in Section 3.4 for collecting and evaluating business key figures.

Example from practice: MIS

Table 8.2-2 gives an overview of important relationships between the aspects of the architecture method described in Section 8.2 and the architectural topics discussed in Chapters 3–7.

Connections between Section 8.2 and Chapters 3–7

Table 8.2-2: Overview of the connections between Section 8.2 and Chapters 3–7

Chapter/ section number	Chapter/section heading	Reason for connection
3.2	From Classic Architecture to Software Architecture (WHAT)	The architecture method is the manifestation of the fact that software architecture is not only the representation of the structures of a system but also a discipline
3.3	Architecture and the System Concept (WHAT)	Thinking in systems is one of the essential prerequisites for executing the architecture method sensibly
3.4	Architecture and the Building Blocks of a System (WHAT)	The architecture method deals with a set of fundamental system building blocks
4.1	Architecture Levels (WHERE)	The activities of the architecture method are performed at different architecture levels
4.2	Architecture Views (WHERE)	Within each activity of the architecture method one or more different architectures views are created or worked out
5	Architecture Requirements (WHY)	While executing the architecture method the architect is guided by requirements throughout all activities and the actions of the activities
6	Architecture Means (WITH WHAT)	While executing the architecture method the architect applies different architecture means corresponding to the activity in question and its actions

Chapter/ section number	Chapter/section heading	Reason for connection
6.6.5	Unified Method Ar- chitecture (UMA)	UMA can be used to model the architecture meth- od in order to embed the activities of the architec- ture method into an overall development process
7.2	Organizations (WHO)	Which development process is chosen also de- pends on the significant basic understandings of an organization. For example, scientific manage- ment understanding tends to prefer the waterfall model
7.3	Individuals (WHO)	The different identities individuals can have influ- ence the way a process is executed and should be considered when choosing a process
7.4	Individuals and Groups (WHO)	Group dynamics and group composition influence the way a process is executed
7.5	Architect as Central Role (WHO)	The architecture method comprises those activi- ties and corresponding actions that are required by the architect's role

8.3 Creating the System Vision

**Basic concepts of the
activity "creating the
system vision"**

Figure 8.3-1 shows the basic concepts of the activity "creating the system vision."
We will look at these in more detail and visualize how they relate to each other.

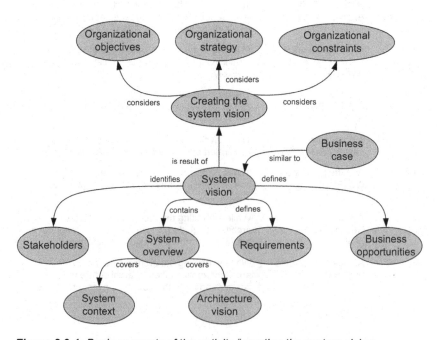

Figure 8.3-1: Basic concepts of the activity "creating the system vision

Figure 8.3-2 illustrates the individual actions of the activity "creating the system vision." This activity is primarily concerned with developing the requirements view of a system (see Section 4.2). Not all of the actions have a primarily architectural nature. However, a system vision must be architecturally feasible. It is therefore important that you participate in all actions and look at the system vision from an architectural point of view. Imagine the following example: The requirement is for a system to be available for productive use at a specific point in time. In order to have the greatest possible freedom for further development, there is the additional requirement for the organization to develop the system in-house. However, the functional scope of the system is so vast that it cannot be developed in-house within the given time frame due to missing development capabilities. It is now your task as the architect to draw attention to the conflict between these individual requirements and to show alternative solutions. In this case, the following alternative solutions could be possible: moving the productive start for the system, or realizing the system by integrating commercial off the shelf products with custom-developed software building blocks. Use custom development in cases where it is important not to be dependent on product lifecycles of a product supplier and where the IT system built should support a business capability that distinguishes it from competitors.

The way to a system vision

In this activity you take on the role of an architectural consultant in a team of experts from different areas. Other team members are domain experts, for example. You can only create an overall system vision by putting together a team with members from the different areas.

Architect as architectural consultant

The term "business case" is sometimes used instead of "system vision." A business case generally highlights the economic benefits more clearly than a system vision. However, it is sometimes difficult to differentiate between them. USDP does differentiate between "business case" and "system vision," but stresses the close connection between the two.

System vision and business case

The business opportunities to be achieved by realizing the system are an important part of the system vision. You should clearly state the benefits of the system and the problems that the system solves. Make the benefits tangible both qualitatively and quantitatively—quantitatively in the form of business key figures, such as "return on investment (ROI), time to market, or time to value."

Describe business opportunities

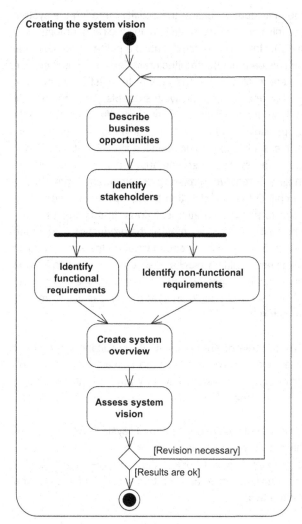

Figure 8.3-2: Creating the system vision

Table 8.3-1 illustrates the business context, the business opportunities, and the problem description for MIS.

Table 8.3-1: Business opportunities and problem description for MIS

Business context	
MIS is embedded in the global department responsible for the enterprise resource planning systems (ERP Support) for the enterprise. This department offers its services to all departments that need ERP systems	
Business opportunities	
The management of ERP Support wants to be able to measure the performance of its global department as well as its regional sub-departments. Therefore, key performance indicators (e.g., number of tickets closed, reopened, rejected) are to be recorded and evaluated. Based on the findings, the management of ERP Support will be able to rectify weaknesses directly and thus improve the overall performance	
Problem description	
Problem	At the moment there is no information available about the qualitative and quantitative performance of the ERP Support department
Concerns	Management Team leaders
Consequences	No management measures can be undertaken to maintain and improve services.
Successful solution	The transparency of the actual performance ability of the department is increased and justified measures can be taken. In the long term, customer satisfaction is increased.
Task of the system	MIS should enable the recording and evaluation of performance indicators.

In addition to describing business opportunities, a system vision also identifies the stakeholders of the system. Since the success of a system depends on its acceptance by the stakeholders, this action is very important [Rozanski and Woods 2005]. The stakeholders include the immediate users of the system, as well as clients, operators, or departments affected. The following questions can be useful in identifying the stakeholders:

Identify stakeholders

> Who uses the system?
> Who is affected by the introduction of the system?
> Who benefits from the system?
> Who operates the system?
> Who maintains the system?
> Who accepts the system?
> What expectations do the stakeholders have?
> What tasks, competencies, and responsibilities do the stakeholders have?

We recommend describing the stakeholders using a standard template that reflects the answers to the questions above.

Expectation management is necessary

Stakeholders are not always positive about the development of a new system. A new system could shift the political power structure between departments, for example. In the worst case, individual stakeholders could boycott the project. Therefore, always be aware that social aspects are also important for you in your role as an architect (see Chapter 7). Address the expectations stakeholders have of the system and the architecture actively. This aspect should be recognized as part of the activity "communicating the architecture" (see Section 8.7).

Table 8.3-2: MIS stakeholders

Stakeholder	Role	Description
ERP management	Represents the interests of management	Analyzes performance indicators and derives actions from them
Central architecture	Represents central architectural guidelines	Assesses the conformity of the MIS architecture with the central guidelines
System operation	Represents operational specifications	Operates MIS (installation, start, stop, update)
Team leader	Represents the requirements of the team leaders	Records data for collecting performance indicators
Administrator	Represents the requirements of the administrators	Manages MIS users. Initiates data imports
Controller	Represents the requirements from controlling	Runs reports and checks performance of the various support teams against defined performance indicators

Identify stakeholders with architectural relevance early

Table 8.3-2 contains the stakeholders for our MIS example. Enterprises often have a central architecture department that defines architectural specifications valid for the whole enterprise. Sometimes this department is identified as a stakeholder too late. You should therefore always analyze the organizational environment and include stakeholders with architectural relevance. These include, for example, system operators who will later operate the system. You can also prioritize the stakeholders in order of their importance to enable you to take their requirements into account correspondingly later on [Oestereich and Bremer 2009]

A system vision should document the significant requirements that the system must satisfy. This ensures that you define the system's functional scope at an early stage. During requirements gathering, you derive detailed requirements within the identified scope. Record the relevant non-functional requirements as well as the functional requirements.

Identifying the functional requirements means defining the functionality the system is to provide (see Chapter 5). The focus should be on the primary functionality. From the significant functional requirements, select those of an architectural nature. For example, you may have to connect external systems in order to realize some requirements. You must therefore investigate the feasibility of integrating these systems. Table 8.3-3 contains some examples of functional requirements for MIS.

Table 8.3-3: Significant functional requirements for MIS

Functional requirement	Description
Log on	Users must authenticate themselves with an ID and a password before MIS grants them access
Enter performance data	Team leaders must be able to enter performance data for their teams. Administrators must be able to enter performance data for any teams
Import incident data	Incident data must be imported into MIS from the Incident Management System (IMS) to determine performance indicators
Import CCM data	Configuration & Change Management (CCM) data must be imported into MIS from the CCM system (CCMS) to determine performance indicators
Create performance reports	Controllers must be able to create performance reports
Manage user accounts	Administrators must be able to manage user accounts
Display performance reports	Managers, team leaders, controllers, and administrators must be able to look at performance reports

Unfortunately, the non-functional requirements that a system must satisfy are often neglected. However, to ensure the system is accepted, you must also recognize these requirements. The direct non-functional requirements determine the expected quality of the functional requirements (see Sections 5.1 and 5.5). For example, a requirement for displaying the input screens of MIS may be that 80% of the screens must appear within 5 s. Indirect non-functional requirements can also have an effect on the system. Such requirements, also known as constraints, restrict your creative freedom as an architect. The central architecture department can specify, for example, that MIS must be implemented based on JEE. This excludes a realization of MIS with PHP or .NET from the very beginning. In particular, you must assess and gather the non-functional requirements at an early stage. Furthermore, you will always be faced with the challenge of identifying undocumented non-functional requirements and agreeing them with stakeholders. Table 8.3-4 contains non-functional requirements for MIS.

Table 8.3-4: Significant non-functional requirements for MIS

Non-functional requirement	Description
Operability	MIS must be connected to the central system management infrastructure
Extensibility	It must be possible to add new performance indicators and performance reports to MIS within an average of ten person days
Time-to-Market	MIS must be developed within six months
Compliance with IT standards	Guidelines issued by the central architecture department must be complied with
Security	Only authenticated users must be able to access functionalities and data for which they have authorization.
Usability	MIS must offer context-sensitive online help for users
Availability	MIS must be available 24/7
Performance	80% of the screens must be displayed within 5 s

Create system overview

Based on the significant requirements identified, you can now start to create the system overview. You will consider the system in its context for the first time. Therefore, you initially view the system as a black box (see Section 3.3) and identify the human and system actors that the system interacts with. The human actors are the users of the system. System actors are the external systems (peripheral systems) that the system communicates with. The system context boundary depicts the relationship between the system under construction and its human actors and system actors. It thus illustrates the system boundary. You refine the system context and make it more concrete later on in the course of the project.

Create a first system context

Figure 8.3-3 illustrates the system context of MIS. It contains the human actors (roles). These were derived from the stakeholders. It also contains the peripheral systems. In this example, these are an Incident Management System (IMS), a Configuration & Change Management System (CCMS), and a System Manage-

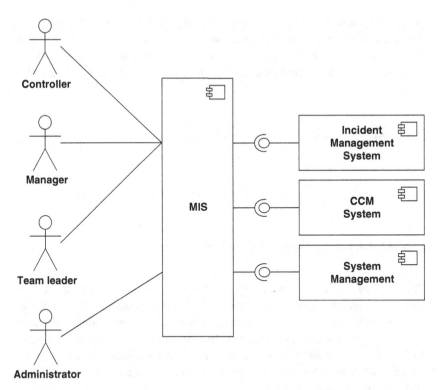

Figure 8.3-3: MIS system context

ment System. The IMS contains information about incidents that the ERP support department processes. These include setting up or unlocking a user account. This information shows how long it took to process an incident. If errors are discovered in ERP, these must be corrected by the development department. The support department sends them to the development department by means of change requests. These changes are managed in CCMS and not in IMS. Since information must be available from both CCMS and IMS for a precise analysis, MIS must also communicate with CCMS. To operate MIS, it must also be connected to the central system management infrastructure (see Section 3.4). This is the result of the non-functional requirement of operability, rather than functional requirements. The corresponding extension of the system context lays the foundation for fulfilling this non-functional requirement later.

During this activity, you create a first approximate decomposition of the system as well as the system context. It corresponds to a first architectural vision. The vision is usually vague. You make it more concrete later during the "designing the architecture" activity. The presentation at this point can be very informal and you can restrict it to the identification of significant building blocks (see Figure 8.3-4).

There is a first architecture vision

So-called "box and line diagrams" are frequently used instead of UML diagrams. These are very informal and make it easier for various stakeholders to understand the architecture vision. This type of diagram is sometimes also used as the basis for more precise and more formal UML diagrams [Rozanski and Woods 2005].

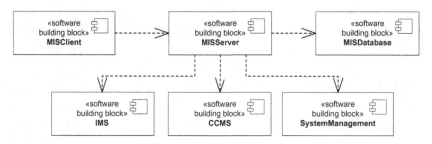

Figure 8.3-4: *First architecture idea of MIS*

Assess system vision

Creating this system overview completes the main actions for creating a system vision. The system vision can now be assessed. It is assessed on one hand by the team that created it and on the other by the stakeholders—in the MIS case, for example, by the ERP management. The requirements could also be critically reviewed in this context. For example, the architect responsible for MIS may notice that the availability requirement does not allow for a maintenance window and could point out this problem.

MIS: Architecture views developed

Table 8.3-5 shows which artefacts have been worked out for the architecture view "requirements view" (see Section 4.2) for MIS during the "creating the system vision" activity.

Table 8.3-5: *Architecture views developed during "creating the system vision"*

Architecture view	MIS artefacts
Requirements view	> Business opportunities and problem description (see Table 8.3-1)
	> MIS stakeholders (see Table 8.3-2)
	> Significant functional requirements (see Table 8.3-3)
	> Significant non-functional requirements (see Table 8.3-4)
Logical view	> MIS system context (see Figure 8.3-3)
	> First architecture idea of MIS (see Figure 8.3-4)

Checklist: Creating the system vision

Have business opportunities and the problem description been documented?
Are all stakeholders clearly agreed on the essential task of the system to be developed?
Have all architecturally significant stakeholders been identified?
Have all significant requirements been documented?
Has sufficient attention been paid to non-functional requirements?
Has a system context been created?
Does the system context cover all human and system actors (peripheral systems)?
Has an architecture vision been created?
Has the system vision been assessed?

Table 8.3-6 gives an overview of important relationships between the aspects of the architecture method described in Section 8.3 and the architectural topics discussed in Chapters 2–7.

Connections between Section 8.3 and Chapters 3–7

Table 8.3-6: Overview of the connections between Section 8.3 and Chapters 3–7

Chapter/section number	Chapter/section heading	Reason for connection
3.3	Architecture and the System Concept (WHAT)	Thinking in systems is applied to work out building blocks required. The system and its environment are the basis for creating the first system context
3.4	Architecture and the Building Blocks of a System (WHAT)	A system and its building blocks are the basis for identifying the first building blocks of the system to be developed
4.1	Architecture Levels (WHERE)	At the organizational level the business opportunities are described and the stakeholders are identified. At the system level the requirements are identified and the system context is created. At building block level the first building blocks of the system are identified
4.2	Architecture Views (WHERE)	The requirements view and the logical view are created
5	Architecture Requirements (WHY)	Functional requirements, qualities, and constraints are considered
6.1	Architecture Principles (WITH WHAT)	Architecture principles (e.g., modularity and loose coupling) are applied to create the system overview and the first building blocks
6.2	Basic Architecture Concepts (WITH WHAT)	Basic architecture concepts (e.g., component orientation) are applied to create the system overview and the first building blocks

Chapter/ section number	Chapter/section heading	Reason for connection
6.6	Architecture Modeling Means (WITH WHAT)	Architecture modeling means (e.g., UML) are applied to document the system overview and the first building blocks
7	Organizations and Individuals (WHO)	The architect has to understand the concerns and needs of the various stakeholders and therefore has to communicate and collaborate with them

Further reading:
Creating the system vision

[Oestereich and Bremer 2009]
Oestereich, Bernd; Bremer, Stefan, *Analyse und Design mit UML 2.3 - Objektorientierte Softwareentwicklung, 9. Auflage,* Oldenbourg Verlag, 2009 (available in German language only)

[Rozanski and Woods 2005]
Rozanski, Nick und Woods, Eoin, *Software Systems Architecture - Working with Stakeholders Using Viewpoints and Perspectives*, Addison-Wesley, 2005

Summary:
Creating the system vision

> In this activity you take on the role of an architectural consultant in a team of experts from different domains.
> The term "business case" is sometimes used instead of "system vision."
> A system vision should contain the business opportunities, the stakeholders, the significant requirements, and a first system overview.
> Identify and prioritize the stakeholders.
> During the creation of the system vision, you must manage the expectations of the individual stakeholders.
> Document the significant functional and non-functional requirements.
> A first system overview should consist of a system context and a first architecture idea.
> At this point the presentation of the architecture idea can be very informal and you can restrict it to the identification of significant building blocks.

8.4 Understanding the Requirements

Basic concepts of the activity "understanding the requirements"

Figure 8.4-1 shows the basic concepts of the activity "understanding the requirements" and visualizes how they relate to each other. We will look at these in more detail in this section.

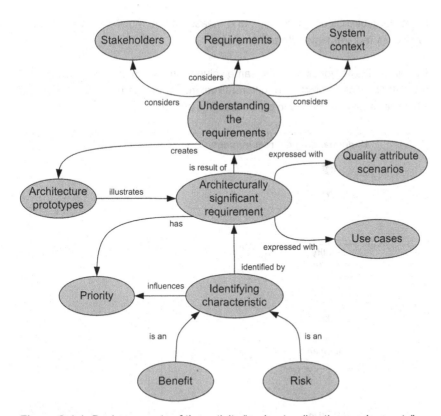

Figure 8.4-1: Basic concepts of the activity "understanding the requirements"

It is important to have a good understanding of the requirements an architecture must satisfy to be able to utilize your creative freedom as an architect when designing the architecture (see Section 8.5). This applies to both functional and non-functional requirements. You cannot design an architecture without a good understanding of architecturally significant requirements. Therefore, the architectural activity "understanding the requirements" consists of the actions shown in Figure 8.4-2. It is primarily concerned with developing the requirements view of a system (see Section 4.2).

Understanding the requirements is the prerequisite for architecture design

Unfortunately, requirements are not always documented clearly. In practice, you are more likely to meet contradictory and imprecise formulations. Some relevant requirements may not even be documented. The requirement that it must be possible to extend our example system MIS is very imprecise: it must be made more concrete. For example, a more precise formulation would be that it must be possible to add new performance indicators and performance reports to MIS within an average of ten person days.

Requirements are not always clear

You have to clear up contradictions and imprecise formulations in the requirements and identify and document missing requirements. Finally, make require-

Requirements must be tangible

ments tangible. Clear, imaginable, and measurable formulations make it easier to discuss requirements with stakeholders.

Requirements must be prioritized

Requirements do not all have the same value. Some will provide a higher benefit than others. The realization of different requirements also bears different risks. Prioritize requirements based on the benefits and the risks.

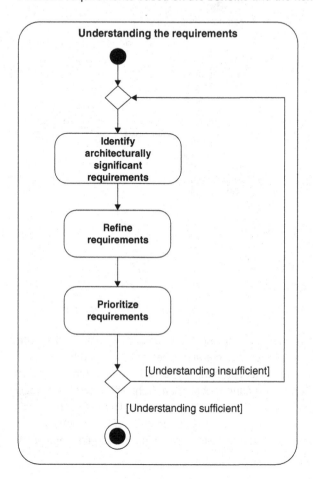

Figure 8.4-2: Understanding the requirements

Identify architecturally significant requirements

Both functional and non-functional requirements can be architecturally significant. In practice, functional requirements that relate to interactions with a system are frequently documented as use cases. Therefore, in this context, we often talk about identifying the architecturally significant use cases. Non-functional requirements can be divided into qualities and constraints. Qualities are a measure for the quality of the realization of the functional requirements. One example of a quality is that MIS should be available 24/7. Constraints define the way functional requirements and qualities can be realized (see Section 5.1). The development period of six months given for MIS is a condition that restricts the architectural creative freedom. It therefore represents a constraint.

In this activity you identify the architecturally significant requirements. But what exactly is an architecturally significant requirement and how can you extract it from the total of all requirements? Often, all of the requirements appear architecturally significant at first glance. It is therefore important that you classify requirements systematically. Requirements are given by different stakeholders, and the stakeholders each have a different priority. You can thus filter the requirements initially according to the priority of the stakeholders. Requirements each have a different relevance for stakeholders because they have different benefits. Furthermore, there are various risks involved in realizing requirements. You can therefore assess requirements using the criteria "benefit" and "risk" (see Figure 8.4-3). Candidates for architecturally significant requirements are requirements with a high benefit for the stakeholders and a low implementation risk. Requirements can have both a high benefit and a high implementation risk—process these requirements with top priority. Requirements that have only a high benefit or only a high implementation risk should be treated as second priority. We will look at this more closely with some examples for MIS.

What is architecturally significant?

Important requirements are the significant requirements with the highest benefit for the stakeholders. For example, the recording of performance data is very important for the MIS stakeholders, since without this feature, it is not possible to create performance reports. In contrast, the sending of e-mail notifications as soon as new performance reports are available is less important.

Identification by benefit

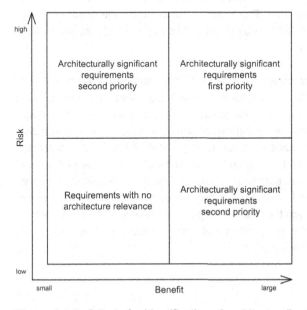

Figure 8.4-3: Criteria for identification of architecturally significant requirements

Identification by risk

Requirements that have a high architectural risk are typically requirements where you have no experience of realization or requirements that affect areas that are not completely under your own control (e.g., building blocks of an external partner). Thus there is a high risk involved in realizing such requirements because you are not sure whether you can feasibly realize them successfully on time and within budget. One example is requirements that involve peripheral systems. If, in the case of MIS, for example, we have to connect the IMS system to its JEE application using a JCA adapter, but have no experience in this area, we have to consider this requirement as high risk and architecturally significant. Requirements where the implementation has a big effect on the system to be realized can also have a high implementation risk. The central specification of IT guidelines has, for example, a great effect on a system to be realized: non-compliance with these guidelines can lead to a refusal by stakeholders to accept the system. Requirements that involve a high effort if they are not considered early enough in the architecture design also belong to this category. For example, it is often important for reasons of security and traceability that you document actions performed within a system. In this context we often speak of auditing. You can only integrate such a requirement at a late stage in the architecture and in the existing system implementation with a high effort. A further feature of such requirements is that they influence many architecturally significant building blocks. A use case where the realization involves building blocks from the presentation logic layer, the business logic layer, and the persistence logic layer (see Section 3.4) is generally architecturally significant. From the wealth of use cases, you have to select candidates that require different architecturally significant building block types.

Refine requirements

Refining the architecturally significant requirements is primarily concerned with making requirements tangible. This includes documenting the requirements effectively, connecting functional and non-functional requirements, as well as demonstrating requirements.

Documentation of qualities with quality attribute scenarios

As already stated, in practice it is usual to describe functional requirements by means of use cases. One means for documenting qualities that is not used so frequently in practice is the so-called quality attribute scenario (see Section 6.3). Some qualities, such as the availability of MIS, are valid for the system as a whole. However, other qualities apply to only some of the functional requirements. For example, with MIS, controllers must be able to create performance reports. MIS should also ensure safe access to data. A combination of these two requirements would lead to controllers only being able to create performance reports for teams for which they have the appropriate authorization. You can use quality attribute scenarios for qualities that apply across the whole system and qualities that are use case-specific.

It therefore seems obvious to connect architecturally significant use cases with architecturally significant qualities. To do this, look at every architecturally significant use case with regard to the level of its qualitative realization. The more different quality features (e.g., security, traceability, performance) a use case has, the greater its architectural character. You can create quality attribute scenarios for each combination. We will discuss this below using the example of creating performance reports in MIS (see Table 8.4-1).

Connecting functional requirements and qualities

Table 8.4-1: Use case-specific quality attribute scenarios

Creating performance reports and security	
Criterion	Meaning
Source	Identified controller
Stimulus	Tries to create a performance report for teams for which he is not authorized
Artefact	Performance report data in the system
Context	System is in normal state
Reaction	System refuses access to the performance data and logs the access attempt
Reaction measurement	System has refused access and a log entry exists

Creating performance reports and traceability	
Criterion	Meaning
Source	Identified controller
Stimulus	Creates performance reports
Artefact	Performance report data in the system
Context	System is in normal state.
Reaction	System creates performance reports and logs the actions executed.
Reaction measurement	Performance reports are available and actions were logged

Creating performance reports and performance	
Criterion	Meaning
Source	Identified controller
Stimulus	Creates performance reports
Artefact	Performance report data in the system
Context	System is in normal state
Reaction	System creates performance reports and logs the actions executed
Reaction measurement	The average time for creation is 5 s

Consider architecturally significant use cases and qualities within the given constraints

You should then investigate how to realize the quality attribute scenarios within the defined constraints. It frequently becomes clear that this is not possible. In this case, point out these contradictions and show stakeholders alternatives.

Demonstrating requirements

You can use various means to demonstrate documented requirements (e.g., prototypes). This shows the requirements in a different light and enables you to gain new insights.

Architecture prototypes make requirements concrete

One way of getting a better understanding for the individual architecturally significant requirements and checking their feasibility is to use prototypes. Prototypes help to minimize the risk of any problems that may arise later. For example, if you are confronted with new technologies, you can use a prototype to assess them. In the case of MIS, the architect could look into the use of JCA as a means of integration. The prototypes in the activity "understanding the requirements" do not reflect the subsequent architecture of the system; they merely help to provide a better understanding of requirements given. It is also common practice to create prototypes to demonstrate the user interface during requirements gathering. Prototypes can also provide valuable architectural findings for usability. For example, if the requirement is that user queries can be aborted (abort feature) or several actions can be canceled (undo feature), these aspects are architecturally significant.

Refining the requirements step-by-step

As shown in Chapter 5, requirements are situated at different architecture levels. The individual requirements are related to one another above and beyond these levels. They thus refine the system to be created step-by-step from architecture level to architecture level. In this activity you therefore refine the requirements of the organizational level, through the system level, down to the building block level, within several iterations.

No complete requirements without the implemented architecture

Architecturally significant requirements only become fully complete and consistent during the design and implementation of an architecture. This is implied by the iterations in the architecture method presented here. During the activities "designing the architecture" and "implementing the architecture," new requirements may arise as feedback or it may become necessary to adjust existing requirements. You should then deal with the new or adjusted requirements in the subsequent iteration during the activity "understanding the requirements."

Prioritize requirements

A further action during the "understanding the requirements" activity is prioritizing the requirements. The prioritization is the result of classifying the requirements according to benefit and risk. Address requirements with a high benefit and a high risk as early as possible. These are requirements that an architecture must satisfy. Tables 8.4-2 and 8.4-3 show an example of the prioritization of the functional and non-functional requirements for MIS. The priority is determined using the following formula: Priority = (Benefit + Risk)/2.

Table 8.4-2: Prioritized functional requirements

Functional requirement	Benefit	Risk	Priority
		(1 = high, 3 = low)	
Display performance reports	1	1	1
Import incident data	1	1	1
Import CCM data	1	1	1
Log on	3	1	2
Enter performance data	1	3	2
Print performance data	2	2	2
Create performance reports	2	3	2.5
Manage user accounts	3	2	2.5
Send e-mail	3	3	3

Table 8.4-3: Prioritized non-functional requirements

Non-functional requirement	Benefit	Risk	Priority
		(1 = high, 3 = low)	
Operability	1	1	1
Extensibility	1	3	2
Time-to-Market	2	3	2.5
Compliance with IT standards	1	1	1
Security	2	2	2
Usability	3	3	3
Availability	2	3	2.5
Performance	1	2	1.5

One risk that architects typically fall for is that they want to make the architecture too perfect. This is the case when you consider certain non-functional require- ments disproportionately heavily although they only play a small role or even no role in the case in question. An example is when the architecture plans for the graphical interface to be replaceable (non-functional requirement "extensibility") even though the system is to be operated exclusively via a desktop interface of

Risk of architectures that are "too good"

a specific platform. Examples of possible negative consequences are unnecessarily complex architectures or systems that are not "finished" or systems that do not sufficiently meet requirements. Therefore, in your own interest, as a measure of discipline, use a table, for example, to explicitly specify which of the generally known direct non-functional requirements are at all relevant for the quality properties of a system. Table 8.4-4 shows this using the example of MIS.

Table 8.4-4: Quality relevance of non-functional requirements

Non-functional requirement	Relevance for the quality (1 = high, 3 = low)
Operability	1
Interoperability	1
Performance	1
Manufacturer independence	2
Portability	2
Availability	2
Security	2
Scalability	2
Testability	2
Maintainability	2
Extensibility	2
Modifiability	2
User-friendliness	3

Prioritization of requirements provides "only" orientation

Note, however, that prioritizing requirements (like other metrics) is a useful tool that provides you with orientation (tendency) but does not dictate the exact direction (see also Section 8.6).

MIS: Architecture view developed

Table 8.4-5 shows which artefacts have been worked out for the "Requirements view" architecture view (see Section 4.2) for MIS during the "understanding the requirements" activity.

Table 8.4-5: *Architecture views developed during "understanding the require-ments"*

Architecture view	MIS artefacts
Requirements view	> Use case-specific quality attribute scenarios (see Table 8.4-1) > Prioritized functional requirements (see Table 8.4-2) > Prioritized non-functional requirements (see Table 8.4-3) > Quality relevance of non-functional requirements (see Table 8.4-4)

Have all architecturally significant requirements been identified?
Has sufficient attention been paid to non-functional requirements?
Are all architecturally significant requirements measurable?
Do any architecturally significant requirements exclude each other?
Have all architecturally significant requirements been prioritized?
Have all architecturally significant requirements been refined?
Have all architecturally significant requirements been documented?
Have the architecturally significant requirements been confirmed by the stakeholders?

Checklist: Understanding the requirements

Table 8.4-6 gives an overview of important relationships between the aspects of the architecture method described in Section 8.4 and the architectural topics discussed in Chapters 3–7.

Connections between Section 8.4 and Chapters 3–7

Table 8.4-6: *Overview of the connections between Section 8.4 and Chapters 3–7*

Chapter/ section number	Chapter/section heading	Reason for connection
3.1	Classic Architecture as Starting Point (WHAT)	Architecture has to cover all requirements in order to be useful. Therefore, architecturally significant requirements have to be identified
4.1	Architecture Levels (WHERE)	Architecturally significant require-ments at system level are identified
4.2	Architecture Views (WHERE)	The requirements view is created

Chapter/ section number	Chapter/section heading	Reason for connection
5	Architecture Require- ments (WHY)	Architecturally significant requirements, qualities, and constraints are analyzed
6.3	Architecture Tactics, Styles, and Patterns (WITH WHAT)	Requirements can be documented system- atically by applying use cases, quality at- tribute scenarios, and requirement patterns
7	Organizations and Indi- viduals (WHO)	To analyze and refine requirements the architect depends on information from different stakeholders. Therefore, he has to communicate and collaborate with them

8.5 Designing the Architecture

Basic concepts of the activity "designing the architecture"

Figure 8.5-1 shows the basic concepts of the activity "designing the architecture" that we will look at in this chapter and visualizes how they relate to each other.

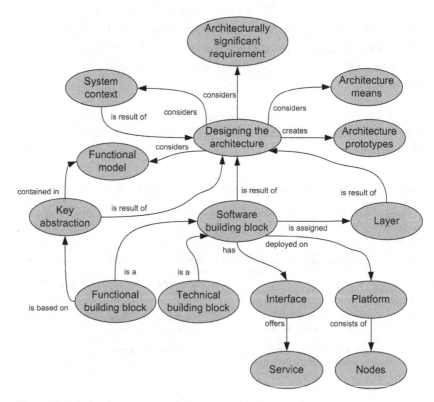

Figure 8.5-1: Basic concepts of the activity "designing the architecture"

Systems are embedded in organizations, are created for specific functional areas or functional domains, and must fulfill dedicated requirements (see Section 3.3). As we can see from Figure 8.5-2, you must take these facts into account when designing the architecture. You identify the architecturally significant requirements and analyze them in more detail during the "understanding the requirements" activity. In the "analysis and design" discipline you create functional models. Since you also design the architecture within this discipline, you also analyze functional models from an architectural perspective during this activity. You also consider and refine the system context. In addition, you use architecture means (e.g., patterns, reference architectures) to design the architecture (see Chapter 6).

Factors that influence the design of an architecture

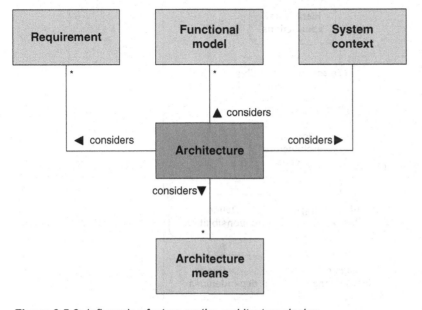

Figure 8.5-2: Influencing factors on the architecture design

The individual actions of this activity are aligned with the influencing factors. Figure 8.5-3 gives an overview of these actions. The result of the first iteration is often referred to as the architecture vision, since you make the significant decisions about the structuring of the system in this iteration. The architecture vision contains the basic system building blocks, their responsibilities, and their interactions. It also defines the technologies (see Section 6.7) for the subsequent implementation. We will look at the different actions in more detail in this section. In this activity, you primarily develop the logical, data, process, and deployment views of a system (see Section 4.2).

Overview of design actions

During the "creating the system vision" activity, you define a first system context (see Section 8.3). In the "designing the architecture" activity, you refine this context and make it more concrete. Often, different architects work on the creation of

Define context

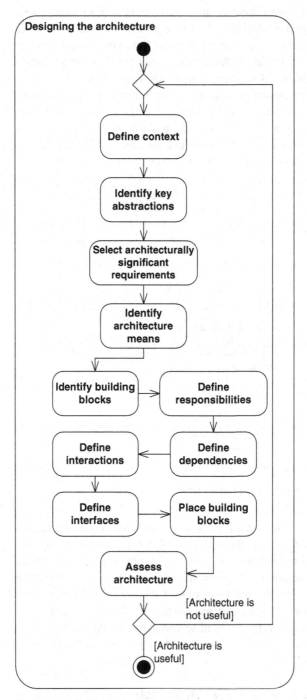

Figure 8.5-3: *Designing the architecture*

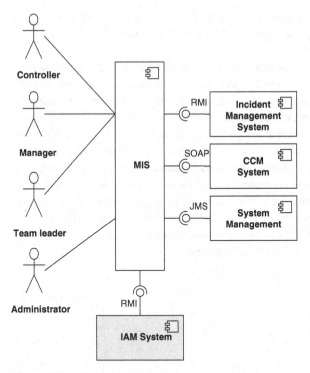

Figure 8.5-4: *Extended MIS system context*

the system vision and the design of the architecture. If this is the case, examine the system context even more closely here to close any possible gaps. In the case of MIS, for example, there are requirements that users must authenticate themselves and that central guidelines must be complied with. One of these guidelines could specify that each system must be connected to the central Identity and Access Management infrastructure (IAM infrastructure). This would mean that the IAM system must be added to the system context (see Figure 8.5-4).

In this activity, you also make the interfaces between the system and its actors more concrete, for example, by considering the following questions:
> Which services do the actors of the system require?
> Which services does the system require from the connected systems?
> Which entities are transferred via the interface and what meaning do these have?
> Which interface technologies are used?

A system context is more than just a diagram: it is an artefact that documents every interface in detail. For more information about the system context, see Section 8.3.3. You can use contexts not only at system level, but also at the level of more finely grained system building blocks (e.g., subsystems). Dedicated

A system context is more than just a diagram

interface agreements can also be derived from the system context. These agreements represent separate artefacts and define an interface.

Identify key abstractions

As stated in Section 3.3, an architecture covers both functional and technical aspects. Therefore, it is usual to design both a functional and a technical architecture. Since the functional architecture is oriented around the functional domains, in this action you analyze these domains with regard to their key abstractions. Key abstractions represent the significant abstractions of a functional domain that must be handled by the system to be realized—examples are abstractions of objects, concepts, locations, or persons [Oestereich and Bremer 2009] In the case of MIS, these are, for example, performance report, service, or support department (see Figure 8.5-5). Terms such as "primary business entity," "primary business object," "core entity," or "core object" are frequently used as synonyms for the term "key abstraction." You can derive the functional architecture from the key abstractions and the functional requirements.

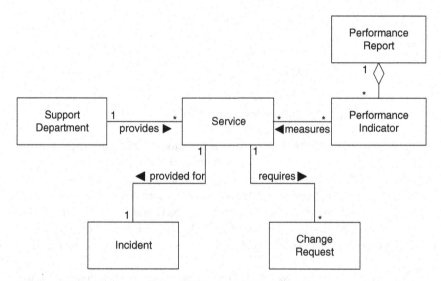

Figure 8.5-5: *Key abstractions of MIS*

Select architecturally significant requirements

In this action you select the architecturally significant requirements that you want to consider in the architecture design in the current iteration. To do this you use the quality attribute scenarios that arose during the "understanding the requirements" activity. Include requirements with a high priority as early as possible in an architecture.

Identify architecture means

Now that you know the key abstractions as well as the requirements and the system context, in a next step you can identify suitable architecture means. You should select them for pure purpose considerations (geared towards the existing requirements). Do not fall into the trap of following hype, the golden hammer syndrome, or the silver bullet syndrome; neither should you give political considerations priority. An architecture means alone does not solve all problems: you have to apply it correctly, adapt it, and if necessary combine it with your own design ideas. This implies that despite selecting an appropriate architecture means, there is still a risk that you might use it incorrectly. Two simple examples should make this clear:

> If you use the MVC pattern [Buschmann et al. 1996], then you can use an MVC framework (e.g., Struts). However, if (e.g., for convenience) you use specific building blocks (e.g., value objects) of this framework in the business logic layer, the result is a close coupling with the presentation layer. It is precisely this coupling that using the MVC pattern was supposed to avoid.

> If you use object orientation in the development of a distributed system (e.g., by means of entity objects with JEE), then there is a risk that the network load will be too high and performance will be lacking. This would happen if you used the individual attributes of the entity objects according to the pure theory of object orientation using methods.

As soon as you have designed the basic structures of the system to be realized, the focus shifts from functionality to technology. This means that the technological architecture means become more important. For example, you define the concrete application servers, databases, or middleware systems.

The focus shifts from functionality to technology

In the case of MIS, it would be ideal to have an existing reference architecture for such a performance indicator system. In many cases this will not be the case. You should then look beyond the project horizons to determine whether other projects have developed similar systems.

Identification of suitable means

To select architecture means for a functional architecture, firstly check whether there is an existing reference architecture for the given functional domain, since this would have the highest level of reusability. Section 6.5.4 gives examples of such reference architectures. Functional reference architectures are similar in nature to analysis patterns [Fowler 1996]. However, in contrast to analysis patterns, they are at the level of coarse grained software building blocks and not classes. A functional reference architecture for the MIS example would specify the functional building blocks required to handle the key abstractions and to fulfill the functional requirements. If there are no suitable reference architectures, you can determine the functional building blocks using the architecture principles, such as separation of concerns, loose coupling, and high cohesion (see Section 6.1).

Identify architecture means for the functional architecture

Why do we break down the software system functionally? Is there a functional requirement for this? As long as the system fulfills the desired functional require-

Why are architecture means required for functional concerns?

ments, how the system is structured functionally should be irrelevant. At first glance this is correct. However, the non-functional requirements also influence the functional architecture. For example, the desire for extensibility of the system or for parallel development by multiple teams forces structuring in sensible, manageable units or building blocks.

Identify architecture means for the technical architecture

The wealth of means for designing technical architecture is larger than that for functional architecture. Therefore, it is generally easier to find suitable architecture means here. The starting point for selecting the means is the non-functional requirements. For example, IT standards in an enterprise often specify the component platform to be used. There are usually suitable platform-specific reference architectures for the respective platform, such as JEE or .NET (see Section 6.5.4). You can reuse them in any project either without changes or with slight adjustments [Siedersleben 2004]. Such reference architectures also define which types of technical building blocks are required to fulfill non-functional requirements. If there are no reference architectures, look at basic architectures (see Section 6.4) as well as architecture tactics, styles, and patterns (see Section 6.3).

Relationship between non-functional requirements and architecture principles

A first step in identifying the correct architecture means is to look at the relationship between certain non-functional requirements and architecture principles (see Section 6.1) frequently used to satisfy the non-functional requirements. Since these architecture principles have an effect in all other architecture means (e.g., tactics and patterns), this relationship provides hints for other possible architecture means. The more specialized architecture principles derived from "high cohesion" and "loose coupling" are particularly interesting. However, this relationship is not complete and precisely unique: it is a trial and error approach that you develop based on your experiences over time. Documenting such trial and error approaches and reusing them in various contexts is very useful. The examples in table 8.5-1 demonstrate the architecture principles that may be relevant for fulfilling some non-functional requirements.

Table 8.5-1: Relationship between non-functional requirements and architecture principles

Non-functional requirement	Architecture principle
User-friendliness	Explicit interfaces, interface segregation, ...
Interoperability	Information hiding, separation of interface and implementation, ...
Robustness	Loose coupling, high cohesion, ...
Security	Information hiding, interface segregation, ...
Testability	Loose coupling, high cohesion, separation of interface and implementation, ...

Non-functional requirement	Architecture principle
Extensibility	Loose coupling, encapsulation, abstraction, separation of concerns, information hiding, ...
Reusability	See Extensibility

You identify the building blocks using the selected architecture means. In the simplest case you can use an existing reference architecture. This specifies the building blocks required. In this case your activity can be restricted to verification: check whether every key abstraction is assigned to exactly one building block. The identification of the building blocks and the definition of their responsibilities are closely related. Therefore, these two actions are handled together.

Identify building blocks

What is the best way to identify functional building blocks? The functional building blocks are concerned with the key abstractions and the associated functional requirements. By identifying a functional building block for functionally related key abstractions, you therefore identify possible candidates for functional building blocks. On one hand you apply the separation of concerns principle, and on the other, the principle of high cohesion. The cohesion within a functional building block is high, since the key abstractions handled by the building block are closely related. A building block identified in this way also takes care of a significant functional concern. Figure 8.5-6 illustrates the functional building blocks of MIS.

Identify functional building blocks

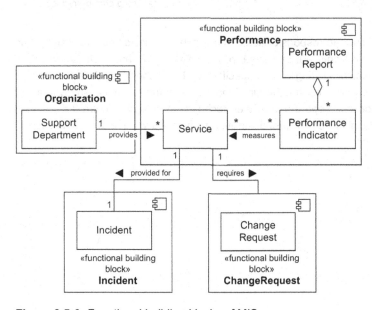

Figure 8.5-6: Functional building blocks of MIS

Functional building blocks of the architecture vision correspond to functional subsystems

In this action you identify the functional subsystems of the system as part of the architecture vision. The functional building blocks from Figure 8.5-6 therefore correspond to the functional subsystems of MIS. In a further step you split the functional subsystems into finer functional building blocks.

Define the responsibilities of the functional building blocks

Functional building blocks realize the functional requirements that are closely related to the key abstractions they handle. Therefore, categorize the architecturally significant requirements according to the key abstractions and assign them to the appropriate functional building blocks. This defines the responsibilities of the building blocks. For MIS these are documented in table 8.5-2.

Table 8.5-2: Functional building blocks of MIS and their responsibilities

Functional building block	Key abstractions	Responsibilities
Organization	Support department	Realizes any functionality for managing support departments or organizational units
Performance	Performance, performance report, performance indicator	Realizes any functionality for managing performance, performance reports, and performance indicators
Incident	Incident	Realizes any functionality for managing incidents
Change request	Change request	Realizes any functionality for managing change requests

You can define the responsibilities in more detail by assigning every step of an architecturally significant use case to a functional building block. Do not think yet about which building blocks specified by the technical architecture realize the step. This ensures that the functional scope of the functional subsystems or building blocks is separate from their technical realization. Figure 8.5-7 visualizes this definition of the responsibilities using the example "Calculate performance indicator."

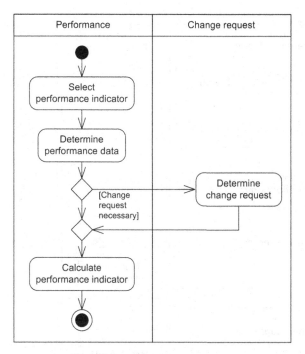

Figure 8.5-7: *Definition of functional responsibilities using the example of MIS*

Functional building blocks alone are not viable: they must be supported by technical building blocks in order to be able to exist on a platform. You must therefore also identify technical building blocks. In the same way as for the functional building blocks, you should also look out for suitable architecture means for the technical building blocks. You will usually use a suitable technical reference architecture. Figure 8.5-8 shows one that is often suitable in practice.

Identify technical building blocks and define their responsibilities

The technical reference architecture from Figure 8.5-8 is an example. Similar illustrations can be found in [Oestereich and Bremer 2009], [Siedersleben 2004], and [Fowler 2003]. We will briefly explain the parts of the reference architecture below. Table 8.5-3 covers the layers and Table 8.5-4 the building blocks.

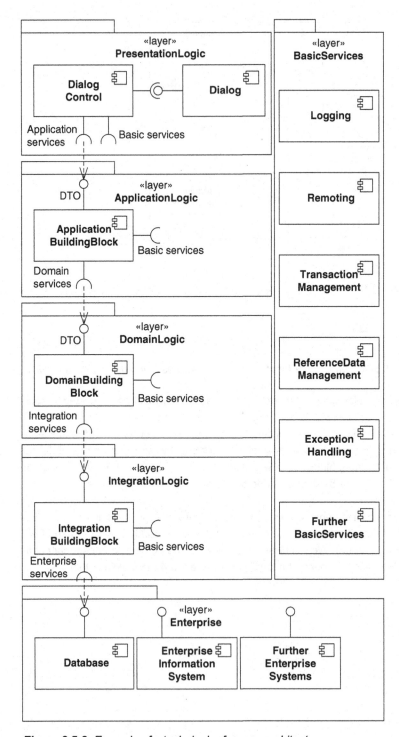

Figure 8.5-8: Example of a technical reference architecture

Table 8.5-3: *Layers and their responsibilities*

Layer	Responsibility
Basic services	Technical building blocks that represent basic functionality are assigned to this layer. They can be used by building blocks from the presentation logic layer, application logic layer, domain logic layer, and integration logic layer. If the layers are distributed beyond the process and network boundaries, plan corresponding call mechanisms (keyword: remoting)
Presentation logic	The presentation logic layer contains building blocks used for communication with the user
Application logic	The application logic layer contains building blocks that realize application logic. Application logic is logic with a very close relationship to the application to be realized and which you often cannot or cannot easily reuse in other contexts. For example, the presentation of a performance indicator in graphical or textual form is dependent on the concrete use case and is difficult to reuse
Domain logic	The domain logic layer contains building blocks that realize domain logic. Domain logic represents functionality that you can reuse across application boundaries. It is therefore application-independent and operates purely on functional abstractions. For example, the calculation of a performance indicator is independent of whether the indicator is displayed graphically or in text form.
Integration logic	The integration logic layer houses building blocks that encapsulate the connection of enterprise systems. One simple example is Data Access Objects that abstract the database access [Fowler 2003].
Enterprise	The enterprise layer, often referred to as the back-end layer, contains systems with which the system to be developed must interact. These can be databases, enterprise information systems, system management systems, etc.

The differentiation between application logic and domain logic is not always obvious and the border between the two is sometimes blurred [Evans 2004]. As stated in Table 8.5-3, the domain logic is application-independent and you can reuse it in various contexts. For example, the calculation of telephone costs is independent of whether the costs are requested from a call center application or a self-service application. The display of the costs, however, is application-specific. Application logic should not spread into the domain logic layer, otherwise there is a danger that the domain logic cannot be reused in other use cases and is difficult to test.

Differentiation between application logic and domain logic

Table 8.5-4: *Building blocks and responsibilities of the technical reference architecture*

Building block	Responsibility
Dialog	A dialog corresponds to the view building block within the model-view-controller architecture pattern [Buschmann et al. 1996]
Dialog control	A dialog control building block corresponds to the controller building block within the model-view-controller architecture pattern [Buschmann et al. 1996]. It uses services from application building blocks
Application building block	An application building block encapsulates application logic and makes it available in a controlled manner. The data is exchanged using data transfer objects (DTO) [Fowler 2003]
Domain building block	A domain building block encapsulates domain logic and makes it available in a controlled manner. The data is exchanged using data transfer objects (DTO)
Integration building block	An integration building block encapsulates integration logic (e.g., database, SAP, LDAP) and makes it available
Basic service building block	A basic service building block provides basic services (e.g., logging, management of reference data)

Making functional subsystems more concrete

Regardless of whether you have been able to use a technical reference architecture or have designed your own technical architecture, you can use the functional subsystems identified and the building block types specified by the technical architecture to derive concrete functional building blocks for the functional subsystems. The technical architecture defines how functional building blocks or subsystems are realized. In the example used here, we can identify the required dialog, dialog control, application, domain, and integration building blocks for every functional subsystem. Table 8.5-5 shows this using the example of the functional subsystem "Performance." It shows only building blocks for the key abstraction "Performance." For the sake of simplicity, we have ignored the performance indicator and performance report.

Table 8.5-5: *Identification of building blocks based on functional and technical architecture using the example of MIS*

Building block	Building block type	Responsibility
Performance dialog	Dialog	Presents performance-related data and receives entries
Performance dialog control	Dialog control	Controls the user interaction for performance-related aspects
PerformanceABB	Application building block	Encapsulates performance-related application logic
PerformanceDBB	Domain building block	Encapsulates performance-related domain logic
PerformanceIBB	Integration building block	Encapsulates performance-related integration logic

The functional building blocks identified in this way structure in total a functional subsystem realized with the concepts of the technical architecture (see Figure 8.5-9).

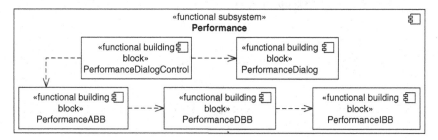

Figure 8.5-9: *Example of a functional subsystem of MIS*

As soon as the functional scope of the functional subsystems has been defined, you can consider the responsibilities in more detail. In other words, you now treat the subsystems as a white box and divide the functionality across the concrete building blocks. In the MIS example, a functional step of a use case can be split into presentation logic, application logic, domain logic, and integration logic. Basic services such as security can also be involved. For example, in MIS, a user must log on before she or he can enter performance data or view performance reports. This produces the concrete responsibilities of the building blocks. The actual calculation of a performance indicator is the responsibility of the domain building block PerformanceDBB, for example.

Refining the responsibilities

Once you have identified the building blocks and documented their responsibilities, you can define their dependencies. The dependencies result on one hand from the functional conditions and on the other from the technical conditions.

Define dependencies

You can derive the functional dependencies from the structural relationships of the functional key abstractions. For example, in the case of MIS, "performance" is related to "incident" and "change request." From this we can define a dependency of the functional building block "performance" to the functional building blocks "incident" and "change request" (see Figure 8.5-10). Thus we get a first dependency diagram. It may well be that due to technical circumstances, the functional dependencies are not immediately visible in the final architecture.

Dependencies from functional conditions

The technical dependencies result from the architecture means you select for designing the technical architecture. Figure 8.5-11 illustrates which building blocks may be in relationship to one another if you use this technical reference architecture. For example, application building blocks may not communicate directly

Dependencies from technical conditions

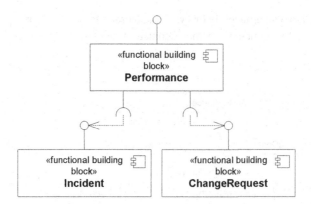

Figure 8.5-10: Functional dependencies using the example of performance

with integration building blocks. Instead, application building blocks interact with domain building blocks, and these in turn interact with integration building blocks. This should achieve the highest possible platform and technology independence (see Section 3.4).

What effect do functional and technical dependencies have?

Figure 8.5-11 visualizes the dependencies of the MIS building blocks using the example of "performance" and "change request," which arise from the functional and technical conditions. What is the effect of the functional dependence of "performance" and "change request?" It becomes clear that the application building block ApplicationABB is dependent on the domain building block ChangeRequestDBB and that there is no dependency between PerformanceDBB and ChangeRequestDBB. The domains "performance" and "change request" are therefore decoupled at the domain building block level. This is an example for the application of the principle of loose coupling (see Section 6.1). The advantage of this decoupling is that functional domains can remain independent from one another as far as possible and thus be developed separately.

Strong vs. loose coupling

The decoupling can vary in strength. You can therefore generally prohibit the communication of domain building blocks across domain boundaries. The consequence of this is that application building blocks must transfer all non-domain data to domain building blocks. For example, if data from the change request domain is required for the calculation of a performance indicator, the application building block PerformanceABB has to get this data from the change request domain and transfer it to the domain building block PerformanceDBB. In the case of a strong decoupling, the change request data in the example must be converted into a form that the domain building block PerformanceDBB expects. If the decoupling is less strong, you can permit some cross-domain dependencies at the domain building block level. For example, if you want to decouple the user of the performance domain from the fact that change requests are required to

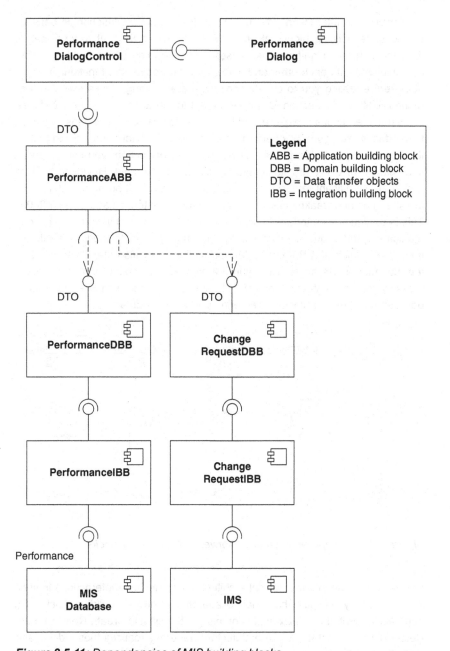

Legend
ABB = Application building block
DBB = Domain building block
DTO = Data transfer objects
IBB = Integration building block

Figure 8.5-11: Dependencies of MIS building blocks

calculate performance indicators, you could permit access to the change request domain from the performance domain. To keep the coupling as low as possible, plan dedicated interface building blocks that act as facades into the external domains [Gamma et al. 1995].

Define interactions

By defining the interactions you document the dynamic relationships between the software building blocks at an architectural level. To do this, you analyze the architecturally significant use cases and determine which building blocks communicate with each other and how in order to realize the functionality to be delivered, enabling you to clearly show how the building blocks exercise their responsibilities. This action is closely related to the definition of the interfaces, since the interactions are expressed by the service calls and the transfer of data to interfaces. You generally perform these actions simultaneously. Even though it will not be possible to portray all facets of an interaction, you should define interactions for every architecturally significant requirement. However, by illustrating the significant features of the interactions, you will be able to determine the strengths and weaknesses of an architecture [Oestereich and Bremer 2009]. This is particularly important for the assessment of the architecture. UML communication and sequence diagrams are frequently used to model the interactions [Oestereich and Bremer 2009]. Interactions can also stretch across system boundaries. As an architect you will also have to define and model these cross-system interactions. Figure 8.5-12 illustrates a very simplified interaction between MIS building blocks for entering performance data.

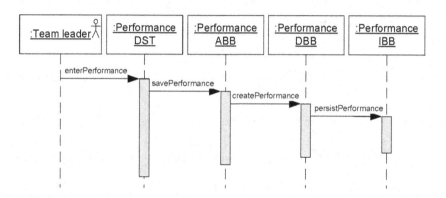

Figure 8.5-12: Simplified interaction between MIS building blocks

Definition of generally accepted interactions

Normally, you can abstract typical architecturally significant interactions in such a way that they visualize the usual collaborations between building blocks at a generally accepted level. Examples of this are the classic Create-Read-Update-Delete (CRUD) operations. An architecture generally realizes these identically, regardless of the concrete abstraction. For example, the recording of data via a user interface is always the same, regardless of whether performance data or support departments are to be recorded. Such interactions may already be documented by the reference architecture you use.

Building blocks communicate with one another via interfaces (see Section 3.4). They offer their services via interfaces and use functionality from other building blocks via their interfaces. Therefore, in this action, you must define both the interfaces offered and the interfaces required. You have two challenges here: firstly, expressing the required and offered functionality using interfaces; secondly, defining the interfaces such that the dependencies between the building blocks are as low as possible. When you defined the dependencies you already defined which building blocks are dependent on one another in principle. The definition of the interfaces determines the degree of dependence. Depending on how the interfaces are designed, building blocks can be more or less strongly dependent on one another. Hence this action deals with some aspects of good interface design. In the following sections we use the term "service" for a piece of functionality that is offered or required by a building block via an interface.

Define interfaces

Interfaces are abstractions of concrete building block implementations (see Section 6.1). Therefore, implementation-specific aspects should not be visible in an interface. This applies even to the naming of services offered by interfaces. Services should clearly express their purpose by reflecting this in their name. In this context we also talk about *intention-revealing interfaces* [Evans 2004]. The name of the service should clearly state what you can achieve with it, and not how it achieves something.

Interfaces should disclose their purpose and not their implementation

There are two types of services: services that do not change the state of a building block and services that do [Evans 2004; Siedersleben 2004]. The former are referred to as functions or queries, and the latter as commands. In contrast to commands, functions have no side effects. They are easier to test and present fewer risks than commands and are also known as idempotent functions. The reading of performance data is an example of a function. In contrast, commands put building blocks into another state and therefore require more extensive testing. The creation of performance data is an example of a command. The definition of the interface should clearly segregate (see Section 6.1) functions and commands by having services represent either functions or commands.

Services should be divided into functions and commands

The preconditions and post-conditions of a service should be documented in order to better express its character. Preconditions are conditions that must be fulfilled before the service can be called. Post-conditions are the conditions that are guaranteed by the service if the preconditions are fulfilled. This corresponds to the Design by Contract principle (see Section 6.1).

Services should document their preconditions and postconditions

A service expects input parameters and returns output parameters. Therefore, clients of the service depend on the data types it declares. This can lead to a close coupling (see Section 6.1) between building blocks if the data types dis-

Services should not disclose any details

close too many details. For the purpose of loose coupling therefore, you should consider the information hiding principle (see Section 6.1) when designing an interface. Depending on the type of interface, you can use different classes of data types (see Table 8.5-6). We can generally say that the coupling within a subsystem should be high (internal coupling), and between subsystems it should be low (external coupling). Therefore, you can use standard data types, entity objects [Evans 2004], and value objects [Fowler 2003] within a subsystem. For the communication between subsystems, however, use data transfer objects instead of entity objects. Entity objects have their own identity within a domain. An incident is an example of an entity object in the MIS case. In contrast, value objects are defined exclusively via their attributes. They do not have their own identity and are immutable. For example, an amount of money can be represented by a value object of the type money. In the MIS case, the monetary costs of an incident could be represented using money value objects. The costs belong to an incident and have no own identity. The difference between entity objects and value objects is domain-specific. For example, the abstraction "address" can be an entity object in one domain, and a value object in another. Data transfer objects are objects that originate from the idea of minimizing the number of client/ server interactions necessary (see Section 6.4) and decoupling clients from the concrete representation of entity objects. In the case of MIS, a performanceDTO could represent the entity "performance," for example.

Table 8.5-6: Use of data types in interfaces

Classes of data types	Examples	Internal	External
Standard data types	Integer, double, string, etc.	X	X
Data transfer objects	PerformanceDTO, change requestDTO, customerDTO, contractDTO, etc.		X
Entity objects	Performance, customer, contract, address	X	
Value objects	Money, color, period	X	X

Data transfer objects within subsystems?

Sometimes you can even use data transfer objects between building blocks of a subsystem. This is the case, for example, if data is to be transported beyond network or process boundaries. You can also select this approach to decouple building blocks of a higher layer from building block details of a lower layer. In the MIS case, for example, domain building blocks could exchange data with application building blocks via data transfer objects instead of entity objects.

Interfaces for entities?

The question of whether interfaces should be defined for entity objects is frequently discussed. There is no one definitive answer to this question. If the entity classes or objects are real objects in the sense of object orientation (see Section 6.2), then the use of interfaces is appropriate. However, if the actual business logic is primarily encapsulated in service providers, the use of interfaces brings only little advantage as the operations are then restricted to the setting and reading of attributes (so-called "setter" and "getter" operations).

Associations between entities have a considerable influence on the coupling of building blocks. In the MIS example, a support department delivers one or more services (see Figure 8.5-5). How should the relationship between support department and service be mapped? The use of real object associations leads to a close coupling between the subsystems, since the data types of the subsystems are communicated via the interfaces. In contrast, the use of logical keys for referencing entities across building block boundaries decouples building blocks from one another. A logical key identifies an entity uniquely without referencing it directly via an object association. To achieve this, every entity receives a unique number or a unique time stamp, for example. Use logical keys for interfaces across subsystem and system boundaries. For internal interfaces object references are preferred.

Associations between entities

You should take the instructions given above into account when you are defining interfaces. However, how do we actually create the interfaces? Interfaces are driven by the concrete requirements. It is not a matter of publishing random services in the interfaces; you must analyze the functional and non-functional requirements precisely and define suitable services for them. If you do not, there is a danger that you will define too many services or incorrect services. Therefore, based on the architecturally significant use cases, play out the interactions and continually ask yourself which services the building block in question specifically requires in this iteration. During the course of the iterations, you revise services by splitting or merging them. You should always follow the instructions given for purposeful interface design.

How do we create interfaces?

You can use various means to specify interfaces. Table 8.5-7 shows some of these means. In many cases, you will use a combination of the means listed.

What means do you use for the specification of interfaces?

Table 8.5-7: Means for specifying interfaces

Means	Description
UML with OCL	In combination with OCL, UML offers suitable options for specifying interfaces (see Section 6.6.2)
IDL	You can use implementation-independent interface description languages, as we know them from CORBA and COM, to specify interfaces
WSDL	An interface can also be specified by the sum of the messages exchanged. This is the case particularly in the SOA environment. WSDL is frequently used there
DSL	You can also use domain-specific languages to specify interfaces. In this case, you create a language closely based on the domain in order to specify the interface

Place building blocks

Once you have defined the interfaces, you place the building blocks on processes or threads and the platform. Thus you work out and complete the process view and the deployment view of the architecture.

Placing the building blocks on the platform

A platform consists of both hardware and software building blocks (see Section 3.4). In this context we also refer to the nodes of a system. In placing the building blocks on the platform, you place the software building blocks on the nodes. Nodes, or platform building blocks, can be both hardware as well as software building blocks. For example, a JEE execution environment can be installed on a hardware server. The software building blocks are then executed in the execution environment on the hardware server. The deployment view also shows the connections between the nodes. It therefore goes beyond the pure placement of the software building blocks on the nodes. Further relevant points are, for example, specifying the dimensions of the hardware server (processor, main memory, disk space, etc.) and the network, as well as specifying the precise software to be used (operating system, application server, database, driver, etc.). These points as a whole are often referred to as operational architecture. They cover more than just software aspects. Designing them requires knowledge of other disciplines, such as the network and system management architecture (see Section 3.2). In this section the focus is on the deployment of the building blocks. Figure 8.5-13 visualizes the deployment view of MIS. The IAM system is not shown here in order to keep the diagram in proportion.

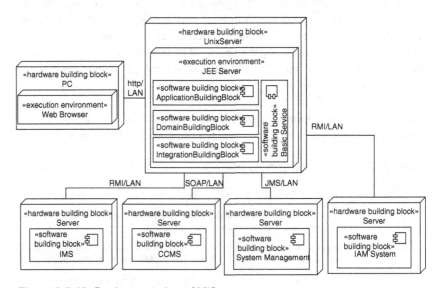

Figure 8.5-13: Deployment view of MIS

Concurrency is an important topic in the design of architectures for software systems today. Component platforms may already offer corresponding services to simplify concurrency management (e.g., remote access, lifecycle management, clustering), but they cannot be relied on alone. This is because these services do not eliminate typical problems, such as race conditions, deadlocks, or data inconsistencies. You have to deal with these topics actively. In this action, therefore, you create concurrent models and state models. Concurrent models illustrate the placement of software building blocks to processes or threads. [Schmidt et al. 2000] contains useful architecture patterns for concurrency. State models articulate the possible states a system can be in and the permitted state transitions, as well as events and actions. Making this information explicit makes it easier to avoid possible concurrency problems. For more information about this topic, see [Rozanski and Woods 2005].

Placing the building blocks on processes

Do not use an architecture without thinking about it thoroughly. Carefully analyze how suitable the architecture is for the intended purpose. And there is always more than one architecture alternative. Therefore, as an architect, you will often be faced with the challenge of selecting the most suitable alternative from those available. You will also be asked to assess existing architectures. Assessing an architecture is relevant during both the elaboration of an initial architecture and during the subsequent development of a system. It enables you to check whether an architecture matches the requirements defined initially or that have been subsequently modified. There are various methods available for assessing architectures [Rozanski and Woods 2005]. We will briefly discuss some of them.

Assess architecture

In a presentation, you present aspects of an architecture to stakeholders informally. Stakeholders can give immediate feedback to the aspects presented.

Presentations

Formal reviews are performed by a group of stakeholders. They analyze the architecture documentation systematically, comment on it formally, and where necessary, decide on actions for rectifying deficiencies.

Formal reviews

Walkthroughs are based on architecturally significant scenarios. These scenarios are played out to determine whether and how an architecture fulfills them. Affected stakeholders take part in walkthroughs. In the MIS case, for example, the use case "Enter performance data" could be played out.

Walkthroughs

You create simulations to provide answers to specific questions, such as the behavior of the system under load, answers to be received, etc., without having to implement the system itself.

Simulations

Architecture proto-types in the architecture assessment

Architecture prototypes are implementations for assessing architecture alternatives or aspects of an architecture. You can use them to realize typical processes of an architecture. In a prototype, you implement an architecture using rudimentary building blocks so that you can test the most important processes to a limited degree. If all relevant system building blocks (e.g., from the user interface right up to persistence) interact successfully, this is often referred to as an architecture "viability prototype." Implement this "viability prototype" as early as possible in order to reduce risks.

Scenario-based methods

The Software Architecture Analysis Method (SAAM) [Kazman et al. 1994] and the Architecture Tradeoff Analysis Method (ATAM) [Kazman et al. 1998] developed further from SAAM are examples of scenario-based methods. They address the problem of room for interpretation for non-functional requirements by working out concrete scenarios that make a non-functional requirement more specific. The individual scenarios are worked out in groups in which all stakeholders—user, client, architect, etc.—are represented. This enables all stakeholders to get a better understanding for the individual requirements. An example scenario for the requirement of extensibility could be as follows: "With a maximum effort of one person year, the system should be integrated in an enterprise-wide portal." Based on the scenarios worked out, an architecture is assessed and the effects of the scenarios on an architecture are evaluated. Using the example scenario, the assessment could produce the following result: "The rules for programming the page sequence are not yet completely defined, meaning that this logic is distributed across the entire presentation view. In the case of a changeover in the user navigation, therefore, all program parts of the presentation layer must be changed." These example scenarios enable a detailed qualitative assessment of an architecture. However, this assessment method is based on the architecture documentation (see Section 8.7). It requires very detailed knowledge of an architecture to be assessed and the changes to be made in order to be able to understand all of the effects of such a scenario.

Checklists

Checklists can be very useful in assessing an architecture. A checklist consists of a list of detailed questions that you can use to assess the various requirements of an architecture. You can use checklists for various assessment methods.

Example of a checklist question

Based on the example of the "extensibility" requirement, the question could be: "Does the architecture allow the subsequent provision of an additional web user interface?" You can use these questions to determine how well an architecture supports the given requirements. The difficulty of this method is that you already need to have a very precise understanding of the requirements when you create the checklist. In the example above, you must already know that extensibility refers to the additional integration of a web user interface and an additional user interface for mobile devices is not required.

Table 8.5-8 shows which artefacts have been worked out for which architecture views (see Section 4.2) for MIS during the "designing the architecture" activity.

Table 8.5-8: *Architecture views developed during "designing the architecture"*

Architecture view	MIS artefacts
Logical view	> Extended system context (see Figure 8.5-4) > Key abstractions (see Figure 8.5-5) > Functional building blocks (see Figure 8.5-6) > Functional building blocks and their responsibilities (see Table 8.5-2) > Definition of functional responsibilities (see Figure 8.5-7) > Identification of building blocks based on functional and technical architecture (see Table 8.5-5) > An example functional subsystem (see Figure 8.5-9) > Functional dependencies using the example of performance (see Figure 8.5-10) > Dependencies of MIS building blocks (see Figure 8.5-11) > Simplified interaction between MIS building blocks (see Figure 8.5-12)
Data view	Use of data types in interfaces (see Table 8.5-6)
Deployment view	Deployment of software building blocks (see Figure 8.5-13)

Are all peripheral systems (even indirect systems, e.g., system management) detailed in the system context?

Are all architecturally significant use cases covered by building blocks?

Is every building block involved in at least one use case?

Are all other kinds of functional requirements (for example, business rules) covered by appropriate means?

Are all non-functional requirements covered by appropriate means?

Has every building block been documented with regard to its responsibility, interface, and interactions with other building blocks?

Has every key abstraction been assigned to a functional building block?

Have functional building blocks been designed according to the reference architecture used?

Have building blocks been planned for crosscutting tasks (e.g., logging)?

Does every building block have a clear responsibility and no overlaps with other building blocks?

Has every building block been assigned to a suitable logical layer?

Do interfaces exist between the system and its peripheral systems?

Do interfaces exist between the subsystems?

Do interactions between building blocks take place exclusively via interfaces?

Are there any unnecessary interactions between building blocks?

Are there any circular dependencies between building blocks?

Has every building block been placed on a node?

Has enough attention been paid to the concern of concurrency?

Has the architecture been assessed?

Have the results of the assessment been integrated into the architecture?

Has sufficient attention been paid to the degree of maturity of the means used?

Have the means used been evaluated?

Are proven means used to design the architecture?

Are standard means used or rather proprietary means?

If proprietary means are used, are the reasons for this documented?

Do the selected means bring any benefit compared to simple proprietary solutions?

Is the additional effort for using the selected means justifiable?

Are the impacts of selected means on architectural properties documented?

Are the impacts of selected means on architectural properties documented?

Is the decision for and the adaption of means sufficiently documented?

Are the selected means sufficiently adaptable as required?

Have the selected means been adapted with respect to the domain in question?

Are alternatives (advantages and disadvantages) to the means selected documented?

Based on the given requirements have all relevant means been considered?

Are all selected means actually in use?

Are there examples for the successful use of the selected means?

Whenever possible, are the most concrete means applied?

Are the reasons for not using means as recommended documented?

Are conflicts between means documented?

Are means selected that allow work directly in the domain in question?

Are means used whose use is necessary as a result of the application of other means?

Are those low level means used that are recommended as advisable for the implementation of chosen high level means?

Is a selected high level means (for example, a reference architecture) based on proven low level means (principles, patterns, styles etc.) and are these documented?

Is the use of means sufficiently documented?

Can structural breaks be avoided through the use of specific means?

Is there a reference implementation for a selected reference architecture and is this accessible (e.g., as Open Source)?

Where useful, are domain-specific languages used?

If domain-specific languages are used, are suitable basic concepts (dynamic languages, scripting languages, MDSD) and technologies used to implement them?

| If a modeling means is used not only for documentation but also for generation or model-driven development, are the models sufficiently formal? |
| Where useful, are domain-specific languages also used for the architecture description, i.e., an ADL? |
| Are sufficient resources provided for measures to improve the architecture as part of reengineering and maintenance? |
| Are there sufficient measures to improve the architecture in reengineering and maintenance? |

Table 8.5-9 gives an overview of important relationships between the aspects of the architecture method described in Section 8.5 and the architectural topics discussed in Chapters 3–7.

Connections between Section 8.5 and Chapters 3–7

Table 8.5-9: Overview of the connections between Section 8.5 and Chapters 3–7

Chapter/section number	Chapter/section heading	Reason for connection
3.2	From Classic Architecture to Software Architecture (WHAT)	For a better separation of different concerns, a distinction should be made between functional, technical, and platform architecture
3.3	Architecture and the System Concept	Thinking in systems is applied to create building blocks required
3.4	Architecture and the Building Blocks of a System (WHAT)	A set of fundamental system building blocks is applied to create the building blocks required
4.1	Architecture Levels (WHERE)	Building blocks are created at system and building block level
4.2	Architecture Views (WHERE)	Logical view, data view, and deployment view are created
5	Architecture Requirements (WHY)	Functional requirements, qualities, and constraints are taken into account for creating building blocks
6	Architecture Means (WITH WHAT)	Different architecture means are used to work out the system context and to create the building blocks.
6.6	Architecture Modeling Means (WITH WHAT)	Architecture modeling means (e.g., UML) are applied to document the system context and the building blocks
7	Organizations and Individuals (WHO)	During the activity designing the architecture the architect interacts with various stakeholders to validate the architecture. Furthermore the architect should involve the developers in designing the architecture and take their inputs into account

8.6 Implementing the Architecture

Figure 8.6-1 shows the basic concepts of the activity "implementing the architecture" that we will look at in this chapter and visualizes how they relate to each other.

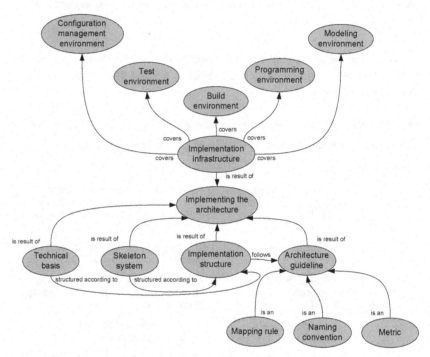

Figure 8.6-1: *Basic concepts of the activity "implementing the architecture"*

Architect is responsible for feasibility

Your work as an architect does not end with the design of the architecture. You are also involved with the implementation of the system, since you have to ensure that it can be implemented based on your architecture. Figure 8.6-2 shows the actions you perform. The activity "implementing the architecture" is primarily concerned with developing the implementation view of a system (see Section 4.2). You do not execute this activity all by yourself—you work with experts from your team (e.g., developers, configuration managers, test managers) and you delegate tasks. However, the architectural responsibility for implementing the architecture lies with you.

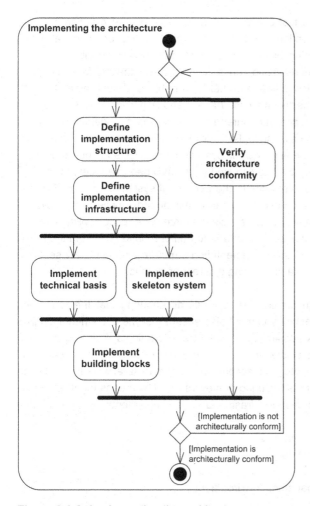

Figure 8.6-2: Implementing the architecture

The logical view of the system created during the design of the architecture must now be reflected in the realization. You therefore define how the building blocks of the logical view are mapped on the building blocks of the implementation view. The result of this action is the implementation structure, which is the decomposition of the source code into manageable units. Your options are restricted by the realization technology you use. For example, if you use Java for the realization, the units package, class, and interface are available. The architect of MIS would therefore have to define how the subsystems, building blocks, and interfaces of MIS are to be mapped onto packages, classes, and interfaces of the Java technology.

Define implementation structure

Defining mapping rules and naming conventions

In addition to defining a first concrete mapping, you must also define mapping rules and naming conventions. You should group all realization units that define the interface of a building block or a subsystem in dedicated interface packages. However, position realization units that implement the interface in internal packages. You must also differentiate between public and published interfaces [Fowler 2002]. Public interfaces are interfaces used within your own source code basis. It is easier to change such interfaces, since you can identify and adapt consumers of the interface using tools. Published interfaces however, are difficult to change, since they are used across system boundaries and you do not control the source code of the systems using your published interfaces. In the MIS example, these are the interfaces to the peripheral systems, such as IMS and CCMS. However, from a certain system size, this already applies for subsystem boundaries, since there may also be a clear source code responsibility here and you cannot make changes easily. For a better differentiation between the public and published interfaces, the implementation structure should clearly separate these interfaces by, for example, using different packages.

Define the implementation infrastructure

When implementing an architecture, as well as ensuring that the realization matches the original design, you must also ensure that the implementation proceeds as efficiently as possible and without any problems. This requires that you take the selection of the architecture means (development environment, programming language, etc.) into account in the architectural work for the implementation, as well as the structuring of the system. The means together are referred to as the implementation infrastructure. The implementation infrastructure includes:
> Programming environments
> Modeling environments
> Build environments
> Configuration management environments
> Test environments

Defining the implementation infrastructure is essential

By defining the programming environment, e.g., Eclipse, you also define which source code formats and templates are to be used, how an application server should be integrated, or how the configuration management repository should be accessed. The definition of the implementation infrastructure is often neglected, resulting in a heterogeneous implementation infrastructure that restricts the efficiency of the implementation.

Enabling efficient collaboration

The aim of selecting the architecture means for the implementation infrastructure is to enable the collaboration between the individual developers on the entire system to be as efficient as possible. To achieve this, you must have standardized procedures that define how, for example:

> Changes are integrated in the entire system
> The individual parts of the entire system are created and installed
> The entire system is tested.

The concrete definition of the procedures is heavily dependent on the respective conditions. In addition to the architecture means used, other factors such as the number of developers involved, or the distribution over one or more development locations, influence the procedures.

Before a system can be realized on a broad scale, you must establish the technical basis. A technical basis includes the basic technical services (see Section 8.5) required and the implementation of the frameworks used to realize the functional building blocks. The actual business logic should be as independent from the basic technical services and frameworks as possible. In other words, the dependency of the functional building blocks on the technical building blocks and frameworks should be as low as possible. The technical basis should also abstract and encapsulate aspects of the platform as far as possible. In MIS, for example, it should be possible to test the functional building blocks both within a JEE server and outside of it. However, you can only create an appropriate technical basis if you have sufficient information about the needs of the functional building blocks. This is one reason for implementing a skeleton system. A skeleton system also clearly shows how the system can be implemented conform to the architecture.

Implement the technical basis

The structure of a skeleton system already corresponds to the architecture of the final system. However, the individual building blocks do not yet provide a complete implementation of the functionality. They usually provide the functionality required to reflect a clearly delineated use case. All other functionalities are either not implemented or defined with temporary implementations (mocks or mockups). Using a skeleton system gives you a "complete, ready-to-run" system as early as possible for a clearly delineated use case. This system contains all fundamental building blocks even if they have not yet been realized completely. The functional scope of the use case is second priority here. However, you must select it such that all fundamental building blocks are also involved in the realization of that use case. Once you have realized the skeleton of the total system, you can develop the individual building blocks further, thus increasing the functional scope of the system further. This approach has the advantage that during the development period, a "ready-to-run" system is available at all times. It enables you to continuously verify the requirements given using the existing system. In addition, you can direct the focus towards critical or complex aspects of the system at the beginning, resulting in a reduction of the risks. A skeleton system enables developers to focus on the actual domain logic of the system since the fundamental structure of the system already exists. Model-driven software development is a real accelerator in this context since the fundamental structure can be generated based on the defined architecture models.

Implement a skeleton system

Developing the technical basis and skeleton system in parallel

Implement the technical basis and the skeleton system in parallel. This enables you to take conclusions obtained from the implementation of the skeleton system into account when you implement the technical basis. The technical basis will always be one iteration ahead of the skeleton system.

Implement building blocks

As an architect, you should be involved not only in the implementation of the technical basis and the skeleton system, but also in the implementation of the concrete functional building blocks as the project progresses. This provides you with immediate feedback on whether your architecture fulfills the intended purpose and you can eliminate weaknesses early. Your involvement also increases your acceptance within the team (see Chapter 7).

Verify architecture conformity

An important task in implementing the architecture, or rather, of architecture guidelines, is the verification and safeguarding of architecture conformity. This is also known as architectural enforcement. The conformity of the deliverables with a defined architecture must be ensured with the first lines of source code written or the first abstraction modeled. If this is not the case, potential architecture erosions are detected too late. An example of an architecture erosion is that the system deviates from the initially defined architecture because changes are executed during maintenance without complying with the architecture. Various means are available to safeguard the conformity of an implemented system with the planned architecture.

Continuous, manual verification

The most simple means is continuous, manual verification that the source code written complies with the architecture. As it is so simple, this means is available quickly and at short notice. The disadvantage of manual verification is the effort it requires and the incomplete coverage of the building blocks verified.

Use of tools for source code and model analysis

You can also use automated checks to verify the source code. The open source range for Java has various tools for this, e.g., FindBugs, Checkstyle, or PMD. In the analysis, include metrics that enable you to make a statement about the quality of the source code. These include, for example:

> Cyclomatic complexity [McCabe 1976]
> Method lengths
> Class lengths
> Inheritance depth and breadth
> Number of attributes and methods of a class
> Cohesion of methods of a class
> Number and scope of Copy&Paste violations

Do not apply metrics blindly

However, do not apply metrics blindly and as the sole assessment criterion to base architectural decisions on. Assess them on a case by case basis, and include further parameters (e.g., special requirements) from the respective context. It is also important to communicate the use of metrics in advance (see

Section 8.7). Such tools can also verify the compliance with guidelines (for programming, naming conventions, etc.) or even enforce compliance. Many modeling environments also enable you to define modeling rules and check them automatically during modeling. This ensures that you can identify potential problems as early as the design stage.

Another option for ensuring that an architecture is implemented correctly is to specify the architecture using a skeleton system as a template. The developers have freedom within the scope of the skeleton system. However, the prerequisite for this is that such a skeleton system actually implements all architectural decisions.

Skeleton system as a template

Frameworks are another option for achieving a good match between architecture and realization (see Section 6.2). Using interfaces and abstract implementations, frameworks give their users guidelines for realizing a solution. These interfaces and abstract implementations reflect the architecture you created. They thus ensure that the solution implemented matches a predefined architecture. You must provide examples of typical use cases of the framework. The developers can use these as a reference to implement their own functionality.

Frameworks

A further option for achieving the best possible match between the system implemented and the predefined architecture is the use of source code generators (see Section 6.2.5) and model-driven software development (see Section 6.2.6). These options enable you to generate source code using specifications. Specifications may be available in the form of models and thus enable a description of the entire system or parts of a system at a higher level of abstraction. The generator uses these models to create source code for larger parts of the total system. It ensures that the source code created for the architecture is compliant by generating all architecturally significant realization building blocks.

Generative approaches and model-driven software development

Is compliance with architecture guidelines checked automatically?
Is correct implementation of the architecture ensured automatically?
Does the documentation contain an example for best and worst case for every metric?
Are there rules for mapping building blocks of the logical view to building blocks of the implementation view?
Is every building block of the logical view also contained in the implementation view?
Have the implementation infrastructure means used been evaluated?
Are proven implementation infrastructure means used?
Are standard implementation infrastructure means used or rather proprietary means?
If proprietary implementation infrastructure means are used, are the reasons for this documented?
Has the implementation infrastructure been aligned with the organizational constraints?
Has the implementation infrastructure been configured in accordance with architecture guidelines?

Checklist: Implementing the architecture

Is there a cookbook for the implementation infrastructure?	
Is there a technical basis?	
Does the technical basis comply with the predefined architecture?	
Does the technical basis cover all architecturally significant use cases?	

Connections between Section 8.6 and Chapters 3–7

Table 8.6-1 gives an overview of important relationships between the aspects of the architecture method described in Section 8.6 and the architectural topics discussed in Chapters 3–7.

Table 8.6-1: Overview of the connections between Section 8.6 and Chapters 3–7

Chapter/ section number	Chapter/section heading	Reason for connection
3.1	Classic Architecture as Starting Point (WHAT)	The Classic architecture definition states that the architect is involved in implementing an architecture too
3.4	Architecture and the Building Blocks of a System (WHAT)	A set of fundamental system building blocks is applied to create the building blocks required for implementing the architectural design
4.2	Architecture Views (WHERE)	Implementation view is created
5	Architecture Requirements (WHY)	Functional requirements, qualities, and constraints are taken into account for creating building blocks implementing the architectural design
6.7	Architecturally Relevant Technologies (WITH WHAT)	Different technologies are chosen and applied to define the implementation structure and infrastructure and to implement the technical basis, skeleton system, and building blocks
6.2	Basic Architecture Concepts	To achieve architectural conformance frameworks, generative approaches and model-driven software development (MDSD) are applied
7	Organizations and Individuals (WHO)	The architect must be actively involved in the implementation of the system and ensure that the system is implemented according to the planned architecture. He therefore has to interact in particular with developers

8.7 Communicating the Architecture

Basic concepts of the activity "communicating the architecture"

Figure 8.7-1 shows the basic concepts of the "communicating the architecture" activity that we will look at in detail in this chapter and visualizes how they relate to each other.

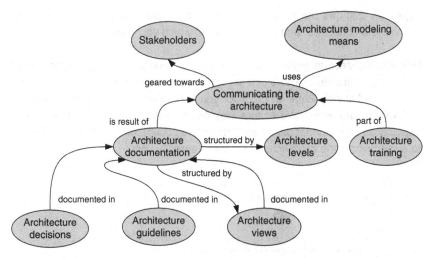

Figure 8.7-1: Basic concepts of the activity "communicating the architecture"

An architecture provides a model for all stakeholders. They can work with this model and thus communicate with one another. However, the prerequisite for this is that you communicate an architecture you have designed to the relevant stakeholders continuously as part of all architectural activities (see Figure 8.2-1). You must communicate the architecture clearly and with reference to the objectives. Thus all stakeholders get an understanding for a system to be realized and the work they have to do as well as the collaboration within the team or the project organization (see Chapter 7). The following examples explain why it is so important to communicate an architecture to all stakeholders [Bass et al. 2003]:

Continuous communication

> Developers must be able to understand how to implement the architecture correctly.
> Testers must be able to understand the building blocks to be tested according to the specifications of an architecture.
> Managers must be able to understand what effect an architecture has on the project planning.
> Customers must be able to understand why the consideration of certain requirements means more effort in the design of an architecture.

Communicating an architecture means involving stakeholders in different aspects of an architecture. To ensure that an architecture is accepted, understood, and correctly implemented, it is very important to involve "your" developers in architectural decisions. With regard to the various other stakeholders, it is important to communicate an architecture because this enables you and the stakeholders to verify whether and how a future system fulfills the given requirements. It also enables you to improve the acceptance of the future system by the stakeholders.

Involve stakeholders

Figure 8.7-2 shows the individual actions of the architectural activity "communicating the architecture" and the sequence in which you execute them.

Document architecture guidelines

Defining architecture guidelines is one of your central tasks. You do this in all architectural activities. There are different architecture guidelines for different aspects and stakeholders. In order for you to be able to communicate effective architecture guidelines and ensure they are applied, you must document them explicitly as an important part of an architecture documentation. It is not sufficient to communicate the architecture guidelines verbally only.

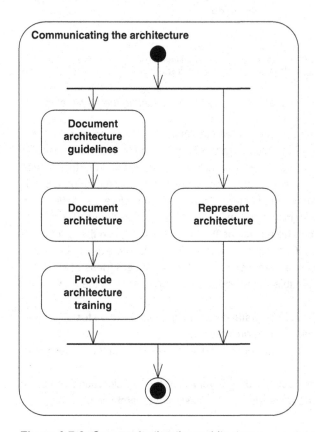

Figure 8.7-2: Communicating the architecture

Purpose of architecture guidelines

Architecture guidelines support you in ensuring the following for an architecture:
> Quality
> Correct implementation
> Communication

You define architecture guidelines for two areas:

> How architecture means are to be used
> How architecture is to be documented (we will look at this more closely later on in this section)

Areas of architecture guidelines

Examples of architecture means for which you have to create architecture guidelines are:

> Use of object-oriented concepts in Java
> Naming conventions, e.g., for building blocks
> Programming in Java
> Use of UML diagrams

Subjects of architecture guidelines

Architecture guidelines must be easy to use in daily work. If they are documented in a bureaucratic creation of endless pages they will not be applied systematically and may even be disregarded. Therefore, restrict architecture guidelines to a manageable number of truly relevant and transparent specifications. Describe these specifications concisely, uniformly, and understandably. Structure the documentation of architecture guidelines such that it can be used without unnecessary effort and supports its communication. It should therefore always consist of at least the following parts:

> The guideline itself
> Reason for the guideline
> Example for the application of the guideline
> Example for the violation of the guideline

How should architecture guidelines be documented?

Table 8.7-1 contains an example guideline for MIS.

Table 8.7-1: Guideline using the example of MIS

Guideline	
Data is exchanged between building blocks across the boundaries of logical layers using data transfer objects (DTO)	
Reason	Better decoupling of the layers and reduction of the network load
Example for application	See Figure 8.5-11
Example for violation	Building blocks for the web framework are used to exchange data between the presentation logic layer and the application logic layer

Before you start creating architecture guidelines, check whether the desired guidelines already exist somewhere else and can be used as a basis. For example, the UML community has rules for writing identifiers as a quasi-standard.

Do not create architecture guidelines where they already exist

However, do not use such standards without further consideration—you have to adapt them to the specific requirements (e.g., project size).

When should architecture guidelines be created?

To use architecture means practically and create artefacts you have to consider architecture guidelines. This means that you have to create architecture guidelines continuously and from an early stage. Creating or considering architecture guidelines retrospectively is only feasible with a high effort, if at all.

Drawing up architecture guidelines for architecture documentation

You must also define architecture guidelines for creating the architecture documentation and using architecture modeling means. Do this before you start creating an architecture documentation. Architecture guidelines should answer the questions below for the architecture documentation (you can add to the list as required):

> What is the content of the architecture documentation?
> How is the architecture documentation structured?
> How is the architecture documentation organized?
> How is the architecture documentation kept up-to-date?
> What rules are there for the style of writing?
> How should architecture modeling means be used?
> Which language should be used for the identifiers (all types)?
> Which styles of writing are to be used for identifiers?

Document architecture

You communicate architecture in presentations, reviews, training, etc. Architecture documentation has an effect on these activities, either directly or indirectly. Therefore, the architecture documentation has a key role in communicating an architecture.

Important objectives

Architecture documentation should be aligned with the following two important objectives [Bredemeyer and Malan 2010]:

> Document an architect's decisions completely and unambiguously.
> Communicate architecture aligned with the various stakeholders or target groups (customer, project lead, software developers, etc.).

Architecture documentation is necessary for correct architecture implementation

An architecture can only be implemented as you planned if the related architecture documentation, created in accordance with the objectives above and according to specific rules, is available and you communicate it actively (see Section 7.5). Only such an explicit architecture can be communicated, understood, and implemented. If an architecture is well thought out but generally only exists in your mind, it can only be partly implemented or may be implemented incorrectly. Alternatively, the related architecture documentation is destined to gather dust on a shelf. An important side effect of the architecture documentation is that creating it often provides important insights into an architecture itself, which may again lead to its improvement. Architecture and its documentation are therefore interdependent.

Architecture documentation should always describe at least the following aspects [Bredemeyer and Malan 2010]:

> Architecture decisions (see Sections 8.2–8.6)
> Architecture views (see Chapter 4)
> Architecture requirements (see Chapter 5 and Sections 8.2 and 8.3)

Aspects that should not be missing in any architecture documentation

Documenting the architecture decisions explicitly is a very important point in an architecture documentation. The architecture decisions that led to a specific architecture can only be understood and justified—especially after a long time—if they are known. Architecture decisions are visualized in the results of the architecture design, which are reflected in the architecture documentation. However, a UML diagram that, for example, shows a logical four layer architecture, does not clearly indicate all underlying architecture decisions. Therefore, you have to document the architecture decisions as well as the results of the architecture design—for example, in the form of a table.

Documenting architecture decisions

Important architecture decisions in MIS are, for example:

> Prioritization of requirements (see Tables 8.4-2 and 8.4-3)
> Interface protocols to the peripheral systems (see Figure 8.5-4)
> Identification of the key abstractions (see Figure 8.5-5)

Important subjects of architecture decisions are:

> Architecturally significant requirements (e.g., scalability)
> Selection of specific architecture means (e.g., selection of a pattern or a platform technology)
> How the selected architecture means are applied (e.g., a specific building block specified by a selected pattern is missing)
> Structure of the building blocks (e.g., certain building blocks collaborate directly, rather than via their interfaces)

Subjects of architecture decisions

This leads to the following questions that can be answered using explicitly documented architecture decisions:

> Which are the architecturally significant requirements and why?
> Why were certain architecture means selected?
> Why were the architecture means applied in this way?
> Why are the building blocks structured in this way?

Figure 8.7-3 shows the context of architecture documentation. We will now look at the facts presented in Figure 8.7-3 that have not been explained more closely yet.

Context of architecture documentation

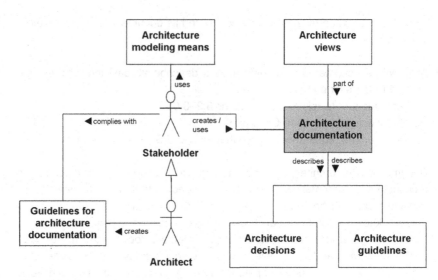

Figure 8.7-3: *Architecture documentation in context*

Architect does not create architecture documentation alone

As the architect you will create large parts of an architecture documentation However, other stakeholders (analysts, developers, etc.) will also contribute to it. The architecture documentation is created taking account of the guidelines you specify.

Architecture documentation must consider target groups

As previously stated, an architecture is important for various stakeholders. The architecture documentation should therefore be available in different forms so that it satisfies the different viewpoints of the different target groups. For example, a slide presentation that shows only the most significant building blocks of a system with simple graphical means (box and line diagrams), without going into detail about technical details such as interfaces, is completely sufficient for the decision-makers target group. Presenting a semi-formal model using the Unified Modeling Language (UML) or an Architecture Description Language (ADL) would not have the desired effect for these stakeholders. In contrast, it would be fatal to design and realize a system based on a slide presentation because important aspects would be missing. Thus you would use a marchitecture (see Section 1.1) for high-level presentations only. Do not leave the selection of the architecture modeling means (see Section 6.6) and the form of an architecture documentation to chance. Instead, select them deliberately and with a specific objective.

Using standard architecture modeling means

The selection of an architecture modeling means is important for the maintenance and communication of an architecture documentation. Using established standards (see Section 6.6) brings considerable benefits:
> Use of the architecture modeling means is documented
> Architecture modeling means has been tested and proven

> Better support for questions and problems
> Support for the architecture modeling means via tools from various manufacturers

There are degrees of flexibility in the use of architecture modeling means (e.g., in the selection of the language for identifiers or the utilization of specific options of an architecture modeling means). If these degrees of flexibility are used without any clear intention, the quality of an architecture documentation can suffer with regard to the following points:

Consequences of incorrect use of architecture modeling means

> Consistency
> Understanding
> Clarity
> Maintainability

"Poor" architecture documentation has wide-reaching, undesirable consequences. It often has a negative effect on an architecture, i.e., the software quality of the system suffers. For example, an awkward naming (e.g., for building blocks) in an architecture documentation can have an effect right down to the source code. The source code then becomes unreadable and thus difficult to maintain.

Poor quality architecture documentation can lead to poor software quality

You can and should use the possibilities of the selected architecture modeling means to describe all views of a system described in Chapter 4. Consider both static and dynamic aspects.

Architecture views are documented

For MIS, for example, part of the requirements view is documented with quality attribute scenarios (see Table 8.4-1) and prioritized requirements (see Tables 8.4-2 and 8.4-3).

Do not mix different architecture levels and views (see Chapter 4) in an architecture documentation. Instead, divide an architecture documentation into the different levels and views explicitly. This makes it easier for someone reading the architecture documentation to get a step-by-step understanding of the different architecture aspects and to find the content relevant for them. The details for the MIS example show this clearly (see Sections 8.2–8.6). If you want to visualize aspects of different architecture levels together, mark the different levels clearly. If this is not possible (in a clear form), use multiple diagrams.

Do not mix different architecture levels and views

There is no one standard for structuring an architecture documentation but there are numerous procedures. For example, you can split up or organize an architecture documentation according to building blocks and/or architecture views. An architecture documentation should be based on the template shown in Table 8.7-2.

Structuring of architecture documentation

Table 8.7-2: *Template for architecture documentation*

Introduction					
Overview					
Selection of require-ments	Selection and application of architecture means			Structure of the building blocks	
Architecture views					
Require-ments view	Logical view	Data view	Implementa-tion view	Pro-cess view	De-ploy-ment view
Crosscutting aspects					
Architecture guidelines		Other			
Architecture assessment					
Project aspects					
Open issues					
Glossary					

This template shows a basic structure based on [IEEE 2007] for architecture documentation. We recommend that you add to and refine this structure as required for a specific project. The main elements of this template have the following contents:

> *Introduction:* Motivation, objectives, target groups, and reader guide.
> *Overview:* Essential architecture aspects grouped with references to in-depth parts in the architecture documentation.
> *Architecture views:* Contents according to the respective viewpoint of a view. Here it is important to document the architecture decisions that led to the artefacts, and not simply list the artefacts.
> *Crosscutting aspects:* Aspects that cannot be assigned to individual architecture views. These include, for example, guidelines for using UML diagrams or the definition of viewpoints.
> *Architecture assessment:* Logs of architecture assessments and rejected architecture alternatives.
> *Project aspects:* Aspects such as iteration planning, task distribution, or training.
> *Open issues:* Points that still require clarification, e.g., unclear requirements.
> *Glossary:* Must always be included! Central terminology and synonyms.

You can use a structure like this both for architecture documentation bundled in a single artefact and documentation distributed over several artefacts. Furthermore, you can base the storage structures (e.g., directory structures in a file system) for the artefacts of an architecture documentation on this basic structure. An architecture documentation should always be structured based on a proven template. One example of such a template is the ANSI/IEEE standard 1471–2000 [IEEE 2007; OpenGroup 2001]. [Bass et al. 2003] also contains useful comments and templates for sensible structuring of architecture documentation.

The terms (in an architecture documentation) are a considerable problem in the use of an architecture documentation if they are interpreted differently by different stakeholders. This is particularly valid for key terms of a domain. To alleviate this problem, [Evans 2004] suggests the following architecture guidelines:

Select terminology carefully

> Use only terms from the domain model.
> Discuss the meaning of alternatives for a term and define which of the terms available for selection should be used as standard in future.
> Make sure that changes with regard to terms used are reflected in the domain model.
> Check terms for correctness (consistency, contradictions, understanding, etc.).

We recommend supplementing the textual architecture documentation with an audio-visual documentation to make it easier to communicate the architecture. There are various media and means available:

Supplementary audio-visual architecture documentation

> Audio books
> Blog
> Freehand drawings
> Livestream
> Podcast
> RSS-Feed
> UML diagrams
> Video/DVD

To document architecture and make it easier to communicate, it is essential to have the significant features of an architecture in visual form as well as in text form in an architecture documentation. You should therefore visualize the model of the system to be developed. The visualized artefacts of a model are an important part of an architecture documentation. Important: visualize the different aspects of an architecture with different artefacts (e.g., UML diagrams). Such visual artefacts make it easier to present, communicate, and discuss an architecture and the effects of changing requirements on this architecture. There are various more or less formal architecture modeling means available for this purpose (see Section 6.6). A visual architecture documentation can never replace a written architecture documentation—it supplements it by providing an overview of the

Visualization of the architecture model supplements written architecture documentation

architecture quickly and enabling the reader to focus on specific aspects without getting lost in the details of a text. The visual display also serves as a means of navigation through the textual description. This has an effect particularly when, for example, as an architect and/or developer you have to familiarize yourself with a new architecture.

Visual architecture documentation

In order for the visual architecture documentation to bring a real benefit, it should not attempt to portray all details of the textual description. Instead, it should highlight the important aspects (e.g., interfaces and layer association). The visual architecture documentation thus makes it easier to access the concepts described in the textual architecture documentation. It should also answer at least the following questions with regard to system building blocks:
> What roles do the building blocks have?
> What relationships exist between the building blocks?
> How do the building blocks communicate with one another?

These aspects are documented in the logical view.

Ensuring simple access to architecture documentation

It is important to ensure fast and easy access to an architecture documentation. Therefore, it is important to have a corresponding technical infrastructure (e.g., use of a CMS or a repository) with the option of version control, since architecture documents are developed further over time.

Scope of architecture documentation

Architecture documentation can vary in scope and can cover different types of artefacts (texts, diagrams, presentations, etc.). How much architecture documentation is necessary? Generally, the scope of an architecture documentation should be selected such that all stakeholders can properly understand an architecture and it can be correctly implemented. The complexity of a project (e.g., requirements, system size, project organization, functional experience of the project team members, etc.) influences the scope of the documentation (see Figure 8.7-4). It is therefore not possible to specify a universal scope The challenge is to maintain the scope to fit the purpose. Remember, however, that most artefacts created must also be maintained in the future. You can partially limit the scope by consistently complying with the following rules:
> Document only architecturally significant aspects (e.g., interfaces).
> Create only artefacts that bring a real added value and that will actually be used (e.g., consider whether it makes sense to create a UML activity diagram for every use case).
> Avoid redundancies (e.g., the documentation of an interface should not be repeated for each building block that implements the interface).
> Remember that sometimes "less is more."
> Architecture documentation must be 100% up-to-date. This means that the scope must not restrict the maintenance of the documentation.

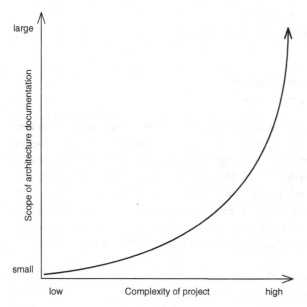

Figure 8.7-4: Correlation between project complexity and architecture documentation scope

You cannot assume that an architecture and the architecture guidelines will be understood and implemented correctly based on the architecture documentation alone (no matter how well-developed it is). As the architect you have to continuously bring the architecture and architecture guidelines into the minds of the respective stakeholders. Architecture and architecture guidelines can only fulfill their intended purpose if the stakeholders consider and correctly apply them. The prerequisite for this is that architecture and architecture guidelines are known, accepted, and understood. Therefore, communicate architecture and architecture guidelines deliberately and with caution. To communicate architecture and architecture guidelines successfully, it is important that you do not refer to them simply by means of an architecture documentation but that they are also communicated or trained verbally. For example, this can take place as part of a team meeting or the establishment of an architecture board. This achieves real acceptance of architecture and architecture guidelines and prevents an incorrect use or understanding that would lead to considerable effort in eliminating consequential errors (e.g., in the implementation of an architecture).

Provide architecture training

Training courses require resources and must be planned. The project lead should not make decisions on this issue alone because the project lead often cannot finally assess the technical facts (e.g., should a different persistence framework be used in the future, or can our Java developers change over to Ruby with no further effort?). Once again you are required to act as a technical consultant and determine the training requirements of the individual stakeholders. The training effort generally increases the more the training is concerned with implementing an architecture.

Planning training courses

Types of training courses	Training courses can be offered as

Training courses can be offered as
> External/internal seminars or workshops
> Blended learning
> Coaching measures
> Presentations in a team meeting
> Participation in an architecture

Represent architecture

As an architect you should always represent your architecture, even in the face of (political) resistance. You do this on various fronts. Dangers for an architecture must be recognized early (e.g., the possible rejection of an architecture decision by an important stakeholder). An architecture, and thus also the architect, is subject to the potentially conflicting opinions of the different stakeholders. Therefore, do not neglect any stakeholders when you are positioning an architecture. For example, you risk not getting your architecture accepted if you do not represent it actively enough to management, claiming to be "just a technician."

Checklist: Communicating the architecture

Are developers involved in architectural decisions?
Is the architecture communicated to all stakeholders?
Are guidelines communicated to the respective stakeholders affected?
Is the architecture represented to all stakeholders?

Checklist: Architecture guidelines

Are there guidelines for using architecture means?
Are there guidelines for creating architecture documentation?
Are architecture guidelines documented?
Are guidelines based on standards?
Are guidelines created continuously and in time?

Checklist: Architecture documentation

Have the architecture modeling means used been evaluated?
Are proven architecture modeling means used?
Are standard architecture modeling means used or rather proprietary means?
If proprietary architecture modeling means are used, are the reasons for this documented?
Is IEEE standard 1471 [IEEE 2007] complied with?
Are at least the requirements, logical, and deployment views documented?
Are at least architecture decisions, architecture views, and architecture requirements documented?
Are different architecture levels and views not mixed?
Is there a supplementary audio-visual architecture documentation?
Does the visual architecture documentation concentrate only on architecturally significant aspects?
Can the architecture documentation be accessed quickly and easily?
Is the scope of the architecture documentation appropriate to the requirements, system size, and project organization?

Does the scope of the architecture documentation still allow unrestricted maintenance of the architecture documentation?
Are architecture guidelines part of the architecture documentation?
Does the architecture documentation include a glossary?
Is version management available for the architecture documentation?
Does the architecture documentation contain context information, such as author(s), change history, version, etc.?

Is a standardized architecture view model used?
Has the selected architecture view model been adapted?
Are all views used specified?
Do any views used have redundancies?
Are all views used coherent?
Are static and dynamic structures considered?

Table 8.7-3 gives an overview of important relationships between the aspects of the architecture method described in Section 8.7 and the architectural topics discussed in Chapters 3–7.

Table 8.7-3: Overview of the connections between Section 8.7 and Chapters 3–7

Chapter/ section number	Chapter/section heading	Reason for connection
3	Architecturs and Architecture Disciplines (WHAT)	The understanding of the definition of software architecture and its major concerns is a key prerequisite for communicating the architecture successfully
4.1	Architecture Levels (WHERE)	Architecture levels are used to structure architecture documentation and to align architecture training to the appropriate audience
4.2	Architecture Views (WHERE)	Architecture views are worked out and used to communicate and document an architecture
5	Architecture Requirements (WHY)	For communicating the architecture appropriate it is required to know the stakeholdes and the corresponding different requirements which led to given architectural decisions
6.6	Architecture Modeling Means (WITH WHAT)	Architecture modeling means are used to work out the architecture documentation
7	Organizations and Individuals (WHO)	The architect has to communicate the architecture to various stakeholders in the right form so that the stakeholders understand the architecture and how it addresses their needs and concerns

8.8 Maintaining the Architecture

Basic concepts of the activity "maintaining the architecture"

Figure 8.8-1 shows the basic concepts of the "maintaining the architecture" activity that we will look at in detail in this chapter and visualizes how they relate to each other.

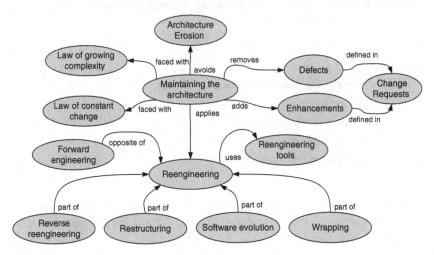

Figure 8.8-1: *Basic concepts of the activity "maintaining the architecture"*

Motivation

Maintenance of software systems deals with changes to the system after it has been delivered. This covers, for example, the correction of errors, the improvement of quality attributes such as performance, and the evolution or further development of the system. According to a study from Nosek and Palvia [Nosek and Palvia 1990], only 20% of the time invested in a software system is concerned with the actual development. In contrast, 40% of the time is spent on understanding, and 40% again on changing the software system—i.e., on typical activities in software maintenance. During maintenance it is especially important to avoid the erosion of the architecture. To do this you will perform the architecture activities presented in this chapter. This means that you will also understand the requirements (often expressed in change requests), determine the impact of the requirements on the architecture, define the necessary changes to the architecture, and ensure that these changes are implemented in order to avoid the erosion of the architecture.

Constant change and growing complexity

In real software development we can observe two important laws [Lehmann and Belady 1985]: the law of constant change and the law of growing complexity. With reference to the maintenance of software architectures, this means that as the architect, you have to constantly contend with changes but still ensure you keep the complexity under control. In reality, this is often difficult for the following reasons:

> It is difficult to be prepared for unexpected changes.
> Knowledge is not documented sufficiently or documentation is lost. In some legacy systems even the source code no longer exists. If the original architects and developers have left the enterprise, it is difficult to get back the knowledge about the system.
> Where changes are quick—in the hectic of daily business—revising the documentation and the design, architecture, and requirements documents is often forgotten. The principle of traceability is violated.
> Quick changes and corrections, in particular when they are performed by persons other than those who originally designed the architecture, tend to violate architectural conventions.

Below we will briefly outline the most important means for software maintenance.

From an architecture view, software reengineering is an important part of software maintenance. It is concerned with the following major tasks [Chikofsky and Cross 1990]:

Reengineering

> *Reverse engineering* covers activities for regaining lost information about existing software systems. The first task is to identify the system building blocks. Their interactions and relationships must also be reconstructed. The goal is the description of a view of a system with a higher level of abstraction. This can be the reconstruction of an architecture based on the code, for example. Many reverse engineering tools use visualizations to illustrate an architecture.
> *Restructuring* covers all activities for changing the structure of a system. This can refer to both the code and to other documents related to the system. This means that architecture documents can also be reconstructed. Restructuring is thus primarily changing a representation into another representation at the same level of abstraction.
> *Software evolution* is the implementation of changes to the software system. Here we can differentiate in particular technologies for bringing in expected and unexpected changes.
> *Wrapping* gives a given system or a building block a new interface but does not change the system itself. It is frequently used for version adjustments or other slight interface changes to software building blocks. It is also used for software evolution: if you want to completely change a large system, it is often unwise to completely rewrite it. Instead, it is better to change it step-by-step. The new and old parts must then communicate with one another, for example, to test the system. A wrapper can provide an old subsystem as a building block in a new system. Wrappers are also sometimes used for

interim solutions if an old system will soon be exchanged. In practice, however, such interim solutions often survive longer than planned.

The term *reengineering* therefore covers all activities for understanding and changing a software system to implement it in a new form.

Areas of use for reengineering

Software reengineering often involves legacy systems, i.e., systems that have existed for a long time but still represent a value for the enterprise. Redeveloping the system is deemed to be more problematic than adjusting the legacy system to new facts—for example, for cost reasons.

However, reengineering is not just about legacy systems. Through their additional abstractions, such as class hierarchies or explicit interfaces, modern object-oriented or component-oriented systems easily enable restructuring, tracing the architecture, or refactoring. This means that as a result of the additional abstraction and modularity, in these systems it is easier to improve and extend the architecture incrementally—which means a strong focus on reengineering activities.

You can use, for example, the means introduced in Section 6.2 such as aspect orientation, generative programming, and model-driven development.

Measures to improve architecture

In practice, unfortunately, relatively little value is placed on measures to improve architecture. This is because these measures often involve a lot of effort but it is not easy to identify the short-term business benefits. For example, improving the modularity can be very important for the modifiability and reusability of the architecture and its ability to be understood. However, a new functionality is still more suitable for convincing a customer to invest in a product.

Reengineering through environmental influences

Therefore, in practice, important tasks in reengineering are influenced more by changes to the "environment." Some examples are:

> Systems are often confronted with new programming languages, new standards, new platforms, new middleware products, databases, and other new environment elements that have to be integrated or to which the systems have to be migrated.

> It can often happen that a system needs a new user interface. For example, mainframe systems are often character-oriented and have to be migrated to graphical user interfaces. Today, many systems receive an (additional) web interface. Mainframe applications are also often changed to client-server architectures or integrated in them.

Architect must work towards measures to improve architecture

Your task as the architect is to pay attention to this and to convince stakeholders to give sufficient weight to measures to improve the architecture as part of maintenance work. In particular, you have to point out the long-term consequences of failure to improve the architecture to the stakeholders. Previous subsections of Chapter 8 deal with this and similar tasks in detail.

In connection with reengineering, the term "forward engineering" is often differentiated. It covers primarily situations in which you develop a new system. In its extreme, with forward engineering, the problem and the possible solution alternatives are still completely unclear and it is difficult to estimate the effort required. You can design the architecture with a great degree of freedom without having to consider dependencies from legacy systems.

Contrast to forward engineering

Reengineering is usually concerned with the opposite situation: there are numerous dependencies but you have already gathered some experience and can estimate the reengineering effort quite well. This ability to estimate the effort better often means in practice that reengineering is preferred to forward engineering—where possible—in order to keep the risks under control.

There are a number of tools for the different reengineering technologies:
> Classic tools are available for the *program analysis*, such as grep, diff, and debugger. However, there are also more extensive tools, for example, for architecture visualizations, analysis tools based on syntax trees or control flows, as well as tools for static and dynamic analysis of characteristics.
> Based on the program analysis tools you can calculate *metrics* automatically, i.e., measured values for the software architecture or the software system.
> With load generators and profilers you can execute performance *analyses*.
> You can use wrapper generators to automate *wrapping*.

Reengineering tools

Tools for refactoring enable you to refine an architecture step-by-step. Modern development environments, such as Eclipse [Eclipse 2010a], already provide simple refactorings, such as "shift method" or "rename class." More extensive tools enable *remodularization*, the *clustering* of structures in order to detect module dependencies, as well as the *analysis and restructuring of inheritance hierarchies*.

8.9 Summary

> The planned and the actual development path deviate from one another due to various influencing factors. Be aware of this and adapt your method accordingly.

Summary: Architecture and development processes

> Methods are guides for structuring individual core disciplines, (architecture) activities, (architecture) actions, and crosscutting tasks. They define the chronological sequence of these aspects in a development process.
> We can differentiate between the waterfall model and iterative, incremental development processes.
> Iterative, incremental development processes provide the best opportunity for reacting to changes during development.
> Create an architecture iteratively and incrementally, rather than in strict sequence.
> As the architect you must support the project lead in planning the iterations in order to ensure that architecturally significant requirements are addressed as early as possible and that risks are therefore minimized.
> You can combine methods. There are process metamodels (e.g., SPEM or UMA) on the market, as well as software tools (e.g., RMC or EPF).
> USDP differentiates between the following phases: inception, elaboration, construction, and transition.

Summary:
Overview of the
architecture method

> As an architect, you need a method to guide you in your project.
> In addition to the method, your own experience is essential for adapting the recommendations of the method to the concrete project situation.
> The architecture method consists of the following activities: creating the system vision, understanding the requirements, designing the architecture, implementing the architecture, and communicating the architecture.
> Execute the activity "communicating the architecture" in parallel to the other activities.
> In the "creating the system vision" activity, it is your responsibility to question requirements critically with regard to their architectural feasibility in the overall or global IT context of an organization. Point out contradictory requirements and indicate alternatives.
> With regard to the architecture method, during the activity "creating the system vision," see yourself as an architectural consultant.
> The activity "understanding the requirements" is dedicated to the identification, prioritization, and detailing of architecturally significant requirements. It is particularly important to consider non-functional requirements thoroughly.
> "Implementing the architecture" is concerned with the definition of development guidelines, with manual reviews, and the establishment of an infrastructure, for example.
> The aim of the activity "communicating the architecture" is to convey the best possible understanding of the architecture and the architecture decisions to the individual stakeholders.

> An important result of the architectural activities is the creation of the different architecture views as described in Chapter 4.
> The ratio of the individual architectural activities changes from iteration to iteration.

> In this activity you take on the role of an architectural consultant in a team of experts from different domains.
> The term "business case" is sometimes used instead of "system vision."
> A system vision should contain the business opportunities, the stakeholders, the significant requirements, and a first system overview.
> Identify and prioritize the stakeholders.
> During the creation of the system vision, you must manage the expectations of the individual stakeholders.
> Document the significant functional and non-functional requirements.
> A first system overview should consist of a system context and a first architecture idea.
> At this point the presentation of the architecture idea can be very informal and you can restrict it to the identification of significant building blocks.

**Summary:
Creating the
system vision**

> Requirements restrict your creative freedom as an architect and are rarely precise.
> Identify and prioritize requirements and make them tangible.
> Identify and prioritize architecturally significant requirements according to benefit and risk.
> Document qualities with quality attribute scenarios.
> Quality attribute scenarios can also document the qualitative nature of functional requirements.
> Consider architecturally significant use cases and qualities within the given constraints.
> Use architecture prototypes to demonstrate architecturally significant requirements.
> In performing the activity "understanding the requirements," refine the requirements of the organizational level, through the system level, down to the building block level, within several iterations.

**Summary:
Understanding the
requirements**

> The design of an architecture is influenced by the architecturally significant requirements, functional models, the system context, and the architecture means to be used.
> The architecture of the first iteration is also known as the architecture vision.

**Summary:
Designing the
architecture**

> In defining the system context, you make the system context contained in the system vision more concrete and document the interfaces. A system context is more than just a diagram.
> Identify the key abstractions of the functional domain for the architecture design.
> Consider requirements with a high priority as early as possible in the design.
> An architecture means alone does not solve all problems. As the architect you have to adapt the means and where applicable combine them with your own design ideas.
> When selecting architecture means, first consider reference architectures and basic architectures. If none of these are suitable, consider tactics, styles, and patterns, as well as concepts and principles.
> During the architecture design, the focus shifts from functionality to technology.
> Define the responsibilities and dependencies of every building block.
> You identify functional building blocks using key abstractions, the functional requirements belonging to the abstractions, and non-functional requirements.
> You can derive dependencies from functional and technical facts.
> Document the interactions between the building blocks.
> Interfaces should disclose their purpose and not their implementation.
> The placement of the building blocks covers their placement on nodes and processes.
> Informal and formal methods are available for assessing an architecture (e.g., presentations, walkthroughs, simulations, architecture prototypes, scenario-based methods).

Summary: Implementing the architecture

> As the architect you are responsible for the implementation of the architecture.
> In the "implementing the architecture" activity you define the implementation structure. It should be derived from the logical view.
> Define mapping rules and naming conventions.
> Define an implementation infrastructure (development environment, programming language, etc.). This infrastructure must enable efficient collaboration.
> Implement the technical basis and the skeleton system. Develop them in parallel, whereby the basis should always be one step ahead of the skeleton system.
> As the architect you should also implement building blocks yourself, in order to get feedback on whether your architecture fulfills the intended purpose and to achieve higher acceptance within the team.

> Verify whether the implementation conforms to the architecture defined. This verification should be automated where possible.

> In order for an architecture to be correctly understood and implemented by the stakeholders, you must communicate it continuously during all architectural activities.
> To ensure that an architecture is accepted, understood, and correctly implemented, it is very important to involve the developers in architectural decisions.
> Communicate architecture verbally, in writing, and visually.
> The architecture documentation plays a key role in communicating an architecture.
> The architecture documentation documents an architecture and architecture guidelines.
> Create and communicate architecture guidelines continuously and in time.
> Important aspects that the architecture documentation must always cover are architecture decisions, architecture views, and architecture requirements.
> The explicit documentation of the architecture decisions is a very important point in an architecture documentation. The architecture decisions that led to a specific architecture can only be understood and justified once they are known.
> Use standardized architecture modeling means to create an architecture documentation.
> When creating an architecture documentation, pay attention to consistency, understanding, clarity, and maintainability. These must be safeguarded by corresponding guidelines.
> It makes sense to supplement the textual architecture documentation with an audio-visual architecture documentation.
> The visual architecture documentation should not attempt to portray all details of the textual description—it should only highlight the important aspects.
> It is important to ensure fast and easy access to an architecture documentation and a corresponding technical infrastructure should be planned.
> The scope of an architecture documentation depends on requirements, system size, and project organization, among other things. You can restrict it by limiting yourself to the truly architecturally significant aspects and strictly avoiding redundancies. With regard to the scope, do not exceed any limits that restrict the maintenance of an architecture documentation with the given resources.

**Summary:
Communicating the
architecture**

**Summary:
Maintaining the
architecture**

> Maintenance of software systems deals with changes to the system after it has been delivered. This covers, for example, the correction of errors, the improvement of quality attributes such as performance, and the evolution or further development of the system.
> 40% of the time invested in a software system is concerned with changing the software system.
> During maintenance it is especially important to avoid the erosion of the architecture
> In real software development we can observe two important laws [Lehmann and Belady 1985]: the law of constant change and the law of growing complexity.
> The architect has to constantly contend with changes but still ensure he keeps the complexity under control.
> Software reengineering deals with the following important tasks: reverse engineering, restructuring, software evolution, and wrapping.
> Reengineering often takes place more as a result of environmental influences.
> Software reengineering often involves legacy systems, i.e., systems that have existed for a long time but still represent a value for the enterprise.
> In practice, unfortunately, relatively little value is placed on measures to improve architecture.
> As the architect you have to work towards measures to improve architecture.
> In connection with reengineering, the term "forward engineering" is often differentiated. It covers primarily situations in which you develop a new system.
> There are a number of tools for the different reengineering technologies (e.g., program analysis, calculation of metrics, performance analyses, and automatic wrapping)
> Tools for refactoring allow to refine an architecture step-by-step

Further Reading

**Further reading:
Architecture and
development
processes**

[Ambler 2010]
Ambler, Scott, *Agile Architecture: Strategies for Scaling Agile Development*, http://www.agilemodeling.com/essays/agileArchitecture.htm, 2010

[Beck 2005]
Beck, Kent, *Extreme Programming Explained – Embrace Change*, Addison-Wesley Longman, Amsterdam, 2005

[V-Modell XT 2009]
V-Modell XT, Specification v. 1.3, *http://v-modell.iabg.de/v-modell-xt-html-english/index.html*, 2009

[Boehm 1998]
Boehm, Barry, *A Spiral Model of Software Development and Enhancement*, IEEE, 21, 61 72, 1998

[Cockburn 2002]
Cockburn, Alistair, *Agile Software Development*, Addison-Wesley, New York, 2002

[Cohn 2010]
Cohn, Mike, *Succeeding with Agile – Software Development Using Scrum*, Addison-Wesley Longman, Amsterdam, 2010

[Cunningham et al. 2001]
Cunningham, Wart et al., *Manifesto for Agile Software Development*, http://agilemanifesto.org/, 2001

[Eclipse 2010c]
Eclipse Process Framework Project (EPF), http://www.eclipse.org/epf/, 2010

[Fowler 2004]
Fowler, Martin, *Is Design Dead?*, http://www.martinfowler.com/articles/designDead.html, 2004

[Jacobson et al. 1999]
Jacobson, Ivar; Booch Grady; Rumbaugh James, *The Unified Software Development Process*, Addison-Wesley, New York, 1999

[Larman 2002]
Larman, Craig, *Applying UML and Patterns – An Introduction to Object-Oriented Analysis and Design and the Unified Process*, Second Edition, Prentice Hall PTR, Upper Saddle River, NJ, 2002

[Oestereich and Weiss 2008]
Oestereich, Bernd; Weiss, Christian, *APM – Agiles Projektmanagement*, dpunkt.verlag, Heidelberg, 2008 (available in German language only)

[OMG 2008c]
Object Management Group, *Software and Systems Process Engineering Metamodel Specification*, v2.0 (Beta 2), http://www.omg.org/spec/SPEM/2.0/, 2008

[Parmer and Felsing 2002]
Palmer, R., Stephen; Felsing, M., John, *A Practical Guide to Feature-Driven Development*, Prentice Hall International, 2002

[Parnas et al. 1986]
Parnas, David L., Clements, Paul, Naval Research Laboratory, *A rational Design Process: How and Why to fake it*, 1986

[Royce 1970]
Royce, Winston, *Managing the Development of Large Systems*, IEEE WESCON Proceedings, 26, 1–9, 1970

Further reading: Overview of the architecture method

[Bass et al. 2003]
Bass, Len; Clements, Paul; Kazman, Rick, *Software Architecture in Practice*, Second Edition, Addison-Wesley, New York, 2003

Further reading: Creating the system vision

[Oestereich and Bremer 2009]
Oestereich, Bernd; Bremer, Stefan, *Analyse und Design mit UML 2.3 – Objektorientierte Softwareentwicklung*, 9. Auflage, Oldenbourg Verlag, 2009 (available in German language only)

Further reading: Designing the architecture

[Rozanski and Woods 2005]
Rozanski, Nick und Woods, Eoin, *Software Systems Architecture - Working with Stakeholders Using Viewpoints and Perspectives*, Addison-Wesley, 2005

[Buschmann et al. 1996]
Buschmann, Frank; Meunier, Regine; Rohnert, Hans; Sommerlad, Peter; Stal, Michael, *Pattern-Oriented Software Architecture Vol. 1, A System of Patterns*, John Wiley & Sons, New York, 1996

[Evans 2004]
Evans, Eric, *Domain-Driven Design – Tackling Complexity in the Heart of Software*, Addison-Wesley, Boston, 2004

[Fowler 2003]
Fowler, Martin, *Patterns of Enterprise Application Architecture*, Addison-Wesley Longman, Amsterdam, 2003

[Gamma et al. 1995]
Gamma, Erich; Helm, Richard; Johnson, Ralph; Vlissides, John, *Design Patterns – Elements of Reusable Object-Oriented Software*, Addison-Wesley, Reading, 1995

[Kazman et al. 1998]
Kazman, R.; Klein, M.; Barbacci, M.; Lipson, H.; Longstaff, T.; Carrière, S.J., *The Architecture Tradeoff Analysis Method*, Proceedings of ICECCS, Monterey, 1998

[Kazman et al. 1994]
Kazman, Rick; Bass, Len; Abowd, Gregory; Webb, Mike, *SAAM: A Method for Analyzing the Properties Software Architectures*, Proceedings of the 16th International Conference on Software Engineering, Sorrento, 1994

[Oestereich and Bremer 2009]
Oestereich, Bernd; Bremer, Stefan, *Analyse und Design mit UML 2.3 – Objektorientierte Softwareentwicklung*, 9. Auflage, Oldenbourg Verlag, 2009 (available in German language only)

[Schmidt et al. 2000]
Schmidt, Douglas C.; Rohnert, Hans; Stal, Michael; Buschmann, Frank, *Pattern-Oriented Software Architecture Vol. 2, Patterns for Concurrent and Networked Objects*, John Wiley & Sons, New York, 2000

[Siedersleben 2004]
Siedersleben, Johannes, *Moderne Software-Architektur – Umsichtig planen, robust bauen mit Quasar*, dpunkt.verlag, Heidelberg, 2004 (available in German language only)

[Fowler 2002]
Fowler, Martin, *Public vs. published Interfaces*, http://www.martinfowler.com/ieeeSoftware/published.pdf, 2002

[McCabe 1976]
McCabe, Thomas J, *A Complexity Measure*, IEEE Transactions on Software Engineering, 2(4), 308–320, 1976

[Bass et al. 2003]
Bass, Len; Clements, Paul; Kazman, Rick, *Software Architecture in Practice*, Second Edition, Addison-Wesley, New York, 2003

[Bredemeyer und Malan 2010]
Bredemeyer, Dana; Malan, Ruth, *Visual Architecting Action Guide Book*, http://www.ruthmalan.com/, 2010

[Evans 2004]
Evans, Eric, *Domain-Driven Design – Tackling Complexity in the Heart of Software*, Addison-Wesley, Boston, 2004

Further reading: Implementing the architecture

Further reading: Communicating the architecture

[IEEE 2007]
IEEE, *Recommended Practice for Architectural Description of Software-intensive Systems*, http://www.iso-architecture.org/ieee-1471/, 2007

[Opengroup 2001]
Opengroup, *Developing Architecture Views – Introduction*, http://www.opengroup.org/public/arch/p4/views/vus_intro.htm, 2001

Further reading:
Maintaining the
architecture

[Chikofsky und Cross 1990]
Chikofsky, Elliot J.; Cross, James H., *Reverse Engineering and Design Recovery: A Taxonomy*, IEEE Software, 7(1), 1990

[Lehmann and Belady 1985]
Lehman, M.M.; Belady, L.A., *Program Evolution – Processes of Software Change*, Academic Press, London, 1985

[Nosek and Palvia 1990]
Nosek, J.; Palvia, P., *Software Maintenance Management: Changes in the Last Decade*, Journal of Software Maintenance, 2(3), 157–174, 1990

Summarizing Figures

Figure: *Software architecture domain*

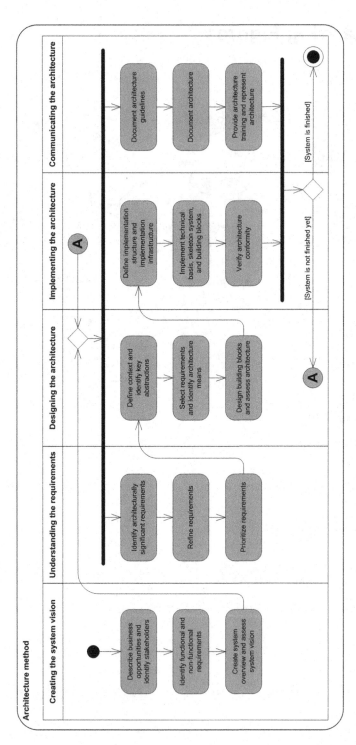

Figure: Architecture method—activities and actions

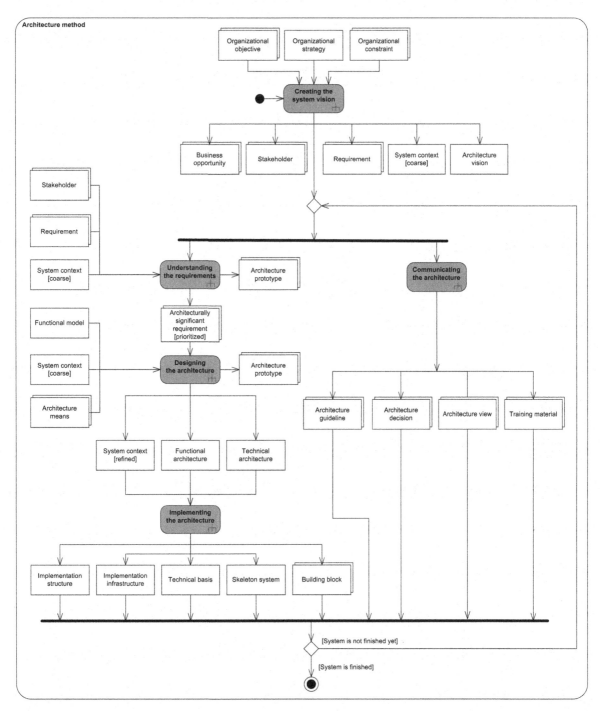

Figure: Architecture method—activities and work products

| Glossary

Term (synonym)	Explanation
.NET	.NET is a Microsoft component platform.
4+1 view model	The 4+1 view model is an architecture view model developed by Philippe Kruchten. It defines five architecture views frequently required in practice.
Abstract syntax	The abstract syntax describes the structure of a formal (modeling) language.
Abstraction	Abstraction means focusing on aspects of a concept that are relevant for a specific purpose and neglecting unimportant details for this particular purpose.
Adjourning stage	The adjourning stage is the fifth stage of group development according to Tuckman. After achieving the group objective, the adjourning stage reflects on the performance and experiences of the group. The group can also dissolve or set a new objective.
Agile method	An agile method is based on an iterative and incremental approach and strives to reduce unnecessary tasks to a minimum (e.g., the creation of superfluous documentation). Examples are XP, Scrum, and FDD.
Apollo team	An Apollo team is a homogeneous group consisting of highly intelligent, analytical people with high mental ability. It generally produces worse results in the achievement of objectives than heterogeneous teams.
Application building block	An application building block encapsulates application logic and makes it available in a controlled manner.
Application logic	Application logic is logic with a very close relationship to the application to be realized and which often cannot or cannot easily be reused in other contexts.
Application server	An application server is a software framework that provides basic services supporting the efficient development of a specific type of applications, as for example web applications (see Web application server).
Architectural awareness	Architectural awareness is a mindset that recognizes the importance of architecture. The quality of this awareness is relevant strategically and in the long term, since an architectural awareness is a basis for lifelong learning and thus for being a successful architect.
Architecturally relevant technology	A technology that has impacts on design and implementation of architecture and therefore belongs to the software architect's "toolbox."
Architecturally significant requirement	An architecturally significant requirement is a requirement with a high benefit for the stakeholders and/or a high implementation risk.
Architecture action (architecture step)	An architecture action is an action within an architecture activity.
Architecture activity	An architecture activity is an activity performed within an architecture method.

Term (synonym)	Explanation
Architecture decision	An architecture decision is a strategic decision about aspects of an architecture. For example, the decision to apply the architecture pattern MVC or the decision to mention the nonfunctional requirement portability is an architecture decision.
Architecture description language (ADL)	An architecture description language is a special DSL (see Domainspecific language) used to describe the architecture of systems precisely to simulate and validate the architecture via software tools.
Architecture dimension	An architecture dimension is a category of the architecture orientation framework. All architecture dimensions together help to systematically breakdown the overall domain "architecture." An architecture dimension thus covers one specific architectural aspect and has a question word assigned to it for clarity and better usability.
Architecture discipline	An architecture discipline deals with certain architectural aspects of a system and comprises corresponding architectural activities. There are different types of architecture disciplines. For example, as well as software architecture, data architecture and security architecture.
Architecture documentation	An architecture documentation covers all artefacts that describe an architecture. It is generally structured according to the following topics: architecture decisions, architecture views, crosscutting aspects, architecture assessment, project aspects, open points, and glossary.
Architecture domain	An architecture domain is a restricted area of knowledge or interest in which "architecture" is of fundamental importance. Typical architecture domains are software architecture, enterprise architecture, or system architecture.
Architecture Erosion	Architecture Erosion describes the fact that architectures erode over time due to changes which are applied in a blindfold manner without thinking about the architectural impact and overall consequences.
Architecture framework	An architecture framework is a collection of standards, specifications, guidelines, best practices, methods, reference models, and architecture view models. Architecture frameworks, such as the Zachman Framework, RMODP, or TOGAF address the enterprise architecture of an organization and are distinguished by their specific scope and design.
Architecture guideline	An architecture guideline is a guideline that should be considered during the design and implementation of an architecture. Guidelines ensure that architectures are correctly designed and implemented.
Architecture level	An architecture level encompasses architecturally significant elements at the same level of abstraction.
Architecture means	Architecture means are applied during the design and implementation of an architecture. The spectrum of possible architecture means ranges from elementary principles to concrete technologies. Architecture means comprise the toolbox of an architect.
Architecture method	An architecture method defines the method for designing and implementing an architecture.

Term (synonym)	Explanation
Architecture modeling means	Architecture modeling means are for documentation, specification, communication, analysis, and validation of architectures, to some extent also to support automatic code generation. The Unified Modeling Language (UML) is an example.
Architecture orientation framework	The architecture orientation framework is a framework in which knowledge and experience of architecture can be embedded. It is structured according to different architecture dimensions.
Architecture pattern (pattern)	An architecture pattern is a threepart rule that expresses the relationship between a certain context, a certain system of forces, and a specific building block configuration. The building block configuration enables the recurring forces arising in the context concerned to disperse.
Architecture pattern language	An architecture pattern language is a specific pattern language (see Pattern language) that offers a set of composable architecture patterns (see Architecture pattern).
Architecture principle	An architecture principle is a proven and tested principle that should be applied in the design and implementation of an architecture.
Architecture prototype	An architecture prototype is generally used to investigate risks. A ready-to-run implementation is created for specific problems, thus enabling a better understanding of the risks. Within the "understanding the requirements" activity, prototypes do not yet reflect the actual architecture. Instead, they are used to obtain a better understanding for the individual architecturally significant requirements and to check their feasibility (for example, to investigate new technologies). As part of the "designing the architecture" activity, prototypes refer to actual architecture and are used to assess architecture alternatives or aspects of an architecture.
Architecture style (style)	An architecture style is a special type of architecture pattern. In particular, styles express the structural organization of a family of systems.
Architecture tactic	An architecture tactic provides guidelines for implementing a quality attribute of the system under construction and its architecture. In principle therefore, an architecture tactic helps you to get a first idea about a design problem.
Architecture type case	The architecture type case is the metaphor used in this book on which the architecture orientation framework is based (see Architecture orientation framework).
Architecture viability prototype	An architecture viability prototype is an architecture prototype that brings together all relevant system building blocks (e.g., from the user interface right up to persistence) for successful interaction. It is developed to prove the viability of the architecture.
Architecture view	An architecture view represents a system from the viewpoint of a set of related concerns.
Architecture view model	An architecture view model defines architecture views and their content.

Term (synonym)	Explanation
Architecture vision	An architecture vision is a first, approximate decomposition of a system. It is usually not clearly defined, and becomes more concrete later during the design of the architecture. The presentation is usually informal.
Aspect orientation (AOP, AO)	Aspect orientation avoids crosscutting concerns being spread across the source code or the design. Instead, solutions are encapsulated in an aspect and thus separated from the system or system building block affected by the aspect.
Authentication	The process of verifying that someone (really) is who he claims he is. "Someone" may be a person, an IT system, a process, etc.
Authorization	Authorization supplements authentication by verifying that an identified user or IT system is entitled to perform a requested action (e.g. read, write, delete, execute) on a targeted resource (e.g., file, database record).
Availability	Availability is a runtime requirement expressed in the relationship of the downtimes to the productive times. The fewer the downtimes compared to the productive times, the higher the availability of the system.
Basic architecture	A basic architecture is a architecture mean that helps to structure entire systems. This mean applies various architecture means and is more conrete than other more generic means like principles or patterns.
Basic architecture concept	An important concept that architects use today to design and implement architectures.
Basic service building block	A basic service building block provides basic services (e.g., logging, management of reference data).
Behavioral science understanding	This understanding places the person at the center of the consideration by perceiving the person as a social being striving for recognition and appreciation rather than as a pure production factor.
Black box	Black box is a form of the information hiding principle. It states that the internal details of a system building block should not be visible for the clients.
Building block level	In macro-architecture, the building block level is the level of architecturally significant system building blocks. In contrast, in microarchitecture, the building block level contains architecturally insignificant system building blocks.
Business case	A business case is similar to a system vision. It generally highlights the economic benefits more clearly than a system vision. The term is sometimes used instead of system vision, but there is no great difference between the two terms.
Business opportunity	A business opportunity is a benefit for an organization that is to be achieved through the realization of the system. It is a significant part of a system vision. The business opportunities include the benefit of the system and the problems that the system solves. The benefit is made tangible both qualitatively and quantitatively—quantitatively in the form of business key figures.

Term (synonym)	Explanation
Centralization	Centralization designates the location of a concern in exactly one system building block. In most cases, there must be a trade-off between centralization and decentralization.
Change Request	A change request defines a change to an IT system or its specifications due to a defect or enhancement.
Checklist	A checklist consists of a list of detailed questions that can be used to assess the various aspects of an architecture. Checklists can be used for various assessment methods.
Circular dependencies, avoidance of	The avoidance of circular dependencies between the building blocks of a system is an important sub-principle of loose coupling. It states, that the graph which results from the dependencies between building blocks must be acyclic.
Client/Server architecture	The classic client/server model is based on a two-tier architecture that partitions tasks or workloads between the providers of a resource or service (servers), and service requesters (clients). A central question in the design of a client/server architecture is how to split up the functionality between the client and the server. This question is known as the decision between a rich client and a thin client.
Closed system	A closed system does not exchange information with its environment. It does, however, have an energetic relationship with its environment.
Cloud Computing	Cloud computing is a model for enabling convenient, on-demand network access to a shared pool of configurable computing resources (e.g., networks, servers, storage, applications, and services) that can be rapidly provisioned and released with minimal management effort or service provider interaction. Different cloud deployment types exist, i.e. private, public and hybrid clouds.
Command	A command is a special type of service offered via an interface. It changes the state of a building block.
Common Object Request Broker Architecture (CORBA)	The Common Object Request Broker Architecture is a standard specified by the Object Management Group (OMG). It defines interoperability between software components written in multiple computer languages and running on multiple computers.
Communicating the architecture	The objective of the architecture activity "communicating the architecture" is to convey the best possible understanding of the architecture and the architecture decisions to the individual stakeholders (e.g., project leads, developers, users, customers).
Communication middleware	A communication middleware is a central technology that connects many distributed systems (see Middleware). It is a platform that offers systems services for all aspects of the distribution, such as distributed calls, efficient access to the network, transactions, and much more.
Completer	Completers investigate content and are good at analyzing. However, they are not good at bringing in their own ideas and motivating other people.

Term (synonym)	Explanation
Component	A component (from the Latin *componere:* to compound) is a coarse-grained system building block with the following features: self-contained, used via defined interfaces (functional and technical), reusable in various contexts, has meta-information. A component consists of finer detailed building blocks (e.g., classes, interfaces) or other components and may be part of a component, a layer, or a subsystem.
Component orientation	Component orientation can be considered as the evolution of object orientation that looks at the development of the components of a system.
Component platform	A component platform is a runtime environment (container) for components. It is based on the separation of technical and functional concerns. The component platform takes over the technical concerns. Examples of technical concerns in the enterprise environment are distribution, security, persistence, transactions, concurrency, and resource management.
Concept	see Basic architecture concepts.
Conceptual view	The conceptual view describes functional aspects of a system without reference to technical details.
Concern	A concern is a matter that affects or touches one; a subject that excites one's interest, attention or care. A concern can also be a requirement, a question, a worry, an objective, or a wish.
Concrete syntax	The concrete syntax provides an instrument for the textual or graphical notation of models.
Consistency	The principle of consistency states that an architecture should follow a standard set of rules from beginning to end: naming convention, communication of the system building blocks, structure of the interfaces, structure of the documentation, etc.
Constraint	see Indirect non-functional requirement.
Convention over Configuration	The Convention over Configuration Principle states that standard assumptions are made and only necessary adjustments have to be configured.
Conway's law	Conway's law states that organizations that design systems are constrained to produce systems whose structures are copies of the communication structures of these organizations.
CORBA component model	The CORBA component model is a standard specified by the Object Management Group (OMG). It defines a component model and is based on the OMG's CORBA standard.
Creating the system vision	The creation of the system vision is the architecture activity that ensures that the system vision is feasible from an architecture perspective.
Crosscutting concern	A crosscutting concern is a technical aspect (e.g., logging) that is orthogonal to functional aspects. Crosscutting concerns are spread across functional building blocks.
Data architecture	Data architecture encompasses the data-oriented aspects of a system. The design of logical or physical data models, the selection of persistence mechanisms (e.g., database or file system), the configuration of a database, or the design of a data warehouse are possible activities of this discipline.

Term (synonym)	Explanation
Data flow architecture	A data flow architecture is a type of architecture that is particularly useful for splitting a complex task into a series of simple tasks and then map it as a combination of independent calls (e.g., pipes and filters).
Data transfer object (DTO)	A data transfer object is an object that minimizes the number of client/server interactions necessary. It is also intended to decouple clients from the concrete representation of entity objects.
Data view	A data view describes aspects of a system with regard to saving, manipulating, managing, and distributing data.
Database	A database is a system intended to organize, store, and retrieve large amounts of data easily.
Database as a Service (DaaS)	Database as a Service (DaaS) provides higher abstraction level access to persistence systems than StaaS usually does.
Dataflow architecture (Pipes and filters, Batch sequential)	A dataflow architecture structures an architecture along the dataflows. It is particularly useful if a complex task can be split into a series of simple tasks and then mapped as a combination of independent calls.
Decentralization	Decentralization is the term for the distribution of a concern to several system building blocks. In most cases, there must be a trade-off between centralization and decentralization.
Defect	A defect characterizes an error or fault in an IT system or its specifications.
Dependency Injection	Dependency Injection is an application of the Inversion of Control Principle. It transfers the responsibility for the creation and linking of building blocks to an externally configurable framework in order to reduce the coupling to the environment of the building block.
Dependency Inversion	Dependency Inversion is an application of the Hollywood Principle or loose coupling: one building block defines an interface with which it works and other building blocks realize the interface.
Deployment view (execution view)	The deployment view describes the physical deployment of system building blocks at runtime.
Design	Design encompasses the process for defining the architecture, building blocks, interfaces, and other properties of a system or a system building block. The design is also the result of this process. Depending on the level of detail of the system building blocks, the design differentiates between macro-architecture and micro-architecture.
Design for change	The principle of design for change states that architecture should be designed such that probable changes to a software system can be implemented easily.
Designing the architecture	The design of the architecture is the architecture activity in which the architecturally significant structures of a system are created. Here specific means are selected from a broad range of architecture means and decisions are taken.
Development process	A development process structures individual disciplines, activities, and tasks and puts them into chronological order.

Term (synonym)	Explanation
Development time requirement	A development time requirement is a quality or constraint that must be specifically considered during the development of a system.
Dialog building block	A dialog building block corresponds to the view building block within the model-view-controller architecture pattern.
Dialog control building block	A dialog control building block corresponds to the controller building block within the model-view-controller architecture pattern. It uses services from application building blocks.
Digital Identity	Digital identity is an IT system level representation of a person, a process, a service, or other resource. Digital identities are introduced so that a single person can be recognized as a singular entity across multiple IT systems.
Direct non-functional requirement (quality, quality attribute)	A direct non-functional requirement is also known as a quality or quality attribute since it reflects the qualitative nature of the functional requirements fulfilled by organizations, IT systems, or building blocks. For example, the desire of customers to receive an order within 24 hours is a non-functional requirement that an organization must satisfy.
Discipline	see Software development discipline.
Domain	A domain is a restricted area of knowledge or interest.
Domain building block	A domain building block encapsulates domain logic and makes it available in a controlled manner.
Domain logic	Domain logic represents functionality that can be reused across application boundaries. It is therefore application-independent and operates purely on domain-specific abstractions.
Domain-specific language (DSL)	A domain-specific language is a special modeling language. It can be used to describe the relevant concepts of a specific, technically motivated domain precisely.
Don't Repeat Yourself (DRY)	The Don't Repeat Yourself (DRY) Principle states that redundancy must be avoided whenever possible.
Dynamic language	A dynamic language is a language at a high level of abstraction that executes many tasks during runtime that other languages execute at compile time.
Emergence	Emergence states that a system has properties that differentiate it from its system building blocks. Accordingly, no one system building block holds these properties alone. They arise from the interaction of the individual system building blocks. Hence, a system is more than the sum of its parts.
Enhancement	An enhancement characterizes the need for additional functionality of an IT system or the need to enhance the IT system's quality attributes or specifications.
Enterprise architecture	Enterprise architecture is a discipline that designs an enterprise-wide IT architecture taking into account business strategies, business processes, and business data.
Entity object	An entity object is an abstraction that has its own identity within a domain. Typical examples are customer, order, and product.

Term (synonym)	Explanation
Evaluator	Evaluators are disciplined and hard-working people who approach problem solutions pragmatically. They cannot, however, adapt to changing situations and accept unverified ideas.
Execution environment	An execution environment is a software building block of a platform that provides services to software building blocks of a system. For example, a JEE application server offers execution environments for JEE components such as Java Servlets or Enterprise JavaBeans.
Explicit interface	An explicit interface is detached from the actual system building block. The concept of the explicit interface is implemented, for example, by technologies such as Enterprise JavaBeans or web services.
Extensibility	Extensibility is a development time requirement that states that it must be possible to extend a system with new functionality. The lower the coupling between system building blocks, the better the extensibility of the system.
eXtensible Markup Language (XML)	The eXtensible Markup Language is a standard defined by the World Wide Web Consortium (W3C) in order to define and represent structured data by means of textual documents. In addition to the core standard, there is a broad set of related standards, tools, complementary languages and typical utilization scenarios around the processing (e.g., editing, transforming etc.) of XML documents.
Extreme Programming (XP)	Extreme Programming is an agile software development method that focuses on the flexible and timely implementation of requirements and prioritizes working source code over documentation.
Facade	A facade is a building block that protects an entire subsystem against direct access from clients. It provides a common interface for the building blocks of a subsystem and this hides the subsystems building blocks from clients.
Feature Driven Development (FDD)	Feature Driven Development is an agile method that covers a collection of proven practices known across industry. It focuses on the timely implementation of the features required in short iterations.
Formal review	A formal review is performed by a group of stakeholders. They analyze the architecture documentation systematically, comment on it formally, and where necessary, decide on actions for rectifying deficiencies.
Forming stage	The forming stage is the first stage of group development according to Tuckman. The members of the group get to know each other and can assess each other. Individual group members can be classified at this stage. The group also distinguishes itself from its environment.
Forward engineering	Forward engineering covers primarily situations in which you develop a new system.
Function (query)	A function is a special type of service offered via an interface. It has no side-effects and is easier to test and carries less risk than a command. It is also known as an idempotent function.

Term (synonym)	Explanation
Functional architecture	A functional architecture defines functional building blocks of a system, which are required to satisfy functional requirements, on a technology-independent level.
Functional building block	A functional building block deals with the key abstractions of a domain and the associated functional requirements.
Functional building block requirement	A functional building block requirement is a functional property that a system building block must possess for the system to be able to fulfill its requirements.
Functional model	A functional model defines the concepts, their responsibilities and relationships of a functional domain. For example, the functional model for the domain customer defines all concepts related to a customer such as customer, customer address, customer relationships, customer preferences, etc.
Functional organizational requirement	A functional organizational requirement is a functional requirement placed on organizations by, for example, their customers, employees, business partners, or by authorities.
Functional requirement	A functional requirement defines required functionality.
Generative creation of a system building block	Generative creation of a system building block automates the recurring creation of building blocks using generators.
Generative programming	Generative programming is the generative creation of system building blocks. The objective of generative programming is to increase the level of automation in the creation of software.
Group	A group is a special form of an organization. It interacts with its environment, pursues a task, has a structure, and develops a culture.
High cohesion	Cohesion is a measurement of the semantic dependencies within a building block. The principle of high cohesion states that these dependencies should be as high as possible.
Holism	Holism considers a system in its entirety. It concentrates on the emergent system properties that arise from the interaction of the system building blocks.
Hollywood Principle	see Inversion of Control.
HOW dimension (architecture method)	The HOW dimension contains the most important architecture activities that an architect performs during his work.
Hygiene factory	Work dissatisfaction is influenced by hygiene factors, such as the relationship to managers and peers as well as politics. If these factors are perceived as positive, they can reduce work dissatisfaction, but do not increase work satisfaction
Identity and Access Management (IAM)	Identity Management (IdM) comprises all technical as well as organizational means which underpin the administration, attestation, and provisioning of identity-related user attributes. Access Management (AM) supplements entitlement-management as well as access control enforcement.
Implementation infrastructure	The implementation infrastructure encompasses architecture means (development environment, programming language, etc.) for the implementation of an architecture.

Term (synonym)	Explanation
Implementation structure	The implementation structure defines how the building blocks of the logical view of a system are mapped on the building blocks of the implementation layer.
Implementation view (development view)	The implementation view describes aspects of a system with regard to implementation, build, configuration, test, delivery, and maintenance.
Implementer	Implementers are conscientious people who complete tasks thoroughly and carefully. They sometimes tend to be perfectionists and can allow themselves to be disturbed by trivialities.
Implementing the architecture	Implementing the architecture is the architecture activity in which the architecture designed is implemented. On one hand the implementation infrastructure is established, and on the other, conformity with the architecture is governed.
Implicit interface	An implicit interface is a direct part of a system building block. A module written in the programming language C is an example of a system building block with an implicit interface.
Increment	An increment is a result that arises at the end of an iteration. It is usually a piece of software that is ready-to-run.
Incrementality	The incrementality principle states that a first architecture design, as well as changes to an existing architecture, should be implemented incrementally as far as possible.
Indirect non-functional requirement (constraint)	An indirect non-functional requirement has an effect on the way the required functionalities and qualities are realized. It represents specifications or facts that must be adhered to or taken into account.
Information as a Service (INFaaS)	Information as a Service (INFaaS) refers to the consumption of information, situated anywhere in the cloud, through a well-defined information interface.
Information hiding	The information hiding principle states that a client can access only those parts of an artefact (e.g., system building block) that are really necessary for the client's task. All remaining parts are hidden from the client.
Infrastructure as a Service (IaaS)	Infrastructure as a Service (i.e., IaaS) primarily relates to services of the type computing power, such as servers and server farms. Beyond this specific use, the term is also often used as an umbrella term to refer to the remaining set of service types in this list (i.e., STaaS and DaaS).
Integration architecture	Integration architecture is concerned with the planning and realization of integrative solutions. Its objective is connecting multiple systems of one or more enterprises.
Integration as a Service (INTaaS)	Integration as a Service (INTaaS) refers to cloud-based offers encapsulating complete integration stacks that support interfacing with applications, semantic mediation, and flow control functionality.
Integration building block	An integration building block encapsulates integration logic (e.g., database, SAP, LDAP) and makes it available.
Integration logic	Integration logic embodies logic for connecting enterprise systems. A simple example is logic for accessing databases.

Term (synonym)	Explanation
Interface	An interface defines a contract between the system building block that offers a functionality and the system building blocks that use the functionality. It also defines the operations offered by the system building block.
Interface Segregation Principle	The Interface Segregation Principle states that a client should never be based on an interface that it does not use. In particular, this also means that you should segregate complex interfaces that multiple client types are based on into multiple individual interfaces.
Intrusion protection	Intrusion protection is the set of all measures that guarantee operating integrity and vitality of IT systems, including an effective defense against threats such as denial-of-service (DoS) attacks.
Inversion of Control (Hollywood Principle)	The Inversion of Control Principle states, that the relationships of building blocks should follow the so-called Hollywood Principle: "don't call us, we'll call you". This means, that application (client) building blocks hand over the control flow to framework (server) building blocks which call back the client building blocks whenever it is necessary.
IT standard and guideline	An IT standard or guideline is a specification across an organization that IT systems being developed within an organization must satisfy.
IT system (system)	A system is a unit that consists of integrated software and hardware building blocks for the purpose of fulfilling a functional objective. To achieve this objective, it communicates with its environment and must take account of the constraints predetermined by the environment.
Iteration	An iteration is an individual development step within an iterative and incremental development process. All of the typical activities of software development, such as analysis, design, etc. are executed within an iteration.
Java Enterprise Edition (JEE)	JEE is an Oracle/SUN component platform.
Key abstraction	A key abstraction represents a significant abstraction of a functional domain that the system under construction must handle. Examples are abstractions of objects, concepts, locations, or persons.
Language support for abstractions	The principle of language support for abstractions states that architectural abstractions, such as components or interfaces, should have language support in both the design language and the programming language.
Law of Demeter	The Law of Demeter states that a system building block should only use closely related building blocks.
Layered architecture	A layered architecture structures a system into layers logically.
Layers	Layers is an architecture pattern that structures the software building blocks of a system logically using layers. Software building blocks of a layer are cohesive and can access software building blocks of a directly subsequent lower layer. Layers are used to develop the logical view.

Term (synonym)	Explanation
Liskov Substitution Principle	The Liskov Substitution Principle states that subtypes must behave exactly as their corresponding basetype. In this way a basetype can be replaced by one of its subtypes without affecting depend clients.
Loose coupling	Loose coupling is a measurement for the degree of coupling of building blocks. The principle of loose coupling states that the coupling between building blocks should be as weak as possible.
Maintainability	Maintainability is a development time requirement that states that errors in a system can be corrected with appropriate efforts. The easier it is to correct an error, the more maintainable the system.
Maintaining the architecture	The maintenance of the architecture is the architecture activity in which the architecture is evolved during the maintenance phase of the system lifecycle. Defects are fixed and enhancements are added.
Maintenance	Maintenance of software systems deals with changes to the system after it has been delivered. This covers, for example, the correction of errors, the improvement of quality attributes such as performance, and the evolution or further development of the system.
Message-oriented middleware	Message-oriented middleware is a widespread type of middleware system (see Communication middleware) that uses asynchronous messages as a central communication means.
Metamodel	A metamodel defines the abstract syntax (that is, model elements and their relationships) of the set of all models conforming to this metamodel. In a broader sense, it may also define the semantics and the concrete syntax (representation), e.g., textual or graphical notation. Models are also known as instances of the related metamodel.
Meta-object facility	The *meta-object facility* (MOF) is the basis of the OMG modeling architecture. The MOF specification defines an abstract syntax and a framework for the construction and handling of technology-independent metamodels, referred to as MOF-based metamodels.
Meta-object protocol	A meta-object protocol (MOP) is a comfortable programming interface that enables a program to access itself.
Metaprogramming	The idea of metaprogramming is to overcome the classical separation of programs and their data. In metaprogramming, programs are considered to be data themselves. Thus, programs can manipulate or at least reflect themselves. The goal is to achieve a higher level of flexibility and control in software systems by means of an additional abstraction layer.
Method	In this book, a method represents the aggregation of method content and development process.
Method content (content)	Method content is a defined procedure instruction for executing a specific software development task or activity.
Micro-architecture	A micro-architecture details a software architecture in which non-fundamental system building blocks and their structure are defined.

Term (synonym)	Explanation
Middleware	Middleware comprises distribution aspects of the architecture of a software system. It offers applications services for all aspects of the distribution, such as distributed calls, efficient access to the network, transactions, and much more.
Model	A models is an abstraction of the original. It doesn't consider all details, only those that are useful to the stakeholder of the model for his or her purposes.
Model-driven software development (MDSD, MDD, MDE)	Model-driven software development does not use models solely for documentation purposes. It treats them as central artefacts of a ready-to-run system. It is a generic term for technologies that create ready-to-run software from models automatically.
Modeling language	Modeling languages are used to specify systems. A modeling language is the aggregation of concrete syntax, abstract syntax, and static and dynamic semantics. The abstract syntax is also known as the metamodel. The terms "well-formedness criteria" and "constraints" are also used as synonyms for static semantics.
Moderator	Moderators are self-confident people with few prejudices and a calm nature. They can integrate other people into the team activity easily and have a strong perception. However, they do not have the usual level of creativity.
Modularity	The modularity principle states that systems should consist of well-defined system building blocks with clearly distinguishable functional responsibilities.
Motivator	Motivators are, for example, work itself, responsibility, and recognition. These increase work satisfaction, but do not reduce work dissatisfaction.
Network architecture	Network architecture is concerned with the network infrastructure of systems. The main tasks of this discipline are the planning and design of the functions, services, building blocks, and protocols of a network.
New Generation Operations Systems and Software (NGOSS) initiative	The New Generation Operations Systems and Software (NGOSS) initiative from TeleManagement Forum defines a comprehensive reference architecture tailored to the telecommunications industry.
Node	A node is a system resource, such as a physical processing unit, an execution environment, or an application server.
Non-functional building block requirement	A non-functional building block requirement expresses the standard of quality that the environment demands in the fulfillment of the functional building block requirements.
Non-functional organizational requirement	A non-functional organizational requirement expresses the standard of quality that the environment demands in the fulfillment of the functional organizational requirements. Delivery within 24 hours or a two year guarantee time are examples of non-functional organizational requirements.
Non-functional requirement	A non-functional requirement reflects an expectation and necessity that stakeholders consider important in addition to the functional requirements. A non-functional requirement always describes a quality aspect demanded (e.g., performance, extensibility) in the implementation of functional requirements.

Term (synonym)	Explanation
Non-functional system require-ment	A non-functional system requirement expresses the standard of quality that the environment demands in the fulfillment of the functional system requirements. Typical non-functional system requirements are performance, availability, extensibility, and plat-form independence.
Non-repudiation	Non-repudiation is the ability to prove security-related events beyond doubt, i.e., in a court of law if necessary.
Norming stage	The norming stage is the third stage of group development ac-cording to Tuckman. The members of the group identify them-selves with the roles worked out and agree on rules for working together.
n-tier architecture	A n-tier architecture is used to structure a system logically in n tiers, where the variable n represents the number of tiers. Two-tier and three-tier architectures are examples of n-tier architecture frequently encountered.
Object orientation	Object orientation is based on the core idea of encapsulating data and the related functionality. This means that object orientation is a further development of the procedural (structured) concept. Today, object orientation is a prevalent architecture concept.
Object-oriented remote procedure call (OORPC) system	An OORPC system is a widespread type of middleware system (see Communication middleware) based on object-oriented, dis-tributed RPC calls.
Object-relational mapping (ORM)	Object-relational mapping enables the integration of an object-ori-ented application with the relational paradigm. ORM also provides an object-oriented database access layer to relational databases for object-oriented application logic. Object-relational mappers, such as Hibernate, are an important technology in this area.
Open system	An open system is in touch with and exchanges information with its environment. The system has to interact with its environment to be able to exist.
Open/closed prin-ciple	The open/closed principle states that system building blocks should be open for changes but closed for the use of their internal details by other system building blocks.
Organization	An organization is a social entity that permanently follows an objective and has a formal structure that enables the activities of the member to be focused on the objective followed.
Organizational constraint	An organizational constraint is a specification, such as budget and time-to-market. Another example is the restrictions that the knowledge and experience within the team place on the design of the architecture.
Organizational culture (culture)	An organizational culture defines the norms and thus the free-dom for the design of the architecture. It can be expressed in the specification of very clear standards and guidelines. The culture of an organization also defines how people within the organization deal with one another and what expectations the organization has of them.
Organizational level	The organizational level encompasses architecturally significant elements at the abstraction level of organizations.

Term (synonym)	Explanation
Pattern	See Architecture pattern.
Pattern language	A pattern language is a collection of semantically related patterns that offer solution principles for problems in a specific context.
Peer-to-peer architecture	A peer-to-peer architecture is a basic architecture that uses a series of equal peers for (distributed) communication.
Performance	Performance is a runtime requirement and describes the capability of a system to react to external events in a certain timeframe.
Performing stage	The performing stage is the fourth stage of group development according to Tuckman. The team spirit that has developed results in goal-oriented, collaborative cooperation. At this point, the group has established itself and achieved its potential.
Phase	A Phase is a certain time segment in a development process, in which certain development activities are carried out. For example, during the construction phase of the Unified Software Development Process (USDP) the IT system is being implemented and tested.
Piecemeal growth	The idea of the principle of piecemeal growth is to let an architecture grow step-by-step. After every step there is an assessment that entails a decision about what to do next. This means that there is little or no planning in advance.
Plant	Plants are people who take unconventional approaches and can contribute to solutions based on their knowledge and powers of imagination. However, they also tend to overlook regulations and have their head in the clouds.
Platform	A platform is a system that can consist of software and, if applicable, hardware building blocks. It executes software building blocks of a system.
Platform architecture	A platform architecture defines the platform building blocks and their structure.
Platform as a Service (PaaS)	Platform as a Service (PaaS) offers readily integrated and coherently set-up application and development platforms. Examples of PaaS offerings are pre-fabricated JEE or .Net environments.
Platform independence (portability)	Platform independence is a development time requirement and requires that a system can be operated on different platforms or can be ported to different platforms.
Polymorphism	Polymorphism is the ability of objects belonging to different classes but to the same type to respond to method, field, or property calls of the same name, each one according to an appropriate type-specific behavior. Polymorphism enables "connector compatibility" based on interfaces. How the connector is realized is irrelevant for the clients.
Presentation	A presentation can be used as an informal means of review. In a presentation, aspects of an architecture are presented to stakeholders informally. Stakeholders can give immediate feedback to the aspects presented.
Presentation logic	Presentation logic is the logic used for communication with the user.
Principle	see Architecture principle.

Term (synonym)	Explanation
Procedural approach	A Procedural approach is a classic approach for structuring architectures using procedures, which are also called sub-program, function, routine, or operation.
Process view	The process view describes concurrency aspects of the system building blocks.
Product line architecture	A product line architecture is a special form of reference architecture that defines the common architecture of multiple similar software products.
Prototyping	The prototyping principle states that you should develop simple prototypes first before developing a product in order to get to know the problem better.
Publish/subscribe architecture	A publish/subscribe architecture is a basic architecture in which calls are not sent to the communication participants directly but are forwarded by an intermediary. In a publish/subscribe architecture, communication is typically via asynchronous events.
Quality	see Direct non-functional requirement.
Quality attribute	see Direct non-functional requirement.
Quality attribute scenario	A quality attribute scenario makes non-functional requirements understandable by describing them according to a specific scheme. Specifically, the focus is on measurability. Quality attribute scenarios can be divided into scenario types. Examples are: availability scenarios, changeability scenarios, performance scenarios etc.
Reductionism (decomposition)	Reductionism investigates system building blocks separately. This view enables concrete statements to be made about the behavior and function of individual system building blocks.
Reengineering	Reengineering is an important part of software maintenance and is concerned with reverse engineering, restructuring, software evolution, and wrapping.
Reengineering tool	A reengineering tool is a piece of software used to perform reengineering activities.
Reference architecture	A reference architecture combines general architecture knowledge and general experience with specific requirements for a coherent architectural solution for a specific problem domain.
Reference model	A reference model contains the specific characteristics of the problem domain addressed (in the context of a reference architecture).
Reference Model for Open Distributed Processing (RM-ODP)	RM-ODP is an ISO standard architecture framework for open, distributed systems. In addition to an architecture view model, it includes an object model and a collection of function definitions.
Reference to use cases	The reference to use cases principle states that an architecture should not be created randomly; rather, its design should be based on the relevant use cases. This ensures that an architecture does not exceed the aim of the desired system.
Reflection	Reflection enables access to meta-information (e.g., type, features) of a building block.

Term (synonym)	Explanation
Remote procedure call (RPC) system	An RPC system is a widespread type of middleware system (see Communication middleware) that uses distributed procedure calls as a central abstraction.
Repository	A repository is a data storage unit. Its main task is to enable different building blocks to access data simultaneously.
Requirement	A requirement is a system capability that the user needs to solve a problem or achieve an objective. Alternatively, a requirement is a capability that the system must possess in order to fulfill a contract, standard, specification, or other formal document.
Requirement pattern	A requirement pattern is a methodological tool that enables the systematic development of requirements.
Requirements catalog	A requirements catalog contains the set of requirements placed on a system. A catalog must be complete and consistent.
Requirements view	The requirements view describes the requirements a system has to fulfill and their context (business opportunities, problem description Stakeholders and business processes).
Resource investigator	Resource investigators seek out challenges and are extroverted and communicative. Their strengths lie in building up personal contacts and researching new topics. In contrast, they tend to lose interest in a topic when it becomes routine.
Restructuring	Restructuring covers all activities for changing the structure of a system.
Reusability	Reusability is a development requirement that states that system building blocks should be designed and implemented such that they can be used or reused in other contexts.
Reverse engineering	Reverse engineering covers activities for regaining lost information about existing software systems.
Runtime requirement	A runtime requirement contains expectations with regard to the behavior of a system at runtime.
Scalability	Scalability is a development time requirement that states that a system must be able to cope with increasing loads. There is a general differentiation between vertical and horizontal scalability. In the case of vertical scalability, for example, a server is replaced with a more powerful server. With horizontal scalability, the load is distributed across several servers.
Scenario-based method	A scenario-based method is a method of assessment that addresses the problem of the scope for interpretation with regard to non-functional requirements. It works out concrete scenarios that make a non-functional requirement more specific. The architecture is assessed based on the scenarios.
Scientific management understanding (Taylorism)	The scientific management understanding has its roots in early industrialization. It is based on the principle of the perfect division of labor. The person as an individual is perceived as a production factor.
Scripting language	In the original sense, a scripting language is a programming language intended to control the software systems. Today, however, scripting languages are used for all other possible purposes (e.g., dynamic websites) as languages at a higher abstraction level.

Term (synonym)	Explanation
Scrum	Scrum is an agile method that encompasses a collection of meetings, artefacts, roles, values, and basic convictions. Here, the work is organized and the means and methods selected to a great extent independently by the project members.
Security	Security is a non-functional requirement with a pervasive nature. It covers confidentiality, authentication, integrity, privacy, non-repudiation, and intrusion protection.
Security architecture	As a discipline, security architecture focuses on guaranteeing security aspects such as identity and authorization checks and the verifiability and non-repudiation of security-relevant operations. As a basic architecture, security architecture refers to an application that is to be protected and an underlying security infrastructure.
Security Infrastructure	Security Infrastructure is an umbrella term which spans all security-related components underpinning the planning, designing, development, as well as operation of IT systems. Samples of security infrastructure are firewalls, intrusion protection systems, as well as IT systems, which offer the authentication of users.
Self-documentation	The self-documentation principle states that the architect or developer of a system building block should try to make every item of information about the system building block part of the system building block itself.
Semantic	Semantic is the study of meaning. It typically focuses on the relation between signifiers (e.g., words) of a language and what they stand for. In addition to the abstract and concrete syntax, as well as the static semantics, every language must also have semantics that precisely define the meaning of the model.
Separation of concerns principle	The separation of concerns principle states that different aspects of a problem (e.g., logging and exceptions) must be separated and each individual problem part treated separately.
Separation of interface and implementation	The separation of interface and implementation principle states that interfaces should be described separately from the implementations so that the client can rely on the interface without knowing any implementation details.
Service (platform service)	A service is a software building block that provides basic functionality that is usually independent of any business functionality realized by the system. In other words, a service provides functionality for satisfying non-functional requirements. A service can also be functionality provided via the interface of a building block.
Service-oriented architecture (SOA)	A service-oriented architecture is a basic architecture that represents software building blocks as reusable, distributed, and loosely coupled services that provide standardized access.
Shaper	Shapers have a dynamic personality with a strong will and are capable of pushing through decisions. They are, however, excitable and have a tendency to provoke.
Shared repository architecture	A shared repository architecture stipulates a system building block that serves as a central data storage unit.

Term (synonym)	Explanation
Simulation	A simulation provides answers to specific questions, such as the behavior of the system under load, without the need to implement the system itself.
Single Sign-On (SSO)	SSO is an attribute of authentication and authorization towards multiple independent IT systems. SSO allows users to log into the SSO system once and gain access to all connected IT systems, transparently (i.e. without being prompted to log in again).
Skeleton system	The structure of a skeleton system already corresponds to the architecture of the final system. However, the individual building blocks do not yet provide a complete implementation of the functionality. They only provide the functionality required to reflect a clearly delineated use case. A skeleton system is evolved into the complete system by adding functionality (use cases) incrementally.
Software architecture (application architecture, macro-architecture, high-level design)	Software architecture$_{total}$ = Software architecture$_{structure}$ + Software architecture$_{discipline}$ Software architecture$_{structure}$: The software architecture of a system is the structure or structures of the system, which comprise software building blocks, the externally visible properties of those building blocks, and the relationship among them and with their environment. Software architecture$_{discipline}$: As a discipline, software architecture covers the architecture activities and the related decisions about the design and implementation of a software architecture.
Software as a Service (SaaS)	Software as a Service (SaaS) is a very broad category of services whose only common feature is that the actual software is delivered via the web and usually accessed through a web browser by an end user. Examples of software offerings that already exist in the cloud are e-mail, calendar, document sharing, or web conferencing. Other examples in the area of business domain-specific software are customer relationship management (CRM) or enterprise resource planning (ERP) types of applications.
Software development discipline	A software development discipline is a set of related activities producing a set of deliverables required by the subsequent discipline. Examples of software development disciplines are business modeling, requirements gathering and analysis.
Software evolution	Software evolution is the implementation of changes to the software system.
Software reengineering	Software reengineering is concerned with the following important tasks: reverse engineering, restructuring, software evolution, and wrapping.
Spiral model	The spiral model is a refinement of the waterfall model that tries to resolve the weaknesses of the latter. Instead of running through the specified disciplines sequentially just once, a software development plan is subdivided into several cycles.
Stakeholder	A stakeholder is a natural or legal person or organization with a concern in a system to be realized. The stakeholders include the immediate users of a system, as well as clients, the state, operators, or departments affected, etc.

Term (synonym)	Explanation
Static semantic	The static semantic define the well-formedness criteria of a language that its syntax cannot define.
Storage as a Service (STaaS)	Storage as a Service (STaaS) offers storage and disk systems on demand.
Storming stage	The storming stage is the second stage of group development according to Tuckman. For each member of the group, this stage decides whether they want to remain in the group.
Strategic decision	A strategic decision is long-term in nature and has a more comprehensive effect.
Structural break	A structural break is an important architectural problem that designates the break between two paradigms. For example, there is a structural break between the object-oriented paradigm of programming languages and the relational paradigm of databases.
Style	see Architecture style.
Subsystem	A subsystem encapsulates coherent functionality and is self-contained. It therefore provides related functionality that satisfies some of the requirements placed on the system.
Superfluous complexity, avoidance of	The avoidance of superfluous complexity is a principle that proclaims to keep architectures as easy as possible because unnecessarily complex architectures are prone to error and are not sufficiently understood.
System architecture	System architecture$_{total}$ = System architecture$_{structure}$ + System architecture$_{discipline}$ System architecture$_{structure}$: The system architecture of a system is the structure or structures of the system, which comprise building blocks (software and hardware building blocks), the externally visible properties of those building blocks, and the relationship among them and with their environment. System architecture$_{discipline}$: As a discipline, system architecture covers the architecture activities and the related decisions about the design and implementation of a system architecture.
System Boundary	A system boundary separates a system from its environment. It allows to draw the line between what belongs to the system and what does not.
System building block (building block)	A system building block represents the abstract type of all concrete building blocks of a system. It can require other system building blocks and can have one or more interfaces or require one or more interfaces of other system building blocks.
System context	A system context encompasses a graphical representation of the system and its environment, including its human actors and surrounding systems. It also documents the interfaces between the system and its human actors and surrounding systems.
System level	The system level encompasses architecturally significant elements at the abstraction level of IT systems.
System management architecture	System management architecture primarily contains the operational aspects of systems. Within this discipline, the tasks of an architect are the design of operating strategies of centralized and decentralized system landscapes and the definition of service level agreements.

Term (synonym)	Explanation
System overview	A system overview consists of a system context and an architecture vision.
System vision	A system vision evaluates the business usefulness of a system, names the stakeholders, defines the essential requirements, and contains a first system overview.
Systemic understanding	The systemic understanding considers the organization as a system with an objective and system limits, and which interacts with its environment.
Tactic	see Architecture tactic.
Team worker	Based on their social nature, team workers have the ability to approach people and cultivate team spirit. In crisis situations they tend to be indecisive.
Technical architecture	A technical architecture is dedicated primarily to the realization of non-functional requirements and defines technical building blocks.
Technical basis	A technical basis includes the basic technical services required and the implementation of the framework used to realize the functional building blocks.
Technical building block	A technical building block encapsulates functionality for non-functional aspects, such as logging, auditing, security, reference data, persistence, and transaction management. It uses services from the platform and abstracts them such that they can be used in a platform-independent way by functional building blocks.
Technology	see Architecturally Relevant Technology.
The Open Group Architecture Framework (TOGAF)	The Open Group Architecture Framework (TOGAF) is a comprehensive and widely used architecture framework for developing enterprise architectures. TOGAF comprises a method (Architecture Development Method (ADM)), a framework for defining the structural content of architecture (Architecture Content Framework (ACF)), as well as tools, reference models, and taxonomies. Numerous best practices, principles, guidelines, and technologies also play a part.
Three-tier architecture	A three-tier architecture expands a two-tier architecture by introducing an intermediate tier between the client and the database server or Enterprise Information System.
Traceability	The principle of traceability states that it should be possible to find the actual architectural structures, as they are implemented in the code or other artifacts.
Transaction processing monitor (TP monitor)	A transaction processing monitor (TP monitor) is one of the oldest forms of middleware. It provides an infrastructure for developing, running, and controlling distributed transactions. Historically, a TP monitor is a widespread form of middleware system (see Communication middleware).
Two-tier architecture	A two-tier architecture consists of two tiers. The classic client/server model, for example, is based on a two-tier architecture.
UML infrastructure	The UML infrastructure specifies the Core package which is the language core of UML.

Term (synonym)	Explanation
UML superstructure	The UML superstructure is based on the Core package of the UML infrastructure. It makes up the UML language definition generally referred to as UML metamodel. The UML superstructure specifies the abstract syntax of UML.
Understanding the requirements	Understanding the requirements is an architecture activity that deals with the identification, prioritization, and refinement of architecturally significant requirements. The conscious examination of non-functional requirements in particular is of great importance, since these are often either weakly formulated or not formulated at all.
Unified Method Architecture (UMA)	The Unified Method Architecture is a special DSL used to specify methods.
Unified Modeling Language (UML)	The Unified Modeling Language is a generic modeling language specified by the Object Management Group (OMG). Its specification is divided into several parts. The UML infrastructure forms the core of the Meta-Object Facility (MOF) and the UML superstructure. The UML superstructure specifies the UML metamodel. UML diagrams are an option for the notation of UML models.
Unified Software Development Process (USDP)	The Unified Software Development Process is an iterative and incremental method that comprehensively defines artefacts, activities, and roles.
Usability	The usability of a system is a measure of the extent to which the user experiences the operation of the system as efficient, ergonomic, and satisfactory.
Use case	A use case is a description of a series of interaction between an actor and the IT system under design. Use cases are usually described according to a predefined description template. They can be described textually and graphically.
Value object	A value object is defined solely by its attributes. It does not have its own identity and is immutable. For example, an amount of money can be represented by a value object of the type money.
View	see Architecture view.
Viewpoint	A viewpoint is the system-independent specification of a specific architecture view.
V-Modell	The V-Modell is a method developed in Germany for projects for public authorities. Its name comes from the V-shaped presentation of the activities.
V-Modell XT	The V-Modell XT is a further development of the V-Modell that permits the adjustment of the method to concrete project demands.
Walkthrough	A walkthrough is based on architecturally significant scenarios. In walkthroughs, these scenarios are played out to determine whether and how an architecture fulfills them. Affected stakeholders take part in walkthroughs.
Waterfall model	The waterfall model is a method that allows for the sequential and one-time processing of different software development disciplines. For example, it runs through the disciplines requirement gathering, analysis, design, and implementation one after the other.

Term (synonym)	Explanation
Web application server	A web application server is a server for web applications that creates dynamic HTML pages and executes the application logic between the client (browser) and downstream systems, such as a database.
Web service	A web service is a technology that implements both the middleware and the SOA basic architecture and focuses heavily on XML and Internet standards.
WHAT dimension (architectures and architecture disciplines)	The WHAT dimension contains architecture basics and definitions. It therefore lays the basis for working as an architect.
WHERE dimension (architecture perspectives)	The WHERE dimension is an architecture dimension that covers the different levels at which architecture takes place and the views with which architecture can be considered.
WHO dimension (organizations and individuals)	The WHO dimension is an architecture dimension that deals with the role of the architect and the influence of individuals and organizations on architecture.
WHY dimension (architecture requirements)	The WHY dimension is dedicated to the requirements placed on IT systems in general and architectures in particular.
WITH WHAT dimension (architecture means)	The WITH WHAT dimension structures the different architecture means an architect can use in his activities.
Wrapping	Wrapping gives a given system or a building block a new interface but does not change the system itself. It is frequently used for version adjustments or other slight interface changes to software building blocks.
XML	see eXtensible Markup Language.
Zachman Framework	The Zachman Framework is a domain-independent and technology-independent architecture framework, originally developed at IBM, that focuses on enterprise architecture. It provides a powerful architecture view model that, in addition to views, defines view aspects and roles that are orthogonal to the views for each view.

List of Abbreviations

Abbreviation	Meaning
2PC	Two-Phase Commit Protocol
3GL	3rd Generation Language
ABLE	Architecture Based Languages and Environment
ACF	Architecture Content Framework
ACID	Atomicity, Consistency, Isolation, Durability
AC-MDSD	Architecture Centric MDSD
ACME	Architectural Description of Component-based Systems
ACS	Ars Digita Community System
ADL	Architecture Description Language
ADM	Architecture Development Method
ADML	Architecture Description Markup Language
Ajax	Asynchronous JavaScript and XML
AM	Access Management
ANSI	American National Standards Institute
AOP	Aspect Oriented Programming
API	Application Programming Interface
ASCET	Advanced Simulation and Control Engineering Tool
ASP	Active Server Pages
ASP	Application Service Provider
AST	Abstract Syntax Tree
ATAM	Architecture Tradeoff Analysis Method
B2B	Business to Business
B2BAI	Business to Business Application Integration
BAM	Business Activity Monitoring
BC	Before Christ
BPEL	Business Process Execution Language
BPEL4WS	Business Process Execution Language for Web Services
BPM	Business Process Management
BPM	Business Process Modeling
BSS	Business Support Systems
CAPEX	Capital Expenditure
CASE	Computer-Aided Software Engineering
CCM	Corba Component Model
CCM	Configuration &Change-Management
CCMS	Configuration & Change-Management-System
CGI	Common Gateway Interface
CICS	Customer and Controller Systems

Abbreviation	Meaning
CIO	Chief Information Officer
CLOS	Common Lisp Object System
CLR	Common Language Runtime
CMS	Content Management System
CMU	Carnegie Mellon University
COBOL	Common Business Oriented Language
COM	Component Object Model
CORBA	Common Object Request Broker Architecture
COTS	Commercial off-the-shelf
CRM	Customer Relationship Management
CRUD	Create, Read, Update, Delete
CTO	Chief Technology Officer or Chief Technical Officer
CVS	Concurrent Versions System
CWM	Common Warehouse Metamodel
DaaS	Database as a Service
DCE	Distributed Computing Environment
DCOM	Distributed Component Object Model
DLL	Dynamic Link Library
DOM	Document Object Model
DoS	Denial-of-Service
DRY	Don't Repeat Yourself
DSL	Domain Specific Language
DTD	Document Type Definition
DTO	Data Transfer Object
DVD	Dissociated Vertical Deviation
EAI	Enterprise Application Integration
EAST	Electronics Architecture and Software Technology
EDA	Event Driven Architecture
EDI	Electronic Data Interchange
EDOC	Enterprise Distributed Object Computing
EJB	Enterprise Java Beans
EMF	Eclipse Modeling Framework
EPF	Eclipse Process Framework
ERP	Enterprise Resource Planning
ESB	Enterprise Service Bus
ETL	Extract Transform and Load
eTOM	Enhanced Telecom Operations Map
FDD	Feature Driven Development
FOP	Formatting Objects Processor
FTP	File Transfer Protocol

Abbreviation	Meaning
GoF	Gang of Four
GPL	General Purpose Language
HTML	Hyper Text Markup Language
HTTP	Hyper Text Transfer Protocol
IaaS	Infrastructure as a Service
IAM	Identity and Access Management
IBM	International Business Machines
IDL	Interface Description Language
IEC	International Electrotechnical Commission
IEEE	Institute of Electrical and Electronics Engineers
IIOP	Internet Inter ORB Protocol
IMS	Incident Management System
INFaaS	Information as a Service
INTaaS	Integration as a Service
IoC	Inversion of Control
ISO	International Organization for Standardization
ISP	Internet Service Provider
IT	Information Technology
ITU	International Telecommunication Union
J2EE	Java 2 Enterprise Edition
JAAS	Java Authentication and Authorization Service
JCA	Java Connector Architecture
JDBC	Java Database Connectivity
JDO	Java Data Objects
JEE	Java Enterprise Edition
JET	Java Emitter Template
JMS	Java Messaging Service
JPA	Java Persistence API
JSF	Java Server Faces
JSP	Java Server Pages
JVM	Java Virtual Machine
LAN	Local Area Network
LDAP	Lightweight Directory Access Protocol
MDA	Model Driven Architecture
MDD	Model Driven Development
MDE	Model Driven Engineering
MDSD	Model Driven Software Development
MIS	Management Information System
MOF	Meta Object Facility
MOM	Message Oriented Middleware

Abbreviation	Meaning
MOP	Meta Object Protocol
MQ	Message Queue
MS	Microsoft
MVC	Model View Controller
NGOSS	Next Generation Operations Support Systems
NIST	National Institute of Standards and Technology
NTLM	NT Lan Manager
OASIS	Organization for the Advancement of Structured Information Standards
OCL	Object Constraint Language
OCM	Open Cloud Manifesto
OMA	Object Management Architecture
OMG	Object Management Group
OMT	Object Modeling Technique
OOA	Object Oriented Analysis
OOD	Object Oriented Design
OODBMS	Object Oriented Database Management System
OOP	Object Oriented Programming
OO-RPC	Object Oriented Remote Procedure Call
OOSA	Object Oriented System Analysis
OOSE	Object Oriented Software Engineering
OPEX	Operational Expenditure
ORB	Object Request Broker
ORM	Object Relational Mapping
OS	Operating System
OSF	Open Software Foundation
OSI	Open Systems Interconnection
OSS	Operations Support System
OSS/J	OSS for Java Initiative
P2P	Peer-to-Peer
PaaS	Platform as a Service
PBM	Policy Based Management
PC	Personal Computer
PDF	Portable Document Format
PHP	PHP Hypertext Preprocessor
PIM	Platform Independent Model
PKI	Public Key Infrastructure
PL	Product Line
PLE	Product Line Engineering
POC	Proof of Concept

Abbreviation	Meaning
POSA	Pattern Oriented Software Architecture
PSM	Platform Specific Model
PSM	Protocol State Machine
PSP	Project Structure Plan
QoS	Quality of Service
QVT	Query, Views, Transformation
QWAN	Quality without a Name
RAM	Random Access Memory
RDBMS	Relational Database Management System
RDF	Resource Description Framework
REST	Representational State Transfer
RMC	Rational Method Composer
RMI	Remote Method Invocation
RM-ODP	Reference Model for Open Distributed Processing
ROI	Return on Investment
RPC	Remote Procedure Call
RSS	Really Simple Syndication
RUP	Rational Unified Process
SA/D	Structured Analysis/Design
SAAM	Software Architecture Analysis Method
SaaS	Software as a Service
SADL	Structural Architecture Description Language
SAP	Systeme, Anwendungen und Produkte
SAX	Simple API for XML
SCM	Supply Chain Management
SCM	Software Configuration Management
SDLM	Software Design Level Model
SEI	Software Engineering Institute
SETI	Search for Extra-Terrestrial Intelligence
SID	Shared Information and Data Model
SLA	Service Level Agreement
SMTP	Simple Mail Transport Protocol
SOA	Service Oriented Architecture
SOAP	Simple Object Access Protocol
SOI	Service Oriented Infrastructure
SPEM	Software Process Engineering Metamodel
SPI	Service Provider Interface
SQL	Structured Query Language
SSF	Software System Family
SSO	Single Sign On

Abbreviation	Meaning
STaaS	Storage as a Service
TAFIM	Technical Architecture Framework for Information Management
Tcl	Tool Command Language
TCP/IP	Transmission Control Protocol/Internet Protocol
TMF	Tele Management Forum
TOGAF	The Open Group Architecture Framework
TP	Transaction Processing
TT	Trouble Ticket
UDDI	Universal Description, Discovery and Integration
UMA	Unified Method Architecture
UML	Unified Modeling Language
UP	Unified Process
URI	Uniform Resource Identifier
USDP	Unified Software Development Process
USE	Unanticipated Software Evolution
VB	Visual Basic
VM	Virtual Machine
WAM	Web Access Management
WBS	Work Breakdown Structure
WSDL	Web Services Description Language
WWW	World Wide Web
XMI	XML Metadata Interchange
XML	eXtensible Markup Language
XP	eXtreme Programming
XSL	eXtensible Stylesheet Language
XSLT	eXtensible Stylesheet Language Transformations

Bibliography

[ABLE 2009]

ABLE, *Architecture Based Languages and Environment,* http://www-2.cs.cmu.edu/afs/cs/project/able/www/able.html, 2009

[ActiveCharts 2007]

ActiveCharts, *UML 2 Activity Diagram Execution and Visualization,* http://activecharts.informatik.uni-ulm.de/publications.html, 2007

[ADML 2002]

ADML, *Architecture Description Markup Language,* http://www.opengroup.org/architecture/adml/adml_home.htm, 2002

[Alexander 1977]

Alexander, Christopher; Ishikawa, Sara; Silverstein, Murray; Jacobson, Max; Fiksdahl-King, Ingrid; Angel, Shlomo, *A Pattern Language,* Oxford University Press, 1977

[Alur et al. 2003]

Alur, Deepak; Crupi, John; Malks, Dan, *Core J2EE Patterns,* Prentice Hall PTR, 2003

[Ambler 2002]

Ambler, Scott, *Agile Enterprise Architecture: Beyond Enterprise Data Modeling,* http://www.agiledata.org, 2002

[Ambler 2010]

Ambler, Scott, *Agile Architecture: Strategies for Scaling Agile Development,* http://www.agilemodeling.com/essays/agilearchitecture.htm, 2010

[Anderson et al. 2002]

Anderson, David P.; Cobb, Jeff; Korpela, Eric; Lebofsky, Matt; Werthimer, Dan, *SETI@home: An Experiment in Public-Resource Computing,* In Communications of the ACM, Vol. 45 No. 11, pp. 56-61, 2002

[Andrews et al. 2003]

Andrews, T.; Curbera; F., Dholakia, H.; Goland, Y. ; Klein, J.; Leymann, F.; Liu, K.; Roller, D.; Smith, D.; Thatte, S.; Trickovic, I. ; Weerawarana, S., *Business Process Execution Language for Web Services,* Version 1.1, http://www.ibm.com/developerworks/webservices/library/ws-bpel, 2003

[Antlr 2005]

Parr, Terence, *ANTLR - ANother Tool for Language Recognition,* http://www.antlr.org, 2005

[AOSD 2005]

Aspect-Oriented Software Association, http://aosd.net, 2005

[Apache 2006]

Apache Software Foundation, *Web Services – Axis,* v.1.4, http://ws.apache.org/axis/, 2006

[Apache 2010a]

Apache Software Foundation, *Formatting Objects Processor (FOP),* http://xml-graphics.apache.org/fop/, 2010

[Apache 2010b]

Apache Software Foundation, *Velocity Project,* http://velocity.apache.org/, 2010

[Ascet 2005]

ETAS GmbH, *ASCET-SD Overview,* http://en.etasgroup.com/products/ascet_sd/, 2005

[Autosar 2005]

The Autosar Consortium, *Automotive Open System Architecture,* http://www.autosar.org, 2005

[Avgeriou and Zdun 2005]

Avgeriou, Paris;Zdun, Uwe. *Architectural Patterns Revisited - A Pattern Language.* In Proceedings of 10th European Conference on Pattern Languages of Programs (EuroPlop 2005), Irsee, Germany, 2005

[Bass et al. 2003]

Bass, Len; Clements, Paul; Kazman, Rick, *Software Architecture in Practice,* Second Edition, Addison-Wesley, New York, 2003

[Beck 2005]

Beck, Kent, *Extreme Programming Explained – Embrace Change,* Addison-Wesley Longman, Amsterdam, 2005

[Beedle and Schwaber 2001]

Beedle, Mike; Schwaber, Ken, *Agile Software Development with Scrum,* Prentice-Hall, Upper Saddle River, NJ, 2001

[Belbin 1993]

Belbin, Meredith, *Team Roles at Work,* Butterworth-Heinemann, 1993

[Boehm 1998]

Boehm, Barry, A Spiral Model of Software Development and Enhancement, IEEE, 21, 61 72, 1998

[Bonér and Vasseur 2004]

Bonér, Jonas; Vasseur, Alexandre, *Aspectwerkz,* http://aspectwerkz.codehaus. org, 2004

[Bosch 2000]

Bosch, Jan, *Design and Use of Software Architectures,* Addison-Wesley, 2000

[Booch et al. 2005]

Booch, Grady; Rumbaugh James; Jacobson, *The Unified Modeling Language,* Addison-Wesley, Amsterdam, 2005

[Booth et al. 2003]

Booth, D.; Haas, H.; McCabe, F.; Newcomer, E.; Champion, M.; Ferris, C.; Or- chard, D., *Web Services Architecture,* W3C Working Draft 8, http://www.w3.org/ tr/2003/wd-ws-arch-20030808/, 2003

[Bouzan and Bouzan 1997]

Bouzan, Tony; Bouzan, Barry, *Das Mind-Map-Buch, Die beste Methode zur Steigerung ihres geistigen Potentials,* mvg-verlag, 1997 (available in German language only)

[Box et al. 2000]

Box, D.; Ehnebuske, D.; Kakivaya, G.; Layman, A.; Mendelsohn, N.; Nielsen, H. F.; Thatte, S.; Winer, D., *Simple object access protocol (SOAP) 1.1,* http:// www.w3.org/tr/soap/, 2000

[Bray et al. 1998]

Bray, T.; Paoli, J.; Sperberg-McQueen, C. M., *Extensible markup language (XML) 1.0,* http://www.w3.org/tr/1998/rec-xml-19980210, 1998

[Bredemeyer and Malan 2010]

Bredemeyer, Dana; Malan, Ruth, *Visual Architecting Action Guide Book,* http://www.ruthmalan.com/, 2010

[Bredemeyer 2002]

Bredemeyer, Dana, *Introduction to Software Architecture,* http://www.bredemeyer.com/papers.htm, 2002

[Briggs and Myers 1995]

Briggs, Isabel; Peter B. Myers, *Gifts Differing: Understanding Personality Type,* Davies-Black Publishing, 1995

[Brooks 1995]

Brooks, F., *The Mythical Man-Month,* Addition Wesley, New York, 1995

[Brown et al. 1998]

Brown, William, J.; Malveau, Raphael, C.; McCormick III, Hays, W., "Skip"; Mowbray, Thomas, J., *Anti Patterns – Refactoring Software Architectures, and Projects in Crisis,* John Wiley & Sons, New York, 1998

[Burke 2004]

Burke, B., *JBoss aspect oriented programming,* http://www.jboss.org/jbossaop, 2004

[Buschmann et al. 1996]

Buschmann, Frank; Meunier, Regine; Rohnert, Hans; Sommerlad, Peter; Stal, Michael, *Pattern-Oriented Software Architecture Vol. 1, A System of Patterns,* John Wiley & Sons, New York, 1996

[Chikofsky and Cross 1990]

Chikofsky, Elliot J.; Cross, James H., *Reverse Engineering and Design Recovery: A Taxonomy,* IEEE Software, 7(1), 1990

[Christensen et al. 2001]

Christensen, E.; Curbera, F.; Meredith, G.; Weerawarana, S., *Web services description language (WSDL) 1.1,* http://www.w3.org/tr/wsdl, 2001

[Chughtai and Vogel 2001]

Chughtai, Arif; Vogel, Oliver, *Software-Wiederverwendung, Theoretische Grundlagen, Vorteile und realistische Beurteilung,* http://www.ovogel.de, 2001 (available in German language only)

[Clements and Northrop 2001]
Clements, P.; Northrop, L., *Software Product Lines: Practices and Patterns,* Addison-Wesley, 2001

[Cockburn 1995]
Cockburn, Alistair, *Growth of Human Factors in Application Development,* http:// alistair.cockburn.us/crystal/articles/gohfiad/growthofhumanfactorsinsd.htm, 1995

[Cockburn 1996]
Cockburn, Alistair, *The Interaction of Social Issues and Software Architecture,* Communications of the ACM, Issue 39, Number 10, 1996

[Cockburn 2000]
Cockburn, Alistair, *Writing Effective Use Cases,* Addison-Wesley, New York, 2000

[Cockburn 2002]
Cockburn, Alistair, *Agile Software Development,* Addison-Wesley, New York, 2002

[Cohn 2010]
Cohn, Mike, *Succeeding with Agile – Software Development Using Scrum,* Addison-Wesley Longman, Amsterdam, 2010

[Conway 1968]
Conway, Melvin E., *How Do Committees Invent?,* Datamation magazine, F. D. Thompson Publications, Inc., April, 1968

[Coplien 2004]
Coplien, James O., *A Pattern Definition,* http://hillside.net/patterns/222-design-pattern-definition, 2004

[Coplien and Harrison 2004]
Coplien, James O.; Harrison, Neil B., *Organizational Patterns of Agile Software Development,* Prentice Hall, Upper Saddle River, NJ, 2004

[Cunningham et al. 2001]
Cunningham, Wart et al., *Manifesto for Agile Software Development,* http:// agilemanifesto.org/, 2001

[Curtis et al. 1988]

Curtis, B.; Krasner H.; Iscoe N., *A Field Study of the Software Design Process for Large Systems,* Communications of the ACM, Issue 31, Number 11, 1988

[Czarnecki and Eisenecker 2000]

Czarnecki, Krysztof; Eisenecker, Ulrich W., *Generative Programming - Methods, Tools and Applications,* Addison-Wesley, 2000

[Czarnecki and Helsen 2006]

Czarnecki K., Helsen S., *Feature-model-based survey of model transformation approaches,* IBM Systems Journal archive, 45(3):621 645, 2006

[Davis 1993]

Davis, Alan, *Software Requirements: Objects, Functions and States, 2nd edition,* Prentice Hall, Upper Saddle River, NJ, 1993

[Dijkstra 1972]

Dijkstra, Edsger W., *The Humble Programmer,* Communications of the ACM, 1972

[Dorfmann and Thayer 1990]

Dorfman, Merlin; Richard H. Thayer, *Guidelines and Examples of System and Software Requirements Engineering,* IEEE Computer Society Press, Los Alamitos CA., 1990

[Dörner 1989]

Dörner, Dietrich, *Die Logik des Mißlingens, Strategisches Denken in komplexen Situationen,* Rowohlt Verlag, Reinbek bei Hamburg, 1989 (available in German language only)

[Drumm 1995]

Drumm, Hans-Jürgen, *Personalwirtschaftslehre,* 3. neu bearbeitete und erweiterte Auflage, Springer-Verlag GmbH, Heidelberg, 1995 (available in German language only)

[DSTG 2010]

Delta Software Technology GmbH, *ANGIE,* http://www.d-s-t-g.de, 2010

[Dyson and Longshaw 2004]

Dyson, Paul; Longshaw, Andrew, *Architecting Enterprise Solutions,* Wiley, 2004

[EAST 2005]

Debruyne, Vincent; Simonot-Lion, Françoise; Trinquet, Yvon, *EAST-ADL - An Architecture Description Language,* in IFIP International Federation for Information Processing (176), Springer, 2005

[Eclipse 2010a]

The Eclipse Project, http://www.eclipse.org/, 2010

[Eclipse 2010b]

Eclipse Modeling Framework Project (EMF), http://www.eclipse.org/modeling/emf/, 2010

[Eclipse 2010c]

Eclipse Process Framework Project (EPF), http://www.eclipse.org/epf/, 2010

[Evans 2004]

Evans, Eric, Domain-Driven Design - Tackling Complexity in the Heart of Software, Addison-Wesley, Boston, 2004

[EWITA 2003]

EWITA, *Enterprise Architecture and Related Definitions,* http://www.ewita.com/ea_overview/definitions/architecturedefinitions.htm, 2003

[Filman and Friedman 2000]

Filman, Robert E.; Friedman, Daniel P., *Aspect-Oriented Programming is Quantification and Obliviousness,* Proceedings of the Workshop on Advanced Separation of Concerns, OOPSLA 2000, Minneapolis, Minnesota, USA, 2000

[FODA 2005]

SEI, *Feature-Oriented Domain Analysis,* http://www.sei.cmu.edu/domain-engineering/foda.html, 2005

[Foote and Yoder 1999]

Foot, Brian; Yoder, Joseph, *Big Ball of Mud,* http://www.laputan.org/mud/mud.html, 1999

[Fowler 1996]

Fowler, Martin, *Analysis Patterns: Reusable Object Models,* Addison-Wesley, 1996

[Fowler 2002]

Fowler, Martin, *Public vs. published Interfaces,* http://www.martinfowler.com/ieeesoftware/published.pdf, 2002

[Fowler 2003]

Fowler, Martin, *Patterns of Enterprise Application Architecture,* Addison-Wesley Longman, Amsterdam, 2003

[Fowler 2004]

Fowler, Martin, *Is Design Dead?,* http://www.martinfowler.com/articles/design-dead.html, 2004

[Fowler 2005a]

Fowler, Martin, *Language Workbenches: The Killer-App for Domain Specific Languages?,* http://martinfowler.com/articles/languageWorkbench.html, 2005

[Fowler 2005b] Fowler, Martin, *The New Methodology,* http://www.martinfowler.com/articles/newmethodology.html, 2005

[Foster et al. 2001]

Foster, I.; Kesselman, C.; Tuecke, S, *The Anatomy of the Grid: Enabling Scalable Virtual Organizations,* International Journal of Supercomputer Applications, 15(3), 2001

[Fugetta et al. 1998]

Fuggetta, A.; Picco, G. P.; Vigna, G., *Understanding code mobility,* IEEE Transactions on Software Engineering, 24(5), 342-361, May 1998

[Fricke and Völter 2000]

Fricke, A.; Völter, M, *SEMINARS – A Pedagogical Pattern Language on how to Teach Seminars Efficiently,* http://www.voelter.de/publications/seminars.html, 2000

[Gamma et al. 1995]

Gamma, Erich; Helm, Richard; Johnson, Ralph; Vlissides, John, *Design Patterns - Elements of Reusable Object-Oriented Software,* Addison-Wesley, Reading, 1995

[Garlan et al. 2000]

Garlan, David; Monroe, Robert T.; Wile, David, *Acme - Architectural Description of Component-Based Systems.* In Leavens, Gary T.; Sitaraman, Murali (Eds.),

Foundations of Component-Based Systems, Cambridge University Press, pp. 47-68, 2000

[Goedicke et al. 2000]

Goedicke, M.; Neumann, G.; Zdun, U., *Object system layer,* Proceedings of 5th European Conference on Pattern Languages of Programs (EuroPlop 2000), 397-410, Universitätsverlag Konstanz, Irsee, Germany, 2000

[Gray 1978]

Gray, J. N., *Notes on Database Operating Systems. Operating Systems: An Advanced Course.* Lecture Notes in Computer Science 60, 393-481, Springer-Verlag, 1978

[Greenfield and Short 2004]

Greenfield, Jack; Short, Keith, *Software Factories,* Wiley, 2004

[Grimes 1997]

Grimes, R.; *Professional DCOM Programming,* Wrox Press Inc., 1997

[Grosso 2001]

Grosso, W., *Java RMI,* O'Reilly & Associates, 2001

[Haumer 2005]

Haumer, Peter, *IBM Rational Method Composer: Part 1: Key concepts,* http://www.ibm.com/developerworks/rational/library/dec05/haumer/#notes, 2005

[Henning and Vinoski 1999]

Henning, Vinosiki, *Advanced CORBA Programming with C++,* Addison-Wesley, 1999

[Herbsleb and Grinter 1999]

Herbsleb, James D.; Grinter, Rebecca E., *Splitting the Organization and Integrating the Code: Conway's Law Revisited,* International Conference on Software Engineering, Los Angeles, 1999

[Herzberg 1966]

Herzberg, Friedrich, *Work and the Nature of Man,* Harpercollins, 1966

[Hofmeister et al. 1999]

Hofmeister, Christine; Nord Robert; Soni Dilip, *Applied Software Architecture,* Addison-Wesley, New York, 1999

[Hohpe and Woolf 2003]

Hohpe, Gregor; Woolf, Booby, Enterprise Integration Patterns: Designing, Building, and Deploying Messaging Solutions, Addison-Wesley, New York, 2003

[IBM 2003]

IBM, *CICS (Customer Information Control System) Family,* http://www.ibm.com/software/htp/cics/, 2003

[IBM 2004]

IBM, WebSphere MQ Family,

http://www-306.ibm.com/software/integration/mqfamily/, 2004

[IBM 2005]

IBM, http://www-306.ibm.com/software/websphere/, 2005

[IBM 2011]

IBM, Getting cloud computing right,

http://public.dhe.ibm.com/common/ssi/ecm/en/ciw03078usen/ciw03078usen.pdf, 2011

[IEEE 1990]

IEEE, *IEEE Standard Glossary of Software Engineering Terminology,*

http://standards.ieee.org/findstds/standard/610.12-1990.html

[IEEE 2007]

IEEE, Recommended Practice for Architectural Description of Software-intensive Systems, http://www.iso-architecture.org/ieee-1471/, 2007

[IEEE 2010]

IEEE, Guide to the Software Engineering Body of Knowledge, http://www.swebok.org/, 2010

[ISO10746 1998]

International Organization for Standardization, *Information technology -- Open Distributed Processing -- Reference model: Overview,* http://www.iso.org/iso/en/cataloguedetailpage.cataloguedetail?csnumber=20696&ics1=35&ics2=80&-ics3=, 1998

[ISO17799 2001]

International Organization for Standardization, *Information technology -- Code of practice for information security management,* http://www.iso.org/iso/en/cataloguedetailpage.cataloguedetail?csnumber=33441&ics1=35&ics2=40&ics3=, 2001

[iText 2010]
The iText Project, http://www.lowagie.com/itext/, 2010

[Jacobson et al. 1999]
Jacobson, Ivar; Booch Grady; Rumbaugh James, *The Unified Software Development Process,* Addison-Wesley, New York, 1999

[JCC 2005]
JavaCC – the Java Compiler Compiler, https://javacc.dev.java.net/, 2005

[Jeckle et al. 2004]
Jeckle, Mario; Rupp, Chris; Hahn, Jürgen; Zengler, Barbara; Queins, Stefan, *UML 2 glasklar,* Hanser, München, 2004 (available in German language only)

[Jini 2007]
The Jini Community, *Jini Community Homepage,* http://www.jini.org/, 2007

[Johnson and Foote 1988]
Johnson, R. E.; Foote, B., *Designing reusable classes,* Journal of object-oriented programming, 1(2), 22-35, 1988

[Jones et al. 1993]
Jones, N. D.; Gomard, C. K.; and Sestoft, P, *Partial Evaluation and Automatic Program Generation,* Prentice Hall, Englewood Cliffs, NJ, 1993

[Jones 2004]
Jones, Judith, *Architecting the Enterprise, Developing Architecture Skills,* http://www.opengroup.org/architecture/0404brus/presents/jones/developing_architecture_skills1.pdf, TOGAF, 2004

[Kazman et al. 1994]
Kazman, Rick; Bass, Len; Abowd, Gregory; Webb, Mike, SAAM: A Method for Analyzing the Properties Software Architectures, Proceedings of the 16th International Conference on Software Engineering, Sorrento, 1994

[Kazman et al. 1998]

Kazman, R.; Klein, M.; Barbacci, M.; Lipson, H.; Longstaff, T.; Carrière, S.J., The Architecture Tradeoff Analysis Method, Proceedings of ICECCS, Monterey, 1998

[Keller 1997]

Keller, Wolfgang, *Mapping Objects to Tables: A Pattern Language,* Proceedings of the 1997 European Pattern Languages of Programming Conference, Irsee, Germany, Siemens Technical Report 120/SW1/FB, 1997

[Keller 2002]

Wolfgang Keller, *Enterprise Application Integration, Erfahrungen aus der Praxis,* dpunkt.verlag, Heidelberg, 2002 (available in German language only)

[Keller and Coldewey 1998]

Keller, Wolfgang; Coldewey, Jens, *Accessing Relational Databases: A Pattern Language,* In Martin, Robert; Riehle, Dirk; Buschmann, Frank (Eds.): Pattern Languages of Program Design 3, Addison-Wesley, 1998

[Kelter et al. 2005]

Kelter, Udo; Wehren, Jürgen; Niere, Jörg, *A Generic Difference Algorithm for UML Models, Proceedings of SE 2005,* Essen, Germany, 2005

[Kiczales et al. 1991]

Kiczales, Gregor; des Rivieres, Jim; Bobrow, Daniel G., *The Art of the Metaobject Protocol,* MIT Press, 1991

[Kiczales et al. 1997]

Kiczales, Gregor; Lamping, John; Mendhekar, Anurag; Maeda, Chris; Videira Lopes, Cristina; Loingtier, Jean-Marc; Irwin, John, *Aspect-Oriented Programming,* ECOOP 1997, 220-242, 1997

[Kiczales et al. 2001]

Kiczales, G.; Hilsdale, E.; Hugunin, J.; Kersten, M.; Palm, J.; Griswold, G., *Getting Started with AspectJ,* Communications of the ACM, 44 (10), 59–65, 2001

[Kieser and Kubicek 1993]

Kieser, Alfred; Kubicek, Herbert, *Organisation,* Schäffer-Poeschel, 1993 (available in German language only)

[Kniesel et al. 2002]

Kniesel, G.; Noppen, J.; Mens, T.; Buckley, J., *The first workshop on unanticipated software evolution (USE 2002),* ECOOP 2002 Workshop Reader, Springer Verlag, LNCS 2548, 2002

[Kruchten 2000]

Kruchten, Philippe, *The Rational Unified Process - An Introduction Second Edition,* Addison-Wesley, Boston, 2000

[Larman 2002]

Larman, Craig, Applying UML and Patterns – An Introduction to Object-Oriented Analysis and Design and the Unified Process, Second Edition, Prentice Hall PTR, Upper Saddle River, NJ, 2002

[Leffingwell et al. 2003]

Leffingwell, Dean; Widrig, Don, *Managing Software Requirements: – A use case approach,* Addison-Wesley Professional, 2003

[Lehmann and Belady 1985]

Lehman, M.M.; Belady, L.A., *Program Evolution - Processes of Software Change,* Academic Press, London, 1985

[Lieberherr and Holland 1989]

Lieberherr, Karl; Holland, Ian, *Assuring Good Style for Object-Oriented Programs,* IEEE Software, 38-48, September 1989

[Lieberman 2007]

Lieberman, Ben, *Analyzing use cases by architectural relevance,* http://citeseer.ist.psu.edu/medvidovic97domains.html, Januar 2007

[Linthicum 2001]

Linthicum, David S.; *B2B Application Integration, e-Business-Enable Your Enterprise,* Addison-Wesley, New York, 2001

[Liskov 1988]

Liskov, B, *Data Abstraction and Hierarchy,* SIGPLAN Notices, 23(5), May 1988

[Maier and Rechtin 2000]

Maier M.; Rechtin E., *The Art of Systems Architecting,* Second Edition, CRC Press, 2000

[Malveau and Mowbray 2001]

Malveau, Raphael; Mowbray, Thomas, J, *Software Architect Bootcamp,* Prentice Hall, London, 2001

[Martin 2000]

Martin, Robert C., *Design Principles and Design Patterns,* http://www.object-mentor.com/resources/articles/principles_and_patterns.pdf, 2000

[Mathworks 2010]

Mathworks, *Matlab/Simulink software products,* http://www.mathworks.com/products/simulink, 2010

[McCabe 1976]

McCabe, Thomas J, *A Complexity Measure,* IEEE Transactions on Software Engineering, 2(4), 308-320, 1976

[Medvidovic and Rosenblum 1997]

Medvidovic, Nenad; Rosenblum, David, S., *Domains of Concern in Software Architectures and Architecture Description Languages,* In Proceedings of the USENIX Conference on Domain-Specific Languages, Santa Barbara, California, 1997

[Medvidovic and Taylor 2000]

Medvidovic, Nenad; Taylor, Richard, N., *A Classification and Comparison Framework for Software Architecture Description Languages,* In: IEEE Transactions on Software Engineering, 26(1), 70-93, 2000

[MetaEdit 2010]

MetaEdit+, http://www.metacase.com, 2010

[Meyer 1997]

Meyer, Bertrand; *Object-Oriented Software Construction, second edition,* New Jersey, Prentice Hall, 1997

[Microsoft 2009]

Microsoft, *Microsoft .NET,* http://www.microsoft.com/net/, 2009

[Microsoft 2010]

Microsoft, *Microsoft COM+ Component Services,* http://msdn.microsoft.com/library/ms685978(vs.85).aspx, 2010

[Microsoft 2011]

Microsoft, *MSMQ Microsoft Message Queue Server,* http://msdn.microsoft.com/en-us/library/ms711472.aspx, 2011

[Miller 1956]

Miller, G., The Magical Number Seven, Plus Or Minus Two: Some Limits on Our Capacity for Processing Information, The Psychological Review, 63(2), 81-97, 1956

[Morgan 1960]

Vitruvius, Morgan Morris (Translator), *Ten Books on Architecture,* Dover Publications, 1960

[NIST 2009]

National Institute of Standards and Technology, *The NIST Definition of Cloud Computing,* http://www.nist.gov/itl/cloud/upload/cloud-def-v15.pdf

[Nosek and Palvia 1990]

Nosek, J.; Palvia, P., *Software Maintenance Management: Changes in the Last Decade,* Journal of Software Maintenance, 2(3), 157-174, 1990

[OASIS 2002]

Organization for the Advancement of Structured Information Standards (OASIS), *UDDI Version 3.0 Published Specification,* http://www.uddi.org/specification.html, 2002

[OAW 2005]

The *openArchitectureWare Generator Framework,* http://www.openarchitectureware.org, 2005

[OCM 2010]

Open Cloud Manifesto, http://www.opencloudmanifesto.org/, 2010

[Oestereich and Bremer 2009]

Oestereich, Bernd; Bremer, Stefan, *Analyse und Design mit UML 2.3 - Objektorientierte Softwareentwicklung,* 9. Auflage, Oldenbourg Verlag, 2009 (available in German language only)

[Oestereich and Weiss 2008]

Oestereich, Bernd; Weiss, Christian, *APM – Agiles Projektmanagement,* dpunkt.verlag, Heidelberg, 2008 (available in German language only)

[OMG 2003]

Object Management Group, *Common Warehouse Metamodel (CWM) Specification,* v.1.1, http://www.omg.org/spec/cwm/1.1/, 2003

[OMG 2005]

Object Management Group, *UML Profile for Enterprise Distributed Object Computing (EDOC),* http://www.omg.org/technology/documents/formal/edoc.htm, 2005

[OMG 2006]

Object Management Group, *CORBA Component Model,* v.4.0, http://www.omg.org/spec/ccm/4.0/, 2006

[OMG 2007a]

Object Management Group, *UML 2.1.2 Superstructure Specification,* http://www.omg.org/spec/uml/2.1.2/Infrastructure/, 2007

[OMG 2007b]

Object Management Group, *UML 2.1.2 Infrastructure Specification,* http://www.omg.org/spec/uml/2.1.2/infrastructure/, 2007

[OMG 2007c]

Object Management Group, *XML Metadata Interchange (XMI),* v2.1.1, http://www.omg.org/spec/xmi/2.1.1/, 2007

[OMG 2008a]

Object Management Group, *Common Object Request Broker Architecture (CORBA/IIOP),* v.3.1, http://www.omg.org/spec/corba/3.1/interfaces/pdf/, 2008

[OMG 2008b]

Object Management Group, *Query/View/Transformation Specification,* v.1.0, http://www.omg.org/spec/qvt/1.0/, 2008

[OMG 2008c]

Object Management Group, *Software and Systems Process Engineering Metamodel Specification,* v2.0 (Beta 2), http://www.omg.org/spec/spem/2.0/, 2008

[OMG 2010a]

Object Management Group, *Object Constraint Language 2.2,* http://www.omg.org/spec/ocl/2.2/, 2010

[OMG 2010b]

Object Management Group, *Meta-Object Facility (MOF),* http://www.omg.org/mof/, 2010

[OMG 2010c]

Object Management Group, *Model Driven Architecture,* http://www.omg.org/
mda/, 2010

[Opengroup 1999]

Opengroup, *Architecture Description Languages: An Overview,* http://www.
opengroup.org/architecture/togaf/bbs/9910wash/adl_over.ppt, 1999

[Opengroup 2001]

Opengroup, *Developing Architecture Views – Introduction,* http://www.open-
group.org/public/arch/p4/views/vus_intro.htm, 2001

[Opengroup 2010]

Opengroup, *The Open Group Architecture Framework,* http://www.opengroup.
org/togaf/, 2010

[Opengroup 2008b]

Opengroup, IT Architect Certification Program http://www.opengroup.org/itac/,
2008

[OPERA 2005]

Opera Software, http://www.opera.com/, 2005

[Oracle 2011a]

Oracle, *Java Blue Prints,* http://www.oracle.com/technetwork/java/blue-
prints-141945.html, 2011

[Oracle 2011b]

Oracle, *Java Message Service (JMS),* http://www.oracle.com/technetwork/java/
index-jsp-142945.html, 2011

[Oracle 2011c]

Oracle, *Java 2 Platform - Enterprise Edition (Java EE),* http://www.oracle.com/
technetwork/java/javaee/overview/index.html, 2011

[Oracle 2011d]

Oracle, *Oracle Tuxedo v.* 11.1.1.2.0, http://www.oracle.com/us/products/middle-
ware/tuxedo/index.html, 2011

[Osek 2005]

OSEK/VDX, http://www.osek-vdx.org/, 2005

[OSF 1991]

Open Software Foundation, *DCE Application Development Guide,* Revision 1.0, Cambridge, MA, 1991

[OSSJ 2004]

OSS through Java Initiative, http://www.ossj.org/, 2004

[Oxford English Dictionary 2007]

Stevenson, Angus (Ed.), *Shorter Oxford English Dictionary,* Sixth Edition, Oxford University Press, 2007

[Parmer and Felsing 2002]

Palmer, R., Stephen; Felsing, M., John, *A Practical Guide to Feature-Driven Development,* Prentice Hall International, 2002

[Parnas 1976]

Parnas, David L., *On the Design and Development of Program Families,* IEEE Transactions on Software Engineering, 1976

[Parnas et al. 1986]

Parnas, David L., Clements, Paul, Naval Research Laboratory, *A rational Design Process: How and Why to fake it,* 1986

[Parnas 1994]

Parnas, David. L., *Software Aging,* In Proceedings of ICSE 1994, Sorrento, Italy, 1994

[Perry and Wolf 1992]

Perry, Dewayne E.; Wolf, Alexander L., *Foundations for the Study of Software Architecture,* ACM SIGSOFT Software Engineering Notes, 17(4), October, 1992

[Petzold and Sieber 1993]

Petzold Hilarion G.; Sieper Johanna, *Integration und Kreation,* Junfermann, 1993 (available in German language only)

[Pohl et al. 2005]

Pohl, Klaus; Böckle, Günter; Van der Linden, Frank, *Software Product Line Engineering. Foundations, Principles, and Techniques,* Springer, Berlin, 2005

[Popma 2004a]

Popma R., *Jet tutorial part 1 - introduction to jet,* http://www.eclipse.org/articles/article-jet/jet_tutorial1.html, 2004

[Popma 2004b]

Popma R., *Jet tutorial part 2 (write code that writes code),* http://www.eclipse.org/articles/article-jet2/jet_tutorial2, 2004

[Pree 1995]

Pree, W., Design Patterns for Object-Oriented Software Development, Addison-Wesley, 1995

[Raistrick et al. 2004]

Raistrick, Chris; Francis, Paul; Wright, John; Carter, Colin; Wilkie, Ian, *Model driven architecture with Executable UML.* Cambridge University Press, 2004

[Rechtin 1991]

Rechtin, Eberhard, Systems Architecting – Creating and building complex systems, CRC Press, 1991

[Roxio 2003]

Roxio, Inc., *The Napster Homepage,* http://www.napster.com, 2003

[Royce 1970]

Royce, Winston, *Managing the Development of Large Systems,* IEEE WESCON Proceedings, 26, 1-9, 1970

[Rozanski and Woods 2005]

Rozanski, Nick; Woods, Eoin, *Software Systems Architecture - Working with Stakeholders Using Viewpoints and Perspectives,* Addison-Wesley, 2005

[Rüping 2004]

Rüping, Andreas, *Insights into Decision Making,* Proceedings of 9th European Conference on Pattern Languages of Programs (EuroPlop 2004), 1-26, Irsee, Germany, 2004

[Samek 2002]

Samek, Miro, *Practical Statecharts in C/C++,* CMP Books, 2002

[Schmidt et al. 2000]

Schmidt, Douglas C.; Rohnert, Hans; Stal, Michael; Buschmann, Frank, *Pattern-Oriented Software Architecture Vol. 2, Patterns for Concurrent and Networked Objects,* John Wiley & Sons, New York, 2000

[Schmidt et al. 2009]

Schmidt, Maik; Wenzel, Sven; Kehrer, Timo, Kelter, Udo, *History-based Merging of Models,* In Proceedings of the 2009 ICSE Workshop on Comparison and Versioning of Software Models, Vancouver, Canada, 2009

[Schneier 2001]

Schneier, Bruce, *Secret & Lies, IT-Sicherheit in einer vernetzten Welt,* dpunkt. verlag, Heidelberg, 2001 (available in German language only)

[Schumacher et al. 2005]

Schumacher, Markus, Fernandez, Eduardo, Hybertson, Duane, Buschmann, Frank, Sommerlad, Peter. *Security Patterns: Integrating Security and Systems Engineering,* John Wiley & Sons, 2005

[SEI 2010]

Carnegie Mellon University Software Engineering Institute, *Community Software Architecture Definitions,* http://www.sei.cmu.edu/architecture/start/ community.cfm, 2010

[Shaw and Garlan 1994]

Shaw, Mary; Garlan, David, *Characteristics of Higher-level Languages for Software Architecture,* Technical Report CMU-CS-94-210, School of Computer Science, Carnegie Mellon University, Pittsburgh, 1994

[Shaw et al. 1995]

M. Shaw, R. DeLine, D.V. Klein et al., *Abstraction for Software Architecture and Tools to Support Them,* IEEE Transactions on Software Engineering, Vol. 21. No. 4., 1995

[Shaw and Garlan 1996]

Shaw, Mary; Garlan, David, *Software Architecture - Perspectives on an Emerging Discipline,* Prentice Hall, Upper Saddle River, N. J., 1996

[Siedersleben 2004]

Siedersleben, Johannes, *Moderne Software-Architektur – Umsichtig planen, robust bauen mit Quasar,* dpunkt.verlag, Heidelberg, 2004 (available in German language only)

[Stachowiak 1973]

Stachowiak, Herbert, *Allgemeine Modelltheorie,* Springer, Wien, 1973

[Stahl 2002]

Stahl, Eberhard, *Dynamik in Gruppen,* BeltzPVU, 2002 (available in German language only)

[Stahl and Völter 2006]

Stahl, Thomas; Völter, Markus, *Model-Driven Software Development,* Wiley, 2006

[Standish 2009]

The Standish Group International Inc., *The CHAOS Summary 2009,* http://www. standishgroup.com/newsroom/chaos_2009.php, 2009

[Steiger and Lippmann 2003]

Steiger, Thomas; Lippmann, Erich (Hrsg.), *Handbuch angewandte Psychologie für Führungskräfte, Führungskompetenz und Führungswissen,* 2. Auflage, Springer, Berlin 2003 (available in German language only)

[Sun 1988]

Sun Microsystems, *RPC: Remote Procedure Call Protocol Specification,* Tech. Rep. RFC-1057, Sun Microsystems, Inc., June 1988

[Sun 2003]

Sun Microsystems, *Project JXTA,* https://jxta.dev.java.net/, 2003

[Szyperski 1998]

Szyperski, Clemens; *Component Software - Beyond Object-Oriented Programming,* Addison-Wesley, 1998

[Tanenbaum and van Steen 2003]

Tanenbaum, Andrew S.; van Steen, Maarten, *Distributed Systems,* Prentice Hall, New York, 2003

[Tarr 2004]

Tarr, P., *Hyper/J,* http://www.research.ibm.com/hyperspace/hyperj/hyperj.htm, 2004

[Taylor 1913]

Taylor, F.W., The principles of scientific management, 1913

[Terplan 2001]

Terplan, Kornel, *OSS Essentials, Support System Solutions for Service Providers,* John Wiley & Sons, New York, 2001

[TIBCO 2011]

TIBCO, *TIBCO Enterprise Message Service,* http://www.tibco.com/products/soa/messaging/enterprise-mesage-service/default.jsp, 2011

[TMF 2004a]

TeleManagement Forum, *Next Generation Operations Support Systems Initiative (NGOSS),* http://www.tmforum.org/browse.asp?catid=1911, 2004

[TMF 2004b]

Strassner, John; Fleck, Joel; Huang, Jenny; Fauer, Cliff; Richardson, Tony, TeleManagement Forum, *TMF White Paper on NGOSS and MDA,* http://www.tmforum.org/browse.asp?catid=1875&snode=1875&exp=y&linkid=28972, 2004

[Van Deursen et al. 2007]

Van Deursen, A.; Visser, E.; Warmer, J., Model-Driven Software Evolution: A Research Agenda, In Dalila Tamzalit (Eds.), Proceedings 1st International Workshop on Model-Driven Software Evolution (MoDSE), Nantes, France, 2007

[Vinoski 2003]

Vinoski, S.; IEEE Internet Computing, *Toward Integration Column: Integration With Web Services,* November/Dezember 2003

[Vogel and Zdun 2002]

Vogel, Oliver; Zdun, Uwe, *Content Conversion and Generation on the Web: A Pattern Language, EuroPLoP,* 2002

[Völter et al. 2002]

Völter, Markus; Schmid, Alexander; Wolf, Eberhard, *Server Component Patterns,* John Wiley & Sons, New York, 2002

[Völter et al. 2004]

Völter, Markus; Kircher, Michael; Zdun, Uwe, Remoting Patterns - Foundations of Enterprise, Internet, and Realtime Distributed Object Middlware, John Wiley & Sons, 2004

[Vroom and Yetton 1976]

Vroom, Victor H.; Yetton, Philip W., *Leadership and Decision-Making,* University of Pittsburgh Press, Pittsburgh, 1976

[V-Modell XT 2009]

V-Modell XT, Specification v. 1.3, http://v-modell.iabg.de/v-modell-xt-html-english/index.html, 2009

[W3C 1999]

W3C XML Path Language (XPath), v. 1.0, http://www.w3.org/tr/xpath, 1999

[W3C 2004]

W3C, XML Schema, http://www.w3.org/xml/schema, v. 1.1, 2004

[W3C 2006]

W3C Extensible Stylesheet Language (XSL) Specification, v. 1.1, http://www.w3.org/tr/xsl/, 2006

[Weiss and Lai 1999]

Weiss, D. M.; Lai, C. T. R., Software Product-Line Engineering: A Family Based Software Development Process, Addison-Wesley, 1999

[Wiegers 2003]

Wiegers, Karl E., *Software Requirements,* Second Edition, Microsoft Press, 2003

[Withall 2007]

Withall, Stephen, *Software Requirement Patterns,* Microsoft Press, 2007

[Wikipedia 2011]

Systemdefinition, http://en.wikipedia.org/wiki/system/, 2011

[Winer 1999]

Winer, D., *XML-RPC Specification,* http://www.xmlrpc.com/spec, 1999

[Yourdon 2004]

Yourdon, Edward, *Death March,* Prentice Hall, New York, 2004d

[Yourdon 1997]

Yourdon, Edward, Death March, The Complete Software Developer's Guide to Surviving "Mission Impossible" Projects, Prentice Hall, Upper Saddle River, N. J., 1997

[Yourdon and Constantine 1978]

Yourdon, E.; Constantine, L., *Structured Design: Fundamentals of a Discipline of Computer Programming and Design,* Prentice Hall, 1978

[Zachman 1987]

Zachman, John, A., *A Framework for Information Systems Architecture,* IBM Publication, 1987

[Zdun 2004]

Zdun, Uwe, Pattern Language for the Design of Aspect Languages and Aspect Composition Frameworks, IEE Proceedings Software, 151(2), 67- 83, 2004

[Zdun et al. 2006]

Zdun, U. Hentrich, C. van der Aalst, W.M.P. *A Survey of Patterns for Service-Oriented Architectures,* International Journal of Internet Protocol Technology, 1(3), Inderscience, 2006

[Zdun and Hendrich 2006]

Hentrich, C. Zdun, Uwe, *Patterns for Process-Oriented Integration in Service-Oriented Architectures,* Proceedings of 11th European Conference on Pattern Languages of Programs (EuroPLoP 2006), Irsee, Germany, 2006

[Zito et al. 2006]

Zito, A.; Diskin, Z.; Dingel, J. *Package merge in UML 2: Practice vs. theory?* Proceedings of the 9th International Conference on Model Driven Engineering Languages and Systems (MoDELS 2006), Genova, Italy, 2006

| Bibliography

Index